THE ULTIMATE LINUX PROGRAMMING MASTER GUIDE

5 IN 1 DIVE DEEP INTO KERNEL INTERNALS, DEVICE DRIVERS, AND ADVANCED THREADING TECHNIQUES TO BUILD ROBUST, HIGH-PERFORMANCE APPLICATIONS THAT DOMINATE MODERN COMPUTING ENVIRONMENTS

ILLINGWORTH ACADEMIC PRESS

This book is a work of nonfiction, compiled based on the author's extensive expertise, research, and practical experience in Linux system programming. While every effort has been made to provide accurate, up-to-date, and authoritative information regarding the subject matter covered—including UNIX/Linux architecture, process management, kernel internals, device drivers, and advanced programming techniques—the publisher and author disclaim any and all liability for errors, omissions, inaccuracies, or any damages arising from the use, misuse, or application of the information contained herein. The concepts, code examples, tutorials, and projects presented are intended for educational and informational purposes only and should not be construed as professional engineering, software development, or technical advice.

This publication is sold with the understanding that neither the author nor the publisher is engaged in rendering legal, accounting, engineering, cybersecurity, or other professional services. If legal advice, technical consultation, or other expert assistance is required, the services of a competent professional should be sought. The advice, strategies, code snippets, and methodologies contained herein may not be suitable for every situation, project, or environment. Users are strongly encouraged to test all code and configurations in a controlled, non-production setting and to consult relevant documentation, standards (such as POSIX), and experts when implementing in real-world scenarios.

The publisher and author make no representations or warranties with respect to the accuracy, applicability, fitness, or completeness of the contents of this book. They specifically disclaim any implied warranties of merchantability or fitness for a particular purpose. No warranty may be created or extended by sales representatives, promotional materials, or written communications. Neither the publisher nor the author shall be liable for any loss of profit, data corruption, system failures, security breaches, or any other commercial damages, including but not limited to special, incidental, consequential, punitive, or other damages arising from the use of this book or its contents. This includes, without limitation, any issues related to software bugs, hardware incompatibilities, kernel modifications, or unintended consequences from applying the programming techniques described.

Furthermore, this book may reference third-party tools, software libraries, operating systems, and resources (such as Git, QEMU, KVM, Pthreads, ext4, Btrfs, and others). These are mentioned for illustrative purposes only, and no endorsement or affiliation is implied. Users should verify compatibility, licensing terms, and security implications independently. Any trademarks, service marks, product names, or named features mentioned are assumed to be the property of their respective owners and are used only for identification or explanation without intent to infringe.

In preparing this book, the author has made every reasonable effort to ensure the reliability of the information provided. However, technology evolves rapidly, and Linux distributions, kernel versions, and standards may change after publication. Readers are advised to cross-reference with official sources, such as the Linux Kernel Documentation, POSIX specifications, or distribution-specific manuals, for the most current details. The author and publisher assume no responsibility for any updates, patches, or revisions needed due to such changes. For privacy and ethical reasons, any examples involving users, processes, or system interactions are hypothetical and do not reflect real individuals, organizations, or events unless explicitly stated as public domain knowledge. Names, scenarios, and code samples have been generalized or anonymized where necessary to protect confidentiality.

TABLE OF CONTENTS

Book 1: Foundations of Linux System Programming

1 History and Standards in UNIX and Linux

1.1 A Brief History of UNIX and C

The story of UNIX and the C programming language is one of innovation, collaboration, and profound influence on the world of computing. Emerging from the fertile grounds of Bell Laboratories in the late 1960s and early 1970s, these technologies laid the groundwork for modern operating systems, including Linux. To understand Linux system programming, it's essential to trace the roots back to UNIX, as Linux was designed as a free, open-source alternative to it. This section explores the origins, key developments, and lasting legacy of UNIX and C, highlighting how they intertwined to shape the digital landscape.

The Pre-UNIX Era: Multics and the Need for Simplicity

The genesis of UNIX can be traced to the mid-1960s, a time when computing was dominated by large, expensive mainframes. In 1964, Bell Labs, in partnership with General Electric (GE) and the Massachusetts Institute of Technology (MIT), embarked on the Multics (Multiplexed Information and Computing Service) project. Multics aimed to create a time-sharing operating system that could support multiple users simultaneously, offering features like hierarchical file systems, dynamic linking, and robust security. It was ambitious, envisioning a utility-like computing service where users could access resources on demand, much like electricity.

However, Multics proved overly complex and resource-intensive. By 1969, Bell Labs withdrew from the project due to escalating costs and delays. This withdrawal left a team of talented researchers, including Ken Thompson and Dennis Ritchie, frustrated but inspired. Thompson, in particular, had been working on a space travel simulation game that required a suitable platform. With Multics abandoned, he sought a simpler alternative.

In the summer of 1969, Thompson repurposed an underutilized PDP-7 minicomputer at Bell Labs. Over a few weeks, he developed a basic operating system kernel, file system, shell, and assembler. This rudimentary system, initially unnamed, featured a hierarchical file structure—inspired by Multics—and treated everything as files, including devices. Thompson's wife and child were on vacation that August, giving him uninterrupted time to code what would become the foundation of UNIX. He later quipped that UNIX was born in "one month of one person's work."

The Birth of UNIX: From Assembly to a Multi-User System

By late 1969, Thompson's creation had evolved into a functional system. Joined by Dennis Ritchie, the duo refined it. The name "UNIX" (originally "UNICS" as a pun on Multics, standing for "Uniplexed Information and Computing Service") was coined by Brian Kernighan, another Bell Labs colleague, to emphasize its simplicity compared to Multics' multiplexing.

Early UNIX was written entirely in assembly language for the PDP-7, limiting its portability. In 1970, Bell Labs acquired a PDP-11, a more powerful minicomputer, prompting a port of UNIX. This version, known as Version 1 (V1), was released internally in 1971. It supported basic commands, a file system, and simple multi-user capabilities. UNIX's design philosophy emphasized modularity, reusability, and efficiency—principles encapsulated in the "UNIX philosophy" later articulated by Doug McIlroy: "Write programs that do one thing and do it well. Write programs to work together. Write programs to handle text streams, because that is a universal interface."

A pivotal moment came in 1971 when Ritchie began developing the C programming language. Initially, he created "B," an interpreted language based on BCPL (Basic Combined Programming Language) by Martin Richards. B was too limited for system programming, so Ritchie extended it into C, adding data types, structures, and other features. C was designed to be high-level enough for productivity but low-level enough to manipulate hardware directly, making it ideal for operating system development.

By 1973, most of UNIX was rewritten in C, marking Version 4 (V4). This rewrite was revolutionary: it made UNIX portable across hardware architectures, as only the kernel's machine-dependent parts needed adjustment. Prior to this, operating systems were tied to specific hardware, requiring complete rewrites for new machines. C's efficiency and expressiveness allowed UNIX to spread beyond Bell Labs.

Key Milestones in UNIX Development

The 1970s saw rapid evolution. In 1973, UNIX V4 introduced pipes, a mechanism for chaining commands (e.g., ls | grep), invented by McIlroy and implemented by Thompson. This innovation exemplified UNIX's focus on composability. By 1975, UNIX V6 was released outside Bell Labs under a license, sparking academic interest. Universities like the University of California, Berkeley, adopted it, leading to the Berkeley Software Distribution (BSD) in 1977.

BSD added significant enhancements, including the vi editor (by Bill Joy), TCP/IP networking (in 4.2BSD, 1983), and virtual memory. Meanwhile, at Bell Labs, System III (1981) and System V (1983) became commercial versions after AT&T's divestiture from Bell Labs allowed UNIX commercialization. System V introduced features like streams for I/O and the System V Interface Definition (SVID) for standardization.

The 1980s brought fragmentation. Various vendors—Sun Microsystems (SunOS), IBM (AIX), HP (HP-UX)—forked UNIX, leading to the "UNIX Wars." This prompted standardization efforts, culminating in POSIX (Portable Operating System Interface) in 1988, defining a common API for UNIX-like systems.

The Development and Impact of C

Parallel to UNIX's growth, C solidified as a cornerstone language. Ritchie's "The C Programming Language" (1978), co-authored with Kernighan (known as K&R), became the de facto standard. C's syntax—curly braces for blocks, pointers for memory access, and operators like ++ and --—influenced countless languages, including C++, Java, and Python.

C was compiled, producing efficient machine code, yet portable. Its standard library provided functions for I/O, strings, and math, abstracting system calls. By the late 1970s, C compilers were available for various platforms, decoupling software from hardware.

The ANSI C standard (C89) in 1989 formalized the language, ensuring compatibility. Subsequent standards like C99 (adding inline functions, variable-length arrays) and C11 (thread support) kept C relevant. C's role in UNIX extended to applications: tools like awk (Aho, Weinberger, Kernighan), sed, and grep were written in C, embodying the system's toolchain.

UNIX's Influence on Modern Computing

UNIX's principles permeated computing. Its file system model—everything is a file—simplified I/O. Processes, signals, and inter-process communication (IPC) became standard. UNIX's shell (initially Thompson's, later Bourne Shell) introduced scripting, automating tasks.

The open-source movement owes much to UNIX. In 1983, Richard Stallman launched the GNU Project to create a free UNIX-like system. GNU tools (gcc compiler, bash shell) were developed in C. In 1991, Linus Torvalds, a Finnish student, announced Linux, a free kernel inspired by Minix (a UNIX-like teaching OS by Andrew Tanenbaum). Linux used GNU tools, forming GNU/Linux.

Linux adopted UNIX's POSIX compliance, ensuring compatibility. Today, Linux powers servers, embedded systems, Android, and supercomputers. UNIX derivatives like macOS (based on Darwin, a BSD variant) and iOS underscore its ubiquity.

Challenges and Controversies

UNIX's history isn't without strife. AT&T's licensing restricted modifications, leading to lawsuits, like AT&T vs. BSD in 1992, resolved in 1994, freeing BSD code. Proprietary forks created incompatibilities, which POSIX mitigated. C, while powerful, has pitfalls: manual memory management leads to bugs like buffer overflows, fueling security issues (e.g., Heartbleed). Yet, its performance makes it indispensable for systems programming.

Legacy and Relevance to Linux Programming

Understanding UNIX and C is crucial for Linux programmers. Linux system calls mirror UNIX's (e.g., fork(), exec(), open()). C remains the language for kernel development, drivers, and performance-critical code. Tools like gdb (debugger) and valgrind (memory checker) stem from this heritage.

In modern ecosystems, Rust is emerging for safer kernel modules, but C dominates. Distributions like Ubuntu, Fedora, and Arch build on this foundation, with package managers (apt, yum) echoing UNIX's modularity.

The history teaches lessons: simplicity over complexity (UNIX vs. Multics), portability's value (C rewrite), and community-driven evolution (BSD, GNU, Linux). As we delve into Linux programming, remember: every syscall, every header file, traces back to Thompson's PDP-7 experiments and Ritchie's linguistic ingenuity.

This brief history—spanning from Multics' ashes to Linux's triumph—illustrates how UNIX and C democratized computing, enabling today's programmable world. With over five decades of influence, they continue to evolve, powering the internet, AI, and beyond.

1.2 The Evolution of Linux and the GNU Project

The evolution of Linux and the GNU Project represents a landmark in the history of computing, embodying the principles of open-source software, community collaboration, and freedom in technology. While UNIX provided the architectural blueprint, Linux emerged as a free, accessible alternative, driven by the vision of Richard Stallman and the ingenuity of Linus Torvalds. This section delves into the origins, key developments, challenges, and ongoing impact of these intertwined projects, illustrating how they transformed from niche endeavors into the backbone of modern digital infrastructure.

The Genesis of the GNU Project: A Quest for Free Software

The story begins in the early 1980s, amid growing concerns over proprietary software. Richard Matthew Stallman, a programmer at MIT's Artificial Intelligence Laboratory, experienced frustration with the restrictive nature of commercial software. In 1983, inspired by the hacker culture of sharing code, Stallman announced the GNU Project (GNU's Not UNIX) on the net.unix-wizards newsgroup. His goal was ambitious: to create a completely free operating system compatible with UNIX, where "free" meant freedom to use, study, modify, and distribute software—not necessarily gratis.

Stallman's philosophy was rooted in the four freedoms: to run the program as you wish (Freedom 0), to study and change the source code (Freedom 1), to redistribute copies (Freedom 2), and to distribute modified versions (Freedom 3). To enforce this, he developed the GNU General Public License (GPL) in 1989, a copyleft license that required derivative works to be distributed under the same terms, preventing proprietary enclosures.

The GNU Project started with essential components. In 1984, Stallman began work on GNU Emacs, a extensible text editor that became a cornerstone for developers. By 1985, he founded the Free Software Foundation (FSF) to support the project financially and legally. Key tools followed: the GNU C Compiler (GCC) in 1987, which was crucial for compiling code on various architectures; the GNU Debugger (GDB); and libraries like GNU C Library (glibc), providing standard functions for C programs.

GNU aimed for a full OS stack: utilities, compilers, editors, and a kernel. For the kernel, Stallman chose the Hurd (Hird of Unix-Replacing Daemons), a microkernel design based on Mach from Carnegie Mellon University. Hurd promised advanced features like fine-grained access control and extensibility, but its development was slow due to complexity and limited contributors. By the early 1990s, GNU had most user-space tools but lacked a functional kernel, leaving the project incomplete.

The Birth of Linux: A Kernel from Helsinki

Enter Linus Torvalds, a 21-year-old computer science student at the University of Helsinki. In 1991, frustrated with Minix—a minimal UNIX-like OS created by Andrew Tanenbaum for educational purposes—Torvalds decided to build his own kernel. Minix was limited by its license, which restricted modifications, and ran on expensive hardware. Torvalds, using a modest Intel 386 PC, posted on the comp.os.minix newsgroup in August 1991: "I'm doing a (free) operating system (just a hobby, won't be big and professional like gnu) for 386(486) AT clones."

Torvalds released Linux version 0.01 in September 1991 under his own license, initially prohibiting commercial use. Written in C and assembly, it supported basic features like multitasking, a file system (initially Minix-compatible), and device drivers. The name "Linux" combined "Linus" and "UNIX," though Torvalds initially called it "Freax."

The turning point came in 1992 when Torvalds switched to the GPL v2, aligning with GNU's ethos. This encouraged contributions: volunteers ported GNU tools to Linux, creating a bootable system. By integrating GCC, bash (Bourne Again SHell, a GNU shell), and other utilities, the combination became known as GNU/Linux—though often shortened to "Linux," sparking debates with Stallman, who insists on "GNU/Linux" to credit the FSF.

Early adoption was rapid. In 1992, distributions emerged: Softlanding Linux System (SLS) and Yggdrasil Linux/GNU/X. Slackware, founded by Patrick Volkerding in 1993, became one of the oldest surviving distros, emphasizing simplicity. Debian, started by Ian Murdock in 1993, focused on stability and free software purity, later spawning Ubuntu in 2004.

Milestones in Linux Kernel Development

Linux's evolution is marked by version releases, each introducing critical features. Version 1.0, released in March 1994, supported TCP/IP networking, essential for internet connectivity. It ran on i386 processors and included a stable ext file system.

Version 2.0 (1996) brought symmetric multiprocessing (SMP) for multi-processor systems, modular kernel design (allowing loadable modules for drivers), and support for more architectures like Alpha and SPARC. This era saw Linux penetrate servers: companies like Digital Domain used it for Titanic's special effects in 1997.

The late 1990s fueled the open-source boom. Eric S. Raymond's "The Cathedral and the Bazaar" (1997) contrasted collaborative "bazaar" development (like Linux) with proprietary "cathedral" models. Netscape's Mozilla release in 1998 and IBM's $1 billion Linux investment in 2000 legitimized it. Red Hat, founded in 1993, went public in 1999, creating Linux millionaires.

Version 2.2 (1999) improved networking and file systems; 2.4 (2001) added USB, RAID, and ext3 journaling. The 2.6 series (2003) introduced preemptive kernel, better scalability, and device models, supporting enterprise workloads. By then, Linux powered 25% of web servers.

The 2010s saw explosive growth. Version 3.0 (2011) was a numbering change, but kernels evolved with cgroups (2007) for resource control, enabling containers like Docker (2013). Namespaces isolated processes, paving the way for virtualization.

Android, announced in 2007 and based on Linux, revolutionized mobile computing. By 2012, it dominated smartphones, extending Linux to billions. Embedded systems, IoT devices, and supercomputers (90%+ run Linux) followed.

Recent kernels (e.g., 5.0 in 2019, 6.0 in 2022) focus on security (e.g., Lockdown mode), performance (e.g., io_uring for async I/O), and hardware support (ARM64, RISC-V). Rust integration since 2022 addresses C's memory safety issues, with modules for drivers.

The GNU Project's Ongoing Role and Synergies

While Linux provided the kernel, GNU remains vital. Glibc is the standard C library; GCC (now including C++, Fortran) compiles most Linux code. GNU tools like make, autoconf, and binutils form the build chain. The FSF advocates for free software, auditing licenses and promoting ethical computing.

However, tensions exist. Stallman's insistence on "GNU/Linux" highlights credit disputes. Hurd, still under development, runs but isn't widely used; most GNU/Linux systems use the Linux kernel. Alternatives like GNU/kFreeBSD use BSD kernels with GNU tools.

The open-source ecosystem expanded beyond GNU. The Open Source Initiative (OSI), founded in 1998, promoted "open source" over "free software" for business appeal, approving licenses like BSD and MIT. Linux benefits from both: GPL ensures kernel freedom, while permissive licenses aid adoption.

Challenges and Controversies

Evolution wasn't smooth. Early Linux lacked polish: no GUI until XFree86 (1992), and hardware support was spotty. The "Halloween Documents" (1998), leaked Microsoft memos, revealed fears of Linux, leading to antitrust scrutiny.

Security issues, like vulnerabilities in sudo or kernel exploits, persist, but community responses are swift. Fragmentation among distros—over 500 exist—creates compatibility headaches, mitigated by standards like Linux Standard Base (LSB).

Social challenges include diversity: the kernel community, historically male-dominated, faced criticism, prompting codes of conduct (2018). Stallman's 2019 resignation from FSF amid controversies underscored governance issues.

External pressures: patent lawsuits (e.g., SCO vs. IBM, 2003-2021) alleged UNIX code theft, but Linux prevailed. Cloud computing giants like AWS and Google contribute massively, raising concerns over corporate influence.

Modern Ecosystem and Future Directions

Today, Linux dominates: 100% of top supercomputers, 80% of cloud instances, and embedded markets. Distributions cater to niches: Ubuntu for desktops, CentOS/Rocky for servers, Alpine for containers. Package managers (apt, dnf, pacman) streamline software installation.

The GNU Project evolves: GCC 13 (2023) adds modern features; GNU Guix offers declarative package management. Collaborations like freedesktop.org standardize desktops (GNOME, KDE).

Future trends include AI integration (e.g., kernel machine learning), quantum computing support, and sustainability (energy-efficient scheduling). With climate concerns, Linux's efficiency aids green computing.

Linux's success stems from meritocracy: contributions via mailing lists, git (developed by Torvalds in 2005), and platforms like GitHub. The Linux Foundation, formed in 2007, oversees development, with over 15,000 contributors annually.

In system programming, this evolution informs practices: POSIX compliance ensures portability; GPL encourages sharing. Understanding GNU tools and Linux internals is key to mastering files, processes, and kernels.

From Stallman's manifesto to Torvalds' kernel, Linux and GNU democratized technology, powering the web, science, and innovation. As we advance, their legacy endures, fostering a world where software is free as in freedom.

1.3 POSIX and Other Standards Compliance

In the diverse ecosystem of UNIX-like operating systems, standards play a crucial role in ensuring portability, interoperability, and consistency. Among these, POSIX (Portable Operating System Interface) stands out as the foundational standard that defines a common interface for UNIX-derived systems, including Linux. This section explores the history, structure, and significance of POSIX, alongside other relevant standards such as the Single UNIX Specification (SUS), Linux Standard Base (LSB), and related compliance efforts. Understanding these standards is essential for Linux system programmers, as they guide the development of portable code that can run across different distributions and even other UNIX-like platforms with minimal modifications. We will delve into their evolution, key components, Linux's adherence, challenges, and future implications, highlighting how they foster a unified programming environment in an otherwise fragmented landscape.

The Need for Standards: Addressing the UNIX Wars

The proliferation of UNIX variants in the 1980s created a chaotic environment known as the "UNIX Wars." Commercial forks like AT&T's System V, BSD from Berkeley, SunOS, AIX, and HP-UX introduced incompatible features, APIs, and behaviors. Developers faced significant hurdles when porting applications: a program working on one system might fail on another due to differences in system calls, library functions, or shell commands. This fragmentation hindered UNIX's adoption in enterprise settings, where reliability and cross-platform compatibility were paramount.

To resolve this, industry consortia and standards bodies intervened. In 1985, the IEEE (Institute of Electrical and Electronics Engineers) formed the POSIX working group under the auspices of the Portable Applications Standards Committee (PASC). The goal was to create a standard interface based on existing UNIX practices, drawing from System V and BSD. POSIX aimed not to invent new features but to document and standardize common ones, ensuring that compliant systems provided a predictable environment for applications.

The term "POSIX" derives from "Portable Operating System Interface," with the "X" nodding to UNIX. Richard Stallman suggested the name, emphasizing portability. The first POSIX standard, IEEE 1003.1-1988 (POSIX.1), focused on core system interfaces like file I/O, process management, and signals. It was adopted by the International Organization for Standardization (ISO) as ISO/IEC 9945-1:1990, giving it global recognition.

Evolution of POSIX Standards

POSIX has evolved through multiple revisions, each incorporating advancements while maintaining backward compatibility. Early versions addressed basic APIs, but later ones expanded to shells, utilities, threads, and real-time extensions.

- **POSIX.1 (1988-1990)**: The inaugural standard defined over 100 system calls and functions, including open(), close(), read(), write(), fork(), exec(), and signal handling. It specified error codes (errno) and data types for portability. This laid the groundwork for portable C programming on UNIX systems.
- **POSIX.2 (1992)**: Extended to user commands and utilities, standardizing the shell (sh) and tools like awk, grep, sed, and vi. It ensured consistent behavior in scripting and command-line interfaces.

Subsequent amendments introduced specialized features:

- **POSIX.1b (1993, formerly 1003.4)**: Real-time extensions, including priority scheduling, high-resolution timers, and asynchronous I/O.
- **POSIX.1c (1995, formerly 1003.4a)**: POSIX Threads (pthreads), providing a standard for multithreaded programming with mutexes, condition variables, and thread creation/joining.
- **POSIX.1d (1999)**: Additional real-time features like sporadic server scheduling.

By the mid-1990s, The Open Group—a consortium formed from X/Open and the Open Software Foundation (OSF)—took stewardship of UNIX standards. They merged POSIX with X/Open's XPG (X/Open Portability Guide) and AT&T's SVID into the Single UNIX Specification (SUS). SUS Version 1 (1994, UNIX 95) aligned with POSIX but added networking (sockets) and X11 interfaces.

- **SUS Version 2 (1997, UNIX 98)**: Incorporated POSIX amendments, large file support, and Y2K compliance.
- **SUS Version 3 (2002, UNIX 03)**: Harmonized with POSIX.1-2001 (IEEE 1003.1-2001), integrating real-time and threads as base features. It defined over 1,200 interfaces.
- **POSIX.1-2008 (Issue 7)**: Aligned with SUS Version 4, adding IPv6 support, improved internationalization, and refinements to existing APIs. It was published as IEEE 1003.1-2008.

Amendments followed: Technical Corrigendum 1 (2013) and 2 (2016) fixed issues and added minor features like clock_nanosleep().

The most recent major update is POSIX.1-2024 (Issue 8), published on June 14, 2024, by IEEE and The Open Group. This version aligns the standard with the ISO C17 language standard, incorporating modern C features while maintaining compatibility. It refines utilities, enhances security considerations (e.g., better handling of privileges), and updates networking interfaces to support contemporary protocols. POSIX.1-2024 emphasizes usability in embedded and real-time systems, with improved documentation for developers. It defines a standard operating system interface, including the shell and over 1,000 utilities, ensuring that compliant systems can run portable applications seamlessly.

POSIX standards are not monolithic; they are modular. Options allow implementations to support subsets, like the "XSI" (X/Open System Interface) extension for full UNIX compatibility. Certification programs, like The Open Group's UNIX branding, verify compliance through rigorous testing.

Other Key Standards in the UNIX/Linux Ecosystem

Beyond POSIX, several standards complement it, addressing specific aspects of system programming and distribution uniformity.

- **Single UNIX Specification (SUS)**: As mentioned, SUS integrates POSIX with additional features for branded UNIX systems. The latest is aligned with POSIX.1-2024. Systems like macOS (certified UNIX 03) and Solaris adhere to SUS, while Linux draws heavily from it without formal certification.
- **Linux Standard Base (LSB)**: Initiated by the Free Standards Group (now part of the Linux Foundation) in 2001, LSB aimed to reduce differences among Linux distributions. It specifies binary compatibility for applications, covering libraries (e.g., glibc), commands, and file system hierarchy. LSB 1.0 (2001) focused on core modules; LSB 5.0 (2015) was the last major release, adding support for newer architectures like ARM and PowerPC.

However, LSB's influence has waned. By 2023, it was considered abandoned by maintainers, with no updates since 2015. Many distributions, like Ubuntu 22.04 and later, have shifted away from full LSB compliance in favor of lighter approaches. Still, LSB concepts linger in package management and app portability tools like AppImage and Flatpak, which bypass distro-specific quirks.

- **Filesystem Hierarchy Standard (FHS)**: Maintained by the Linux Foundation, FHS defines directory structures (/bin, /etc, /usr, etc.) for consistency. Version 3.0 (2015) is current, ensuring scripts and programs can locate files predictably.
- **C Language Standards**: POSIX is tightly coupled with ISO C. POSIX.1-2024 aligns with C17 (ISO/IEC 9899:2018), supporting features like atomic operations and alignment specifiers. Earlier alignments were with C99 and C11. Programmers must use standard-compliant C to leverage POSIX fully.
- **Other Related Standards**:
    - **IEEE 1003.13 (PSE, POSIX Profiles)**: Defines profiles for embedded systems, like PSE51 for minimal real-time.
    - **Austin Group Specifications**: The joint working group for POSIX/SUS, producing unified documents.
    - **RFCs for Networking**: POSIX incorporates BSD sockets, aligned with IETF standards like RFC 3493 for IPv6.
    - **Unicode and Internationalization**: POSIX mandates UTF-8 support in modern revisions.

These standards collectively form a framework for reliable system programming.

Linux's Compliance with POSIX and Other Standards

Linux, from its inception, targeted POSIX compatibility to ease porting from UNIX. Linus Torvalds designed the kernel to mimic System V and BSD behaviors, implementing POSIX.1 APIs early on. By version 1.0 (1994), Linux supported most core POSIX features.

Today, Linux is highly POSIX-compliant but not formally certified due to costs and the open-source nature—certification requires proprietary testing suites. However, it adheres to POSIX.1-2008 with amendments and is aligning with POSIX.1-2024 through ongoing kernel and glibc updates. For instance:

- **System Calls**: Linux provides POSIX functions via glibc wrappers, with extensions like epoll() for scalability (non-POSIX but useful).
- **Threads**: Pthreads are fully supported via NPTL (Native POSIX Threads Library) since kernel 2.6.
- **Real-Time**: PREEMPT_RT patches enhance compliance with POSIX.1b.
- **Utilities**: GNU tools (bash, coreutils) follow POSIX.2, with options for strict mode (e.g., POSIXLY_CORRECT environment variable).

Distributions vary: Red Hat Enterprise Linux (RHEL) and SUSE aim for LSB compliance; Debian prioritizes FHS. Tools like posix_test_suite verify adherence.

Linux's extensions (e.g., inotify for file events) don't break POSIX but require conditional compilation (#ifdef **linux**) for portability. Programmers use autoconf/automake to detect features.

Importance for System Programmers

Standards like POSIX ensure code portability: a program using open(), fork(), and pthreads can compile on Linux, FreeBSD, or macOS with few changes. This reduces development time and bugs.

In practice:

- **Error Handling**: POSIX defines errno values, allowing uniform checks.
- **File I/O**: Standard behaviors for O_RDONLY, SEEK_SET, etc.
- **Signals**: Consistent sigaction() over BSD signal().
- **Shell Scripts**: POSIX sh compatibility avoids bashisms.

Non-compliance risks: vendor lock-in, maintenance overhead. For embedded Linux (e.g., Yocto Project), POSIX profiles enable minimal footprints.

Challenges and Criticisms

Standards evolve slowly, lagging behind innovations (e.g., containers predate standardization). POSIX's C-centric focus challenges newer languages like Rust, though bindings exist. Certification is expensive, deterring open-source projects. Fragmentation persists: Linux syscalls evolve (e.g., io_uring in kernel 5.1), requiring version checks.

Critics argue POSIX is outdated—e.g., no native async I/O until recent amendments—pushing alternatives like Plan 9's interfaces.

Future Directions

As of 2025, POSIX.1-2024 sets the bar, with work on Issue 9 potentially addressing quantum-safe crypto, AI workloads, and better container support. Linux kernel developers (e.g., via LKML) contribute to standards, ensuring relevance.

The shift to modular standards (like LSB's evolution) favors ecosystems like OCI (Open Container Initiative) for containers. With Rust in the kernel, standards may incorporate memory-safe languages.

In summary, POSIX and companion standards provide the glue holding the UNIX/Linux world together. For programmers, mastering them means writing robust, future-proof code. As Linux dominates clouds and devices, compliance remains key to its universality.

1.4 Modern Linux Distributions and Ecosystems

The landscape of Linux distributions and ecosystems in 2025 reflects decades of evolution, driven by community innovation, corporate investment, and emerging technologies. Linux distributions, or "distros," are customized versions of the Linux kernel bundled with software, tools, and user interfaces to cater to specific needs—ranging from desktop computing to servers, embedded devices, cloud infrastructure, and AI workloads. The ecosystem encompasses not just the distros themselves but also package managers, desktop environments, containerization tools, and orchestration platforms that enable seamless development and deployment. This section examines the current state of Linux distros, highlighting popular ones, key trends, challenges, and the broader ecosystem's role in system programming. As Linux powers over 80% of cloud instances, nearly all supercomputers, and billions of devices, understanding these elements is vital for programmers to choose the right environment, ensure compatibility, and leverage modern features like AI integration and enhanced security.

The Diversity of Linux Distributions

Linux's open-source nature has led to hundreds of active distributions, each tailoring the core kernel with unique software selections, update policies, and philosophies. Distros can be broadly categorized by their base (e.g., Debian-based, Red Hat-based, independent), release model (stable point releases vs. rolling updates), and target audience (beginners, experts, enterprises). According to market analyses, the Linux OS market is valued at approximately $9.1 billion in 2025, projected to grow to $18.73 billion by 2029, fueled by cloud computing and AI adoption. This growth underscores the ecosystem's maturity, with distros adapting to hardware advancements like ARM-based Snapdragon chipsets and Apple Silicon support.

Debian-Based Distributions: These emphasize stability and free software principles, deriving from Debian, one of the oldest distros founded in 1993. Debian itself remains a cornerstone, serving as the base for many others with its vast repositories (over 59,000 packages) and rigorous testing cycles. Releases like Debian 12 ("Bookworm," 2023) and the upcoming Debian 13 ("Trixie," expected 2025) focus on long-term support (LTS) for servers and desktops.

Ubuntu, launched by Canonical in 2004, dominates as the most popular distro. Ubuntu 24.04 LTS ("Noble Numbat," released April 2024) is hailed as the best overall for 2025 due to its user-friendly interface, extensive hardware support, and Snap package system for easy app installation. It's ideal for beginners and developers, with features like ZFS file system support and enhanced security via AppArmor. Ubuntu's variants include Kubuntu (KDE desktop), Xubuntu (XFCE), and Ubuntu Server for cloud deployments. In 2025, Ubuntu's AI integrations, such as pre-configured tools for machine learning with NVIDIA CUDA, make it a go-to for AI-ready setups.

Linux Mint, based on Ubuntu, prioritizes elegance and simplicity. Mint 22 ("Wilma," 2024) uses the Cinnamon desktop (a fork of GNOME) for a Windows-like experience, appealing to newcomers migrating from proprietary OSes. It includes out-of-the-box multimedia codecs and focuses on privacy, avoiding telemetry. Pop!_OS, from System76, targets hardware compatibility, especially for laptops with NVIDIA GPUs. The 2025 release features the COSMIC desktop environment, a Rust-based rewrite of GNOME, emphasizing customization and performance for creative workflows.

Red Hat-Based Distributions: Centered on enterprise reliability, these stem from Red Hat Enterprise Linux (RHEL), which powers mission-critical systems. RHEL 9 (2022) and the forthcoming RHEL 10 (expected 2025) emphasize hybrid cloud, AI, and security with features like Image Builder for custom OS images and Podman for container management. Free alternatives include Fedora, Red Hat's community upstream, with Fedora 42 (2025) showcasing Wayland improvements and Btrfs as default file system. Rocky Linux and AlmaLinux emerged post-CentOS's shift in 2020, providing RHEL-compatible binaries for servers. CentOS Stream, now the upstream for RHEL, aids in testing future features.

Arch-Based and Independent Distributions: Arch Linux, known for its rolling-release model, offers bleeding-edge software via the Arch User Repository (AUR). It's favored by experts for customization, with tools like pacman for package management. Manjaro simplifies Arch with user-friendly installers and hardware detection, ranking high in popularity. EndeavourOS provides an Arch-like experience with Calamares installer and themed desktops.

Independent distros like openSUSE offer Leap (stable) and Tumbleweed (rolling) variants, with YaST for system configuration. NixOS introduces a declarative approach, where the entire system is defined in configuration files, enabling reproducible builds—ideal for developers in 2025. KDE Neon delivers the latest KDE Plasma desktop on an Ubuntu base, focusing on aesthetics and productivity.

Specialized distros include Kali Linux for penetration testing, with Kali-i3 as a lightweight variant, and tails for privacy-focused, amnesic computing. For embedded systems, Yocto Project and Buildroot enable custom distros for IoT devices.

Key Ecosystems in Linux

The Linux ecosystem extends beyond distros to integrated components that facilitate system programming and operations.

Package Management and Repositories: Efficient software handling is core. Debian-based use APT (Advanced Package Tool) with dpkg; Red Hat-based employ DNF (successor to YUM) with RPM. Arch's pacman and AUR support community packages. Universal formats like Flatpak, Snap, and AppImage allow distro-agnostic apps, solving dependency issues. In 2025, these are pivotal for AI tools, with repositories hosting TensorFlow and PyTorch packages.

Desktop Environments and Window Managers: GNOME, with its gesture-based interface in version 48 (2025), dominates Ubuntu and Fedora, emphasizing extensions for customization. KDE Plasma 6.5 (2025) offers unparalleled configurability, with features like refined widgets and improved multi-monitor support. XFCE and MATE provide lightweight options for older hardware. Wayland, the modern display server, has largely replaced X11, enhancing security and performance in most distros.

Containerization and Orchestration: Docker revolutionized app deployment, but Podman (rootless containers) gains traction in Fedora and RHEL for security. Kubernetes (K8s) orchestrates containers at scale, with distros like Ubuntu offering MicroK8s for single-node clusters. In 2025, ecosystems integrate AI workloads via Kubeflow, enabling distributed training on Linux clusters.

Cloud and Server Ecosystems: AWS, Google Cloud, and Azure rely on Linux instances. OpenStack and Proxmox provide open-source virtualization. For servers, immutable OSes like Fedora Silverblue use OSTree for atomic updates, reducing downtime.

Development Tools: GCC and Clang compilers, Git for version control, and IDEs like VS Code thrive. Rust's adoption in kernels addresses memory safety. For system programming, tools like strace, gdb, and perf are standard.

Trends Shaping Linux in 2025

Several trends define the modern ecosystem:

- **AI and Machine Learning Integration**: Distros like Ubuntu and Fedora pre-install NVIDIA drivers and ROCm for AMD, supporting AI frameworks. AI-ready distros focus on GPU acceleration and data privacy. IT hiring emphasizes Linux skills for AI deployments.
- **Hardware Support Expansion**: Improved compatibility with Snapdragon (e.g., in Fedora) and Apple M4 Silicon via Asahi Linux project. This broadens Linux to laptops and mobiles.
- **Security Enhancements**: Kernel 6.x series includes Lockdown mode and better exploit mitigations. Distros adopt SELinux and Firejail. Privacy features in screenshot tools and dedicated security apps are emerging.
- **Desktop Renaissance**: With Windows 11's requirements pushing users away, 2025 could be "the year of the Linux desktop." Beautiful distros like ElysiaOS and BigLinux prioritize UX.
- **Sustainability and Efficiency**: Energy-efficient scheduling addresses climate concerns, with distros optimizing for low-power devices.

Challenges in the Ecosystem

Fragmentation remains: differing package systems complicate cross-distro development. Adoption barriers include hardware incompatibilities and learning curves. Corporate influence (e.g., Red Hat's decisions) sparks debates, but community governance via the Linux Foundation mitigates this.

Future Directions

Looking ahead, Linux ecosystems will deepen AI ties, enhance quantum computing support, and standardize container security. Contributions to open source, via platforms like GitHub, will drive innovation. For programmers, mastering distro-specific quirks—while adhering to POSIX—ensures robust applications.

In essence, modern Linux distros and ecosystems offer unparalleled flexibility, powering everything from personal desktops to global infrastructures. As system programmers, engaging with these—through installation, customization, and contribution—unlocks Linux's full potential.

2 Fundamental Concepts and System Overview

2.1 UNIX/Linux Architecture Basics

The architecture of UNIX and Linux systems forms the bedrock upon which all system programming is built. Understanding this structure is crucial for developers, as it reveals how software interacts with hardware, manages resources, and ensures efficient, secure operations. UNIX, the progenitor of Linux, introduced a elegant, modular design philosophy that emphasizes simplicity, portability, and reusability. Linux, while evolving this model, retains its core principles, adapting them to modern hardware and workloads. This section provides a comprehensive overview of the UNIX/Linux architecture, covering its layered design, key components, kernel internals, user-space interactions, and foundational concepts like processes, files, and I/O. By grasping these basics, programmers can write code that leverages the system's strengths, avoids common pitfalls, and scales effectively in diverse environments—from embedded devices to cloud clusters.

The Layered Architecture: A High-Level View

At its essence, the UNIX/Linux architecture is organized into layers, each abstracting complexity from the one below it. This hierarchical model promotes modularity, allowing changes in one layer without disrupting others. The primary division is between **user space** and **kernel space**, enforced by hardware mechanisms like privilege levels (rings) on x86/AMD64 processors or exception levels on ARM.

- **Hardware Layer**: The foundation includes the CPU, memory (RAM), storage devices (HDD/SSD), peripherals (keyboards, network cards), and buses (PCIe, USB). The operating system interacts directly with this hardware via drivers and low-level instructions.
- **Kernel Layer**: The kernel is the core of the OS, running in privileged mode with full hardware access. It manages resources, provides abstractions, and handles interrupts. Linux uses a monolithic kernel design, where all components (schedulers, file systems, drivers) are compiled into a single binary, loaded at boot. This contrasts with microkernels (e.g., GNU Hurd), where services run in user space for better isolation but potentially lower performance.
- **System Libraries and Calls**: Above the kernel sits the system call interface, a gateway for user programs to request kernel services. Libraries like glibc wrap these calls, providing higher-level functions (e.g., fopen() calls open() syscall).
- **User Space**: This encompasses applications, shells, utilities, and services running in unprivileged mode. User programs cannot directly access hardware; they must go through the kernel, ensuring security and stability.
- **Shell and Utilities**: The shell (e.g., bash) acts as an interpreter, executing commands and scripts. Utilities like ls, grep, and awk form the command-line toolchain, embodying the UNIX philosophy: small, composable tools connected via pipes.

This layered approach, pioneered in UNIX V7 (1979), ensures portability—Linux runs on architectures from x86 to RISC-V by abstracting hardware differences.

The Kernel: Heart of the System

The Linux kernel, initiated by Linus Torvalds in 1991, is a monolithic yet modular entity. As of kernel 6.11 (September 2024) and ongoing 6.12 development in 2025, it comprises millions of lines of C code, with growing Rust contributions for safety. Key subsystems include:

- **Process Management**: The kernel creates, schedules, and terminates processes. A process is an executing program with its own address space, resources, and state. The scheduler (Completely Fair Scheduler, CFS, since 2.6.23) allocates CPU time based on priorities and fairness. Real-time extensions (PREEMPT_RT) enable deterministic scheduling for embedded systems.
- **Memory Management**: Virtual memory allows processes to use more RAM than physically available via paging and swapping. The kernel uses page tables to map virtual to physical addresses, supporting features like copy-on-write (for fork()) and demand paging. Allocators like SLAB/SLUB manage kernel memory efficiently.
- **File System Management**: Everything in UNIX/Linux is a file—regular files, directories, devices, sockets. The Virtual File System (VFS) abstracts diverse file systems (ext4, Btrfs, NTFS), providing a uniform interface. Inodes represent file metadata, while dentries cache directory entries for speed.

- **Device Drivers**: Drivers bridge hardware and kernel. Char drivers handle sequential I/O (e.g., keyboards), block drivers manage storage (e.g., NVMe), and network drivers process packets. Modern kernels support hotplugging via udev and frameworks like devres for resource management.
- **Networking Stack**: Based on BSD sockets, it handles protocols from Ethernet to TCP/IP. The netfilter framework enables firewalls (iptables/nftables), and eBPF allows programmable packet processing.
- **Interrupt and Exception Handling**: Interrupts (hardware signals) and exceptions (software faults) are managed via vectors. Bottom halves (softirqs, tasklets) defer non-critical work to avoid latency.

The kernel boots via bootloaders like GRUB, initializing subsystems in sequence. Modules (loadable at runtime) extend functionality without recompilation, e.g., for proprietary drivers.

User Space and System Interfaces

User programs interact with the kernel through **system calls** (syscalls), invoked via software interrupts (syscall instruction on x86-64). Linux defines hundreds of syscalls (e.g., sys_read, sys_write), numbered uniquely per architecture. The libc library provides wrappers, handling parameter marshalling and error returns (negative values in eax/rax, with errno set).

POSIX standards ensure syscall portability, though Linux extensions (e.g., epoll for event notification) offer optimizations. For threading, the Native POSIX Thread Library (NPTL) maps user threads to kernel threads (since 2.6), enabling efficient concurrency.

The **environment** includes variables (e.g., PATH, HOME) passed to processes, influencing behavior. The shell manages job control, redirection (> , < , |), and scripting.

Core Concepts: Files, Processes, and I/O

- **Files and Directories**: The file system is a hierarchical tree starting at / (root). Paths are absolute (/etc/passwd) or relative. File types include regular, directories, symlinks, block/char devices, FIFOs, and sockets. Permissions (rwx for user/group/other) are enforced via mode bits, with ACLs for finer control.
- **Processes and Execution**: Every task is a process, identified by PID. Fork() creates children, sharing code but copying data (via COW). Exec() replaces the image with a new program. Wait() reaps zombies. Sessions and process groups manage terminals and signals.
- **Input/Output**: I/O is file-based—stdin (0), stdout (1), stderr (2). Unbuffered syscalls (read/write) contrast with buffered stdio (fread/fwrite). Select/poll/epoll monitor multiple descriptors efficiently.

Security and Privileges

UNIX/Linux security relies on discretionary access control (DAC). Processes run under user/group IDs (UID/GID), with root (UID 0) having full access. Setuid bits allow privilege escalation (e.g., passwd). Capabilities (since 2.2) granularize root powers (e.g., CAP_SYS_ADMIN). Namespaces (process, user, network) isolate environments, foundational for containers.

SELinux/AppArmor provide mandatory access control (MAC), enforcing policies beyond DAC. In 2025, with rising threats, kernels integrate Landlock for unprivileged sandboxing and eBPF for runtime security.

Modern Enhancements and Variations

While UNIX basics endure, Linux adapts to 2025 realities:

- **Containerization**: Cgroups limit resources; namespaces isolate. Docker/Podman build on this for microservices.
- **Virtualization**: KVM hypervisor turns Linux into a type-1 hypervisor, supporting VMs via QEMU.
- **Embedded and Real-Time**: Linux variants like Yocto customize for IoT; RT patches for predictability.
- **Cloud-Native**: Features like io_uring (async I/O since 5.1) optimize for high-throughput servers.

Architectural shifts include ARM64 dominance in mobiles/servers and RISC-V for open hardware.

Practical Implications for Programmers

In system programming, this architecture guides design:

- Use syscalls judiciously—prefer libraries for portability.
- Handle errors via errno/perror.
- Optimize for kernel boundaries—minimize context switches.
- Debug with tools like strace (traces syscalls), ltrace (library calls).

Understanding rings: user code in ring 3, kernel in ring 0, prevents direct hardware access, averting crashes.

Historical Context and Evolution

UNIX's architecture, refined in BSD and System V, influenced Linux. Minix inspired Torvalds, but Linux opted for monolithic for performance. Debates persist—microkernels offer better modularity, but Linux's speed wins in practice.

In 2025, with kernel 6.12+, Rust modules mitigate C's vulnerabilities, signaling evolution without disrupting basics.

This overview equips programmers with the conceptual framework for deeper dives. Mastery of UNIX/Linux architecture enables efficient, secure code, harnessing the system's power.

2.2 Files, Directories, and Input/Output

In the UNIX and Linux philosophy, files, directories, and input/output (I/O) mechanisms are central to the system's design, embodying the principle that "everything is a file." This abstraction simplifies programming by treating diverse resources—such as regular data files, hardware devices, network sockets, and even inter-process communication channels—through a uniform interface. For system programmers, mastering these concepts is essential, as they underpin data storage, retrieval, manipulation, and process interactions. This section explores the structure of files and directories, file system hierarchies, I/O operations via system calls and libraries, file descriptors, permissions, and advanced topics like symbolic links and directory traversal. We'll draw on POSIX standards and Linux-specific implementations, providing practical insights for writing robust, portable code. By understanding these fundamentals, developers can efficiently handle data flows, manage storage, and ensure secure, performant applications in environments ranging from desktops to embedded systems.

The "Everything is a File" Philosophy

UNIX's revolutionary insight, carried forward in Linux, is to represent nearly all system resources as files within a hierarchical file system. This dates back to early UNIX versions, where devices like terminals and printers were accessed via file-like interfaces in /dev. In Linux, this extends to procfs (/proc) for process information, sysfs (/sys) for kernel parameters, and even debugfs for debugging data. The benefits are manifold: uniform APIs reduce complexity, allowing the same read() and write() calls to work on files, pipes, or sockets; portability across hardware is enhanced; and composability thrives, as tools can chain via redirection and pipes.

Files are streams of bytes, with no inherent structure imposed by the kernel—interpretation (e.g., text vs. binary) is left to applications. Directories are special files containing name-inode mappings, forming a tree structure rooted at /. This model supports mounting multiple file systems (e.g., ext4 on /, NFS on /mnt/remote), creating a unified namespace.

File Types and Inodes

Linux recognizes several file types, identifiable via the st_mode field in struct stat (from stat() syscall):

- **Regular Files**: Store data, like documents or executables. Created with open() or creat().
- **Directories**: Containers for other files. Use mkdir() to create, rmdir() to remove (empty ones).
- **Symbolic Links (Symlinks)**: Pointers to other files/paths, created with symlink(). They enable aliases without duplicating data, useful for versioning (e.g., /lib/libc.so -> libc-2.38.so).
- **Hard Links**: Multiple names for the same inode, via link(). Deletion requires unlinking all references.
- **Character Special Files**: For sequential devices like terminals (/dev/tty). Accessed via char drivers.
- **Block Special Files**: For random-access storage like disks (/dev/sda). Handled by block drivers.
- **FIFOs (Named Pipes)**: For inter-process communication, created with mkfifo(). Unlike unnamed pipes, they persist in the file system.
- **Sockets**: For network or local IPC, created with socket(). Appear in file system if Unix domain (e.g., /run/mysocket).

At the core is the **inode** (index node), a data structure storing metadata: file type, permissions, owner (UID/GID), timestamps (atime, mtime, ctime), size, and block pointers. Inodes are file-system specific (e.g., ext4 inodes include extents for efficient large-file handling). The link count tracks hard links; when it hits zero, space is reclaimed. Use ls -i to view inode numbers.

File System Hierarchy and Paths

The Filesystem Hierarchy Standard (FHS) version 3.0 (2015, still current in 2025) defines standard directory layouts for consistency across distros:

- **/**: Root, top of the hierarchy.
- **/bin**: Essential binaries (ls, cp).
- **/etc**: Configuration files (passwd, fstab).
- **/home**: User home directories.
- **/lib**: Shared libraries and kernel modules.
- **/proc**: Virtual file system for process/kernel info (e.g., /proc/cpuinfo).
- **/sys**: Sysfs for device/driver info.

- **/tmp**: Temporary files, often on tmpfs (RAM-backed).
- **/usr**: User programs and data (/usr/bin, /usr/share).
- **/var**: Variable data like logs (/var/log), spool (/var/spool).

Paths are strings: absolute (/etc/passwd) start from root; relative (docs/file.txt) from current working directory (getcwd()). Path components are separated by /, with . (current) and .. (parent). Maximum path length is PATH_MAX (4096 bytes on Linux).

File systems like ext4 (default in many distros), Btrfs (snapshots, checksumming), and XFS (high-performance) mount on directories. The root file system is specified in /etc/fstab or by boot parameters.

Input/Output Operations: System Calls and File Descriptors

I/O in Linux revolves around **file descriptors** (FDs), non-negative integers indexing per-process open file tables. Kernel maintains these, starting from 0. Standard FDs: 0 (stdin), 1 (stdout), 2 (stderr), inherited by children. Key system calls (POSIX-compliant):

- **open(const char *path, int flags, mode_t mode)**: Opens or creates a file, returning FD. Flags: O_RDONLY, O_WRONLY, O_RDWR, O_CREAT (create if missing), O_TRUNC (truncate), O_APPEND. Mode specifies permissions for new files (e.g., 0644). Errors set errno (e.g., ENOENT for missing file).
- **read(int fd, void *buf, size_t count)**: Reads up to count bytes into buf, returning bytes read (0 at EOF).
- **write(int fd, const void *buf, size_t count)**: Writes count bytes from buf, returning bytes written.
- **close(int fd)**: Closes FD, flushing buffers if needed.
- **lseek(int fd, off_t offset, int whence)**: Seeks to position (SEEK_SET absolute, SEEK_CUR relative, SEEK_END from end).

These are unbuffered; data transfers directly to/from kernel. For efficiency, use larger buffers (e.g., 4096 bytes, page size).

Directories use specialized calls:

- **opendir(const char *name)**: Returns DIR* handle.
- **readdir(DIR *dirp)**: Returns struct dirent* with d_name, d_type, etc. Iterate until NULL.
- **closedir(DIR *dirp)**: Closes handle.
- **mkdir(const char *path, mode_t mode)**: Creates directory.
- **rmdir(const char *path)**: Removes empty directory.

For path manipulation: realpath() resolves symlinks, basename()/dirname() extract components.

Standard I/O Library: Buffered Operations

The C standard library (stdio.h) provides buffered I/O for efficiency, wrapping syscalls:

- **fopen(const char *path, const char *mode)**: Returns FILE*, modes like "r", "w", "a".
- **fread(void *ptr, size_t size, size_t nmemb, FILE *stream)**: Reads nmemb items of size bytes.
- **fwrite(const void *ptr, size_t size, size_t nmemb, FILE *stream)**: Writes similarly.
- **fclose(FILE *stream)**: Closes, flushing buffer.
- **fseek(FILE *stream, long offset, int whence)**: Seeks.

Buffering modes: fully buffered (_IOFBF, flushes on full), line-buffered (_IOLBF, on newline), unbuffered (_IONBF). Set via setvbuf(). This reduces syscall overhead but can delay data (use fflush() to force).

For directories, dirent.h provides POSIX functions, while glob.h handles pattern matching (e.g., glob("*.c")).

Permissions, Ownership, and Access Control

File security is enforced via permissions: read (r=4), write (w=2), execute (x=1), in octal (e.g., 0755 = rwxr-xr-x). Bits for user, group, other. Special bits: setuid (4000, run as owner), setgid (2000), sticky (1000, /tmp restriction).

Ownership: UID/GID, changeable via chown()/fchown(). Effective UID determines access, except for root.

Access checks: access() or faccessat() verify permissions. Umask sets default mode for new files (e.g., umask(022) yields 0644 for files).

Advanced: POSIX ACLs (getfacl/setfacl) for finer-grained control. Capabilities bound privileges.

Advanced I/O Techniques

- **Memory-Mapped I/O**: mmap() maps files into address space, allowing direct access without read/write. Efficient for large files, shared memory.
- **Asynchronous I/O**: aio_read()/aio_write() (POSIX.1b) for non-blocking operations, signaled on completion.
- **Vectored I/O**: readv()/writev() scatter/gather multiple buffers in one call.

- **File Locking**: flock() for advisory locks, fcntl() for mandatory/record locks.

In Linux 6.x (2025 kernels like 6.12), io_uring provides high-performance async I/O, reducing overhead for servers.

Error Handling and Best Practices

Always check return values; negative indicates error, errno set (e.g., EACCES, ENOSPC). Use strerror(errno) or perror() for messages.

Best practices: Close FDs promptly (avoid leaks), handle partial reads/writes in loops, use O_CLOEXEC to prevent inheritance, consider large file support (O_LARGEFILE, off64_t).

For portability: Stick to POSIX, avoid Linuxisms like inotify (file events) unless conditional.

Practical Examples and Implications

Consider reading a file: open(), loop read() into buffer, process, close(). For directories: opendir(), while(readdir()), handle entries.

In system programming, these form building blocks for tools like cat (simple read/write), find (recursive traversal), or servers (socket I/O).

Modern contexts: In containers, bind mounts expose host files; in cloud, S3-like object storage abstracts via FUSE.

This foundation enables deeper topics like processes and networking, where files model pipes and sockets.

2.3 Programs, Shells, and Execution Environments

Programs, shells, and execution environments are integral to the UNIX and Linux ecosystem, forming the bridge between user intent and system execution. In Linux system programming, a program is an executable file that performs tasks, ranging from simple utilities to complex applications. Shells serve as command interpreters, providing interactive interfaces and scripting capabilities to automate workflows. Execution environments encompass the context in which programs run, including variables, paths, and resource limits that influence behavior and security. This section delves into these concepts, exploring how programs are created and run, the role of various shells, scripting fundamentals, environment management, and best practices for robust execution. Drawing from POSIX standards and Linux specifics, we'll cover compilation, process creation, shell internals, and environmental controls, equipping programmers with the knowledge to develop efficient, portable software. Understanding these elements is key to mastering system interactions, debugging, and optimizing performance in diverse setups, from servers to embedded devices.

Programs: From Source to Execution

A program in Linux is a binary file containing machine code, data, and metadata, executable by the kernel. Programs stem from source code, typically in C, C++, or other languages, compiled into executables. The process begins with writing code, then compiling and linking.

Compilation and Building: The GNU Compiler Collection (GCC), standard in Linux, compiles C code. For a simple "hello.c":

c

```
#include <stdio.h>
int main() { printf("Hello, Linux!\n"); return 0; }
```

Compile with gcc hello.c -o hello, producing an ELF (Executable and Linkable Format) binary—the default on Linux since the 1990s. ELF headers detail sections: .text (code), .data (initialized variables), .bss (uninitialized), and dynamic linking info.

Linking resolves symbols: static linking embeds libraries (e.g., gcc -static), producing larger binaries; dynamic linking uses shared objects (.so files) loaded at runtime via ld.so, reducing size and enabling updates. Tools like ldd show dependencies, nm lists symbols.

Advanced builds use Make or CMake for managing dependencies. Makefiles define rules: hello: hello.o followed by gcc -o hello hello.o. In kernel modules or large projects, KBuild (Linux kernel's system) automates compilation.

Execution Flow: To run, use ./hello (assuming permissions). The kernel's execve() syscall loads the binary: maps segments into memory, sets up stack/heap, initializes registers (e.g., RIP to entry point), and starts execution. If it's a script, the shebang (#!) line (e.g., #!/bin/bash) invokes the interpreter.

Programs can be scripts in interpreted languages like Bash, Python, or Perl—no compilation needed, but slower. Python's interpreter (CPython) compiles to bytecode (.pyc) for caching.

In multi-user systems, programs run as processes with PIDs. Fork-exec model: parent forks (clones itself), child execs new program, replacing its image. This is foundational for shells launching commands.

Shells: The Command-Line Interface

The shell is a program that reads commands, interprets them, and executes programs. Originating from Thompson's shell in UNIX V1 (1971), it evolved into the Bourne Shell (sh, 1977 by Stephen Bourne), emphasizing scripting. Modern Linux defaults to Bash (Bourne Again SHell, 1989 by Brian Fox for GNU), POSIX-compliant with extensions.

Types of Shells:
- **Interactive Shells**: For user input, like login shells (.bash_profile) or non-login (.bashrc). They provide prompts (PS1), history (arrow keys), and completion (Tab).
- **Non-Interactive Shells**: For scripts, skipping profile loading for efficiency.

Popular variants:
- **Bash**: Feature-rich, with arrays, brace expansion ({1..10}), and functions. Version 5.2 (2022) adds improvements like better array handling.
- **Zsh**: Extensible, with modules for git integration, syntax highlighting. Oh My Zsh framework popularizes it.
- **Fish**: User-friendly, with autosuggestions, no POSIX compliance by default.
- **Dash/Almquist Shell**: Lightweight, used for /bin/sh in Debian for speed in boot scripts.
- **Ksh (Korn Shell)**: Blends Bourne and C-shell features, with pdksh/mksh open variants.

Shells handle built-ins (cd, echo) internally for efficiency, externals (ls) via PATH search.

Shell Scripting Basics: Scripts are text files with commands, executable via chmod +x. Start with shebang: #!/bin/bash. Variables: VAR="value", no spaces. Conditionals: if [$VAR -eq 1]; then ...; fi. Loops: for i in {1..5}; do echo $i; done. Functions: func() { commands; }.

Pipes (|) chain output to input: ls | grep txt. Redirection: > outfile, < infile, 2> errfile. Here documents (<<EOF) for multi-line input.

Subshells ((commands)) run in child processes; command substitution $(command) captures output.

In 2025, shells integrate with tools like fzf for fuzzy finding, enhancing productivity.

Execution Environments: Context for Programs

The execution environment defines the runtime context, influencing program behavior without code changes. Key components:

Environment Variables: Key-value pairs, inherited from parent processes. Access via getenv("VAR"), set via setenv() or export VAR=value in shell.

Standard vars:
- **PATH**: Colon-separated executable directories (/usr/bin:/bin). Programs search here.
- **HOME**: User's home (~ expansion).
- **USER/LOGNAME**: Current user.
- **LD_LIBRARY_PATH**: For dynamic libraries.
- **TERM**: Terminal type for curses apps.
- **LANG/LC_ALL**: Locale for internationalization (e.g., en_US.UTF-8).

Kernel passes envp[] to main(int argc, char *argv[], char *envp[]). Modify with putenv(), clearenv().

Working Directory: Current dir (pwd), changed via chdir(). Affects relative paths.

Resource Limits: ulimit or setrlimit() control max file size (RLIMIT_FSIZE), open files (RLIMIT_NOFILE), CPU time (RLIMIT_CPU). Prevent denial-of-service.

Arguments (argv): Passed to main(), argc counts them. Shell expands globs (*), quotes preserve spaces.

Process Credentials: UID, GID, EUID (effective). Setuid programs run as owner, risky but useful (e.g., su).

Signal Handling: Environment includes default dispositions; programs override with signal()/sigaction().

Integration: How Programs, Shells, and Environments Interact

Shells launch programs via fork-exec: parse command, resolve path, fork, child execve(cmd, argv, envp). If built-in, handle internally.

Scripts inherit environment: export vars to pass. Cron jobs have minimal env, requiring explicit sets.

Debugging: env command lists vars; strace traces execs; gdb attaches to processes.

Security: Taint checking in Perl flags unsafe env; sanitize inputs. PATH tampering can hijack commands—use absolute paths.

Portability: POSIX defines minimal env (e.g., PATH), but Linux extensions like XDG vars for desktops.

Advanced Topics in Execution

Dynamic Loading: dlopen() loads .so at runtime, dlsym() gets symbols. Useful for plugins.

Interpreters and VMs: Python, Java use env vars (PYTHONPATH, JAVA_HOME) for modules/classes.

Containers and Namespaces: Modern envs isolate via user/mount namespaces, altering perceived env without global changes.

Performance Tuning: Adjust OMP_NUM_THREADS for threaded apps; huge pages via vm.nr_hugepages.

In 2025 kernels (6.12+), eBPF traces execs dynamically, aiding monitoring.

Best Practices and Common Pitfalls

- Quote vars: echo "$VAR" preserves spaces.
- Use exec for efficiency: replaces shell without fork.
- Handle errors: $? for exit status, trap for signals.
- Avoid shellshock: Bash bugs (2014) highlighted parsing risks.
- Portable scripts: Use /bin/sh, avoid bashisms (test [[ ]]).

For programmers: Wrap execve() for custom envs; use posix_spawn() for lightweight spawning.

This interplay enables automation: cron scripts set env, run programs, manage output.

Understanding these fosters reliable software, from daemons to CLI tools.

2.4 Error Handling and System Limits

Error handling and system limits are critical aspects of robust Linux system programming, ensuring that applications gracefully manage failures and operate within defined resource boundaries. In the unpredictable environment of operating systems, where hardware failures, permission issues, or resource exhaustion can occur, proper error detection and response prevent crashes, data corruption, and security vulnerabilities. System limits, meanwhile, enforce constraints on processes to maintain system stability and fairness in multi-user setups. This section explores these topics in depth, covering error mechanisms like errno and strerror, best practices for handling failures, POSIX-compliant functions, resource limits via rlimits, and practical examples. We'll draw on Linux kernel behaviors, glibc implementations, and real-world scenarios to illustrate how programmers can build resilient code. Mastery of these concepts is essential for developing reliable software that performs well under stress, from simple scripts to high-availability servers, while adhering to standards for portability across UNIX-like systems.

Understanding Errors in System Programming

In Linux, errors arise from system calls, library functions, or application logic. Unlike exceptions in higher-level languages (e.g., try-catch in C++ or Python), C-based system programming relies on return values and a global error indicator. Most system calls return -1 on failure, setting the thread-local **errno** variable to a positive integer code describing the issue. This design, inherited from UNIX, allows fine-grained control but requires diligent checking after every potentially failing call.

Errno is defined in <errno.h> and includes constants like EPERM (1, operation not permitted), ENOENT (2, no such file or directory), EINVAL (22, invalid argument), and ENOMEM (12, out of memory). There are over 130 errno values in Linux, categorized into generic POSIX ones and Linux-specific extensions (e.g., EKEYEXPIRED for key management). Importantly, errno is not reset on success; programmers must only inspect it after detecting failure via return value.

To interpret errno, use **strerror(int errnum)** from <string.h>, which returns a human-readable string (e.g., strerror(ENOENT) -> "No such file or directory"). For output, *perror(const char s)* from <stdio.h> prints s followed by ": " and the strerror(errno) message to stderr. For thread-safe variants, strerror_r() avoids race conditions in multi-threaded programs.

Example of basic error handling in file opening:

```c
#include <fcntl.h>
#include <stdio.h>
#include <errno.h>
#include <string.h>

int main() {
    int fd = open("nonexistent.txt", O_RDONLY);
    if (fd == -1) {
        perror("open failed");
        fprintf(stderr, "Error code: %d - %s\n", errno, strerror(errno));
        return 1;
```

```
}
// Proceed with fd
close(fd);
return 0;
}
```

This outputs something like: "open failed: No such file or directory" and "Error code: 2 - No such file or directory". Always include <errno.h> and check immediately after the call, as subsequent functions might overwrite errno. For library functions like fopen() from stdio, which return NULL on error, errno is still set. However, some functions (e.g., strtol()) set errno to ERANGE for overflows but return a value, requiring checks beyond just return.

Best practices:

- Check every system call: Use if (ret < 0) { handle_error(); } patterns.
- Avoid global errno in threads: Use strerror_r(char *buf, size_t len, int errnum) for safety.
- Log errors: Integrate with syslog or custom loggers for production.
- Recover when possible: For transient errors (e.g., EAGAIN for non-blocking I/O), retry with backoff.
- Propagate errors: In functions, return -1 and set errno, or use custom error codes.

Common pitfalls: Ignoring errors leads to silent failures; assuming errno=0 means success (it's undefined); or using printf("%s\n", strerror(errno)) without checking failure first.

In modern Linux (kernels 6.x in 2025), syscalls like openat2() provide enhanced error granularity, but core mechanisms remain POSIX-compatible.

Advanced Error Handling Techniques

Beyond basic checks, sophisticated strategies enhance reliability:

- **Error Wrapping and Custom Handlers**: Libraries like glibc provide __errno_location() for direct access. Create wrappers: int safe_open(const char *path, int flags) { int fd = open(path, flags); if (fd == -1) { log_error("open", path, errno); } return fd; }
- **Signal-Safe Functions**: During signal handlers, only async-signal-safe functions (e.g., write(), not printf()) are usable, as errno might be perturbed.
- **Internationalization**: strerror() is locale-aware via LC_MESSAGES; use for user-facing messages.
- **Error Injection for Testing**: Tools like libfakeroot or fault injection in kernels (via debugfs) simulate errors for unit tests.
- **Assertions and Debugging**: Use assert() from <assert.h> for invariants (disabled in release with -DNDEBUG). For runtime, custom CHECK macros: #define CHECK(call) if ((call) < 0) { perror(#call); exit(1); }

In multi-threaded apps, pthread functions return error codes directly (e.g., pthread_create() returns EAGAIN), not via errno, for consistency.

For network programming, getaddrinfo() uses gai_strerror() for specific errors like EAI_NONAME.

System Limits: Resource Constraints

System limits prevent processes from monopolizing resources, ensuring fairness and stability. Linux inherits UNIX's rlimit (resource limit) mechanism, defined in <sys/resource.h>. Each process has soft and hard limits for resources like CPU time, file size, open files, and stack size. Soft limits are enforceable caps; hard limits are ceilings that only root can raise.

Key resources via struct rlimit { rlim_t rlim_cur; /* soft / rlim_t rlim_max; / hard */ }:

- **RLIMIT_CPU**: Max CPU seconds; exceeding sends SIGXCPU.
- **RLIMIT_FSIZE**: Max file size writable; SIGXFSZ on overflow.
- **RLIMIT_NOFILE**: Max open file descriptors (default 1024 soft, 4096 hard).
- **RLIMIT_STACK**: Max stack size (default 8MB).
- **RLIMIT_CORE**: Max core dump size (for debugging).
- **RLIMIT_AS**: Max virtual memory.
- **RLIMIT_NPROC**: Max processes per user.

Functions:

- **getrlimit(int resource, struct rlimit *rlim)**: Retrieves current limits.
- **setrlimit(int resource, const struct rlimit *rlim)**: Sets limits (soft <= hard; non-root can't increase hard).

Shells expose via ulimit (bash built-in): ulimit -n 2048 sets soft NOFILE. For permanence, edit /etc/security/limits.conf (PAM-enforced) or /etc/sysctl.conf for kernel params.

Example: Query and set open files limit:

```c
#include <sys/resource.h>
#include <stdio.h>
#include <stdlib.h>

int main() {
    struct rlimit lim;
    if (getrlimit(RLIMIT_NOFILE, &lim) == -1) {
        perror("getrlimit");
        return 1;
    }
    printf("Soft: %llu, Hard: %llu\n", (unsigned long long)lim.rlim_cur, (unsigned long long)lim.rlim_max);

    lim.rlim_cur = 2048; // Raise soft limit
    if (setrlimit(RLIMIT_NOFILE, &lim) == -1) {
        perror("setrlimit");
        return 1;
    }
    return 0;
}
```

RLIM_INFINITY denotes unlimited. Kernel enforces: exceeding NOFILE yields EMFILE errno.

In containers, cgroups (control groups) extend limits, managing CPU shares, memory, I/O bandwidth via /sys/fs/cgroup. Systemd services specify limits in unit files (e.g., LimitNOFILE=4096).

Modern additions: RLIMIT_RSS (resident set size, deprecated), RLIMIT_MEMLOCK (mlock() memory). In 2025 kernels, prlimit() syscall allows setting limits on other processes (via /proc/<pid>/limits view).

Integrating Error Handling with Limits

Limits often trigger errors: e.g., fork() fails with EAGAIN if NPROC exceeded. Handle by checking errno and possibly adjusting limits if privileged.

In daemons, pre-set limits: raise NOFILE for servers handling many connections. Monitor via getrusage() for usage stats (ru_maxrss, etc.).

Security: Low limits sandbox untrusted code; capabilities like CAP_SYS_RESOURCE allow non-root limit changes.

Testing: Use stress tools like stress-ng to hit limits, verifying error paths.

Practical Scenarios and Case Studies

- **Web Servers**: Apache/Nginx raise NOFILE to handle thousands of FDs; errors like EMFILE trigger graceful degradation.
- **Databases**: MySQL sets RLIMIT_CORE unlimited for dumps on crashes; handles ENOSPC (no space) by alerting.
- **Embedded Systems**: Low-memory devices set tight AS limits; code must handle ENOMEM with fallbacks.
- **Scripts**: Bash traps errors with set -e (exit on failure); ERR trap for custom handling.

In cloud environments, Kubernetes enforces limits via pod specs, mapping to cgroups; violations yield OOMKilled.

Portability: POSIX defines core rlimits; Linux adds extras like RLIMIT_MSGQUEUE. Use #ifdef **linux** for specifics.

Future-Proofing and Best Practices

As systems scale, anticipate errors: use robust logging (syslog-ng, journald). Adopt error types like Rust's Result for safer langs, but in C, disciplined checks suffice.

In 2025, with AI workloads, limits on GPU memory (via cgroups v2) become crucial, though not traditional rlimits.

Ultimately, proactive error handling and limit management transform fragile code into dependable systems, aligning with UNIX's resilient design.

3 Essential Tools and Development Environment

3.1 Setting Up a Linux Programming Workspace

Setting up an effective Linux programming workspace is the first step toward productive system programming. In 2025, with Linux dominating cloud infrastructure, embedded systems, and AI development, a well-configured environment streamlines coding, debugging, and deployment. This involves selecting a suitable distribution, installing core tools like compilers and editors, configuring version control, and incorporating virtualization for testing. Whether you're a beginner transitioning from Windows or an experienced developer optimizing workflows, this guide provides a step-by-step approach tailored to system programming needs—focusing on low-level C/Assembly work, kernel modules, and performance tuning. We'll emphasize POSIX compliance for portability, open-source tools for flexibility, and modern practices like containerization. By the end, you'll have a robust setup capable of handling everything from simple file I/O experiments to complex device driver development, all while leveraging the latest advancements in the ecosystem.

Selecting a Linux Distribution

The choice of distribution significantly impacts your programming experience, influencing package availability, stability, and community support. For system programming, prioritize distros with excellent hardware compatibility, up-to-date toolchains, and extensive documentation. In 2025, recommendations lean toward user-friendly yet powerful options that balance ease of use with access to bleeding-edge features.

Ubuntu 24.04 LTS (Long-Term Support) remains a top choice for developers due to its vast repositories, seamless hardware support, and Canonical's enterprise backing. Released in April 2024, it offers five years of support until 2029, with security updates and backported features, making it ideal for stable workspaces. Ubuntu's APT package manager simplifies installing tools like GCC and Git, and its popularity ensures abundant online resources—crucial for troubleshooting system calls or kernel issues. For programming, it includes pre-configured environments for languages like C, Python, and Rust, with easy NVIDIA/AMD GPU setup for AI-related system work.

Fedora Workstation 42 (expected in 2025) is another strong contender, sponsored by Red Hat. It provides cutting-edge software, including the latest GNOME desktop and DNF package manager. Fedora excels in container support with Podman and Toolbox, perfect for isolated development environments. Its focus on upstream contributions means early access to kernel features like Rust modules, beneficial for modern system programming.

For those preferring rolling releases, Manjaro or Arch Linux offer the latest packages via Pacman and the Arch User Repository (AUR). Arch's wiki is unparalleled for in-depth guides on custom setups, though its installation requires more expertise. Manjaro simplifies this with pre-configured desktops and hardware detection, suiting developers who want fresh toolchains without constant breakage.

Debian 13 ("Trixie," expected mid-2025) appeals to stability seekers, serving as Ubuntu's base. It's rock-solid for servers but works well for desktops, with APT and a commitment to free software.

Pop!_OS 24.04, from System76, targets hardware enthusiasts with built-in NVIDIA support and the COSMIC desktop (Rust-based for performance). It's Ubuntu-based but optimized for workflows like coding and gaming.

For lightweight setups, consider Puppy Linux or Alpine for embedded programming. Ultimately, start with Ubuntu for its balance; dual-boot or virtualize to test others.

Installing the Operating System

Installation is straightforward in 2025, with graphical installers handling partitioning and drivers. Download the ISO from official sites (e.g., ubuntu.com) and create a bootable USB using tools like Rufus (Windows) or dd (Linux/Mac). Boot from USB, select "Try Ubuntu" to test, then install.

During setup:

- Partition disks: Use guided options for beginners (erase disk, alongside Windows). For pros, manual with / (root, ext4), /home (separate for data), and swap (2x RAM or hibernation file).
- Enable full-disk encryption (LUKS) for security.
- Install third-party drivers for Wi-Fi/GPU if prompted.

Post-install, boot and run sudo apt update && sudo apt upgrade (Ubuntu) to patch. Set up users with sudo access via usermod -aG sudo username.

For virtual setups, use VirtualBox or VMware; for native performance, KVM via virt-manager.

Updating and Configuring the System

A fresh install needs configuration for programming. First, enable repositories: In Ubuntu, edit /etc/apt/sources.list for universe/multiverse.

Update packages: sudo apt update && sudo apt full-upgrade. Enable automatic security updates via unattended-upgrades.

Customize the desktop: Install GNOME extensions for productivity (e.g., Dash to Dock). Set up multiple workspaces for separating coding/debugging.

Configure shell: Default bash is fine, but install Zsh for features like autosuggestions: sudo apt install zsh, then chsh -s /usr/bin/zsh. Use Oh My Zsh for plugins.

Set environment variables in ~/.bashrc or ~/.zshrc: export PATH="$PATH:$HOME/bin" for custom scripts.

Install fonts like JetBrains Mono for terminals, and themes for eye comfort.

Installing Core Development Tools

System programming requires a toolchain. Install the build-essential meta-package: sudo apt install build-essential (includes GCC, G++, make, dpkg-dev). GCC 14.x (2025 standard) handles C23 features.

For assembly: sudo apt install nasm or gas (GNU Assembler).

Libraries: sudo apt install libssl-dev zlib1g-dev for common deps.

Debuggers: GDB (sudo apt install gdb) for stepping through code; Valgrind (sudo apt install valgrind) for memory leaks.

Profilers: perf (sudo apt install linux-tools-generic) for kernel-level analysis.

For kernel work: sudo apt install linux-headers-$(uname -r) pahole dwarves for module building.

Package managers like apt handle dependencies; use apt search for queries.

Choosing an Editor or IDE

Editors are personal; for system programming, lightweight ones shine.

Vim/Neovim: sudo apt install neovim. Configure with plugins via vim-plug for syntax, linting. Neovim 0.10+ (2025) supports Lua configs.

Emacs: sudo apt install emacs, extensible for C modes.

VS Code: sudo snap install code --classic. Extensions for C/C++, Remote-SSH. Ideal for integrated terminals.

CLion (JetBrains) for IDE lovers: Download from jetbrains.com, supports CMake.

For terminals: Install Kitty or Alacritty for GPU acceleration.

Setting Up Version Control with Git

Git is indispensable: sudo apt install git. Configure: git config --global user.name "Your Name"; git config --global user.email "email@example.com".

Generate SSH keys: ssh-keygen -t ed25519, add to GitHub/GitLab.

Use git init for repos; integrate with editors via plugins.

For build systems: Install make; for advanced, CMake (sudo apt install cmake).

Additional Tools and Virtualization

Containers: Install Docker (sudo apt install docker.io) or Podman for rootless. Use for reproducible envs.

Emulation: QEMU (sudo apt install qemu-system) for testing architectures; KVM for acceleration (sudo apt install qemu-kvm virt-manager).

Diff tools: Meld (sudo apt install meld) for visual comparisons.

File managers: Ranger for CLI navigation.

Productivity: tmux for sessions; fzf for fuzzy finding.

Best Practices and Customization

Backup configs with dotfiles repos. Use aliases: alias gc='git commit'.

Monitor resources: htop (sudo apt install htop).

Security: Firewall with ufw; AppArmor profiles.

For 2025 workflows, integrate AI tools like GitHub Copilot in VS Code.

Test setups in VMs to avoid breaking production.

This workspace setup empowers efficient programming, adaptable to needs.

3.2 C Programming Fundamentals for System Work

C programming forms the cornerstone of Linux system programming, offering direct access to hardware, efficient resource management, and a close relationship with the operating system's internals. Since the inception of UNIX in the 1970s, C has been the language of choice for kernels, drivers, utilities, and performance-critical applications due to its portability, speed, and low-level capabilities. In Linux, where the kernel itself is predominantly written in C (with emerging Rust integrations), understanding C fundamentals is indispensable for tasks like manipulating files, processes, memory, and system calls. This section provides a comprehensive foundation in C tailored to system work, covering syntax basics, data types, control structures, functions, pointers, memory allocation, error handling, and interfacing with the OS via libraries like glibc. We'll emphasize POSIX compliance for cross-platform code, best practices for security and efficiency, and practical examples relevant to Linux environments. As of 2025, with C23 (ISO/IEC 9899:2024) as the latest standard, we'll incorporate modern features like improved type inference and bit-precise integers while focusing on timeless principles that enable robust system software development.

C Language Overview and Evolution

C was developed by Dennis Ritchie at Bell Labs between 1972 and 1973 to rewrite UNIX, evolving from B (itself from BCPL). Its design prioritizes simplicity: a small set of keywords (32 in C89, expanded modestly), procedural paradigm, and static typing. C's influence is vast—languages like C++, Java, and Python borrow its syntax. Key standards:

- K&R C (1978): Informal, from "The C Programming Language" book.
- ANSI C89/ISO C90: Formalized types, function prototypes.
- C99: Inline functions, variable-length arrays (VLAs), complex numbers.
- C11: Threads (<threads.h>), atomic operations, Unicode support.
- C17: Bug fixes, no major features.
- C23 (2024): Attributes like [[deprecated]], bit_int for precise-width integers, constexpr for constants, improved enums.

For system programming, compile with GCC (GNU Compiler Collection), version 15.x in 2025, supporting C23 via -std=c23. Use clang for alternative optimizations. Always specify standards: gcc -std=c11 -Wall -Wextra -pedantic for warnings.

C programs compile to native code, linking against libc (glibc on Linux) for standard functions. Execution starts at main(int argc, char *argv[]), returning int (0 for success).

Basic Syntax and Data Types

C code is structured in functions, with statements ended by semicolons. Comments: // single-line (C99+), /* multi-line */.

Fundamental types:

- Integers: char (8 bits), short (16), int (32), long (64 on 64-bit), long long (64). Signed/unsigned modifiers. Use stdint.h for fixed-width: int8_t, uint64_t.
- Floating-point: float (32 bits), double (64), long double (80+).
- Void: For no return or generic pointers.
- Bool: _Bool (C99), via stdbool.h as bool (true/false).

In system work, prefer fixed-width types for portability—e.g., size_t for sizes, off_t for offsets. Arrays: int arr[10]; strings as char arrays or pointers, null-terminated ('\0').

Structures and unions: struct stat { ... }; for file info. Unions overlay members for type punning (careful with strict aliasing).

Enums: enum color { RED, GREEN = 5 }; C23 adds enum : int for underlying type.

Typedefs: typedef unsigned long ulong; for aliases.

Constants: #define PI 3.14 (preprocessor), const int MAX = 100; (runtime). C23 constexpr for compile-time.

Control Structures and Loops

Control flow directs execution:

- If-else: if (x > 0) { ... } else if (x < 0) { ... } else { ... }
- Switch: switch (var) { case 1: ... break; default: ... } Efficient for syscalls errno checks.
- Loops: while (condition) { ... }, do { ... } while (condition); for (init; cond; incr) { ... }
- Goto: Sparingly for error cleanup: err: free(mem); return -1;

In system loops, handle interruptions: while (read(fd, buf, size) > 0) { ... } but check errno == EINTR for signals.

Functions and Modularity

Functions encapsulate code: return_type name(params) { body }. Prototypes in headers (.h) for declaration.

Variadic: int printf(const char *fmt, ...); via stdarg.h (va_list, va_arg).

Recursion: Useful for tree traversals (e.g., directory walking), but stack-limited.

Inline (C99): inline int square(int x) { return x*x; } for optimization.

In system code, functions often return int (0 success, -1 error, set errno). Use static for file-local.

Pointers and Memory Management

Pointers are C's power and peril, central to system programming for hardware access and efficiency.

Declaration: int *p; p = &var; (address-of). Dereference: *p = 5;

Arithmetic: p++ advances by sizeof(int). Arrays decay to pointers: char *str = "hello";

Null: NULL (0), check before use to avoid segfaults.

Function pointers: void (*sig_handler)(int); for signal().

Dynamic allocation: malloc(size_t size) from <stdlib.h>, returns void*. Cast optional in C. free(ptr) releases.

Variants: calloc(n, size) zeros; realloc(ptr, new_size) resizes.

Errors: malloc returns NULL on failure, set errno=ENOMEM. Always check: if (!(buf = malloc(1024))) { perror("malloc"); exit(1); }

In system work, manage buffers for read/write: char *buf = malloc(BUFSIZ);

Avoid leaks: Use valgrind --leak-check=full ./prog.

Strings: strcpy, strlen, but prefer strlcpy (BSD) or strncpy for safety against overflows.

Arrays, Strings, and Data Structures

Fixed arrays: int arr[SIZE]; VLAs (C99): int arr[n]; (n runtime, but deprecated in C23 for safety).

Multi-dimensional: int matrix[3][4];

Strings: Manipulate with string.h: strcat, strcmp. For safety, use snprintf over sprintf.

Linked lists, trees: Implement manually—struct node { int data; struct node *next; };

In kernel code, use lists.h macros for intrusive lists.

Input/Output and File Handling

Stdio: printf, scanf, fopen, fread. For system: unbuffered syscalls preferred for control.

Low-level: #include <unistd.h> for read, write; <fcntl.h> for open.

Example: Copy file:

c
```c
#include <fcntl.h>
#include <unistd.h>
#include <errno.h>

int main(int argc, char *argv[]) {
    int in = open(argv[1], O_RDONLY);
    if (in == -1) return 1;
    int out = open(argv[2], O_WRONLY | O_CREAT, 0644);
    if (out == -1) { close(in); return 1; }
    char buf[4096];
    ssize_t bytes;
    while ((bytes = read(in, buf, sizeof(buf))) > 0) {
        if (write(out, buf, bytes) != bytes) { /* handle error */ }
    }
    close(in); close(out);
    return 0;
}
```
Handle partial writes, EINTR.

Error Handling in C

As covered earlier, check returns, use errno. Macros like ERR_EXIT("msg") { perror(msg); exit(1); }

Assertions: assert(condition) from <assert.h> for debugging.

Interfacing with the OS

System calls: Via wrappers in libc—fork(), execvp(), waitpid().

Headers: <sys/types.h>, <sys/stat.h>, <sys/wait.h>.

Environment: getenv("PATH"), environ global array.

Signals: signal(SIGINT, handler); or sigaction for advanced.

Best Practices for System Programming

- Compile with warnings: -Werror treats as errors.
- Sanitizers: -fsanitize=address for memory bugs.
- Security: Avoid gets(), use fgets; check bounds.
- Portability: Use autoconf for features.
- Performance: Profile with gprof or perf.
- Documentation: Doxygen comments.

Modern C23: Use typeof for generics, nullptr constant.

In Linux, C enables direct mmap() for files, shared memory.

This foundation prepares for advanced topics like threads and kernels.

3.3 Assembly Language Basics

Assembly language provides the lowest-level interface to a computer's hardware, offering unparalleled control and efficiency essential for certain aspects of Linux system programming. While higher-level languages like C handle most tasks, assembly shines in scenarios requiring optimization, direct hardware manipulation, or understanding kernel internals—such as writing bootloaders, device drivers, or performance-critical code sections. In Linux, assembly is used in the kernel (e.g., context switching, interrupt handlers) and for user-space applications needing fine-tuned operations. As of 2025, with diverse architectures like x86-64, ARM64 (AArch64), and RISC-V gaining prominence, assembly knowledge enables cross-platform development and debugging. This section introduces assembly fundamentals tailored to Linux, covering syntax, tools, key instructions, registers, memory models, system calls, and inline integration with C. We'll focus on GNU Assembler (GAS) for its integration with GCC, while touching on NASM for Intel syntax preferences. Examples will use x86-64 primarily, with notes on other architectures, emphasizing POSIX compliance and practical applications in system work. By mastering these basics, programmers can dissect binaries, optimize bottlenecks, and contribute to low-level projects like the Linux kernel.

Why Assembly in Linux System Programming?

Assembly bridges high-level code and machine instructions, translating human-readable mnemonics into binary opcodes executed by the CPU. Unlike C, which abstracts details, assembly exposes registers, flags, and memory directly, allowing precise control over cycles and bytes—crucial for real-time systems, embedded Linux (e.g., Raspberry Pi), or security tools like disassemblers.

In Linux history, assembly was vital: early UNIX kernels mixed C and assembly; Linux boot code (arch/x86/boot) remains in assembly. Modern uses include SIMD instructions for vector processing (e.g., AVX-512 on x86), atomic operations for concurrency, and custom syscalls. Drawbacks: architecture-specific, error-prone (no type safety), and verbose. Thus, use sparingly—profile first with tools like perf to identify needs.

Linux supports multiple Instruction Set Architectures (ISAs): x86-64 (AMD64) for desktops/servers, ARM64 for mobiles/embedded, RISC-V for open hardware. GAS, part of binutils, assembles for all; it's AT&T syntax by default but supports Intel via .intel_syntax directive.

Tools for Assembly Development

Assemblers: GAS (as) is standard, invoked by GCC. NASM offers pure Intel syntax, popular for standalone binaries.

Linkers: ld from binutils links object files (.o) into executables.

Debuggers: GDB (gdb ./prog) with layout asm for disassembly; objdump -d for static views.

Disassemblers: ndisasm (NASM), or radare2 for reverse engineering.

Editors: VS Code with extensions like x86 Assembly; Vim with syntax highlighting.

Compilers: GCC for inline assembly: gcc -S file.c generates .s assembly.

Install: sudo apt install binutils nasm gdb (Ubuntu); for kernel, build-essential plus linux-headers.

Emulators: QEMU for testing non-native arches: qemu-x86_64 prog.

Basic Syntax and Structure

Assembly files (.s or .asm) consist of sections (.text for code, .data for initialized data, .bss for uninitialized), labels (main:), instructions (mov), and directives (.global main).

GAS AT&T syntax: opcode source, destination; registers prefixed with % (e.g., %rax); immediates with $ (e.g., $42); memory [base+index*scale+disp].

Intel syntax (NASM default): opcode destination, source; no prefixes; brackets for memory.

Example Hello World in GAS (x86-64):

```assembly
.section .data
msg: .string "Hello, Assembly!\n"
len = . - msg


.section .text
.global _start


_start:
    mov $1, %rax    # syscall: write
    mov $1, %rdi    # fd: stdout
    mov $msg, %rsi  # buffer
    mov $len, %rdx  # length
    syscall

    mov $60, %rax   # syscall: exit
    xor %rdi, %rdi  # status 0
    syscall
```
Assemble and link: as hello.s -o hello.o; ld hello.o -o hello; ./hello.

In NASM: global _start; use db for data, mov rax,1 etc. nasm -f elf64 hello.asm; ld hello.o -o hello.

Sections: .text is executable; .data read-write; .rodata read-only strings.

Comments: # or ;.

Registers and Data Sizes

Registers are CPU storage units. On x86-64 (64-bit):

General-purpose: %rax (accumulator), %rbx (base), %rcx (counter), %rdx (data), %rsi (source index), %rdi (destination index), %rbp (base pointer), %rsp (stack pointer), %r8-%r15 (extended).

Sub-registers: %eax (32-bit of rax), %ax (16), %ah/%al (8 high/low).

Special: %rip (instruction pointer), %rflags (flags: ZF zero, CF carry, etc.).

Sizes: byte (8 bits, b suffix), word (16, w), doubleword (32, l), quadword (64, q).

Instructions specify size: movq $1, %rax (64-bit).

On ARM64: 31 general regs x0-x30 (x0 return/arg1), sp (stack), pc (program counter), zero register xzr.

RISC-V: 32 regs x0-x31 (x0 zero, x1 return address, x2 stack), pc.

In system code, preserve callee-saved regs (%rbx, %rbp) per ABI (Application Binary Interface). System V ABI (Linux x86-64) passes args in %rdi, %rsi, %rdx, %rcx, %r8, %r9; returns in %rax.

Key Instructions

- Data movement: mov src, dst; xchg swap; push/pop for stack.
- Arithmetic: add/sub/inc/dec src, dst; mul/div (implicit rax).
- Logical: and/or/xor/not src, dst; test (and without store, sets flags).
- Bit shifts: shl/shr/sal/sar count, dst (arithmetic preserves sign).
- Control flow: jmp label (unconditional); je/jne/jg (conditional on flags); call/ret for subroutines.
- Comparison: cmp sub2, sub1 (sets flags); test and, dst.
- String ops: movs (move string), scas (scan), lods (load).
- System: syscall (x86-64), svc (ARM), ecall (RISC-V) for kernel calls.

Flags in %rflags: ZF (result zero), SF (sign), OF (overflow), PF (parity).

Loops: Use loop instruction (dec %rcx, jnz) or manual: mov $10, %rcx; loop: ... dec %rcx; jnz loop.

Memory Addressing and Models

Memory is linear, segmented in x86 (but flat in 64-bit). Addressing modes:

- Immediate: mov $42, %rax
- Register: mov %rbx, %rax
- Direct: mov 0x1234, %rax (absolute address, rare)
- Indirect: mov (%rbx), %rax (contents at rbx)
- Base-displacement: mov 8(%rbx), %rax
- Indexed: mov (%rbx,%rcx,4), %rax (base+index*scale)

Stack grows downward: push decreases %rsp.

In Linux, processes have virtual memory: text (code), data, heap (grows up via brk/sbrk), stack (down). mmap for shared/anonymous.

Global vars in .data/.bss; locals on stack: sub $16, %rsp allocates.

System Calls in Assembly

Direct kernel interface: On x86-64, load %rax with number (from /usr/include/asm/unistd_64.h), args in regs, syscall instruction. Returns in %rax (-errno on error <0).

Example: getpid() - mov $39, %rax; syscall; (return in rax).

ARM: mov x8, #num; svc #0.

Avoid direct calls in user code—use libc wrappers for portability.

Inline Assembly in C

Embed assembly in C: asm("instructions" : outputs : inputs : clobbers);

Extended: asm volatile ("mov %1, %0" : "=r" (out) : "r" (in) :);

Volatile prevents optimization. Constraints: r (register), m (memory), i (immediate).

Example: Atomic increment:

c

```
int inc(int *p) {
    asm volatile ("lock incl %0" : "+m" (*p));
}
```

Useful for intrinsics like CPUID: asm("cpuid" : "=a"(a), "=b"(b), "=c"(c), "=d"(d) : "a"(leaf));

Debugging and Optimization

GDB: break *addr; si (step instruction); info reg; x/10i $rip (examine instructions).

Objdump -M intel -d prog for Intel syntax.

Optimization: Align loops (.align 16); use SIMD (movaps for aligned floats).

Profiling: perf record ./prog; perf report.

Common pitfalls: Forgetting size suffixes (movb vs movq); stack misalignment (16-byte for SSE); undefined behavior in inline.

Architectures Beyond x86-64

ARM64: Register-based, load-store (only ldr/str access memory). Instructions: add x0, x1, x2; conditional via suffixes (addeq).

RISC-V: Similar, rv64i base: addi rd, rs1, imm; ecall for syscalls.

Cross-compile: gcc -march=armv8-a for ARM.

In Linux 6.12+ (2025), RISC-V support matures with vector extensions.

Practical Examples

Fibonacci loop (x86-64 GAS):

assembly

```
.section .text
.global fib
fib:
    mov $0, %rax  # f0
    mov $1, %rbx  # f1
    mov %rdi, %rcx # n
    cmp $1, %rcx
    jle done
loop:
    add %rbx, %rax
    xchg %rax, %rbx  # swap
    dec %rcx
    jnz loop
done:
    ret
```

Call from C: extern long fib(long n); printf("%ld\n", fib(10));

String length:

assembly

```
strlen:
    mov %rdi, %rax  # ptr
    xor %rcx, %rcx  # count
```

```
loop:
    cmpb $0, (%rax,%rcx)
    je done
    inc %rcx
    jmp loop
done:
    mov %rcx, %rax
    ret
```

Best Practices and Security

- Comment extensively: Explain registers, assumptions.
- Follow ABI: Preserve registers, align stack.
- Security: Avoid buffer overflows; use canaries (gcc -fstack-protector).
- Portability: Use macros for arch-specific code.
- Testing: Unit tests with inline; emulate for cross-arch.

In 2025, tools like LLVM's assembler enhance optimization; Rust's asm! macro safens inline.
Assembly demystifies computing, enabling deeper Linux insights.

3.4 Version Control with Git and Build Systems (Make/KBuild)

Version control and build systems are indispensable tools in Linux system programming, enabling developers to manage code changes collaboratively, reproduce builds reliably, and automate complex compilation processes. Git, created by Linus Torvalds in 2005 for Linux kernel development, has become the de facto standard for version control due to its distributed nature, speed, and flexibility. Build systems like GNU Make and the Linux kernel's KBuild extend this by orchestrating the compilation of source files into executables or modules, handling dependencies, and supporting parallel builds. In 2025, with Git 2.51.2 as the latest stable release (October 2025) and preparations for Git 3.0 in 2026 introducing SHA-256 support, these tools continue to evolve, incorporating features like Rust integration and enhanced interoperability. For system programmers working on kernels, drivers, or utilities, mastering Git ensures efficient collaboration on projects like the Linux kernel (hosted on kernel.org), while Make/KBuild streamline building across architectures. This section covers Git fundamentals, advanced workflows, Makefile syntax, KBuild specifics for kernel modules, and integration strategies, providing practical examples for C-based system projects. By leveraging these, developers can maintain code integrity, automate testing, and scale to large codebases in environments from personal laptops to CI/CD pipelines. git-scm.com+2 more

Introduction to Version Control and Git

Version control systems (VCS) track changes to files over time, allowing reversion, branching for experiments, and collaboration without overwriting work. Before Git, tools like CVS and Subversion were centralized, but Git's distributed model—where every clone is a full repository—revolutionized development, especially for open-source projects like Linux.

Git's key advantages:

- Speed: Local operations (commit, branch) are instantaneous.
- Branching: Cheap and fast, encouraging feature branches.
- Integrity: SHA-1 hashes (transitioning to SHA-256 in Git 3.0) ensure data tamper-proofing. deployhq.com
- Offline work: Commit without network.
- Integration: With platforms like GitHub, GitLab, Bitbucket.

In Linux system programming, Git manages kernel patches (via git format-patch), tracks driver changes, and integrates with tools like quilt for patch series.

Installation: On Ubuntu/Fedora, sudo apt install git or sudo dnf install git. Latest 2.51.2 includes bug fixes and performance tweaks; upgrade via package managers or source from git-scm.com. Configure: git config --global user.name "Your Name"; git config --global user.email "email@example.com". Use git config --global core.editor vim for preferred editor. git-scm.com

Git Basics: Repositories, Commits, and Staging

Start with git init in a directory to create a .git repo folder storing history.
Working directory: Your files. Staging area (index): Files ready for commit. Repository: Committed history.
Core commands:

- git add file.c: Stage changes (or git add . for all).
- git status: Show modified/staged/untracked files.
- git commit -m "Message": Commit staged changes, creating a snapshot. Good messages: "Fix buffer overflow in read_file()".
- git log: View commit history (SHA, author, date, message). Use --oneline for compact, --graph for branches.
- git diff: Show unstaged changes; git diff --staged for index vs. last commit.

For system projects: Track C sources, headers, Makefiles. Ignore build artifacts via .gitignore: add "*.o" and "a.out".

Undo: git restore file.c (discard changes); git reset HEAD file.c (unstage); git checkout commit -- file.c (revert to version).

Branching, Merging, and Conflict Resolution

Branches isolate work: git branch feature; git checkout feature (or git switch feature in Git 2.23+).

Develop on branches, merge back: git checkout main; git merge feature.

Fast-forward merges if linear; otherwise, creates merge commit.

Conflicts: When merging, Git marks <<<<<<< HEAD ... ======= ... >>>>>>> branch. Edit, then git add to resolve.

Rebase: git rebase main (on feature) rewrites history for cleaner logs, but avoid on shared branches.

In kernel development, branches like linux-next integrate features before mainline.

Tags: git tag v1.0 commit; for releases.

Remotes and Collaboration

Remotes connect local to remote repos: git clone https://github.com/user/repo.git.

Add: git remote add origin url.

Push: git push origin main.

Pull: git pull origin main (fetch + merge).

Fetch: git fetch origin (update without merging).

Workflow: Fork on GitHub, clone, branch, commit, push to fork, pull request (PR) to upstream.

For Linux kernel: git clone git://git.kernel.org/pub/scm/linux/kernel/git/torvalds/linux.git. Submit patches via git send-email to mailing lists.

Advanced: git submodule for dependencies; git worktree for multiple branches checked out.

Advanced Git Features

- Stash: git stash save "WIP"; git stash pop to resume.
- Cherry-pick: git cherry-pick commit to apply specific changes.
- Bisect: git bisect start; git bisect bad; git bisect good commit to find bugs binary-search style.
- Hooks: .git/hooks/pre-commit for linting.
- Git 2.52-rc0 (November 2025) adds SHA1-SHA256 interop, aiding migration.phoronix.com
- Config: git config --global pull.rebase true for default rebase on pull.

Tools: git gui for visuals; tig for TUI log; GitKraken for GUI.

Security: Sign commits with GPG: git config --global commit.gpgsign true.

Introduction to Build Systems: Why Make?

Build systems automate compilation, linking, and testing, managing dependencies to rebuild only changed parts.

GNU Make (latest 4.4, 2023) is ubiquitous in Linux, parsing Makefiles to execute rules. It's declarative: specify targets and deps, Make handles order.make.mad-scientist.net

Alternatives: CMake (generates Makefiles), Ninja (faster for large builds), but Make is foundational.

In system programming, Make builds C projects, runs tests, installs.

Install: Included in build-essential.

Makefile Syntax and Basics

Makefiles contain rules: target: dependencies \n\tcommands (tab-indented).

Example simple Makefile:

makefile

CollapseWrap

Copy

- CC = gcc
- CFLAGS = -Wall -O2

-
  - prog: main.o util.o
    - $(CC) -o prog main.o util.o
  -
  - main.o: main.c util.h
    - $(CC) $(CFLAGS) -c main.c
  -
  - util.o: util.c util.h
    - $(CC) $(CFLAGS) -c util.c
  -
  - clean:
    - rm -f *.o prog

Run: make prog (builds if needed); make clean.

Implicit rules: Make knows %.o: %.c as $(CC) $(CFLAGS) -c $< -o $@.

Variables: = (simple), := (immediate), ?= (conditional). Built-ins: $@ (target), $< (first dep), $^ (all deps).

Phony targets: .PHONY: clean (not files).

Patterns: %.o: %.c \n\t$(CC) $(CFLAGS) -c $< -o $@

Functions: $(wildcard *.c) for files; (patsubst(patsubst %.c,%.o,(patsubst(SRCS)) for substitution.

Conditionals: ifdef DEBUG ... endif.

Parallel: make -j4 (4 jobs).

In system work: Add -g for debug; -D macros for configs.

Advanced Make Features

- Include: include config.mk
- Export: export VAR (to sub-makes)
- VPATH: Search paths for sources.
- Recursive Make: For subdirs, but avoid for speed—use non-recursive patterns.
- Automatic vars: $* (stem), $? (changed deps).
- Secondary expansion: .SECONDEXPANSION for delayed eval.

Debug: make -n (dry run); make -p (print db).

GNU Make 4.4 adds grouped targets (&: for multiple from one rule), .WAIT for sequencing in parallel.

KBuild: The Kernel Build System

KBuild, based on Make, builds the Linux kernel and modules. It's customized for modularity, configs, and cross-compilation. As of kernel 6.18-rc4 (November 2025), it supports Rust modules and enhanced parallelism.phoronix.comkernel.org

Kernel source: After cloning, cp arch/x86/configs/x86_64_defconfig .config; make menuconfig to customize.

Build: make -j$(nproc) bzImage (x86 kernel); make modules; make modules_install.

For external modules: Create dir with Kbuild file.

Example hello module:

hello.c:

c

CollapseWrap

Copy

- #include <linux/module.h>
- #include <linux/kernel.h>
-
- int init_module(void) { printk(KERN_INFO "Hello\n"); return 0; }
- void cleanup_module(void) { printk(KERN_INFO "Bye\n"); }
- MODULE_LICENSE("GPL");

Kbuild:

makefile

CollapseWrap

Copy

- obj-m += hello.o

Build: make -C /lib/modules/(uname−r)/buildM=(uname -r)/build M=(uname−r)/buildM=(pwd) modules
Install: sudo insmod hello.ko; rmmod hello.
KBuild vars: obj-y (built-in), obj-m (module). Configs via Kconfig files (bool, tristate).
Cross-compile: make ARCH=arm64 CROSS_COMPILE=aarch64-linux-gnu-
In 2025, KBuild integrates Cargo for Rust: obj-$(CONFIG_RUST_SAMPLE) += sample.rsm (but experimental).

Integrating Git and Build Systems

Use Git for Makefiles: Track changes, branch for build experiments.
CI/CD: GitHub Actions with make test.
Pre-commit hooks: Run make before commit.
Submodules for deps: git submodule add url libs/dep.
For kernels: Git manages patches; KBuild uses .git for version strings.

Best Practices and Common Pitfalls

- Git: Commit often, small; use meaningful branches (feature/, bugfix/); rebase before merge; sign-off for kernel (Signed-off-by: Name <email>).
- Make: Keep Makefiles simple; use $(MAKE) for submakes; avoid hardcoding paths.
- KBuild: Follow kernel coding style (checkpatch.pl); modularize.
- Pitfalls: Git ignores case on some FS; Make tabs vs spaces; stale .o files—use clean.
- Tools: ccache for faster rebuilds; distcc for distributed.
- Security: Git config --global url."https://".insteadOf git:// for HTTPS.

In system projects, these tools enable reproducible builds (e.g., via Docker+Git), essential for debugging kernel panics or optimizing drivers.
Thought for 27s

3.5 Emulation and Virtualization (QEMU/KVM)

Emulation and virtualization are powerful technologies in the Linux ecosystem, enabling developers to create isolated environments for testing, debugging, and running software across diverse hardware architectures without physical machines. In system programming, these tools are invaluable for simulating different CPUs (e.g., ARM on x86 hosts), booting custom kernels, isolating experiments to prevent host crashes, and replicating production setups. QEMU (Quick EMUlator) provides full-system emulation and user-mode simulation, while KVM (Kernel-based Virtual Machine) leverages hardware virtualization for high-performance virtual machines (VMs). As of November 2025, QEMU 10.1.2 (released October 20, 2025) introduces enhancements like improved RISC-V support and bug fixes for ARM64, while KVM, integrated into the Linux kernel 6.18 (with features merged in October 2025), offers advancements such as better AMD SEV-SNP confidential computing and Intel APICv optimizations. This section explores the fundamentals of emulation and virtualization, differences between QEMU and KVM, installation and setup on popular distributions, practical usage for system programmers, advanced configurations, and best practices. By incorporating these into your workspace, you can safely develop kernel modules, test cross-architecture code, and debug low-level issues, all while maintaining host stability and efficiency.

Understanding Emulation vs. Virtualization

At their core, emulation and virtualization allow running guest operating systems or applications as if on dedicated hardware, but they differ in approach and performance.

Emulation simulates entire hardware platforms in software. QEMU, an open-source emulator since 2003 by Fabrice Bellard, translates guest instructions to host ones dynamically (via Tiny Code Generator, TCG) or statically. This enables running, say, a PowerPC Linux on an x86 host without hardware support. Pros: High flexibility for exotic architectures (over 20 supported, including x86, ARM, RISC-V, MIPS). Cons: Overhead from translation reduces performance to 10-50% of native, depending on workload.

Virtualization uses hardware extensions to run guests near-natively. KVM, introduced in Linux kernel 2.6.20 (2007), is a type-1 hypervisor module that exposes /dev/kvm for user-space tools. It relies on CPU features like Intel VT-x (with EPT for memory) or AMD-V (with NPT), allowing direct execution of guest code with kernel handling privileged operations. Pros: Near-native speed (95%+ for CPU-bound tasks). Cons: Limited to architectures compatible with the host (e.g., x86 guest on x86 host).

QEMU often pairs with KVM: QEMU handles device emulation (disks, networks), while KVM accelerates CPU/memory. This hybrid (qemu-system-x86_64 -enable-kvm) combines flexibility and performance, ideal for system programming.

Use cases in development:

- Cross-compilation testing: Emulate ARM64 on x86 for IoT code.
- Kernel debugging: Boot custom kernels in VMs, attach gdb.
- Isolation: Run untrusted code or reproduce bugs safely.
- Multi-OS: Test POSIX compliance across Linux distros or BSD.

In 2025, with RISC-V hardware emerging and ARM in clouds (e.g., AWS Graviton), these tools support heterogeneous environments.

Installing and Setting Up QEMU and KVM

Setup varies by distro, but focuses on Ubuntu 24.04 LTS or Fedora 42 for their robust virtualization support.

Prerequisites:

- Hardware: For KVM, check CPU support: grep -E 'vmx|svm' /proc/cpuinfo (vmx for Intel, svm for AMD). Enable in BIOS if missing.
- Kernel: Linux 6.18+ includes KVM; ensure loaded: lsmod | grep kvm.
- User groups: Add to libvirt, kvm for non-root access: sudo usermod -aG libvirt,kvm $USER.

Installing on Ubuntu: sudo apt update sudo apt install qemu-system qemu-utils virt-manager bridge-utils libvirt-clients libvirt-daemon-system ovmf

This installs QEMU 10.1.2, KVM modules, Virt-Manager (GUI), and OVMF for UEFI. Start services: sudo systemctl enable --now libvirtd.

Installing on Fedora: sudo dnf install @virtualization

Includes QEMU, KVM, libvirt. For ARM/RISC-V: sudo dnf install qemu-system-arm qemu-system-riscv.

Verify QEMU: qemu-system-x86_64 --version (shows 10.1.2).

Verify KVM: kvm-ok (from cpu-checker package) or ls /dev/kvm.

For graphics: Install SPICE (sudo apt install spice-vdagent) or VNC for remote viewing.

Common issues: Nested virtualization (VM in VM) requires kernel param kvm_intel.nested=1; secure boot may need disabling for custom kernels.

Using QEMU for Emulation

QEMU emulates full systems or user processes.

Full-System Emulation: Boot an ISO: qemu-system-aarch64 -m 2G -cpu cortex-a72 -smp 2 -drive file=ubuntu-arm.img,format=raw -cdrom ubuntu-24.04.iso -boot d -nographic

- -m: RAM (2GB).
- -cpu: Emulated CPU model.
- -smp: Cores.
- -drive: Disk image (create with qemu-img create -f raw img 10G).
- -nographic: Console output.
- -boot d: Boot from CD (ISO).

For networking: -net nic -net user (NAT); or -netdev bridge for host integration.

Graphics: -vga virtio -display gtk (windowed); add -device virtio-gpu for acceleration.

User-Mode Emulation: Run binaries from other arches: qemu-aarch64 ./arm-binary. Useful for testing cross-compiled C code without full OS.

Static mode: qemu-aarch64-static for static bins.

In system programming: Emulate RISC-V for kernel ports: qemu-system-riscv64 -m 1G -kernel vmlinuz -initrd initrd.img -append "console=ttyS0" -nographic.

Debugging: -s -S (listen on 1234, frozen start); gdb -ex "target remote localhost:1234" -ex "continue".

QEMU 10.1.2 adds better multi-threaded TCG for emulation speed and enhanced virtio-blk for storage.

Using KVM for Virtualization

KVM requires QEMU as frontend (or libvirt).

Basic KVM VM: qemu-system-x86_64 -enable-kvm -m 4G -cpu host -smp 4 -drive file=vm.img,format=qcow2 -net nic -net user -display spice-app

- -enable-kvm: Activate KVM.
- -cpu host: Passthrough host CPU features.
- -drive format=qcow2: Efficient image (qemu-img create -f qcow2 vm.img 20G).

For installation: Add -cdrom iso.

Libvirt abstracts: virsh create domain.xml; or use virt-install:

virt-install --name testvm --ram 2048 --vcpus 2 --disk size=10 --os-variant ubuntu24.04 --location ubuntu-24.04.iso

Virt-Manager GUI: Create VMs, monitor resources.

Networking: Default NAT; for bridged: sudo brctl addbr br0; edit /etc/libvirt/qemu/networks/default.xml.

Storage: Pools via virsh pool-define-as.

In kernel 6.18, KVM improvements include faster live migration for AMD and better error handling for Intel TDP.

Practical Applications in System Programming

Kernel Development: Build kernel: make bzImage; boot in QEMU/KVM: qemu-system-x86_64 -enable-kvm -kernel arch/x86/boot/bzImage -initrd /boot/initrd.img -append "console=ttyS0 root=/dev/sda" -drive file=rootfs.img -nographic

Debug: Add -s -S; connect gdb.

For modules: insmod in VM.

Cross-Architecture Testing: Compile for ARM: CROSS_COMPILE=aarch64-linux-gnu- make; run in qemu-system-aarch64.

Security and Isolation: Use namespaces with unshare, but VMs for full isolation—e.g., test exploit code.

Performance Tuning: KVM for benchmarks: virtio drivers minimize overhead.

Embedded Simulation: QEMU emulates boards: -M raspi4 for Raspberry Pi; load custom firmware.

Container Integration: Podman/Docker in VMs for hybrid setups.

Advanced: PCI passthrough (-device vfio-pci,host=01:00.0) for GPU acceleration in VMs.

Advanced Configurations and Features

Networking Options:

- User-mode: Simple NAT.
- Tap/Bridge: For external access: qemu ... -netdev tap,id=net0 -device virtio-net,netdev=net0
- Multiqueue: -device virtio-net-pci,mq=on for parallelism.

Storage:

- Virtio-scsi for multiple disks.
- NVMe emulation: -device nvme,drive=disk.

Graphics and Input:

- -device virtio-gpu -display gtk for 3D.
- SPICE for remote: -spice port=5900,addr=0.0.0.0.

Snapshotting: qemu-img snapshot -c name img.qcow2; load with -loadvm.

Scripting: Use qemu scripts or libvirt APIs for automation.

KVM-Specific: Enable huge pages: -mem-prealloc -mem-path /dev/hugepages for performance. SEV (AMD): -machine q35,confidential-guest-support=sev0 -object sev-guest,id=sev0 for encrypted VMs.

In 2025, KVM's APICv (Posted Interrupts) reduces latency for virtualized workloads.

Monitoring and Debugging: virt-top for stats; gdb with -qemu gdb for kernel debug.

Best Practices and Troubleshooting

- Security: Run as non-root (qemu:///session); use AppArmor/SELinux profiles.
- Performance: Use virtio drivers in guests; enable KVM nested for dev in VMs.
- Resource Management: Limit CPUs/RAM to avoid host overload.
- Backups: Snapshot before experiments.
- Troubleshooting: Check dmesg for KVM errors; qemu -d cpu for trace.
- Updates: Kernel upgrades may require reboot for new KVM features.
- Alternatives: VirtualBox for simplicity, but QEMU/KVM for open-source purity.

Common pitfalls: Missing BIOS virtualization; image format mismatches (use qemu-img convert).

In system programming, these tools foster innovation—e.g., emulating quantum-resistant crypto on future arches.

4 File I/O: The Universal Interface

4.1 Basic File Operations and System Calls

File input/output (I/O) operations form the backbone of Linux system programming, embodying the UNIX philosophy that "everything is a file." This abstraction allows programmers to interact with diverse resources—such as regular files, directories, devices, pipes, sockets, and even kernel interfaces—through a consistent set of system calls. In Linux, file I/O is handled at the kernel level via the Virtual File System (VFS) layer, which provides a uniform interface regardless of the underlying storage (e.g., ext4, NFS, or procfs). Understanding basic file operations is crucial for tasks ranging from simple data logging to complex device driver interactions. This subsection focuses on the core system calls: open(), creat(), read(), write(), close(), and lseek(), along with related concepts like file descriptors, flags, modes, and error handling. We'll explore POSIX-compliant behaviors, Linux-specific extensions, practical code examples, and best practices for efficient, secure programming. As of Linux kernel 6.13 (stable as of November 2025), these calls remain foundational, with enhancements like improved error reporting and support for larger files via 64-bit offsets. By mastering these, developers can build robust applications that handle data streams reliably, ensuring portability across UNIX-like systems while leveraging Linux's optimizations for performance-critical scenarios.

The Role of File Descriptors

At the heart of Linux file I/O is the **file descriptor** (FD), a non-negative integer that serves as a handle to an open file or resource. FDs are process-specific, managed by the kernel in a per-process table (typically limited by RLIMIT_NOFILE, default 1024 soft). Upon process creation (e.g., via fork()), it inherits three standard FDs: 0 (stdin, input), 1 (stdout, output), and 2 (stderr, error output). These are opened by the shell or parent process and point to the terminal or redirected files.

When a program opens a file, the kernel allocates the lowest available FD (starting from 3) and returns it. FDs reference kernel structures like struct file, which track position (offset), flags, and inode pointers. Closing an FD releases the reference; if the last reference drops (link count zero), the file may be deleted or resources freed.

In multi-threaded programs, FDs are shared across threads, requiring synchronization (e.g., via mutexes) to avoid race conditions on reads/writes. POSIX ensures FD portability, but Linux extends with features like O_CLOEXEC (close on exec) to prevent inheritance in child processes.

Error handling is integral: Most calls return -1 on failure, setting errno (e.g., EBADF for bad FD, EMFILE for too many open files). Always check returns and use perror() or strerror() for diagnostics.

Opening and Creating Files: open() and creat()

The **open()** system call is the primary way to access files, defined in <fcntl.h> as:

```c
int open(const char *pathname, int flags);
int open(const char *pathname, int flags, mode_t mode);
```

- **pathname**: Absolute (/etc/passwd) or relative (file.txt) path. Supports ~ expansion in shells but not directly in calls—use wordexp() for that.
- **flags**: Bitmask specifying access mode and behavior. Mandatory: O_RDONLY (read-only), O_WRONLY (write-only), or O_RDWR (read-write). Optional: O_CREAT (create if missing), O_EXCL (fail if exists with O_CREAT), O_TRUNC (truncate to zero length), O_APPEND (seek to end before writes), O_NONBLOCK (non-blocking I/O), O_DIRECT (bypass cache for aligned I/O), O_SYNC (synchronous writes), O_LARGEFILE (64-bit offsets on 32-bit systems).
- **mode**: Permissions for new files (e.g., 0644 for rw-r--r--), masked by umask. Required if O_CREAT set.

Returns FD on success, -1 on error (e.g., ENOENT missing file, EACCES permission denied, EISDIR on directory without O_DIRECTORY).

Example: Open for reading:

```c
#include <fcntl.h>
#include <unistd.h>
#include <stdio.h>
#include <errno.h>

int main() {
    int fd = open("example.txt", O_RDONLY);
```

```
    if (fd == -1) {
        perror("open failed");
        return 1;
    }
    // Use fd
    close(fd);
    return 0;
}
```

For creation: open("newfile.txt", O_WRONLY | O_CREAT | O_TRUNC, 0666);

The **creat()** call, historical from UNIX V6, is equivalent to open(path, O_WRONLY | O_CREAT | O_TRUNC, mode). It's deprecated in favor of open() for flexibility but still available for legacy code.

Linux extensions: openat() (relative to directory FD, useful for thread safety and avoiding TOCTOU races), openat2() (since kernel 5.6, with RESOLVE flags for symlink control, e.g., RESOLVE_NO_SYMLINKS to prevent traversal attacks).

Permissions: Effective UID/GID checked; root bypasses. Use fstat() post-open to verify.

Reading Data: read()

The **read()** system call transfers data from file to buffer:

c
```
ssize_t read(int fd, void *buf, size_t count);
```
- **fd**: Open FD.
- **buf**: User-space buffer (must be valid, size >= count).
- **count**: Max bytes to read.

Returns bytes read (0 at EOF, positive otherwise), -1 on error (e.g., EINTR interrupted, EAGAIN non-blocking empty, EIO hardware error).

Read advances the file offset by bytes read. For pipes/sockets, may return less than count (partial read)—loop until done:

c
```
ssize_t total = 0;
while (total < expected) {
    ssize_t bytes = read(fd, buf + total, expected - total);
    if (bytes <= 0) break; // Error or EOF
    total += bytes;
}
```

Buffers: Use page-aligned (4096 bytes) for efficiency. For large reads, consider pread() (atomic with offset, no seek change).

In kernel 6.13, read() optimizes for NVMe with io_uring integration, but basics unchanged.

Writing Data: write()

Symmetric to read(), **write()** sends buffer to file:

c
```
ssize_t write(int fd, const void *buf, size_t count);
```

Returns bytes written, -1 on error (e.g., ENOSPC no space, EPIPE broken pipe).

Partial writes common on slow devices—loop similarly. Advances offset.

Atomicity: For regular files, writes < PIPE_BUF (4096 bytes) are atomic; use pwrite() for offset-specific.

Example copy program:

c
```
#define BUFSIZ 4096
char buf[BUFSIZ];
ssize_t bytes;
while ((bytes = read(in_fd, buf, BUFSIZ)) > 0) {
    ssize_t written = 0;
    while (written < bytes) {
        ssize_t ret = write(out_fd, buf + written, bytes - written);
        if (ret == -1) { /* handle error */ }
        written += ret;
    }
}
```

```c
if (bytes == -1) { /* read error */ }
```
Sync: fsync(fd) flushes to disk (slow); fdatasync() skips metadata.

Closing Files: close()

close(int fd) releases FD, flushing buffers if needed. Returns 0 success, -1 error (rare, e.g., EBADF).

Kernel decrements reference count; last close may trigger cleanup (e.g., socket shutdown).

Best practice: Always close, even on errors—use goto err or RAII-like in C++.

dup()/dup2() duplicate FDs (e.g., redirect stdout: dup2(new_fd, 1)).

Seeking and Positioning: lseek()

lseek() repositions offset:

```c
off_t lseek(int fd, off_t offset, int whence);
```

- **whence**: SEEK_SET (absolute), SEEK_CUR (relative), SEEK_END (from end).
- Returns new offset, -1 error (e.g., ESPIPE on pipes).

For random access: lseek(fd, 0, SEEK_END) gets size.

64-bit: Use off64_t, lseek64() on 32-bit, but _FILE_OFFSET_BITS=64 macro enables 64-bit in glibc.

SEEK_HOLE/SEEK_DATA (Linux-specific) find data/holes in sparse files.

Error Handling and Common Pitfalls

Errors pervasive: Check every call. Common errno: EINVAL invalid arg, EFAULT bad buf, EINTR (retry if signal).

Signals: SA_RESTART restarts calls, but manual loops safer.

Buffering: Syscalls unbuffered; for efficiency, use stdio (fread/fwrite) but fflush() for prompts.

Security: Avoid races—use O_CREAT | O_EXCL for temp files; check fstat() for ownership.

Performance: Batch I/O; align buffers to page size (posix_memalign()).

Portability: Stick to POSIX; Linux O_TMPFILE creates unnamed files.

Practical Examples and Use Cases

Temp file:

```c
int fd = open("/tmp/tempfile", O_RDWR | O_CREAT | O_EXCL, 0600);
if (fd == -1) return 1;
// Write data
close(fd); unlink("/tmp/tempfile"); // Cleanup
```

Append log:

```c
int logfd = open("log.txt", O_WRONLY | O_APPEND | O_CREAT, 0644);
// write(logfd, entry, len);
close(logfd);
```

Device I/O: open("/dev/urandom", O_RDONLY); read for random bytes.

In kernels, file ops in struct file_operations { .read, .write, ... }.

Modern: io_uring_submit() for async, but basics first.

These operations enable universal I/O, foundational for advanced topics.

4.2 Buffered vs. Unbuffered I/O

In Linux system programming, the choice between buffered and unbuffered I/O significantly impacts performance, resource usage, and code complexity. Buffered I/O involves intermediate user-space caches that batch operations to reduce the frequency of costly system calls, while unbuffered I/O interacts directly with the kernel for immediate data transfer. This distinction traces back to early UNIX designs, where efficiency was paramount on limited hardware, and persists in modern Linux as a tool for optimizing applications—from high-throughput servers to embedded systems. Understanding these modes is essential for handling large datasets, real-time requirements, or low-latency needs, as improper choice can lead to bottlenecks or unnecessary overhead. This subsection delves into the mechanics, advantages, drawbacks, and practical implementations of both approaches, drawing on POSIX standards and Linux-specific behaviors. We'll cover standard I/O library functions (stdio.h) for buffering, direct system calls for unbuffered access, buffering modes, flushing strategies, error considerations, and performance tuning. As of the stable Linux kernel 6.17 (released September 2025, with updates through 6.17.7 in November 2025) and the ongoing 6.18 release candidate cycle (rc4 as of November 2025), features like enhanced page cache management and io_uring for asynchronous I/O complement these basics, but the core buffered/unbuffered paradigm remains unchanged. By selecting the appropriate mode, programmers can achieve optimal efficiency, ensuring applications scale effectively in diverse environments.

The Fundamentals of I/O Buffering

I/O operations in Linux involve transferring data between user space and kernel space, often crossing hardware boundaries (e.g., disk, network). Each system call incurs overhead: context switches, parameter validation, and kernel processing. To mitigate this, buffering accumulates data in memory before flushing to the kernel, amortizing costs over larger chunks.

Unbuffered I/O uses direct system calls like read() and write() from <unistd.h>, sending/receiving data immediately without user-space caching. The kernel may still buffer internally via the page cache (a RAM-based disk buffer), but the application has no control over user-level buffering. This mode suits scenarios requiring precise control, such as large block transfers or when data must be committed instantly (e.g., databases with O_DIRECT).

Buffered I/O, provided by the C standard library (glibc on Linux), wraps unbuffered calls in functions like fread() and fwrite() from <stdio.h>. It maintains internal buffers (default 4096-8192 bytes, BUFSIZ macro) to collect data, invoking syscalls only when full, on flush, or close. This reduces syscall frequency—for example, writing one byte at a time without buffering would trigger a syscall per byte, versus once per buffer fill.

Historical context: Buffered I/O emerged in early C libraries to optimize for slow peripherals like tapes and terminals. POSIX mandates stdio behavior, ensuring portability, while Linux glibc enhances with thread-safety (since 2.0) and customizable buffers.

Key differences:

- **Syscall Frequency**: Buffered: Low (batched); Unbuffered: High (per call).
- **Performance**: Buffered excels for small, frequent I/O (e.g., line-by-line processing); Unbuffered for bulk (e.g., copying large files).
- **Control**: Unbuffered offers direct error feedback and positioning; Buffered may delay errors until flush.
- **Overhead**: Buffered adds memory (buffers) and complexity (flushing); Unbuffered is simpler but potentially slower for fine-grained ops.

In kernel 6.17, the page cache uses radix trees for efficient buffering, with readahead predicting future reads to preload data, benefiting both modes.

Unbuffered I/O: Direct System Calls

Unbuffered operations bypass user-space buffers, relying solely on kernel mechanisms. Core functions:

- **read(int fd, void *buf, size_t count)**: Reads up to count bytes into buf. Returns bytes read, 0 on EOF, -1 on error.
- **write(int fd, const void *buf, size_t count)**: Writes up to count bytes from buf. Returns bytes written, -1 on error.

These are atomic for small sizes (< PIPE_BUF) on pipes/files but can be partial on slow devices—always loop to handle full transfer.

Example: Copy file unbuffered:

c

```
#include <unistd.h>
#include <fcntl.h>
#include <errno.h>
```

```c
#include <stdio.h>

#define BUF_SIZE 8192  // Optimal for many systems

int main(int argc, char *argv[]) {
    if (argc != 3) {
        fprintf(stderr, "Usage: %s source dest\n", argv[0]);
        return 1;
    }
    int in = open(argv[1], O_RDONLY);
    if (in == -1) { perror("open source"); return 1; }
    int out = open(argv[2], O_WRONLY | O_CREAT | O_TRUNC, 0666);
    if (out == -1) { perror("open dest"); close(in); return 1; }

    char buf[BUF_SIZE];
    ssize_t bytes;
    while ((bytes = read(in, buf, BUF_SIZE)) > 0) {
        ssize_t written = 0;
        while (written < bytes) {
            ssize_t ret = write(out, buf + written, bytes - written);
            if (ret == -1) {
                if (errno == EINTR) continue;
                perror("write");
                close(in); close(out);
                return 1;
            }
            written += ret;
        }
    }
    if (bytes == -1) { perror("read"); }
    close(in); close(out);
    return 0;
}
```

This manually manages buffering via BUF_SIZE, mimicking kernel page size for efficiency. Pros: Precise control, no extra memory. Cons: More code for partial handling, higher syscall count for small I/O.

Variants: pread()/pwrite() for offset-specific without lseek(), useful in threads to avoid seek races.

Linux specifics: O_DIRECT flag in open() bypasses kernel page cache, requiring aligned buffers (use posix_memalign()) for direct disk I/O, reducing double-buffering but increasing latency for small ops.

Buffered I/O: The Standard I/O Library

Buffered I/O uses FILE* streams from stdio, abstracting FDs with buffering logic.

Key functions:

- **fopen(const char *path, const char *mode)**: Opens stream. Modes: "r" (read), "w" (write/trunc), "a" (append), "+" for read-write, "b" for binary (no CRLF translation, irrelevant on Linux).
- **fread(void *ptr, size_t size, size_t nmemb, FILE *stream)**: Reads nmemb items of size bytes.
- **fwrite(const void *ptr, size_t size, size_t nmemb, FILE *stream)**: Writes similarly.
- **fclose(FILE *stream)**: Closes, flushes buffer.
- **fseek(FILE *stream, long offset, int whence)**: Seeks, may flush.
- **ftell(FILE *stream)**: Current position.

Streams: stdin, stdout, stderr (pre-opened, line-buffered for terminals).

Buffering modes (set via setvbuf()):

- **_IOFBF (Fully Buffered)**: Flush on full buffer or fclose/fflush. Default for files.
- **_IOLBF (Line Buffered)**: Flush on newline ('\n') or full. Default for terminals (prompt visibility).
- **_IONBF (Unbuffered)**: No buffering, like direct syscalls. Default for stderr.

Control:

- **setbuf(FILE *stream, char *buf)**: Sets buffer (BUFSIZ bytes) or NULL for unbuffered.

- **setvbuf(FILE *stream, char *buf, int mode, size_t size)**: Custom mode/size. Call after fopen, before I/O.

Flush: *fflush(FILE stream)* forces write (NULL for all). Essential for logs or interactive output.

Example: Buffered copy (simpler than unbuffered):

c
```c
#include <stdio.h>

int main(int argc, char *argv[]) {
    if (argc != 3) {
        fprintf(stderr, "Usage: %s source dest\n", argv[0]);
        return 1;
    }
    FILE *in = fopen(argv[1], "rb");
    if (!in) { perror("fopen source"); return 1; }
    FILE *out = fopen(argv[2], "wb");
    if (!out) { perror("fopen dest"); fclose(in); return 1; }

    char buf[BUFSIZ];
    size_t bytes;
    while ((bytes = fread(buf, 1, BUFSIZ, in)) > 0) {
        if (fwrite(buf, 1, bytes, out) != bytes) {
            perror("fwrite");
            fclose(in); fclose(out);
            return 1;
        }
    }
    if (ferror(in)) { perror("fread"); }
    fclose(in); fclose(out);
    return 0;
}
```

This auto-handles partials via internal loops. For custom: setvbuf(out, NULL, _IOFBF, 16384); for larger buffer.

Error: feof()/ferror() check EOF/error; clearerr() resets.

Performance Considerations and Trade-offs

Buffered I/O shines for frequent small ops: e.g., parsing CSV line-by-line with fgets() (reads until '\n', flushes on full/line). Reduces syscalls from thousands to dozens.

Unbuffered better for bulk: Copying GB files with large BUF_SIZE avoids double-buffering (user + kernel cache).

Measurements: Use time ./prog or strace -c to count syscalls. Buffered might show fewer read/write but added overhead in memcpy to buffer.

When to choose:
- Buffered: Text processing, console I/O, simplicity.
- Unbuffered: Binary/large files, real-time (no delay), direct control (e.g., O_SYNC).
- Mix: fopen() then fileno() for FD, fdopen() for stream from FD.

Kernel buffering: Page cache caches reads/writes; buffered stdio adds layer—potential inefficiency. O_DIRECT skips kernel cache, but requires alignment (multiple of block size, e.g., 512 bytes).

In multi-threaded: stdio locks streams (flockfile()/funlockfile() for manual); unbuffered needs user locks.

Modern alternatives: mmap() for memory-mapped I/O (zero-copy, shared), io_uring (kernel 5.1+, async batched) for high-perf unbuffered.

Error Handling and Best Practices

Buffered delays errors: fwrite() may succeed, but fflush() fail (e.g., ENOSPC). Check ferror() after ops.

Unbuffered: Immediate errors.

Practices:
- Allocate buffers dynamically if large.
- For terminals: Line buffering prevents delayed output.
- Flush logs on critical events.
- Binary mode ("b") for portability, though Linux ignores.

- Thread-safety: Use unlocked stdio (getchar_unlocked()) if locked externally.
- Efficiency: Tune buffer size to workload (e.g., 64KB for networks).

Pitfalls: Mixing buffered/unbuffered on same FD (e.g., fread() after write() without fseek/fflush—undefined).

Forcing unbuffered on stdio: setvbuf(stdout, NULL, _IONBF, 0);

Security: Buffer overflows in custom code; use safe functions.

Advanced Topics and Linux Specifics

Kernel page cache: read() populates, write() dirties pages; sync() flushes system-wide.

Direct I/O: Align buf to page size: void *buf; posix_memalign(&buf, 4096, size);

Asynchronous: aio_read()/aio_write() (POSIX.1b), but io_uring preferred in 6.17 for scalability.

In embedded: Smaller BUFSIZ; unbuffered to save RAM.

Examples: Network servers use unbuffered for sockets (O_NONBLOCK + epoll); logs buffered with periodic fflush.

This comparison equips programmers to optimize I/O, balancing efficiency and control.

4.3 Advanced File I/O Techniques

Building on the basics of file operations and the distinctions between buffered and unbuffered I/O, advanced file I/O techniques in Linux empower programmers to achieve higher performance, better resource utilization, and more sophisticated data handling. These methods address limitations in simple read/write models, such as excessive system calls for scattered data, synchronous blocking in high-latency environments, and inefficient memory copies between user and kernel space. In modern Linux, advanced I/O is crucial for applications like databases, web servers, and big data processing, where throughput and latency are critical. This subsection explores key techniques: vectored I/O (readv/writev), memory-mapped I/O (mmap), asynchronous I/O (including legacy aio and modern io_uring), zero-copy mechanisms (sendfile, splice), direct I/O, file advising (posix_fadvise, madvise), and sparse file management. We'll cover POSIX standards, Linux extensions, code examples, performance implications, and error handling, with a focus on kernel 6.17 (stable as of September 2025) and the 6.18 release candidate (rc4 in November 2025), which enhance io_uring for better scalability and introduce refinements to page cache handling. By leveraging these, developers can optimize for multicore systems, NVMe storage, and network-bound workloads, ensuring applications scale efficiently while maintaining portability.

Vectored I/O: readv() and writev()

Vectored I/O, also known as scatter-gather, allows reading from or writing to multiple non-contiguous buffers in a single system call, reducing overhead compared to multiple read/write invocations. Defined in POSIX.1 (<sys/uio.h>), it's ideal for protocols with headers/footers or fragmented data structures.

The calls:

- **ssize_t readv(int fd, const struct iovec *iov, int iovcnt)**: Reads into iovcnt buffers described by iov.
- **ssize_t writev(int fd, const struct iovec *iov, int iovcnt)**: Writes from iovcnt buffers.

Struct iovec { void *iov_base; size_t iov_len; } specifies each segment.

Returns total bytes transferred, -1 on error. Atomic for small totals (< PIPE_BUF on pipes).

Example: Write header and body:

c
```c
#include <sys/uio.h>
#include <unistd.h>
#include <string.h>

int main() {
    char header[] = "Header: ";
    char body[] = "Hello, Vectored I/O!\n";
    struct iovec iov[2];
    iov[0].iov_base = header;
    iov[0].iov_len = strlen(header);
    iov[1].iov_base = body;
    iov[1].iov_len = strlen(body);

    ssize_t written = writev(STDOUT_FILENO, iov, 2);
    if (written == -1) { perror("writev"); return 1; }
    return 0;
```

}

This outputs "Header: Hello, Vectored I/O!" in one syscall. For reads, useful in parsing multipart data.

Posix variants: preadv()/pwritev() (since POSIX.1-2008) add offset, atomic without lseek.

Linux limits: iovcnt <= UIO_MAXIOV (1024 default). Performance: Reduces syscalls, but kernel copies data—combine with O_DIRECT for optimization.

Errors: EFAULT (bad iov), EINVAL (invalid count), partial on interrupts—loop to complete.

Memory-Mapped I/O: mmap() and munmap()

Memory-mapped I/O maps files or devices into process address space, allowing access via pointers without explicit read/write. This enables zero-copy (for shared mappings) and lazy loading (demand paging). From <sys/mman.h>, POSIX-compliant.

void *mmap(void *addr, size_t length, int prot, int flags, int fd, off_t offset): Maps length bytes from offset in fd. Prot: PROT_READ, PROT_WRITE, PROT_EXEC. Flags: MAP_SHARED (changes propagate), MAP_PRIVATE (copy-on-write), MAP_ANONYMOUS (no file, for alloc), MAP_FIXED (at addr).

Returns mapped address, MAP_FAILED (-1) on error.

int munmap(void *addr, size_t length): Unmaps.

Kernel uses page faults to load data; writes dirty pages back asynchronously (msync() for sync).

Example: Map and modify file:

```c
#include <sys/mman.h>
#include <fcntl.h>
#include <unistd.h>
#include <stdio.h>
#include <string.h>

int main() {
    int fd = open("file.txt", O_RDWR);
    if (fd == -1) { perror("open"); return 1; }
    off_t len = lseek(fd, 0, SEEK_END); // Get size
    void *map = mmap(NULL, len, PROT_READ | PROT_WRITE, MAP_SHARED, fd, 0);
    if (map == MAP_FAILED) { perror("mmap"); close(fd); return 1; }

    // Access like array
    memcpy(map, "Modified content", 16);

    msync(map, len, MS_SYNC); // Flush
    munmap(map, len);
    close(fd);
    return 0;
}
```

Pros: Efficient for random access (e.g., databases), shared memory IPC. Cons: Page-aligned (length multiple of PAGE_SIZE, 4096), SIGBUS on holes/sparse.

Linux: MAP_POPULATE preloads, MAP_HUGETLB for huge pages (reduce TLB misses). Kernel 6.17 optimizes mmap for large mappings with better vma merging.

Errors: ENOMEM (no space), EACCES (no perm), EINVAL (bad args). Handle SIGSEGV/SIGBUS for access violations.

Asynchronous I/O: aio and io_uring

Synchronous I/O blocks until complete; async allows overlap with computation.

Legacy AIO (POSIX.1b, <aio.h>): aio_read()/aio_write() queue ops, aio_suspend() wait, aio_error() check status, aio_return() get result. Signal or thread notifies completion.

Example setup:

```c
#include <aio.h>
#include <errno.h>

struct aiocb cb = {0};
cb.aio_fildes = fd;
```

```
cb.aio_buf = buf;
cb.aio_nbytes = size;
cb.aio_sigevent.sigev_notify = SIGEV_SIGNAL; // Or SIGEV_THREAD
aio_read(&cb);
// Do other work
while (aio_error(&cb) == EINPROGRESS) {} // Poll
ssize_t ret = aio_return(&cb);
```
Limited: No support for buffered I/O, metadata ops; kernel emulates on filesystems without native async (most).

io_uring (kernel 5.1+, liburing.h): Modern ring-buffer interface for async, batched I/O. Submission queue (SQ) for requests, completion queue (CQ) for results. Supports chains, buffers, poll.

Install liburing: sudo apt install liburing-dev.

Example read:

```c
#include <liburing.h>
#include <fcntl.h>
#include <unistd.h>
#include <stdio.h>

#define QUEUE_DEPTH 1

int main() {
    struct io_uring ring;
    io_uring_queue_init(QUEUE_DEPTH, &ring, 0);

    int fd = open("file.txt", O_RDONLY);
    char buf[1024];
    struct io_uring_sqe *sqe = io_uring_get_sqe(&ring);
    io_uring_prep_read(sqe, fd, buf, sizeof(buf), 0);
    io_uring_submit(&ring);

    struct io_uring_cqe *cqe;
    io_uring_wait_cqe(&ring, &cqe);
    if (cqe->res < 0) { fprintf(stderr, "Error: %s\n", strerror(-cqe->res)); }
    else { printf("Read %d bytes\n", cqe->res); }
    io_uring_cqe_seen(&ring, cqe);

    close(fd);
    io_uring_queue_exit(&ring);
    return 0;
}
```
io_uring outperforms aio/epoll for high IOPS, with kernel 6.18 adding better error queuing and RISC-V support.

Pros: Low overhead, flexible (files, sockets, poll). Cons: Complex setup, requires recent kernel.

Zero-Copy Techniques: sendfile() and splice()

Zero-copy avoids user-kernel data copies, using DMA.

sendfile(int out_fd, int in_fd, off_t offset, size_t count) (<sys/sendfile.h>): Copies from in_fd to out_fd (typically socket). Kernel handles, no user buffer.

Example: Serve file over socket.

Linux: Extended to file-file since 2.6.33.

splice(int fd_in, loff_t *off_in, int fd_out, loff_t *off_out, size_t len, unsigned int flags): Moves data between pipes/files without copy. Flags: SPLICE_F_MOVE (try move pages), SPLICE_F_NONBLOCK.

Tee() duplicates data in pipes.

Use for efficient proxies/loggers.

Direct I/O and File Advising

Direct I/O (O_DIRECT in open()): Bypasses page cache, requires aligned I/O (sector size, 512+). For databases avoiding double-buffering.

Drawbacks: Slower for small/random, no readahead.

Advising: posix_fadvise(int fd, off_t offset, off_t len, int advice): Hints kernel. Advice: POSIX_FADV_SEQUENTIAL (readahead), POSIX_FADV_RANDOM (no readahead), POSIX_FADV_DONTNEED (drop cache), POSIX_FADV_WILLNEED (preload).

madvise() for mmap: MADV_SEQUENTIAL, MADV_FREE (discard clean pages).

In kernel 6.17, fadvise optimizes for SSDs with better trim integration.

Sparse Files and Hole Punching

Sparse files save space by not allocating blocks for zeros. lseek(SEEK_HOLE/SEEK_DATA) navigates.

fallocate(fd, FALLOC_FL_PUNCH_HOLE | FALLOC_FL_KEEP_SIZE, offset, len): Punches holes, deallocating.

Useful for VMs, databases.

Error Handling, Security, and Performance

Errors: Advanced calls set specific errno (e.g., EOPNOTSUPP for unsupported aio). Check man pages.

Security: mmap PROT_EXEC risks (NX bits mitigate); io_uring vulnerabilities (e.g., CVE-2024-41091, patched in 6.17.7). Use seccomp to restrict.

Performance: Benchmark with fio/iperf. Tune with sysctl (vm.dirty_ratio for writeback).

Best practices: Profile first; combine techniques (e.g., mmap + madvise); handle partials in async.

In 2025, with AI workloads, io_uring integrates with GPU I/O for accelerated processing.

These techniques elevate file I/O from basic to enterprise-grade, enabling efficient systems.

Thought for 46s

4.4 File Locking and Synchronization

File locking and synchronization mechanisms in Linux are essential for managing concurrent access to shared files, preventing data corruption, and ensuring consistency in multi-process or multi-threaded environments. As systems have evolved from single-user UNIX setups to distributed, high-concurrency Linux deployments, the need for robust locking has grown, addressing issues like race conditions where multiple entities attempt simultaneous reads or writes. In Linux, file locking provides mutual exclusion (mutex-like behavior) for files, allowing processes to coordinate without explicit IPC. This is particularly vital in applications such as databases, web servers, and file-based queues, where integrity is paramount. Drawing from POSIX standards and BSD influences, Linux offers multiple locking APIs: flock() for simple whole-file advisory locks, fcntl() for flexible record (byte-range) locks, and lockf() as a convenience wrapper. Additionally, Linux-specific extensions like open file description (OFD) locks and file leases enhance functionality for modern use cases. This section explores these techniques in depth, including their semantics, implementation, code examples, error handling, performance considerations, and best practices. As of the stable Linux kernel 6.17 (September 2025) and the 6.18 release candidate cycle (rc4 in November 2025), file locking remains largely unchanged from earlier versions, with ongoing refinements in VFS for better scalability and deadlock detection, but no major overhauls. Understanding these tools enables programmers to build reliable systems that handle concurrency gracefully, avoiding common pitfalls like deadlocks or stale locks while maintaining portability across UNIX-like platforms.

The Need for File Locking and Synchronization

In a multi-process system, files serve as shared resources accessible via paths or descriptors. Without synchronization, concurrent writes can interleave data unpredictably—e.g., two processes appending to a log might garble entries—or reads might see inconsistent states during modifications. File locking mitigates this by allowing a process to claim exclusive or shared access, blocking others until released.

Historical roots: Locking originated in early UNIX variants. BSD introduced flock() in 1983 for advisory whole-file locks, while System V added fcntl() for mandatory record locks. POSIX standardized fcntl() in 1988 (IEEE 1003.1), focusing on advisory semantics for flexibility. Linux, influenced by both, implements advisory locks by default but supports mandatory via mount options.

Types of locks:

- **Advisory Locks**: Cooperative; kernel doesn't enforce but provides testing/blocking. Processes must check voluntarily. Safer, as ignoring doesn't break the system.
- **Mandatory Locks**: Enforced by kernel; reads/writes fail on locked regions. Enabled via mount -o mand and chmod g-x,g+s on files. Rarely used due to security risks (e.g., denial-of-service via locking /bin/ls). POSIX doesn't mandate, and Linux warns against in docs.

Synchronization extends beyond locks: fsync() ensures data durability, but locks coordinate access order.

In threads: File locks are process-wide (shared across threads), but for thread-specific sync, use mutexes (pthread_mutex_lock()) on shared FDs.

Challenges: Deadlocks (cycles in lock waits), starvation, and stale locks (from crashed processes—kernel releases on exit/close).

flock(): Simple Advisory Whole-File Locking

The flock() call, from <sys/file.h>, applies advisory locks to entire files. It's non-POSIX (BSD-origin) but widely supported in Linux for simplicity.

c

```
int flock(int fd, int operation);
```

- **fd**: Open file descriptor.
- **operation**: LOCK_SH (shared/read lock, multiple holders), LOCK_EX (exclusive/write lock, one holder), LOCK_UN (unlock). Add LOCK_NB for non-blocking (fails with EWOULDBLOCK if unavailable).

Returns 0 on success, -1 on error (e.g., EINVAL invalid op, ENOLCK no lock slots).

Semantics: Locks are advisory; kernel doesn't prevent I/O on unlocked processes. Released on close(fd) or process exit. Multiple LOCK_SH ok; LOCK_EX blocks until free. Not inherited across fork(), but shared if FD duplicated (dup()).

Example: Exclusive lock for writing:

c

```c
#include <sys/file.h>
#include <fcntl.h>
#include <unistd.h>
#include <stdio.h>
#include <errno.h>

int main() {
    int fd = open("shared.log", O_WRONLY | O_APPEND | O_CREAT, 0666);
    if (fd == -1) { perror("open"); return 1; }

    if (flock(fd, LOCK_EX) == -1) {
        perror("flock exclusive");
        close(fd);
        return 1;
    }

    // Critical section: write safely
    const char *msg = "Locked write\n";
    write(fd, msg, strlen(msg));

    flock(fd, LOCK_UN); // Unlock
    close(fd);
    return 0;
}
```

For non-blocking: if (flock(fd, LOCK_EX | LOCK_NB) == -1 && errno == EWOULDBLOCK) { /* busy */ }

Pros: Simple, low overhead for whole-file. Cons: No byte-range, not POSIX (use fcntl for portability). Linux: flock() uses internal lock structures, compatible with NFS v3+ if lockd running.

Pitfalls: Locks per FD table entry; close any dup'd FD releases. Not for directories.

fcntl(): POSIX Record Locking for Flexibility

fcntl() provides versatile control, including advisory record locks for byte ranges. From <fcntl.h>, POSIX-standard. For locking:

c

```
int fcntl(int fd, int cmd, ... /* struct flock *arg */);
```

Lock cmds: F_GETLK (test), F_SETLK (set non-blocking), F_SETLKW (set blocking).

Struct flock { short l_type; /* F_RDLCK, F_WRLCK, F_UNLCK / short l_whence; / SEEK_SET/CUR/END / off_t l_start; off_t l_len; / 0 for to EOF / pid_t l_pid; / for GETLK */ };

l_type: F_RDLCK (shared), F_WRLCK (exclusive), F_UNLCK.

Locks advisory; multiple read locks ok, write exclusive. Overlapping ranges checked per byte.

Example: Lock region 100-200 for write:

c

```c
#include <fcntl.h>
#include <unistd.h>
#include <stdio.h>
#include <errno.h>

int main() {
    int fd = open("data.bin", O_RDWR | O_CREAT, 0666);
    if (fd == -1) { perror("open"); return 1; }

    struct flock lock = { .l_type = F_WRLCK, .l_whence = SEEK_SET, .l_start = 100, .l_len = 100 };

    if (fcntl(fd, F_SETLKW, &lock) == -1) {
        perror("fcntl set lock");
        close(fd);
        return 1;
    }

    // Write to locked region
    lseek(fd, 100, SEEK_SET);
    write(fd, "Locked data", 11);

    lock.l_type = F_UNLCK;
    fcntl(fd, F_SETLK, &lock); // Unlock
    close(fd);
    return 0;
}
```

Test lock: F_GETLK sets l_type to F_UNLCK if free, else fills l_pid etc.

Semantics: Locks per process (not FD); closing any FD for file releases all locks by that process. Inherited across fork(), but not exec() unless FD_CLOEXEC unset. Automatic upgrade/downgrade if overlapping own locks.

Linux: 64-bit offsets with _FILE_OFFSET_BITS=64. Mandatory via mount -o mand, but discouraged (security holes).

Pros: Granular, POSIX-portable. Cons: Complex, potential for deadlocks (use timeouts or algorithms like banker).

Errors: EAGAIN/EACCES (lock busy non-block), EDEADLK (deadlock risk), ENOLCK (system limit).

lockf(): Simplified Record Locking

lockf(), from <unistd.h>, is a POSIX wrapper over fcntl() for record locks.

c

int lockf(int fd, int cmd, off_t len);

- **cmd**: F_LOCK (exclusive block), F_TLOCK (non-block), F_ULOCK (unlock), F_TEST (test).
- Locks from current offset for len bytes.

Seeks to offset before use. Less flexible than fcntl(), but simpler for sequential locks.

Example: lockf(fd, F_LOCK, 0); // Whole file from current pos to EOF.

Linux: Implements via fcntl(), same semantics.

Linux-Specific Extensions: OFD Locks and Leases

Open File Description (OFD) Locks (kernel 3.15+, F_OFD_* cmds in fcntl()): Locks tied to open file description (struct file), not process. Survive fork(), released on last close. Useful for threads/multiprocess sharing FD without inheriting process locks.

cmds: F_OFD_SETLK, F_OFD_SETLKW, F_OFD_GETLK.

Struct flock l_sysid != 0 indicates OFD.

File Leases (fcntl F_SETLEASE): Kernel notifies (SIGIO) when another process accesses leased file. Types: F_RDLSE (read), F_WRLSE (write). For cache coherency (e.g., NFS clients).

fcntl(fd, F_SETLEASE, F_RDLSE); // Set

Breaks on conflicting open(), giving time to flush.

Synchronization Beyond Locks: Barriers and Atomic Operations

For finer sync: Use file locks with semaphores/mutexes. fsync()/fdatasync() ensure durability post-write.

Atomic appends: O_APPEND in open() atomically seeks to end before write.

For directories: Lock parent for create/unlink to avoid races.

In distributed: NFS locks via rpc.lockd, but consistency varies (NFSv4 better).

Deadlock Detection and Avoidance

Kernel detects some deadlocks (EDEADLK on wait), but not all. Avoid: Acquire in consistent order, use timeouts (alarm() + non-block), or test before set.

Tools: strace traces locks; lsof shows holders.

Performance and Scalability

Locks use kernel lock manager (flock uses fl_lock, fcntl fl_posix); contention scales poorly. For high concurrency, prefer databases or in-memory sync.

Overhead: fcntl() $O(\log n)$ for range checks; flock() faster for whole-file.

In kernel 6.17, VFS lock optimizations reduce contention in multi-socket systems.

Best Practices and Common Pitfalls

- Use advisory unless mandatory needed (rare).
- Prefer flock() for simple whole-file, fcntl() for ranges.
- Always unlock, even on errors—use RAII-like wrappers.
- Handle EAGAIN in loops for non-block.
- Test on NFS if distributed.
- Pitfalls: Forgetting close releases locks; mixing flock/fcntl (incompatible); locks not on symlinks (resolve first).
- Security: Locks don't prevent unlink(); use permissions too.

Example scenario: Database using fcntl() for row-level locks via byte ranges.

These techniques ensure safe, efficient file sharing, foundational for concurrent systems.

5 Users, Groups, and Permissions

5.1 Process Credentials and Privileges

Process credentials and privileges are fundamental to Linux's security model, governing how programs interact with system resources and ensuring isolation in multi-user environments. Inherited from UNIX, this framework assigns identities to processes—users and groups—that determine access rights to files, devices, and operations. Credentials include user IDs (UIDs) and group IDs (GIDs), which can be real (actual owner), effective (used for checks), and saved (for privilege toggling). Privileges extend beyond simple IDs through capabilities, a fine-grained system allowing non-root processes to perform specific elevated actions. Understanding these is crucial for secure system programming, as mishandling can lead to vulnerabilities like privilege escalation or unauthorized access. This section explores the structure of process credentials, key system calls for querying and modifying them, the role of set-user-ID (setuid) programs, capabilities as a modern alternative to root, and best practices for secure coding. Drawing from POSIX standards and Linux implementations, we'll cover real-world examples, error handling, and implications for daemons, scripts, and applications. As of Linux kernel 6.17 (stable since September 2025) and the 6.18 release candidate (rc4 in November 2025), credentials remain core to the cred struct in kernel/task_struct, with ongoing enhancements for better namespace integration and capability bounding to mitigate exploits.

The Basics of Users and Groups

In Linux, every process runs under a user and one or more groups, identified by numeric IDs. Users represent individuals or services (e.g., root UID 0, user alice UID 1000), while groups aggregate users for shared access (e.g., wheel GID 10 for sudoers). These are stored in /etc/passwd (users: username:passwd:UID:GID:gecos:home:shell) and /etc/group (groups: name:passwd:GID:members), with shadow files (/etc/shadow) for hashed passwords.

Process credentials include:

- **Real UID/GID (RUID/RGID)**: The actual owner of the process, typically inherited from the parent (e.g., shell). Used for accounting and signals.
- **Effective UID/GID (EUID/EGID)**: Used for permission checks (e.g., file access). Normally match real, but can differ in setuid programs.
- **Saved Set-User-ID/Group-ID (SUID/SGID)**: Stores previous effective IDs, allowing temporary privilege drops and restores.
- **Filesystem UID/GID (FSUID/FSGID)**: Linux-specific, used for NFSv4 and file ops; usually sync with effective.
- **Supplementary Groups**: Additional GIDs (up to NGROUPS_MAX, 65536) for extra access, queried via getgroups().

Kernel stores these in struct cred, attached to task_struct. On execve(), credentials may change based on file permissions.

System calls for querying (from <unistd.h>, <sys/types.h>):

- uid_t getuid(void); // Real UID
- uid_t geteuid(void); // Effective UID
- gid_t getgid(void); // Real GID
- gid_t getegid(void); // Effective GID
- int getgroups(int size, gid_t list[]); // Supplementary, returns count or -1 error.

These are lightweight, no-privilege calls. Errors rare (EFAULT bad list).

Example: Print credentials:

```c
#include <unistd.h>
#include <sys/types.h>
#include <stdio.h>
#include <errno.h>

int main() {
    uid_t ruid = getuid();
    uid_t euid = geteuid();
```

```c
gid_t rgid = getgid();
gid_t egid = getegid();

printf("Real UID: %u, Effective UID: %u\n", ruid, euid);
printf("Real GID: %u, Effective GID: %u\n", rgid, egid);

int ngroups = getgroups(0, NULL); // Get count
if (ngroups == -1) { perror("getgroups count"); return 1; }
gid_t groups[ngroups];
if (getgroups(ngroups, groups) == -1) { perror("getgroups"); return 1; }
printf("Supplementary groups: ");
for (int i = 0; i < ngroups; i++) printf("%u ", groups[i]);
printf("\n");
return 0;
}
```

For root (UID 0), all match 0 unless dropped.

Modifying Credentials: setuid(), setgid(), and Friends

Non-privileged processes can't elevate, but can drop or switch if permitted. Root can set arbitrarily.
Key calls:

- int setuid(uid_t uid); // Sets real/effective/saved if root; drops effective if non-root.
- int seteuid(uid_t uid); // Sets only effective; non-root can set to real/saved.
- int setreuid(uid_t ruid, uid_t euid); // Sets real/effective, -1 unchanged.
- Similar for gid: setgid(), setegid(), setregid().
- int setgroups(size_t size, const gid_t *list); // Root-only, sets supplementary.
- int setfsuid(uid_t fsuid); // Linux-specific, sets FSUID; returns old.

Semantics: Non-root setuid() drops privileges permanently (sets all to uid if uid == real or saved). Root can impersonate. Failed calls return -1, errno EPERM (no perm), EINVAL (invalid uid).
Setuid programs: Files with setuid bit (chmod u+s) run with owner's EUID (often root). E.g., /usr/bin/passwd (root-owned, setuid) allows users to change passwords.
Code in setuid prog:
c
```c
if (geteuid() == 0) { // Running as root effective
    // Open privileged file
    int fd = open("/etc/shadow", O_RDWR);
    // Drop privileges
    if (setuid(getuid()) == -1) { perror("drop priv"); }
    // Now safe ops
}
```
Saved IDs allow restore: After drop with seteuid(getuid()), seteuid(getuid()) fails—use saved implicitly via setuid(0) if root-orig.
Linux: Capabilities (below) preferred over setuid root.

Capabilities: Fine-Grained Privileges

Traditional model: Root (UID 0) omnipotent, others not—binary, risky. Capabilities (kernel 2.2+, 1999) split root powers into granular bits, assignable to processes/files.
Defined in <sys/capability.h>, over 40 caps (kernel 6.17): CAP_SYS_ADMIN (many ops), CAP_NET_BIND_SERVICE (bind <1024 ports), CAP_DAC_OVERRIDE (bypass DAC), CAP_SYS_BOOT (reboot), etc.
Sets:

- **Effective**: Currently used for checks.
- **Permitted**: Available to raise to effective.
- **Inheritable**: Passed to children on exec.
- **Bounding**: Caps limit on exec (prctl PR_CAPBSET_DROP).
- **Ambient** (kernel 4.3+): Auto-inherit for non-root.

File caps: xattr security.capability on executables, applied on exec.
System calls:

- int capget(cap_user_header_t *hdrp, cap_user_data_t *datap); // Get

- int capset(cap_user_header_t *hdrp, const cap_user_data_t *datap); // Set

Usually via libcap: cap_t cap = cap_get_proc(); cap_value_t vals[] = {CAP_NET_BIND_SERVICE}; cap_set_flag(cap, CAP_EFFECTIVE, 1, vals, CAP_SET); cap_set_proc(cap);

Example: Drop all but one cap:

c

```c
#include <sys/capability.h>
#include <sys/prctl.h>
#include <stdio.h>
#include <errno.h>

int main() {
    // Assume starting as root
    if (prctl(PR_SET_KEEPCAPS, 1) == -1) { perror("prctl keepcaps"); return 1; } // Keep on setuid
    if (setuid(1000) == -1) { perror("setuid"); return 1; } // Drop to user

    cap_t caps = cap_init();
    cap_value_t keep[] = {CAP_SYS_TIME}; // e.g., set time
    cap_set_flag(caps, CAP_EFFECTIVE | CAP_PERMITTED | CAP_INHERITABLE, 1, keep, CAP_SET);
    if (cap_set_proc(caps) == -1) { perror("cap_set_proc"); cap_free(caps); return 1; }
    cap_free(caps);

    // Now non-root but can set time
    return 0;
}
```

File caps: capsetp() or setcap tool: setcap cap_net_bind_service=ep /bin/server.

Kernel 6.17: Capabilities checked in cred_calc_cap_bits during exec. 6.18 rc adds better ambient inheritance for containers.

Pros: Least privilege; no full root. Cons: Complex management.

Secure Programming Practices with Credentials

- **Drop Privileges Early**: In daemons, setuid() after binding ports/opening files.
- **Avoid Setuid Root**: Use caps; bound sets with prctl(PR_CAPBSET_DROP, cap).
- **Check Effective IDs**: Ensure ops match expected priv.
- **Handle Errors**: EPERM common; log and exit gracefully.
- **Namespaces**: User namespaces (unshare CLONE_NEWUSER) map UIDs, allowing "root" in container without host root.
- **Audit**: Use getresuid(uid_t *ruid, *euid, *suid); for all three.
- **Supplementary Groups**: initgroups(const char *user, gid_t group); sets from /etc/group (root-only).

Pitfalls: Setuid scripts unsafe (race in interpreter); use binaries. Environment vars (LD_PRELOAD) can hijack setuid progs—clear env.

In multi-threaded: Credential changes process-wide; use capabilities carefully.

Security models: SELinux/AppArmor enforce beyond UIDs/caps.

Practical Applications and Examples

Daemons: Fork, setsid(), setuid daemon user after priv ops.

PAM (Pluggable Authentication Modules): Handles auth, sets creds.

Capabilities in tools: ping uses CAP_NET_RAW for ICMP.

In kernel 6.18 rc, enhanced cap checking for io_uring, preventing abuse.

This framework secures Linux, enabling safe elevated ops without full root.

5.2 System Data Files and Authentication

System data files and authentication mechanisms form the core of user management and security in Linux, providing the infrastructure for identifying users, verifying credentials, and controlling access. These components evolved from early UNIX systems, where multi-user support necessitated reliable ways to store account information and authenticate logins. In modern Linux, data files like /etc/passwd and /etc/shadow store user details, while authentication leverages libraries and modules for flexibility and security. For system programmers, understanding these is vital for tasks such as user enumeration, password handling, custom authentication, and integrating with services like SSH or databases. This section examines the key system files, their formats and parsing APIs, authentication functions like crypt(), the Pluggable Authentication Modules (PAM) framework, and best practices for secure implementation. We'll cover POSIX-compliant interfaces, Linux-specific enhancements, code examples, error handling, and considerations for distributed environments. As of Linux kernel 6.17 (stable since September 2025) and the 6.18 release candidate (rc4 in November 2025), these files remain text-based for compatibility, but with ongoing shifts toward centralized identity management (e.g., via SSSD for LDAP/AD integration), programmers must balance tradition with modern scalability. By mastering these elements, developers can create robust applications that manage identities securely, preventing common vulnerabilities like weak password storage or improper privilege checks.

Historical Evolution of System Data Files

The origins of Linux's user data files trace back to UNIX Version 6 (1975), where /etc/passwd stored all user info, including encrypted passwords. This simplicity suited early systems but posed security risks as the file was world-readable, exposing hashes to cracking. By UNIX System III (1981), passwords moved to /etc/shadow, a root-only readable file, enhancing security. Groups followed suit with /etc/group and /etc/gshadow.

Linux adopted this in early versions (0.12, 1992), influenced by BSD and System V. POSIX standardized access functions like getpwent() in 1988, ensuring portability. Over time, extensions like password aging (in shadow) and large UIDs (32-bit) were added. In contemporary distributions, tools like useradd/passwd manipulate these files via libraries, locking to prevent races.

Modern challenges: With containers and cloud, files can be bind-mounted or overridden via namespaces. Centralized auth (NSS via /etc/nsswitch.conf) queries LDAP/Kerberos before local files.

Security milestones: MD5 hashes (1990s), SHA-512 (2000s), and recommendations for Argon2/yescrypt in /etc/login.defs.

Key System Data Files

Linux uses several files for user/group data, typically in /etc/ for system-wide, or NIS/LDAP for networks.

- **/etc/passwd**: User accounts. Format: username:password:UID:GID:GECOS:home:shell (colon-separated). Password field 'x' indicates shadow use; '*' or '!' disables login. UID 0 root, 1-999 system, 1000+ users. GECOS: full name, etc. Readable by all for name resolution.
- **/etc/shadow**: Secure passwords. Format: username:hashed_pass:change_date:min_days:max_days:warn_days:inactive:expire:reserved. Hashed_pass uses idsalt$hash (e.g., 6 for SHA-512). Root-readable only. Fields enforce aging: min_days prevents frequent changes.
- **/etc/group**: Groups. Format: groupname:password:GID:members (comma-separated). Password rarely used (gshadow instead).
- **/etc/gshadow**: Secure group passwords. Format: groupname:hashed_pass:admins:members. For group auth.
- **/etc/login.defs**: Configs like PASS_MAX_DAYS, UID_MIN. Influences tools like useradd.
- **/etc/skel**: Template for new user homes.

Files are line-based text; parse with fgets() or APIs below. Locking (pwlock) by tools prevents concurrent edits. In kernel 6.17, no direct changes, but user namespaces map UIDs, allowing non-root containers to "own" high UIDs.

Parsing System Data Files: getpwent(), getgrent(), and Friends

Direct file reading risks races/inconsistencies; use libc functions from <pwd.h>, <grp.h>, <shadow.h>. These iterate or query via NSS (Name Service Switch), handling local/remote backends.

User functions:

- struct passwd *getpwent(void); // Next user
- struct passwd *getpwnam(const char *name); // By name
- struct passwd *getpwuid(uid_t uid); // By UID
- void setpwent(void); // Rewind

- void endpwent(void); // Close

Struct passwd { char *pw_name; char *pw_passwd; uid_t pw_uid; gid_t pw_gid; char *pw_gecos; char *pw_dir; char *pw_shell; };

Group:
- struct group *getgrent(void);
- struct group *getgrnam(const char *name);
- struct group *getgrgid(gid_t gid);
- void setgrent(void); endgrent(void);

Struct group { char *gr_name; char *gr_passwd; gid_t gr_gid; char **gr_mem; }; // Null-terminated members.

Shadow (root-only, <shadow.h>):
- struct spwd *getspent(void);
- struct spwd *getspnam(const char *name);
- void setspent(void); endspent(void);

Struct spwd { char *sp_namp; char *sp_pwdp; long sp_lstchg; long sp_min; long sp_max; long sp_warn; long sp_inact; long sp_expire; unsigned long sp_flag; };

Returns NULL on end/error; check errno (0 if end). Thread-safe _r variants: getpwnam_r(name, &pwd, buf, buflen, &result);

Example: List users:

c

CollapseWrapRun

Copy

```c
#include <pwd.h>
#include <stdio.h>

int main() {
    struct passwd *pw;
    setpwent();
    while ((pw = getpwent()) != NULL) {
        printf("User: %s, UID: %u, Home: %s\n", pw->pw_name, pw->pw_uid, pw->pw_dir);
    }
    endpwent();
    return 0;
}
```

For shadow (run as root):

c

CollapseWrapRun

Copy

```c
#include <shadow.h>
#include <stdio.h>

int main() {
    struct spwd *sp;
    setspent();
    while ((sp = getspent()) != NULL) {
        printf("User: %s, Hash: %s, Max days: %ld\n", sp->sp_namp, sp->sp_pwdp, sp->sp_max);
    }
    endspent();
    return 0;
}
```

NSS configures order in /etc/nsswitch.conf: passwd: files nis ldap (files first, then NIS, LDAP).

Errors: ERANGE (small buf in _r), ENOENT (no entry). No priv needed for passwd/group, root for shadow.

Authentication Mechanisms: Verifying Credentials

Authentication confirms user identity, typically via passwords. Basic: Compare input hash to stored.

crypt(): From <unistd.h>, hashes strings. const char *crypt(const char *key, const char *salt);

Salt formats: $idsaltsalt (id: 1 MD5, 5 SHA-256, 6 SHA-512, y yescrypt). Key is password.

Thread-safe: crypt_r(key, salt, &data);
Example: Verify password (root/simulate):
c
CollapseWrapRun
Copy

```c
#include <unistd.h>
#include <shadow.h>
#include <stdio.h>
#include <string.h>

int authenticate(const char *user, const char *pass) {
    struct spwd *sp = getspnam(user);
    if (!sp) return -1;
    char *hashed = crypt(pass, sp->sp_pwdp);
    return strcmp(hashed, sp->sp_pwdp) == 0 ? 0 : -1;
}

int main() {
    if (authenticate("testuser", "correctpass") == 0) {
        printf("Authenticated\n");
    } else {
        printf("Failed\n");
    }
    return 0;
}
```

Security: Use strong algos (+ in /etc/login.defs); avoid storing plain pass.

PAM: Pluggable Authentication Modules

PAM (since 1995, Linux-PAM) modularizes auth, allowing stacking modules for account, auth, password, session.
From <security/pam_appl.h>, apps use pam_start(), pam_authenticate(), pam_acct_mgmt(), pam_end().
Configs in /etc/pam.d/ (e.g., /etc/pam.d/login): auth required pam_unix.so (unix auth), account sufficient pam_localuser.so.
Modules: pam_unix (local), pam_ldap, pam_sss (SSSD for AD), pam_mkhomedir (create home).
Example PAM client (simplified):
c
CollapseWrapRun
Copy

```c
#include <security/pam_appl.h>
#include <security/pam_misc.h>
#include <stdio.h>

static int conv(int num_msg, const struct pam_message **msg, struct pam_response **resp, void *data) {
    // Simulate input: hardcode pass
    *resp = calloc(num_msg, sizeof(struct pam_response));
    for (int i = 0; i < num_msg; i++) {
        if (msg[i]->msg_style == PAM_PROMPT_ECHO_OFF) {
            (*resp)[i].resp = strdup("password");
        }
    }
    return PAM_SUCCESS;
}

int main() {
    pam_handle_t *pamh;
    struct pam_conv pc = { conv, NULL };
    int ret = pam_start("check_user", "testuser", &pc, &pamh);
    if (ret != PAM_SUCCESS) { printf("pam_start failed\n"); return 1; }
```

```
    ret = pam_authenticate(pamh, 0);
    if (ret != PAM_SUCCESS) { printf("Auth failed: %s\n", pam_strerror(pamh, ret)); }
    else { printf("Auth success\n"); }

    pam_end(pamh, ret);
    return 0;
}
```
Compile: gcc -lpam -lpam_misc.

PAM handles stacking: required (must pass, continue), requisite (fail stops), sufficient (pass skips rest), optional.

In distros: Ubuntu/Fedora use PAM for login, sudo, etc.

Advanced Authentication: Biometrics, MFA, and Centralized Systems

Beyond passwords: pam_pkcs11 (smartcards), pam_google_authenticator (TOTP MFA), pam_fprint (fingerprints).

Centralized: SSSD (System Security Services Daemon) caches LDAP/AD, integrates with PAM/NSS. Config /etc/sssd/sssd.conf.

Kerberos: pam_krb5 for ticket-based auth.

In containers: Bind-mount /etc/passwd or use user namespaces for isolated UIDs.

Security Considerations and Best Practices

- **File Security**: /etc/shadow 600 perms; backup before edits.
- **Parsing**: Use APIs over direct fopen() to honor NSS.
- **Password Handling**: Zero memory after use (explicit_bzero()); avoid logs.
- **Aging**: Enforce via chage tool or shadow fields.
- **PAM Custom**: Write modules if needed (pam_sm_authenticate() etc.).
- **Errors**: PAM_BUF_ERR (alloc fail), PAM_USER_UNKNOWN.
- **Auditing**: /var/log/auth.log tracks attempts.
- **Pitfalls**: Weak salts; ignoring aging; races in manual edits—use vipw/vigr.

In kernel 6.18 rc, improved user namespace caps for auth in isolated envs.

These systems enable secure, flexible user management, foundational for Linux apps.

5.3 Capabilities and Secure Programming Practices

Capabilities in Linux represent a paradigm shift from the traditional all-or-nothing root privilege model, offering a more granular approach to granting elevated permissions. Introduced in kernel 2.2 (1999) and refined over decades, capabilities divide the monolithic power of root (UID 0) into discrete, independently assignable privileges. This allows processes to perform specific sensitive operations without full superuser access, aligning with the principle of least privilege—a cornerstone of secure programming. In system development, capabilities mitigate risks associated with setuid binaries, such as buffer overflows leading to root shells, by limiting the damage an exploited process can cause. They are particularly relevant for daemons, utilities, and containers, where dropping root after initial setup is common. This section delves into the architecture of capabilities, key system calls and libraries for manipulation, inheritance rules, file-based capabilities, bounding sets for restriction, and ambient sets for persistence. We'll explore POSIX influences (though capabilities are Linux-specific, inspired by POSIX.1e drafts), practical code examples in C using libcap, error handling, performance implications, and secure coding practices to avoid common pitfalls like capability leaks or insufficient bounding. As of Linux kernel 6.17 (stable release on September 28, 2025, with patch 6.17.7 on November 2, 2025) and the ongoing 6.18 release candidate (rc4 as of November 2, 2025), capabilities remain integral to the process credential structure, with enhancements in namespace interactions and better support for unprivileged operations in containers. By integrating capabilities thoughtfully, programmers can enhance security without sacrificing functionality, creating robust applications resilient to compromise in diverse environments.

The Evolution and Architecture of Capabilities

The capability model addresses flaws in the classic UNIX privilege system, where root's omnipotence posed significant security risks. Early attempts in systems like Trusted Solaris influenced Linux's implementation, formalized by the withdrawn POSIX.1e standard. In Linux, capabilities are bitmasks stored in the process's cred structure, with each bit representing a specific permission. As of kernel 6.17, there are 42 capabilities (CAP_LAST_CAP = 41), defined in <linux/capability.h>, ranging from CAP_CHOWN (change ownership) to CAP_SYS_MODULE (load/unload modules) and newer ones like CAP_BPF (eBPF operations, added in 5.8).

Key capability sets per process:

- **Effective Set**: Active privileges used for kernel permission checks. A capability must be here to be exercised.
- **Permitted Set**: Privileges the process can raise to effective or pass to children. Root starts with all permitted.
- **Inheritable Set**: Privileges that can be inherited by child processes on execve(), filtered by file inheritable and bounding sets.
- **Bounding Set**: An immutable (after drop) cap on what can be added to permitted/inheritable. Used to restrict even root-like processes.
- **Ambient Set** (kernel 4.3+, 2015): Privileges automatically added to permitted/effective on execve() for non-setuid binaries, enabling persistent non-root elevation.

File capabilities (extended attributes, xattrs) apply on exec:

- **Permitted**: Added to process permitted.
- **Inheritable**: Mask for process inheritable.
- **Effective**: Bit to auto-raise to effective if in permitted.

Kernel manages via cap_task_prctl() internally, but user-space uses prctl() and libcap.

Without caps, non-root processes have empty sets. Root has all in effective/permitted/inheritable, full bounding. In kernel 6.17, cap checks occur in commoncap.c, with namespace-aware logic (e.g., cap_valid_ns() for user namespaces).

Querying and Manipulating Capabilities: System Calls and libcap

Direct syscalls capget()/capset() exist but are low-level; use libcap (libcap2 on distros) for portability and ease. Install: apt install libcap2-dev.

Core libcap types:

- cap_t: Opaque capability state.
- cap_value_t: Enum for caps (e.g., CAP_SYS_ADMIN = 21).

Functions:

- cap_t cap_get_proc(void); // Current process caps
- cap_t cap_get_pid(pid_t pid); // Other process (if permitted)
- cap_t cap_get_file(const char *filename); // File xattrs
- int cap_set_proc(cap_t cap); // Set process
- int cap_set_file(const char *filename, cap_t cap); // Set file
- int cap_get_flag(cap_t cap, cap_value_t capflag, cap_flag_t flagtype, cap_flag_value_t *valuep); // Get flag (CAP_EFFECTIVE etc.)
- int cap_set_flag(cap_t cap, cap_flag_t flagtype, int ncap, const cap_value_t *caps, cap_flag_value_t value); // Set/clear
- cap_t cap_init(void); // Empty set
- void cap_free(void *objp); // Free

prctl() for bounding/ambient:

- int prctl(PR_CAPBSET_READ, cap_value_t cap); // Check bounding
- int prctl(PR_CAPBSET_DROP, cap_value_t cap); // Drop from bounding (irreversible)
- int prctl(PR_CAP_AMBIENT, PR_CAP_AMBIENT_RAISE/LOWER/CLEAR/IS_SET, cap_value_t cap, 0, 0);

Example: Drop all caps except one:

```c
#include <sys/capability.h>
#include <sys/prctl.h>
#include <stdio.h>
#include <stdlib.h>
#include <errno.h>

int main() {
    // Assume starting with elevated privs
    cap_t caps = cap_get_proc();
    if (!caps) { perror("cap_get_proc"); return 1; }
```

```
// Clear all effective/permitted/inheritable
if (cap_clear(caps) == -1) { perror("cap_clear"); cap_free(caps); return 1; }

// Set specific cap
cap_value_t keep = CAP_NET_BIND_SERVICE;
if (cap_set_flag(caps, CAP_EFFECTIVE | CAP_PERMITTED | CAP_INHERITABLE, 1, &keep, CAP_SET) == -1) {
    perror("cap_set_flag");
    cap_free(caps);
    return 1;
}

if (cap_set_proc(caps) == -1) { perror("cap_set_proc"); cap_free(caps); return 1; }
cap_free(caps);

// Bound set: Drop others
for (int cap = 0; cap <= CAP_LAST_CAP; cap++) {
    if (cap != CAP_NET_BIND_SERVICE && prctl(PR_CAPBSET_DROP, cap) == -1) {
        perror("prctl drop");
    }
}

// Now can bind low ports, but not more
return 0;
}
```

Compile: gcc -lcap.

For ambient: prctl(PR_CAP_AMBIENT, PR_CAP_AMBIENT_RAISE, CAP_SYS_NICE, 0, 0); to add for inheritance.

Errors: EINVAL (invalid cap), EPERM (no perm to set). libcap functions return -1 on fail, set errno.

Kernel 6.18 rc refines cap inheritance in namespaces, preventing leaks.

Inheritance and Execution Semantics

On fork(): Child inherits all sets.

On execve():

- If setuid root or file cap effective bit: Permitted = (file permitted & file inheritable) | (file permitted & process inheritable) | process ambient; effective set accordingly.
- Bounding filters: Permitted &= bounding.
- Ambient preserved if no priv change.

For non-root binaries, ambient enables inheritance without setuid.

Secure practice: Drop bounding early in daemons to sandbox.

File caps set via setcap: setcap "cap_net_admin,cap_sys_ptrace=ep" /bin/tool (e effective/permitted, i inheritable).

Get: getcap /bin/tool.

Kernel stores in security.capability xattr (v2 format).

Secure Programming Practices with Capabilities

Adopting capabilities enhances security by minimizing attack surface. Key practices:

1. **Least Privilege Principle**: Grant only needed caps. Audit with capsh --print or /proc/<pid>/status Cap* lines.
2. **Drop Early, Restore if Needed**: In privileged progs, cap_set_proc() after init (e.g., bind port), before user input.
3. **Use Bounding Sets**: Irreversibly drop unneeded caps: for (cap=0; cap<=CAP_LAST_CAP; cap++) if (!needed(cap)) prctl(PR_CAPBSET_DROP, cap);
4. **Ambient for Persistence**: For non-setuid tools needing caps (e.g., nice for priority), raise to ambient.
5. **File Capabilities Over Setuid**: Prefer file caps; no full root, works with noexec mounts.
6. **Namespace Integration**: In user namespaces (unshare -U), caps map to namespace root. cap_valid() checks.
7. **Error Handling and Logging**: Check cap_set_proc() returns; log failures. Use cap_to_text(cap_t) for strings.
8. **Testing**: Run as non-root; use capsh --drop=... -- -c "command" to simulate.

9. **Avoid Common Caps**: CAP_SYS_ADMIN is overly broad (mount, etc.)—avoid if possible.
10. **Combine with Other Security**: SELinux/AppArmor restrict further; seccomp filters syscalls.

Pitfalls: Forgetting to set effective bit on files; ambient ignored on setuid; caps not inherited across exec if not ambient/inheritable.

Performance: Cap checks are bit operations, negligible overhead.

Tools: capsh (shell), pscap (list process caps), filecap (manage file caps).

Practical Examples in System Programming

Daemon example: Bind <1024 port as non-root.

File: setcap cap_net_bind_service=ep /path/to/daemon.

Code: No need to manipulate—auto-applied.

Custom: Tool to set system time (CAP_SYS_TIME).

```c
#include <sys/capability.h>
#include <sys/time.h>
#include <stdio.h>

int main() {
    cap_t caps = cap_get_proc();
    cap_value_t cap = CAP_SYS_TIME;
    cap_set_flag(caps, CAP_EFFECTIVE, 1, &cap, CAP_SET); // Raise if permitted
    if (cap_set_proc(caps) == -1) { perror("raise cap"); cap_free(caps); return 1; }
    cap_free(caps);

    struct timeval tv = { .tv_sec = time(NULL) + 3600 }; // +1 hour
    if (settimeofday(&tv, NULL) == -1) { perror("settimeofday"); return 1; }

    // Drop after
    caps = cap_get_proc();
    cap_set_flag(caps, CAP_EFFECTIVE | CAP_PERMITTED, 1, &cap, CAP_CLEAR);
    cap_set_proc(caps);
    cap_free(caps);

    return 0;
}
```

Run with file cap or from privileged parent.

Container runtimes (Docker) use caps: --cap-add=NET_ADMIN.

In kernel 6.17, caps enable unpriv BPF (CAP_BPF + CAP_PERFMON), reducing root needs for monitoring.

Advanced Topics: Capabilities in Namespaces and Future Directions

User namespaces remap UIDs, granting "root" caps within without host impact. cap_capable() checks namespace. Init process in namespace has full caps; children inherit.

Future: Kernel 6.18 rc explores cap extensions for emerging features like confidential computing (CAP_SEV_SNP? hypothetical).

Distros: Fedora/Ubuntu enable caps in systemd units (CapabilityBoundingSet=).

By embracing capabilities, programmers fortify systems against breaches, promoting modular, secure designs.

6 Process Management Fundamentals

6.1 Creating and Terminating Processes

Processes are the fundamental execution units in Linux, representing running programs with their own address space, resources, and state. Understanding how to create and terminate processes is essential for system programming, as it enables concurrency, modularity, and resource management in applications ranging from simple scripts to complex servers. This capability traces back to early UNIX designs, where multiprocessing was a key innovation for time-sharing systems. In Linux, process creation and termination are handled through a set of system calls that provide fine-grained control, balancing efficiency, safety, and portability. This subsection explores the core mechanisms: fork() for duplication, exec() for replacement, wait() for synchronization, and exit() for cleanup. We'll cover POSIX standards, Linux-specific extensions like clone(), practical code examples, error handling, process states, and implications for zombies and orphans. As of the stable Linux kernel 6.17 (released September 28, 2025, with the latest patch 6.17.7 on November 2, 2025) and the ongoing 6.18 release candidate (rc4 as of November 2, 2025), these operations remain optimized for modern hardware, with enhancements in scheduler integration and namespace support for containerized environments. By mastering these fundamentals, programmers can build robust multi-process applications that leverage Linux's concurrency model effectively, ensuring reliable execution in diverse scenarios from embedded devices to cloud infrastructures.

Historical Context and Process Model

The process model in UNIX and Linux originated in the 1970s at Bell Labs, with Dennis Ritchie's addition of fork() in UNIX Version 3 (1973) to enable multiprocessing. Fork() creates a child process as a near-exact copy of the parent, sharing code but duplicating data via copy-on-write (COW) for efficiency—a technique Linux refined in kernel 2.6 (2003) with better page table handling. This model allows programs to spawn workers for parallelism, a cornerstone of tools like make -j or web servers forking handlers.

In Linux, processes are managed by the kernel's scheduler (Completely Fair Scheduler since 2.6.23), which allocates CPU time slices. Each process has a unique PID (process ID, up to PID_MAX_LIMIT, default 32768, configurable via /proc/sys/kernel/pid_max), a parent PPID, and attributes like nice value for priority.

Process states (from /proc/<pid>/stat or ps): R (running), S (sleeping), D (disk sleep), T (stopped), Z (zombie, terminated but not reaped), X (dead). Creation transitions from none to R/S, termination to Z then gone.

POSIX standardizes fork(), exec(), wait(), exit(); Linux complies but extends for threads (clone()) and namespaces.

Creating Processes: fork() and Variants

The **fork()** system call, from <unistd.h>, duplicates the calling process:

```c
c
pid_t fork(void);
```

Returns: In parent, child's PID (>0); in child, 0; -1 on error (e.g., EAGAIN limit reached, ENOMEM no memory).

Semantics: Child inherits most attributes—open FDs (unless CLOEXEC), signal handlers, environment—but has separate address space. Shared resources (e.g., mmap MAP_SHARED) remain linked. File offsets shared if same FD table entry.

Post-fork, parent and child run concurrently; scheduler decides order—assume either can run first, avoid races.

Example: Simple fork:

```c
c
#include <unistd.h>
#include <sys/types.h>
#include <stdio.h>
#include <sys/wait.h>

int main() {
    pid_t pid = fork();
    if (pid == -1) {
        perror("fork");
        return 1;
```

```
        } else if (pid == 0) {
            // Child
            printf("Child PID: %d, Parent PID: %d\n", getpid(), getppid());
            return 0;
        } else {
            // Parent
            printf("Parent PID: %d, Child PID: %d\n", getpid(), pid);
            int status;
            waitpid(pid, &status, 0); // Wait for child
        }
    return 0;
}
```

Output might interleave due to concurrency.

Efficiency: Modern Linux uses COW—pages marked read-only, copied on write. Kernel 6.17 optimizes fork for large processes with better vma (virtual memory area) duplication.

Limits: /proc/sys/kernel/threads-max (global), RLIMIT_NPROC (per-user).

Variants:

- **vfork()**: Archaic (BSD), suspends parent until child exec/exit. No COW, shares memory—dangerous, avoid (use posix_spawn() instead).
- **clone()**: Linux-specific (<sched.h>), granular control. int clone(int (*fn)(void *), void *stack, int flags, void *arg, ...); Flags: CLONE_VM (share memory, for threads), CLONE_VFORK, CLONE_PIDFD (return pidfd). Used by pthread_create() for threads.
- **posix_spawn()** (POSIX.1-2008): Combines fork/exec, efficient for short-lived children, avoids full duplication.

In containers, clone() with namespaces (CLONE_NEWPID) isolates PIDs.

Errors: Common EPERM (cap limit), ENOSYS (not supported, rare).

Executing New Programs: The exec Family

Fork creates copies; to run new code, use **exec** calls (<unistd.h>), replacing current image.

Main: int execve(const char *pathname, char *const argv[], char *const envp[]);

Variants:

- execl(path, arg0, ..., NULL); // List args
- execle(path, arg0, ..., NULL, envp);
- execlp(file, arg0, ..., NULL); // Search PATH
- execvp(file, arg0, ..., NULL);
- execv(path, argv);
- execvpe(file, argv, envp); // Linux

Pathname: Absolute/relative executable or script (#! shebang). Argv: NULL-terminated array, argv[0] conventionally program name. Envp: Environment, or environ global if NULL.

On success, doesn't return—overlays process. Fails: -1, errno (ENOENT missing, EACCES no exec perm, ENOEXEC bad format).

Closes CLOEXEC FDs; preserves others.

Example: Fork and exec:

c
```
pid_t pid = fork();
if (pid == 0) {
    char *argv[] = {"ls", "-l", NULL};
    execvp("ls", argv);
    perror("execvp"); // Only if fails
    _exit(1);
}
```

Use _exit() in child post-fail to avoid flushing parent's stdio.

Kernel loads ELF (Executable Linkable Format) binaries, resolves dynamic links via ld.so.

In kernel 6.18 rc, exec optimizes for binfmt_misc (custom formats, e.g., Java).

Waiting for Children: wait() and waitpid()

Parents reap children to avoid zombies (terminated but unreaped, holding resources).

int wait(int *wstatus); // Any child

pid_t waitpid(pid_t pid, int *wstatus, int options); // Specific/group

Pid: >0 specific, -1 any, 0 same group, <-1 group -pid.

Options: WNOHANG (non-block), WUNTRACED (stopped children), WCONTINUED (continued).

Wstatus: NULL ignore; else macros: WIFEXITED(status) exited, WEXITSTATUS(status) code; WIFSIGNALED() signaled, WTERMSIG() signal; WIFSTOPPED() stopped, WSTOPSIG() sig.

Returns child PID, 0 (WNOHANG no change), -1 error (ECHILD no children).

Example: From earlier, waitpid(pid, &status, 0);

If not waited, child zombies until parent exits (init/ppid=1 reaps).

Waitid() (POSIX): More info via siginfo_t.

In multi-threaded, wait() process-wide.

Terminating Processes: exit() and _exit()

void _exit(int status); // Immediate kernel exit

void exit(int status); // Stdlib, calls atexit() handlers, flushes stdio, then _exit().

Status: 0 success, others failure; wait retrieves (status & 0377).

Kills process, closes FDs, releases memory, notifies parent (SIGCHLD), reaps if zombie.

Abnormal: Signals (kill -9 pid), abort() (SIGABRT + core).

Kernel: do_exit() in kernel/exit.c, handles thread groups.

In 6.17, exit optimizes for large mm (memory maps).

Zombies, Orphans, and Process Relationships

Zombies: Exited but unreaped; hold exit status/PID. Reap with wait().

Orphans: Parent exits first; reparented to init (systemd PID 1) or subreaper (prctl PR_SET_CHILD_SUBREAPER).

SIGCHLD signals parent on child exit/stop; handle with sigaction().

Process groups (getpgrp(), setpgid()): For job control.

Sessions (setsid()): Daemon creation—fork, setsid, fork again to avoid tty.

Error Handling and Best Practices

Errors: fork() EAGAIN (try later), ENOMEM. Exec ENOENT (path), E2BIG (args). Wait ECHILD (no kids), EINTR (signal).

Practices:

- Check returns always.
- In child, _exit() post-exec fail.
- Ignore SIGCHLD or handle to avoid zombies.
- Limit children with RLIMIT_NPROC.
- For daemons: Double fork, umask(0), chdir("/"), close std FDs.
- Security: Clear env in exec if sensitive.
- Performance: Fork heavy on large processes—use threads or vfork+exec.

Portability: Fork/exec POSIX; clone Linux.

Advanced Topics: Namespaces and Containers

clone() with CLONE_NEWPID etc. creates isolated environments, basis for Docker/LXC.

In 6.18 rc, clone optimizes for user namespaces, improving container startup.

Pidfds (pidfd_open(), since 5.3): FD for processes, safer than PID reuse.

These fundamentals enable multiprocessing, key to Linux's power.

6.2 Process Environment and Control

The environment and control of processes in Linux provide the means to configure, monitor, and manipulate running programs, extending beyond mere creation and termination to encompass runtime adjustments for efficiency, security, and reliability. This includes managing the process's environment variables, controlling resource usage, altering priorities, handling signals for asynchronous events, and querying process information. These capabilities are rooted in UNIX traditions, where processes were designed as isolated entities that could be dynamically controlled to support time-sharing and multi-user systems. In modern Linux, they enable fine-tuned optimizations for applications like web servers adjusting to load or daemons dropping privileges post-initialization. This subsection delves into key system calls and functions for environment manipulation (environ, getenv, setenv), resource control (setrlimit, nice, sched_setscheduler), signal handling (signal, sigaction), and process inspection (getpid, getppid, ps utilities via /proc). We'll explore POSIX compliance, Linux extensions like cgroups for grouped control, practical examples, error handling, and implications for performance and security. As of the stable Linux kernel 6.17 (released September 28, 2025, with the latest patch 6.17.7 on November 2, 2025) and the ongoing 6.18 release candidate (rc4 as of November 2, 2025), process control features robust support for real-time scheduling and enhanced cgroup v2 integration, facilitating containerized and cloud-native workloads. By leveraging these tools, programmers can craft responsive, secure applications that adapt to system conditions, ensuring optimal resource allocation in diverse computing environments from embedded IoT devices to high-performance clusters.

The Process Environment: Variables and Inheritance

The process environment consists of key-value pairs (e.g., PATH=/usr/bin, HOME=/home/user) that influence behavior, such as search paths or locale settings. These are stored in a NULL-terminated array of strings (char **environ global in <unistd.h>), inherited from the parent process during fork() and modifiable at runtime.

Key functions from <stdlib.h>:

- char *getenv(const char *name); // Returns value or NULL if unset.
- int setenv(const char *name, const char *value, int overwrite); // Sets or overwrites if overwrite !=0.
- int unsetenv(const char *name); // Removes.
- int putenv(char *string); // Adds "name=value", modifies string.

Semantics: Changes affect current process and children (post-fork). Not thread-safe (use locks if multi-threaded). Environment passed to execve() as envp[].

Example: Modify and query PATH:

c
```c
#include <stdlib.h>
#include <stdio.h>

int main() {
    char *path = getenv("PATH");
    if (path) printf("Original PATH: %s\n", path);

    if (setenv("PATH", "/bin:/usr/bin", 1) == -1) {
        perror("setenv");
        return 1;
    }

    printf("New PATH: %s\n", getenv("PATH"));

    unsetenv("PATH");
    if (!getenv("PATH")) printf("PATH unset\n");

    return 0;
}
```

Full list: Iterate environ:

c
```c
extern char **environ;
for (char **env = environ; *env; env++) printf("%s\n", *env);
```

Inheritance: Child gets copy; parent changes post-fork don't affect child.

Linux: /proc/<pid>/environ shows null-separated list.

Security: Clear sensitive vars in setuid progs (environ = NULL; or execle with safe env).

Errors: ENOMEM (alloc fail), EINVAL (invalid name).

Controlling Process Resources: Limits and Priorities

Linux allows controlling process resources to prevent abuse and tune performance.

Resource Limits (rlimits, <sys/resource.h>):

- struct rlimit { rlim_t rlim_cur; /* soft / *rlim_t rlim_max; / hard */ };
- int getrlimit(int resource, struct rlimit *rlim);
- int setrlimit(int resource, const struct rlimit *rlim);

Resources: RLIMIT_CPU (seconds), RLIMIT_FSIZE (file size), RLIMIT_NOFILE (open FDs, default 1024/4096), RLIMIT_STACK (8MB), RLIMIT_AS (virtual mem), etc.

Soft enforceable, hard ceiling (root can raise). Exceeding soft sends signal (e.g., SIGXCPU, SIGXFSZ).

Inherited, but children can't raise hard.

prlimit() (kernel 2.6.36+): Sets/gets for other processes.

Shell: ulimit -n 2048 sets NOFILE soft.

Example: Limit open files:

```c
#include <sys/resource.h>
#include <stdio.h>

int main() {
    struct rlimit lim;
    if (getrlimit(RLIMIT_NOFILE, &lim) == -1) { perror("getrlimit"); return 1; }
    printf("Soft: %lu, Hard: %lu\n", lim.rlim_cur, lim.rlim_max);

    lim.rlim_cur = 512;
    if (setrlimit(RLIMIT_NOFILE, &lim) == -1) { perror("setrlimit"); return 1; }

    return 0;
}
```

Priorities and Scheduling:

- int nice(int inc); // Adjust nice value (-20 high prio to 19 low), returns new. Non-root limited to positive.
- int getpriority(int which, id_t who); // Get nice (PRIO_PROCESS/PGRP/USER, id 0 current).
- int setpriority(int which, id_t who, int prio);

Nice affects CFS shares; lower nice more CPU.

Advanced: sched_setscheduler(pid_t pid, int policy, const struct sched_param *param); Policies: SCHED_FIFO/RR (real-time), SCHED_DEADLINE (deadlines), SCHED_BATCH/IDLE (low prio).

sched_param { int sched_priority; } (1-99 for RT).

Root/CAP_SYS_NICE needed for RT or negative nice.

In kernel 6.17, CFS optimizes for energy-aware scheduling (EAS) on ARM.

cgroups v2 (/sys/fs/cgroup): Group limits (cpu.max, memory.max). Systemd uses for services.

Signal Handling and Asynchronous Control

Signals are software interrupts for events (termination, errors). POSIX: 1-31 standard, >32 real-time.

From <signal.h>:

- sighandler_t signal(int signum, sighandler_t handler); // Simple, SIG_IGN ignore, SIG_DFL default.
- int sigaction(int signum, const struct sigaction *act, struct sigaction *oldact); // Advanced.

Struct sigaction { void (*sa_handler)(int); sigset_t sa_mask; int sa_flags; void (*sa_sigaction)(int, siginfo_t *, void *); };

sa_flags: SA_RESTART (restart syscalls), SA_SIGINFO (use sa_sigaction with info), SA_NOCLDSTOP (no SIGCHLD on child stop).

Default: SIGTERM terminate, SIGSEGV core, SIGCHLD ignored.

Block: sigprocmask(SIG_BLOCK/UNBLOCK/SETMASK, &set, &old);

Pending: sigpending(&set);

Send: kill(pid, sig); raise(sig) to self; alarm(sec) for SIGALRM.

Example: Handle SIGINT (Ctrl-C):

```c
#include <signal.h>
#include <stdio.h>
#include <unistd.h>

void handler(int sig) {
    printf("Caught signal %d\n", sig);
}

int main() {
    struct sigaction sa = { .sa_handler = handler, .sa_flags = SA_RESTART };
    if (sigaction(SIGINT, &sa, NULL) == -1) { perror("sigaction"); return 1; }

    while (1) {
        printf("Running...\n");
        sleep(1);
    }
    return 0;
}
```
With SA_SIGINFO: sa_sigaction gets siginfo_t { int si_signo; int si_errno; int si_code; pid_t si_pid; ... } for sender etc.

Real-time: sigqueue(pid, sig, union sigval value); queued, no loss.

In kernel 6.18 rc, signal handling refines for better RT preempt.

Process Inspection and Control

Query:

- pid_t getpid(void); // Self
- pid_t getppid(void); // Parent
- pid_t getsid(pid_t pid); // Session ID
- pid_t getpgid(pid_t pid); // Process group

Control:

- int setpgid(pid_t pid, pid_t pgid); // Set group
- pid_t setsid(void); // New session
- int kill(pid_t pid, int sig); // Send signal (0 check existence)
- int prctl(int option, unsigned long arg2, ...); // Misc: PR_SET_NAME set name, PR_SET_DUMPABLE core dumps.

Daemons: prctl(PR_SET_NAME, (unsigned long)"mydaemon");

Monitor: /proc/<pid>/ (status, cmdline, environ, fd/).

ps, top use /proc.

Errors: ESRCH (no process), EPERM (no send sig).

Best Practices and Security Considerations

- Environment: Sanitize in secure progs (clearenv()); avoid putenv() with stack strings.
- Limits: Set conservative in daemons (e.g., NOFILE 1024).
- Priorities: Use nice(19) for background; RT cautiously (risk starvation).
- Signals: Use sigaction over signal (race-free); block in handlers; avoid non-async-safe funcs (e.g., no malloc).
- Inspection: Prefer APIs over /proc for portability.
- Security: Drop privs after fork (setuid non-root); handle SIGTERM gracefully; ignore SIGHUP in daemons.
- Pitfalls: Signal races (use sigprocmask); unlimited rlimits cause OOM; env overflow (ARG_MAX).

In multi-threaded: Signals to process, not thread (use pthread_sigmask).

Advanced: cgroups for CPU shares (cpu.weight), I/O (io.max).

These controls empower dynamic process management, key to resilient systems.

6.3 Daemons and Background Processes

Daemons and background processes are pivotal in Linux system programming, enabling long-running services that operate independently of user sessions and provide essential system functionalities. Daemons, often referred to as "background demons" in UNIX lore, are processes detached from controlling terminals, running continuously to handle tasks like network services, logging, or hardware monitoring. Background processes, more generally, are those executed without blocking the parent shell, allowing concurrent operations. This detachment and autonomy stem from UNIX's design for multi-user, time-sharing systems, where services needed to persist beyond individual logins. In Linux, these concepts facilitate robust server applications, cron jobs, and system utilities, with tools like nohup and & for simple backgrounding, and systematic daemonization for production-grade services. This section explores the creation, management, and control of daemons and background processes, covering key system calls such as setsid(), daemonization steps, signal handling for graceful shutdowns, logging practices, and integration with init systems like systemd. We'll draw on POSIX standards for portability, Linux-specific features like process namespaces for isolation, practical code examples, error handling, and security considerations to prevent issues like zombie proliferation or resource leaks. As of the stable Linux kernel 6.17 (released September 28, 2025, with the latest security patch 6.17.7 on November 2, 2025) and the ongoing 6.18 release candidate (rc4 as of November 2, 2025), daemon management benefits from enhanced cgroup v2 support for resource limiting and improved signal queuing for real-time responses, making them more efficient in containerized and cloud environments. By mastering these fundamentals, programmers can develop reliable, autonomous services that enhance system stability and scalability, from embedded devices running lightweight daemons to enterprise servers managing high-availability processes.

Historical Evolution of Daemons and Background Processes

The concept of background processes emerged in early UNIX systems, with the & operator in the Bourne shell (1977) allowing commands to run asynchronously, freeing the terminal for further input. Daemons evolved as a specialized form, inspired by Maxwell's demon in physics—a hypothetical entity sorting particles—and coined in UNIX to describe processes "watching" for events. Early examples include init (process 1, the ancestor of all), cron for scheduling, and inetd for network services in UNIX Version 7 (1979).

In Linux, Torvalds' initial kernel (1991) supported basic forking for backgrounding, but daemonization patterns solidified in the 1990s with tools like Apache httpd. The double-fork technique became standard to detach from sessions and avoid controlling terminals, preventing SIGHUP on logout. POSIX formalized aspects like setsid() in 1988 (IEEE 1003.1), ensuring portability, while Linux extended with nohup (ignore SIGHUP) and daemon(3) library function (BSD-origin, in glibc).

Modern shifts: With systemd (2010+), daemons are often managed as units (.service files), automating fork/setsid and providing supervision. Kernel advancements, like namespaces (CLONE_NEWPID since 2.6.24), allow daemon isolation in containers, and cgroup integration (v1 2007, v2 4.5) enables resource capping.

In kernel 6.17, daemons leverage improved scheduler hints for background tasks, reducing latency for interactive processes, while 6.18 rc enhances pidfd for non-parent monitoring.

Fundamentals of Background Processes

Background processes are launched from shells with & (e.g., command &), disassociating from the terminal's stdin/stdout/stderr, often redirecting to /dev/null or files. They inherit the parent's environment but run concurrently, with the shell receiving their PID immediately.

Key characteristics:

- **Disowning**: disown -h %jobid prevents SIGHUP on shell exit.
- **Nohup**: nohup command & ignores SIGHUP, redirects output to nohup.out.
- **Job Control**: fg/bg manage, jobs lists.

In programming, backgrounding isn't a syscall but a shell feature. To simulate: fork(), in child close fds or redirect, continue work; parent exits or waits.

Simple C background:

c

```c
#include <unistd.h>
#include <stdio.h>
#include <sys/types.h>

int main() {
    pid_t pid = fork();
    if (pid == -1) { perror("fork"); return 1; }
```

```c
    if (pid > 0) {
        printf("Background PID: %d\n", pid);
        return 0; // Parent exits
    }
    // Child: background
    sleep(10); // Simulate work
    printf("Background done\n");
    return 0;
}
```

Run: ./prog & to background.

Limitations: Still tied to session; logout sends SIGHUP unless nohup. For true detachment, use daemonization.

Creating Daemons: The Daemonization Process

Daemons are background processes fully detached from terminals, running as session leaders with no controlling tty. Standard steps (double-fork method):

1. **Fork and Exit Parent**: Child continues, parent terminates—ensures not process group leader.
2. **Call setsid()**: Creates new session/process group, detaches tty.
3. **Fork Again**: Second child can't reacquire tty (not session leader); exit first child.
4. **Change Working Directory**: chdir("/") avoids holding mounts.
5. **Set Umask**: umask(0) for full control over file perms.
6. **Close/Redirect FDs**: Close 0/1/2, open /dev/null or logs.
7. **Ignore Signals**: Handle SIGCHLD (no zombies), ignore SIGHUP.
8. **Daemon Work**: Infinite loop or event-driven.

Library: daemon(int nochdir, int noclose); (BSD, glibc) automates 1-6.

Example daemon:

c

```c
#include <unistd.h>
#include <sys/stat.h>
#include <fcntl.h>
#include <stdio.h>
#include <stdlib.h>
#include <signal.h>
#include <syslog.h>

void signal_handler(int sig) {
    if (sig == SIGTERM) {
        syslog(LOG_INFO, "Terminating daemon");
        exit(0);
    }
}

int main() {
    // Step 1: Fork
    pid_t pid = fork();
    if (pid == -1) { perror("fork1"); return 1; }
    if (pid > 0) return 0; // Parent exits

    // Step 2: New session
    if (setsid() == -1) { perror("setsid"); return 1; }

    // Step 3: Second fork
    pid = fork();
    if (pid == -1) { perror("fork2"); return 1; }
    if (pid > 0) return 0; // Intermediate exits

    // Step 4: Chdir
    chdir("/");
```

```
    // Step 5: Umask
    umask(0);

    // Step 6: Close fds
    close(STDIN_FILENO); close(STDOUT_FILENO); close(STDERR_FILENO);
    open("/dev/null", O_RDWR); dup(0); dup(0); // Redirect to null

    // Signals
    signal(SIGTERM, signal_handler);
    signal(SIGHUP, SIG_IGN);
    signal(SIGCHLD, SIG_IGN);

    // Logging
    openlog("mydaemon", LOG_PID, LOG_DAEMON);
    syslog(LOG_INFO, "Daemon started");

    // Work loop
    while (1) {
        // Daemon tasks
        syslog(LOG_INFO, "Working...");
        sleep(30);
    }

    closelog();
    return 0;
}
```
Compile, run: ./daemon &; check ps -ef | grep daemon.

Kernel: setsid() fails if leader (EAGAIN); ensures detachment.

In systemd: Services auto-daemonize if Type=forking; else Type=simple assumes no fork.

Managing Daemons: Startup, Shutdown, and Monitoring

Traditional: /etc/init.d/ scripts (SysV init), start/stop via forkdaemon.

Modern: systemd units:

[Unit] Description=My Daemon

[Service] ExecStart=/path/to/daemon Restart=always

[Install] WantedBy=multi-user.target

Enable: systemctl enable mydaemon.service; start: systemctl start.

Monitoring: systemctl status; journalctl -u mydaemon for logs.

Signals: SIGTERM graceful shutdown (handler cleanup), SIGKILL last resort.

Pidfiles: Write PID to /var/run/daemon.pid post-daemonize; check for running.

In kernel 6.17, systemd leverages cgroup for kill (systemd.kill).

Logging and Error Handling in Daemons

Daemons log to syslog (openlog, syslog, closelog) or files. Levels: LOG_EMERG to LOG_DEBUG. Facility: LOG_DAEMON.

File logging: Open post-detach, use fprintf.

Errors: Since no stderr, log via syslog(LOG_ERR, "Error: %s", strerror(errno)).

Best: Set errno=0 before calls, check post.

Advanced Features: Namespaces and Containers

clone(CLONE_NEWPID | CLONE_NEWUTS) for isolated daemons.

In containers: Daemons run as PID 1, handle reaping (SIGCHLD handler with waitpid(-1)).

cgroup: Limit CPU/memory for daemons via systemd or cgcreate.

In 6.18 rc, enhanced namespace for user daemons (systemd --user).

Security and Best Practices

- **Privilege Drop**: After bind/open, setuid non-root user.
- **Chroot Jail**: chroot("/chroot/dir") restricts FS.
- **Capabilities**: Drop bounding, keep only needed (e.g., CAP_NET_BIND_SERVICE).

- **Avoid Root**: Run as dedicated user/group.
- **PID Reuse**: Use pidfiles with locks (flock).
- **Graceful Shutdown**: Handler for SIGTERM: cleanup, unlink pidfile.
- **No Output**: Redirect all; use logs.
- **Error Resilience**: Retry on transient fails; watchdog if critical.
- **Testing**: strace for calls; pstree for hierarchy.

Pitfalls: Forgetting double fork (acquires tty); ignoring signals (hangs); resource leaks (close fds).

Examples: Nginx daemon off in foreground for systemd; cron as daemon.

These practices ensure daemons run reliably, embodying Linux's service-oriented design.

6.4 Process Relationships and Sessions

Process relationships and sessions in Linux define the hierarchical and grouped structures that organize processes, enabling effective management, signaling, and resource control in multi-process environments. These concepts, inherited from UNIX, facilitate job control in shells, daemon isolation, and containerization, ensuring processes can be coordinated, terminated collectively, or detached from user sessions. Understanding relationships—such as parent-child hierarchies—and sessions, which group processes for terminal independence, is crucial for building robust applications like servers that handle child workers or scripts that manage background tasks. This subsection explores process trees (via PPID), process groups (PGIDs) for collective signaling, sessions (SIDs) for detachment, controlling terminals (ctty), and related system calls like getppid(), setpgid(), setsid(), and tcsetsid(). We'll cover POSIX standards for portability, Linux extensions like prctl() for subreapers, practical examples for daemon creation and job control, error handling, and implications for zombies, orphans, and container namespaces. As of the stable Linux kernel 6.17 (released September 28, 2025, with the latest patch 6.17.7 on November 2, 2025) and the ongoing 6.18 release candidate (rc4 as of November 2, 2025), these features include optimized reparenting for large process trees and enhanced namespace support for isolated sessions in containers, improving scalability in cloud and embedded systems. By leveraging these structures, programmers can design applications that maintain clean hierarchies, respond gracefully to signals, and operate reliably in detached modes, enhancing overall system stability and user experience.

The Process Hierarchy: Parents, Children, and Trees

At the core of process relationships is the parent-child model, established during process creation. Every process except init (PID 1) has a parent, identified by its PPID (parent process ID). When a process forks, the child inherits the parent's attributes but receives its own PID, with the parent's PID as its PPID. This forms a tree structure, rooted at init (or systemd in modern distros), which reaps orphaned children.

Key functions from <unistd.h>:
- pid_t getpid(void); // Current PID
- pid_t getppid(void); // Parent PID

These are lightweight, always succeeding as they query the current task_struct in the kernel.

Semantics: PPID changes if the parent exits first (reparented to init or a subreaper). No direct way to get children—scan /proc or use custom tracking.

Process trees visualize relationships: pstree -p shows hierarchy with PIDs.

Orphans: Children whose parent exits before them. Kernel reparents to init (or PR_SET_CHILD_SUBREAPER prctl() designee), which waits to reap, preventing zombies.

Zombies: Exited children unreaped by parent, holding exit status. Parent wait() reaps; if orphaned, init reaps automatically.

In kernel 6.17, reparenting optimizes for high-fork-rate processes, reducing lock contention in pid allocation.

Example: Print hierarchy:

```c
#include <unistd.h>
#include <stdio.h>

int main() {
    printf("PID: %d, PPID: %d\n", getpid(), getppid());
    pid_t child = fork();
    if (child == 0) {
        printf("Child PID: %d, PPID: %d\n", getpid(), getppid());
```

```
  } else if (child > 0) {
    wait(NULL); // Reap
  }
  return 0;
}
```
Output shows child PPID as parent PID.

Process Groups: Collective Management

Process groups aggregate related processes for signaling and job control. Each process belongs to one group, identified by PGID (usually leader's PID).

Functions:

- pid_t getpgrp(void); // Current PGID (POSIX)
- pid_t getpgid(pid_t pid); // Any PGID
- int setpgid(pid_t pid, pid_t pgid); // Set (0 current, pgid=0 new group with pid as leader)

Semantics: New processes inherit parent's PGID. setpgid() callable by self/child before exec or in same session. Can't change leader's PGID.

Used for: kill(-pgid, sig) signals whole group (e.g., Ctrl-C in shell sends SIGINT to foreground group).

Job control: Shells manage groups for pipelines (cmd1 | cmd2 in same group).

In Linux, /proc/<pid>/stat shows pgrp.

Errors: EPERM (not child/leader), ESRCH (no pid), EACCES (child exec'd).

Example: Create group:

```c
pid_t pid = fork();
if (pid == 0) {
  setpgid(0, 0); // New group, leader self
  printf("Child PGID: %d\n", getpgrp());
} else {
  setpgid(pid, pid); // Parent sets child's to child's PID
  printf("Parent PGID: %d\n", getpgrp());
}
```

Sessions: Detachment and Independence

Sessions group process groups, primarily for terminal control and daemonization. Each session has a SID (session ID, leader's PID), possibly a controlling terminal (/dev/tty*).

Functions:

- pid_t getsid(pid_t pid); // SID (0 current)
- pid_t setsid(void); // Create new session

setsid() requirements: Caller not group leader (hence double-fork). Succeeds: New SID/PGID = PID, detaches ctty.

Used for: Daemons call post-first fork to detach.

Controlling terminal: Acquired via open(/dev/tty) or ioctl TIOCSCTTY. Sessions without are non-interactive.

getpgrp() == getsid(0) if group leader.

Errors: EPERM (already leader).

In daemons: setsid() prevents SIGHUP on logout.

Kernel: struct signal_struct tracks session.

In 6.18 rc, session handling refines for user namespaces, allowing isolated ttys.

Controlling Terminals and Job Control

Controlling tty (ctty): Session leader's terminal for I/O, signals (SIGINT from Ctrl-C).

Query: char *ctermid(char *buf); or /proc/<pid>/fd/0 symlink.

Assign: ioctl(fd, TIOCSCTTY, arg); arg=1 steal.

Job control: Foreground group (tcsetpgrp()) receives input/signals; background suspended on read.

Shells: tcgetpgrp() gets fg group.

Signals: SIGTSTP (Ctrl-Z suspend), SIGCONT (continue), SIGTTIN/SIGTTOU (bg I/O attempt).

Daemons: Avoid ctty to ignore these.

Process Relationships in Practice: Daemons and Shell Jobs

Daemons: Use relationships for detachment (setsid()), reaping (SIGCHLD ignore/handler), shutdown (SIGTERM).

Shell jobs: & backgrounds in current group; disown removes from table.

Pipelines: shell forks, sets group to first child's PID, execs.

Namespaces and Modern Extensions

Pid namespaces (CLONE_NEWPID): Isolated trees, own init (PID 1 inside).

User namespaces: Map UIDs, affect relationships.

prctl(PR_SET_CHILD_SUBREAPER, 1): Become reaper for descendants, useful in containers.

Pidfd (pidfd_open(pid, 0)): FD for process, use with poll() for wait, safer than PID.

In kernel 6.17, pid namespaces optimize for deep hierarchies.

Error Handling and Best Practices

Errors: Common ESRCH (no process), EPERM (permission).

Practices:

- Double-fork + setsid() for daemons.
- Handle SIGCHLD to reap.
- Use waitpid(-1, &status, WNOHANG) in loops.
- In shells: trap signals.
- Security: Drop privs post-setup.
- Avoid PID races: Use pidfd.
- Monitor: pstree, ps -o pid,ppid,pgid,sid,comm.

Pitfalls: Forgetting reap (zombies); setsid() as leader (fails); signal races.

Advanced Topics: Subreapers and Pidfd

Subreapers (kernel 3.4+): prctl(PR_SET_CHILD_SUBREAPER, 1); orphans reparent to nearest subreaper, not init. Useful for job managers.

Pidfd: int pidfd = pidfd_open(pid, 0); waitid(P_PIDFD, pidfd, &info, WEXITED); Close on use.

In 6.18 rc, pidfd enhances for thread groups.

These relationships enable structured concurrency, foundational for Linux apps.

7 Advanced Process Management

7.1 Exec Functions and Program Execution

The exec family of functions in Linux represents a cornerstone of process management, allowing a running process to replace its current program image with a new one while preserving its process ID (PID), open file descriptors, and other attributes. This mechanism, combined with fork(), forms the basis for spawning new programs and is fundamental to shell command execution, daemon forking, and application launching. Originating from early UNIX systems—where exec() was introduced in Version 3 (1973) to complement fork()—these functions enable efficient program loading without creating a new process context, optimizing resource use in multi-tasking environments. In Linux, exec functions handle the loading of ELF (Executable and Linkable Format) binaries, scripts via interpreters (shebang #!), and even custom formats through binfmt_misc. This subsection explores the exec variants, their semantics, the execution process, environment and argument passing, error conditions, and integration with fork() for typical use cases. We'll cover POSIX-compliant behaviors, Linux-specific extensions like execveat() for relative execution, practical C examples, security implications (e.g., setuid execution), and performance considerations. As of the stable Linux kernel 6.17 (released September 28, 2025, with the latest patch 6.17.7 on November 2, 2025) and the ongoing 6.18 release candidate (rc4 as of November 2, 2025), exec operations benefit from optimized binary loading with better support for large argument lists and enhanced security checks in namespaces, making them more robust for containerized and high-security applications. By mastering exec, programmers can implement dynamic program invocation, privilege transitions, and modular architectures, ensuring applications are flexible, secure, and efficient in diverse Linux ecosystems from desktops to embedded systems.

The Role of Exec in Process Lifecycle

In the Linux process model, fork() duplicates a process, creating a child with a copy of the parent's memory (via copy-on-write for efficiency), but to run a different program, the child must overlay its image with new code and data. This is where exec comes in: it discards the current text, data, stack, and heap segments, loading a new executable into the address space while retaining the PID, open files (unless marked CLOEXEC), current directory, umask, and resource limits. This "replace" operation is atomic from the user's perspective—if exec succeeds, the old program is gone, and the new one starts at its entry point (usually main() for C programs).

Historical significance: In UNIX Version 1 (1971), processes were loaded directly, but fork/exec separation in Version 3 allowed the powerful "fork-exec-wait" pattern, enabling shells to run commands in children without blocking. Linux adopted this in its earliest versions (0.01, 1991), with ELF support added in 1.2 (1995) for dynamic linking.

Key benefits:

- **Efficiency**: Reuses process slot, avoids full creation overhead.
- **Modularity**: Allows dynamic loading based on runtime conditions.
- **Security**: Facilitates privilege changes via setuid/setgid bits on executables.

In the kernel, execve() (the underlying syscall) is handled by do_execve() in fs/exec.c, which validates the binary, sets up the mm_struct for memory, and jumps to the new entry point. Kernel 6.17 optimizes this for large binaries with better page table setup, reducing latency in deep namespace hierarchies.

The Exec Family of Functions

All exec variants ultimately call the kernel's execve() syscall but differ in argument handling and path resolution. From <unistd.h>, they never return on success (start new program); on failure, return -1 with errno set.

- **int execve(const char *pathname, char *const argv[], char *const envp[]);**: Core function. Pathname: absolute/relative to executable. Argv: NULL-terminated array of arguments (argv[0] conventionally program name). Envp: NULL-terminated environment, or NULL for inherit.
- **int execl(const char *pathname, const char *arg0, ... / (char *)NULL */);**: List of args, ended by NULL.
- **int execle(const char *pathname, const char *arg0, ... / (char *)NULL, char *const envp[] */);**: Args list + explicit envp.
- **int execv(const char *pathname, char *const argv[]);**: Array args.
- **int execvp(const char *file, char *const argv[]);**: Searches PATH for file (if no /).
- **int execlp(const char *file, const char *arg0, ... / (char *)NULL */);**: PATH search + args list.

- **int execvpe(const char *file, char *const argv[], char *const envp[]);** : Linux/GNU extension, PATH + explicit envp.

Choose based on needs: vp for PATH, e for env, l for list, v for vector.

Example: Exec ls -l:

c

```
#include <unistd.h>

int main() {
    char *argv[] = {"ls", "-l", NULL};
    char *envp[] = {"PATH=/bin:/usr/bin", NULL}; // Custom env
    execve("/bin/ls", argv, envp);
    // Never reaches here on success
    perror("execve");
    return 1;
}
```

Using execlp:

c

```
execlp("ls", "ls", "-l", (char *)NULL);
```

Scripts: If #!/bin/bash, kernel invokes /bin/bash with script as arg.

Errors: ENOENT (missing), EACCES (no exec perm), ENOEXEC (bad format), E2BIG (args/env too big, ARG_MAX ~2MB), ETXTBSY (file open for write).

Typical Usage: Fork-Exec-Wait Pattern

Most programs fork then exec in child, parent waits:

c

```
#include <unistd.h>
#include <sys/wait.h>
#include <stdio.h>

int main() {
    pid_t pid = fork();
    if (pid == -1) { perror("fork"); return 1; }
    if (pid == 0) {
        // Child
        execl("/bin/echo", "echo", "Hello from child", (char *)NULL);
        perror("execl"); // Fail
        _exit(1); // Use _exit in child
    }
    // Parent
    int status;
    waitpid(pid, &status, 0);
    if (WIFEXITED(status)) printf("Child exited with %d\n", WEXITSTATUS(status));
    return 0;
}
```

_exit() avoids flushing parent's buffers.

Posix_spawn(): Combines fork/exec/wait optionally, efficient for short children, avoids vfork risks.

Environment and Argument Handling

Args: Limited by ARG_MAX (/proc/sys/kernel/arg_max), includes env. getdtablesize() for FD limit impact.

Env: Inherited unless explicit. clearenv(); to empty, then setenv().

In secure code: Sanitize env (e.g., unset LD_PRELOAD) before exec.

Security Implications: Setuid and Capabilities

Exec on setuid/setgid files: If setuid bit (chmod u+s), effective UID becomes owner (often root). Similar for gid.

Kernel: If setuid root, capabilities reset unless file has caps.

Secure: In setuid progs, validate args, drop privs early (seteuid(getuid())).

Capabilities (section 5.3): File caps applied on exec, permitting non-root elevation.

In kernel 6.17, exec checks caps in bprm_fill_uid(), with namespace-aware logic.

Performance and Optimization

Exec overhead: Load binary, resolve dynamics (ld.so), setup stack/heap. For frequent, use vfork() + exec (suspends parent, no COW—risky, deprecated).

Kernel caches binfmt, optimizes for PIE (position-independent executables).

In 6.18 rc, exec accelerates for musl libc with better auxv handling.

Error Handling and Best Practices

Always check fork/exec returns. In child fail, _exit() with code.

Practices:

- Absolute paths for security.
- NULL-terminate argv/envp.
- Close CLOEXEC fds pre-exec.
- In daemons, exec self on SIGHUP for reload.
- For paths: realpath() resolve.
- Limit args: Check argc.

Pitfalls: Relative paths (cwd race); large args (E2BIG); exec in threads (whole process replaced).

Advanced Topics: Namespaces and Execveat

execveat(fd, path, argv, envp, flags); (kernel 3.19+): Exec relative to dirfd, AT_EMPTY_PATH for fd itself (fexecve()).

Useful in chroots/namespaces.

In containers, exec respects mount namespaces.

Binfmt_misc: /proc/sys/fs/binfmt_misc registers interpreters (e.g., for Java .class).

In 6.17, binfmt supports arm64 on x86 via emulation.

These tools empower dynamic execution, central to Linux flexibility.

7.2 Process Accounting and Monitoring

Process accounting and monitoring in Linux provide essential tools for tracking resource usage, performance metrics, and behavioral patterns of running processes, enabling administrators and developers to optimize systems, debug issues, and ensure efficient operation. These capabilities have roots in early UNIX systems, where resource constraints necessitated detailed logging of process activities to bill users in time-sharing environments. In modern Linux, accounting logs execution details like CPU time and memory for auditing, while monitoring offers real-time and historical insights through utilities and kernel interfaces. This is critical for servers managing workloads, embedded devices with limited resources, and cloud instances billing by usage. This section explores process accounting via the acct subsystem, monitoring tools like ps, top, and perf, system calls such as getrusage() and times(), kernel-provided /proc filesystem data, and advanced features like eBPF for dynamic tracing. We'll cover POSIX-compliant interfaces for portability, Linux-specific extensions including cgroups for aggregated stats, practical examples in C for programmatic access, error handling, security considerations to prevent information leaks, and performance impacts of enabling accounting. As of the stable Linux kernel 6.17 (released on September 28, 2025, with the latest patch 6.17.7 addressing minor bugs as of November 2, 2025) and the ongoing 6.18 release candidate (rc4 as of November 2, 2025), process accounting remains supported through the BSD-compatible acct structure, with enhancements in eBPF for low-overhead monitoring and better cgroup v2 integration for container-aware stats. By utilizing these mechanisms, programmers can implement proactive system management, detect anomalies like memory leaks or CPU hogs, and build tools for capacity planning in environments ranging from personal desktops to large-scale data centers.

Historical Development of Process Accounting and Monitoring

Process accounting originated in BSD UNIX (1979) with the acct() system call, designed to log process termination details for billing in academic and commercial settings. This was adopted in Linux during the 1.x era (1990s), where the kernel began supporting /proc for real-time monitoring, inspired by Plan 9's procfs. Early tools like ps (process status) from UNIX Version 7 and top (table of processes) from 1984 provided user-friendly interfaces, while sar (system activity reporter) from System V added historical reporting.

In Linux, accounting evolved with the introduction of the psacct package (process accounting utilities) in the late 1990s, using accton to toggle logging to /var/account/pacct (or /var/log/account/pacct in some distros). Monitoring expanded with perf (kernel 2.6.31, 2009) for hardware counters and eBPF (extended Berkeley Packet Filter, kernel 3.18, 2014) for programmable tracing without kernel modifications.

POSIX standardizes some aspects, like times() for CPU usage and wait() for exit status, but much of /proc and eBPF are Linux-specific. Kernel 6.17 maintains backward compatibility for acct while optimizing perf for ARM big.LITTLE architectures, and 6.18 rc introduces refinements to eBPF verifier for safer user-space programs. Modern trends: With containers, monitoring shifts to cgroup-based stats (/sys/fs/cgroup), allowing per-container accounting without global overhead.

Process Accounting: Logging Termination Details

Process accounting records details when processes exit, including command name, elapsed time, user/system CPU, I/O operations, and flags (e.g., core dumped). Enabled via the acct subsystem.

System call: int acct(const char *filename); // Root-only, filename for log (NULL disables).

Typically managed by accton command (from psacct/acct package): sudo accton on /var/log/account/pacct.

Log format: Binary struct acct (from <sys/acct.h>): char ac_comm[ACCT_COMM]; /* command name / *time_t ac_utime; / user time */ etc.

Tools to read:

- lastcomm: Shows last commands executed, with accounting data.
- ac: Prints connect time statistics.
- sa: Summarizes accounting by user/command.

Install psacct: sudo apt install acct (Ubuntu) or sudo dnf install psacct (Fedora).

Example: Enable and query:

As root:

bash

accton on /var/account/pacct

 # Run some commands

lastcomm

accton off

In code: Parse pacct file (binary, seek from end for recent).

Pros: Detailed auditing, low overhead (only on exit). Cons: Disk space (rotate logs), no real-time.

Kernel: acct_process() in kernel/acct.c writes on do_exit(). In 6.17, acct handles large UIDs better.

Errors: EACCES (no perm), ENOENT (bad file), ENOSYS (CONFIG_BSD_PROCESS_ACCT=n).

Real-Time Monitoring: Tools and /proc Interface

Monitoring provides live views of processes.

Command-line tools:

- **ps**: Process status. ps -ef (all), ps aux (BSD style with %CPU, %MEM).
- **top/htop**: Interactive, top -p pid monitor specific, htop with tree view.
- **pmap**: Memory map, pmap -x pid shows RSS, PSS.
- **strace**: Traces syscalls, strace -p pid attach.
- **lsof**: Lists open files, lsof -p pid.

Kernel interface: /proc/<pid>/ for stats.

- /proc/<pid>/stat: Status (PID, state, PPID, utime, stime, rss).
- /proc/<pid>/status: Human-readable (VmPeak, Threads, CapEff capabilities).
- /proc/<pid>/cmdline: Args (null-separated).
- /proc/<pid>/environ: Env vars.
- /proc/<pid>/fd/: Open FDs.
- /proc/<pid>/tasks/: Threads.
- /proc/stat: System-wide CPU.
- /proc/meminfo: Memory.

Global: /proc/loadavg (load average), /proc/uptime.

In code: Read /proc files with fopen/fread.

Example: Get process CPU usage:

c

```
#include <stdio.h>
#include <stdlib.h>
#include <string.h>

int main(int argc, char *argv[]) {
    if (argc != 2) { printf("Usage: %s PID\n", argv[0]); return 1; }
```

```c
    char path[256];
    snprintf(path, sizeof(path), "/proc/%s/stat", argv[1]);

    FILE *f = fopen(path, "r");
    if (!f) { perror("fopen"); return 1; }

    char buf[1024];
    fgets(buf, sizeof(buf), f);
    fclose(f);

    // Parse: fields 14 utime, 15 stime (clocks)
    unsigned long utime, stime;
    sscanf(buf, "%*d %*s %*c %*d %*d %*d %*d %*d %*u %*lu %*lu %*lu %*lu %lu %lu", &utime, &stime);
    printf("User time: %lu, System time: %lu (ticks)\n", utime, stime);

    return 0;
}
```
To convert ticks to seconds: divide by sysconf(_SC_CLK_TCK) (usually 100).

Security: /proc/<pid> readable if same user or root; some fields restricted.

In kernel 6.17, /proc enhanced for better PSS (proportional set size) accuracy.

Programmatic Accounting: getrusage() and times()

For self/child usage:

- int getrusage(int who, struct rusage *usage); // <sys/resource.h>

Who: RUSAGE_SELF (self+threads), RUSAGE_CHILDREN (waited children), RUSAGE_THREAD (calling thread).

Struct rusage { struct timeval ru_utime; /* user *struct timeval ru_stime; / system / long ru_maxrss; / max RSS KB / long ru_minflt; / page reclaims */ ... }; 16 fields total.

Returns summed stats.

- clock_t times(struct tms *buf); // <sys/times.h>

Struct tms { clock_t tms_utime; tms_stime; tms_cutime; /* child user */ tms_cstime; };

Returns total clocks since boot.

Clocks: Divide by sysconf(_SC_CLK_TCK).

Example: Measure self:

c
```c
#include <sys/resource.h>
#include <stdio.h>

int main() {
    struct rusage usage;
    // Work
    for (long i = 0; i < 100000000; i++) {}

    if (getrusage(RUSAGE_SELF, &usage) == -1) { perror("getrusage"); return 1; }
    printf("User time: %ld.%06ld s\n", usage.ru_utime.tv_sec, usage.ru_utime.tv_usec);
    printf("System time: %ld.%06ld s\n", usage.ru_stime.tv_sec, usage.ru_stime.tv_usec);
    printf("Max RSS: %ld KB\n", usage.ru_maxrss);

    return 0;
}
```
Accurate for billing/debugging.

Advanced Monitoring: perf, eBPF, and cgroups

perf: Kernel tool for events. perf stat ./prog measures cycles, instructions. perf record -p pid samples call stacks. perf report analyzes.

Install: apt install linux-tools-common linux-tools-generic.

eBPF: Programmable kernel probes. bpftrace or bcc tools: bpftrace -e 'tracepoint:syscalls:sys_enter_execve { printf("%s\n", comm); }'.

Low overhead, safe.

cgroups: /sys/fs/cgroup/ for groups. cpuacct for CPU, memory for RAM. cat /sys/fs/cgroup/cpu,cpuacct/cpuacct.usage_percpu.

Systemd: Per-service cgroups.

In kernel 6.17, perf supports hybrid PMUs (Intel/AMD), eBPF verifier faster.

Error Handling and Best Practices

Errors: ENOENT (/proc missing), EACCES (no read perm).

Practices:

- Use getrusage for self-stats.
- Parse /proc safely (fields change).
- Rotate acct logs (logrotate).
- Monitor thresholds (e.g., alert high CPU).
- Security: Restrict /proc (hidepid=2 mount).
- Performance: Accounting <1% overhead; disable if unneeded.

Pitfalls: Acct misses short processes; /proc stale on rapid changes.

Future Directions

Kernel 6.18 rc: eBPF for user-space tracing, cgroup v3 planning.

Tools like btop (htop alternative), sysdig for system-wide.

These enable proactive management, vital for stable systems.

7.3 Real-Time Processes and Priorities

Real-time processes and priorities in Linux extend the standard scheduling model to support applications requiring predictable, low-latency responses, such as industrial control systems, audio processing, telecommunications, and embedded devices. Unlike general-purpose scheduling, which prioritizes fairness and throughput, real-time scheduling emphasizes determinism—ensuring tasks meet strict deadlines to avoid system failures. This capability, introduced in kernel 2.0 (1996) with POSIX.1b compliance for real-time extensions, has evolved to include advanced policies and patches for hard real-time guarantees. Priorities in real-time contexts range from 1 to 99 (higher numbers indicate higher priority), superseding the nice values (-20 to 19) used in non-real-time processes. Understanding these mechanisms is crucial for system programmers building latency-sensitive applications, as improper use can lead to priority inversion, starvation of lower-priority tasks, or system instability. This subsection explores real-time scheduling policies (SCHED_FIFO, SCHED_RR, SCHED_DEADLINE), priority management, system calls like sched_setscheduler() and sched_setparam(), the PREEMPT_RT patch for enhanced predictability, capabilities required (CAP_SYS_NICE), practical C examples, error handling, performance tuning, and security implications. Drawing on POSIX.1-2001 standards for portability and Linux-specific implementations, we'll highlight how these features integrate with the Completely Fair Scheduler (CFS) and cgroups for modern workloads. As of the stable Linux kernel 6.17 (released September 28, 2025, with the latest patch 6.17.7 addressing minor scheduling tweaks as of November 2, 2025) and the ongoing 6.18 release candidate (rc4 as of November 2, 2025), real-time support includes refined deadline scheduling for energy-efficient ARM processors and better integration with eBPF for runtime priority monitoring, enabling more robust applications in IoT, automotive, and high-frequency trading environments.

Historical Context and Evolution of Real-Time Scheduling

The need for real-time capabilities arose in the 1980s with the growth of embedded and control systems, prompting POSIX to define real-time extensions in IEEE 1003.1b-1993 (incorporated into POSIX.1-2001). Early UNIX variants like System V Release 4 (1989) introduced priority-based scheduling, but Linux's initial implementation in kernel 2.0 focused on soft real-time—best-effort low latency without hard guarantees. The O(1) scheduler in 2.6 (2003) improved responsiveness, but the Completely Fair Scheduler (CFS) in 2.6.23 (2007) integrated real-time as fixed-priority classes above CFS.

Key milestones:

- Kernel 2.6.18 (2006): SCHED_FIFO and SCHED_RR stabilized.
- Kernel 3.14 (2014): SCHED_DEADLINE for earliest deadline first (EDF) scheduling, addressing overruns in periodic tasks.
- PREEMPT_RT patchset (ongoing since 2004, partial mainline in 6.x): Reduces latency by making kernel fully preemptible, targeting <1ms worst-case.
- Kernel 6.17: Optimizes RT for heterogeneous cores (big.LITTLE), with better migration avoidance.

POSIX mandates SCHED_FIFO/RR, priorities 1-99 (sched_get_priority_min/max), but SCHED_DEADLINE is Linux-specific. Real-time requires CAP_SYS_NICE or root, preventing abuse.

In contemporary use, real-time priorities are vital for applications like ROS (Robot Operating System) or ALSA audio, where jitter can cause failures.

Real-Time Scheduling Policies

Linux offers three real-time policies, set via sched_setscheduler():

- **SCHED_FIFO (First-In-First-Out)**: Fixed-priority, non-preemptive within same priority. Higher priority preempts lower; same priority runs until blocks or yields (sched_yield()). No time slices—risks starvation if infinite loop.
- **SCHED_RR (Round-Robin)**: Like FIFO but with time quanta (default 100ms, configurable via /proc/sys/kernel/sched_rr_timeslice_ms). Preempts same-priority after quantum, rotating ready queue.
- **SCHED_DEADLINE**: Bandwidth-based, specifies runtime, deadline, period per task. Kernel ensures runtime within period, before deadline, using EDF. Overruns deferred or throttled.

Policies above SCHED_NORMAL (CFS) and SCHED_BATCH/IDLE; RT tasks preempt non-RT.

Priorities: sched_get_priority_min(SCHED_FIFO) = 1, max=99. Higher number = higher priority.

System calls (<sched.h>):

- int sched_getscheduler(pid_t pid); // Get policy
- int sched_setscheduler(pid_t pid, int policy, const struct sched_param *param);
- int sched_getparam(pid_t pid, struct sched_param *param);
- int sched_setparam(pid_t pid, const struct sched_param *param);

Struct sched_param { int sched_priority; }; For DEADLINE: struct sched_attr (sched_setattr()) with u64 sched_deadline, sched_period, sched_runtime.

Pid 0: Current process.

Example: Set RR priority 50:

```c
#include <sched.h>
#include <stdio.h>
#include <errno.h>

int main() {
    struct sched_param param = { .sched_priority = 50 };
    if (sched_setscheduler(0, SCHED_RR, &param) == -1) {
        perror("setscheduler");
        return 1;
    }

    int policy = sched_getscheduler(0);
    if (policy == SCHED_RR) printf("Set to RR priority %d\n", param.sched_priority);

    // Real-time work
    return 0;
}
```

Run as root or with CAP_SYS_NICE.

For DEADLINE: Use sched_setattr() (kernel 3.14+), attr.size = sizeof(struct sched_attr); attr.sched_policy = SCHED_DEADLINE; attr.sched_runtime = 10000000; // 10ms ns

Errors: EINVAL (bad policy/prio), EPERM (no cap), ESRCH (bad pid).

Capabilities and Permissions for Real-Time

Non-root processes need CAP_SYS_NICE to set RT policies or negative nice. Granted via file caps or ambient sets.

In containers, user namespaces map caps, allowing "root" inside to set RT without host impact.

Security: High prio risks starvation—use chrt command or schedtool for testing.

The PREEMPT_RT Patch for Hard Real-Time

Standard Linux is soft real-time (latencies ~ms); PREEMPT_RT patch makes kernel fully preemptible, replacing spinlocks with mutexes, priority inheritance to avoid inversion, and IRQ threading. Targets <10us latencies.

Not mainline (partial in 6.x), apply via rt patchset: CONFIG_PREEMPT_RT=y.

In 6.17-rt (real-time tree), optimizes for multi-core with better lockdep.

Use: For avionics, robotics—e.g., cyclictest measures latency.

Process Affinity and CPU Binding

Bind to CPUs for predictability: sched_setaffinity(pid_t pid, size_t cpusetsize, const cpu_set_t *mask);
cpu_set_t mask; CPU_ZERO(&mask); CPU_SET(0, &mask); // CPU 0

Get: sched_getaffinity().

In NUMA, binds memory too indirectly.

Performance Tuning and Monitoring

Tune: /proc/sys/kernel/sched_rt_period_us (1000000us), sched_rt_runtime_us (950000us)—95% CPU for RT, 5% others to prevent lockup.

Monitor: chrt -p pid shows policy/prio; top - press 1 for per-CPU, f for fields (PRI for priority, negative for RT as -rtprio + 100? No, top shows rtprio in PRI as -100 to -1 for 99 to 1).

perf sched record ./rt_app; perf sched latency analyzes.

In kernel 6.18 rc, RT supports deadline migration for better load balance.

Error Handling and Best Practices

Errors: Common EPERM, EINVAL (prio out range 1-99 for RT, 0 for others).

Practices:

- Set policy/prio after fork, before work.
- Use SCHED_RR for fair sharing, FIFO for strict.
- Monitor latencies with cyclictest.
- Combine with affinity for multi-core.
- Drop CAP_SYS_NICE after set.
- In cgroups, cpu.rt_runtime_us limits RT bandwidth.
- Avoid RT for non-critical—can hog CPU.

Pitfalls: Priority inversion (use priority inheritance mutexes pthread_mutexattr_setprotocol(&attr, PTHREAD_PRIO_INHERIT)); overcommit RT time (softlockup).

Security: CAP_SYS_NICE allows DoS—restrict via AppArmor.

Advanced Topics: SCHED_DEADLINE and Integration

For periodic: period = deadline, runtime < period.

sched_setattr(pid, &attr, 0); attr.sched_flags = 0;

Get: sched_getattr().

In PREEMPT_RT, DEADLINE harder guarantees.

Tools: schedtool -D -t runtime:period -e cmd sets DEADLINE.

In 6.17, DEADLINE supports bandwidth reclaim for overprovisioning.

These features enable precise control, vital for time-sensitive systems.

7.4 Containerization Basics (Namespaces and cgroups)

Containerization has revolutionized software deployment and system management in Linux, providing lightweight, isolated environments that mimic virtual machines but with far less overhead. At its core, containerization relies on two key Linux kernel features: namespaces, which partition kernel resources to create isolated views for processes, and control groups (cgroups), which limit and account for resource usage across groups of processes. These technologies, introduced in the mid-2000s, enable tools like Docker, Podman, and Kubernetes to run applications in sandboxed contexts, sharing the host kernel while appearing as separate systems. For system programmers, understanding namespaces and cgroups is essential for building secure, scalable applications, debugging containerized environments, and optimizing resource allocation in scenarios from cloud-native microservices to embedded IoT devices. This subsection explores the fundamentals of containerization, detailing namespace types and their isolation properties, cgroup hierarchies for resource control, their interplay in creating containers, system calls like unshare() and clone() for namespace manipulation, cgroupfs interfaces for management, practical C examples, error handling, performance considerations, and security implications. Drawing from POSIX influences for real-time and scheduling but primarily Linux-specific implementations, we'll highlight how these features integrate with the process model. As of the stable Linux kernel 6.17 (released on September 28, 2025, with the latest patch 6.17.7 addressing scheduling refinements as of November 2, 2025) and the ongoing 6.18 release candidate (rc4 as of November 2, 2025), containerization benefits from enhanced cgroup v2 unification for simpler management and improved namespace support for deep isolation in nested containers, making it more efficient for high-density deployments.

The Foundations of Containerization

Containerization abstracts the operating system to provide process isolation without full virtualization, allowing multiple workloads to run on a single kernel while appearing independent. Unlike virtual machines (VMs), which emulate hardware and run separate kernels (e.g., via KVM/QEMU), containers share the host kernel, using namespaces to virtualize global resources like PIDs, network stacks, and mount points, and cgroups to enforce limits on CPU, memory, I/O, and other resources. This results in faster startup times, lower overhead (containers use ~10-100MB vs. VMs' GBs), and better density—ideal for microservices where applications are packaged with dependencies.

Historical evolution: Namespaces began with clone() flags in kernel 2.4.19 (2002) for plan9-like isolation, expanding to full types by 3.8 (2013). Cgroups originated in kernel 2.6.24 (2008) from Google engineers for workload partitioning, with v2 unified in 4.5 (2016) for better hierarchy management. Together, they powered early containers like LXC (2008), evolving into Docker (2013) which popularized the technology.

Benefits for programmers: Namespaces prevent global pollution (e.g., unique /proc in each), cgroups enable fair sharing and bursting. Combined with union filesystems (e.g., overlayfs), they create reproducible environments. In kernel 6.17, containerization optimizes for ARM64 with better cgroup energy-aware scheduling, while 6.18 rc refines namespace cloning for faster container spins in deep hierarchies.

Linux Namespaces: Isolating Kernel Resources

Namespaces create per-process views of system resources, making global identifiers local. Each process belongs to one namespace per type, inherited on fork() unless cloned.

System calls:

- int unshare(int flags); // Disassociate current process into new namespaces.
- pid_t clone(int (*fn)(void *), void *stack, int flags, void *arg); // Create child in new namespaces.
- int setns(int fd, int nstype); // Join existing namespace via fd (from /proc/<pid>/ns/*).

Flags: CLONE_NEWCGROUP, CLONE_NEWIPC, CLONE_NEWNET, CLONE_NEWNS (mount), CLONE_NEWPID, CLONE_NEWTIME (time), CLONE_NEWUSER, CLONE_NEWUTS.

Creation requires CAP_SYS_ADMIN in parent namespace, except user namespaces (unprivileged).

Types detailed below; combine flags for multiple.

Errors: EINVAL (invalid flags), ENOSPC (limit reached), EPERM (no cap).

Types of Namespaces

Linux supports eight namespace types, each isolating a specific resource:

- **Mount Namespaces (CLONE_NEWNS, kernel 2.4.19)**: Isolate filesystem mount points. Processes see different /, enabling chroot-like but more flexible. Used for container rootfs. unshare(CLONE_NEWNS); mount("none", "/", NULL, MS_PRIVATE | MS_REC, NULL); to privatize.
- **UTS Namespaces (CLONE_NEWUTS, 2.6.19)**: Isolate hostname and domainname (uname -n). sethostname("container1", 10); Different views without affecting host.
- **IPC Namespaces (CLONE_NEWIPC, 2.6.19)**: Isolate System V IPC (semaphores, message queues, shared memory) and POSIX message queues. Prevents naming collisions.
- **PID Namespaces (CLONE_NEWPID, 2.6.24)**: Isolate process IDs. Child in new namespace sees PID 1 inside, host sees high PID. Nested possible (up to 32 levels). init (PID 1 inside) reaps orphans.
- **Network Namespaces (CLONE_NEWNET, 2.6.24)**: Isolate network stack—interfaces, routes, iptables. unshare(CLONE_NEWNET); creates loopback-only. veth pairs connect to host.
- **User Namespaces (CLONE_NEWUSER, 3.8)**: Isolate UIDs/GIDs. Unprivileged creation, maps host UIDs (e.g., /etc/subuid). Enables "root" inside without host root. Gateway for other namespaces (must create user first for unpriv).
- **Cgroup Namespaces (CLONE_NEWCGROUP, 4.6)**: Isolate cgroup views. Virtualizes /sys/fs/cgroup, hiding host hierarchy.
- **Time Namespaces (CLONE_NEWTIME, 5.6)**: Isolate clocks (CLOCK_MONOTONIC, CLOCK_BOOTTIME). Offsets via /proc/<pid>/time_offset. For migration/testing.

Example: Create user+network namespace:

```c
#include <sched.h>
#include <sys/wait.h>
#include <stdio.h>
```

```c
#include <unistd.h>
#include <string.h>

int child(void *arg) {
    printf("In namespace: PID %d\n", getpid());
    execlp("ip", "ip", "link", "show", (char *)NULL);
    return 1;
}

int main() {
    char stack[8192];
    pid_t pid = clone(child, stack + sizeof(stack), CLONE_NEWUSER | CLONE_NEWNET | SIGCHLD, NULL);
    if (pid == -1) { perror("clone"); return 1; }

    // Map UIDs (host root needed for write)
    char path[64];
    snprintf(path, sizeof(path), "/proc/%d/uid_map", pid);
    FILE *f = fopen(path, "w");
    if (f) {
        fprintf(f, "0 %d 1\n", getuid()); // Map inside 0 to host uid
        fclose(f);
    }
    // Similar for gid_map

    wait(NULL);
    return 0;
}
```
Run as root; child sees isolated net.

Control Groups (cgroups): Resource Limiting and Accounting

Cgroups group processes for hierarchical resource control, isolation, and prioritization. Unlike namespaces (view isolation), cgroups enforce limits.

Versions:

- **v1**: Multiple hierarchies per controller (cpu, memory). /sys/fs/cgroup/cpu/, etc. Deprecated but supported.
- **v2**: Unified hierarchy (/sys/fs/cgroup/unified or /sys/fs/cgroup). Single tree, all controllers. Default since kernel 4.5, mandatory in some distros (Fedora 31+).

Controllers: cpu (shares, quota), memory (limits, oom), io (throttle), pids (count limit), etc.

Interface: Filesystem-based. mkdir /sys/fs/cgroup/mygroup; echo pid > mygroup/tasks (v1) or cgroup.procs (v2).

Limits: echo 100000 > mygroup/cpu/cpu.cfs_quota_us (100ms/period).

Accounting: cat mygroup/cpu/cpu.stat (usage).

Systemd: Auto-creates cgroups per service.

Libcgroup or cgmanager APIs, but direct fs often sufficient.

Example: Limit CPU:

As root:

```
mkdir /sys/fs/cgroup/cpu/limited
echo 50000 > /sys/fs/cgroup/cpu/limited/cpu.cfs_quota_us # 50ms per 100ms period
echo $$ > /sys/fs/cgroup/cpu/limited/tasks # Add self
```

Run CPU-intensive task, limited to 50%

In code: Use mkdir, open/write/close.

Kernel 6.17: cgroup v2 optimizes for large systems with better delegation.

Interplay Between Namespaces and cgroups

Containers use both: Namespaces isolate views (e.g., own /sys/fs/cgroup), cgroups limit resources.

Docker/Podman: Create cgroup per container, attach namespaces.

unshare(CLONE_NEWCGROUP) virtualizes cgroup view.

In unpriv user namespaces, delegate cgroups via cgroup.controllers.

Error Handling and Best Practices

Errors: EPERM (no cap for clone), ENOSPC (nest limit), EINVAL (bad flags).

Practices:

- Start with user namespace for unpriv.
- Combine namespaces (flags |).
- Handle reparenting in init.
- For cgroups, use v2; delegate subtrees.
- Monitor with cgget, ps -o cgroup.
- Security: Bound caps in containers; restrict delegate.
- Performance: Namespaces low overhead; cgroups add accounting (~1-5%).

Pitfalls: Deep namespaces slow (fixed in 6.17); cgroup v1/v2 mix.

Tools: nsenter -t pid -n ip link (enter net ns); cgexec -g cpu:limited cmd.

In 6.18 rc, cgroup enhances io.latency for better SSD control.

These basics empower container building, transforming Linux into virtualization platform.

8 Threads and Multithreading

8.1 POSIX Threads (Pthreads) Interface

Threads represent a lightweight mechanism for concurrency within a single process, allowing multiple execution flows to share the same address space, resources, and data while operating in parallel. In Linux system programming, the POSIX Threads (Pthreads) interface provides a standardized API for creating, managing, and synchronizing threads, enabling efficient utilization of multi-core processors and responsive applications. Introduced in the POSIX.1c standard (IEEE 1003.1c-1995), Pthreads has been the de facto threading model in UNIX-like systems, including Linux since kernel 2.6 (2003) with the Native POSIX Thread Library (NPTL) replacing the older LinuxThreads. This shift brought full POSIX compliance, better scalability, and lower overhead, making threads suitable for high-performance computing, web servers, and real-time systems. Understanding Pthreads is crucial for programmers dealing with concurrent tasks, as it addresses challenges like data races, deadlocks, and resource sharing that arise when moving beyond single-threaded designs. This subsection explores the core Pthreads API, including thread creation with pthread_create(), attributes via pthread_attr_t, joining and detaching with pthread_join() and pthread_detach(), self-identification with pthread_self(), and termination options like pthread_exit() and pthread_cancel(). We'll cover POSIX semantics for portability, Linux-specific implementations with kernel threads (futexes for efficiency), practical C examples, error handling, performance considerations, and introductory synchronization to prevent common pitfalls. As of the stable Linux kernel 6.17 (released on September 28, 2025, with the latest patch 6.17.7 addressing minor futex optimizations as of November 2, 2025) and the ongoing 6.18 release candidate (rc4 as of November 2, 2025), Pthreads benefits from enhanced scheduler affinity for threads and better integration with eBPF for tracing concurrent behaviors, facilitating development of scalable, thread-safe applications in diverse environments from desktops to cloud clusters.

Historical Background and Threading Models

The evolution of threading in UNIX and Linux reflects the growing need for intra-process concurrency as hardware advanced from single-core to multi-core processors. Early UNIX lacked native threads, relying on processes for parallelism, which incurred high overhead due to separate address spaces. The POSIX threads standard emerged in the 1990s to address this, defining a portable API for user-level threads mapped to kernel entities. Initial Linux implementations used LinuxThreads (1996), which treated threads as separate processes (clone() with shared memory), leading to non-compliance issues like per-thread signals and scalability limits.

The breakthrough came with NPTL in kernel 2.6 (2003), developed by Ulrich Drepper and Ingo Molnar, using futexes (fast userspace mutexes, kernel 2.5.7) for synchronization and true 1:1 kernel threading (each pthread maps to a kernel task). This achieved M:N-like efficiency (many user threads to fewer kernel threads) while fully complying with POSIX. NPTL reduced context switch times and supported up to thousands of threads per process, limited mainly by memory.

POSIX.1-2001 (incorporating 1003.1c) mandates the API in <pthread.h>, ensuring portability across UNIX systems. Linux glibc implements it, with kernel providing underlying syscalls like clone() for creation and futex() for waits.

In contemporary kernels, threading integrates with the CFS scheduler, where threads are scheduled as individual tasks. Kernel 6.17 optimizes thread migration across cores with better load balancing, while 6.18 rc explores enhanced thread-local storage (TLS) for faster access in large-scale applications.

Alternative models like user-level threads (e.g., GNU Portable Threads) exist but lack kernel awareness, leading to blocking issues—Pthreads' kernel-backed approach is preferred for most uses.

Core Pthreads Functions: Creation and Management

Pthreads creation and basic management revolve around a few key functions, with threads starting execution in a user-provided routine.

- **int pthread_create(pthread_t *thread, const pthread_attr_t *attr, void *(*start_routine)(void *), void *arg);**: Creates a new thread, storing its ID in *thread. Attr for attributes (NULL default), start_routine the entry function (returns void exit code), arg passed to it.

Returns 0 on success, positive error (EAGAIN limit, EINVAL bad attr, ENOMEM no memory).

Thread ID (pthread_t, opaque, often unsigned long) unique within process.

Start routine: Runs concurrently; shared data needs sync.

- **pthread_t pthread_self(void);**: Current thread ID.
- **int pthread_equal(pthread_t t1, pthread_t t2);**: Compare IDs.

- **void pthread_exit(void *value_ptr);**: Terminate thread, return value_ptr (like return from start). Implicit at routine end.
- ****int pthread_join(pthread_t thread, void value_ptr);**: Wait for thread, store exit value in *value_ptr (NULL ignore). Like waitpid().
- **int pthread_detach(pthread_t thread);**: Mark detachable—no join needed, resources auto-reclaimed on exit.

Default threads joinable; detach for fire-and-forget.

Example: Basic threaded sum:

```c
#include <pthread.h>
#include <stdio.h>
#include <stdlib.h>

void *thread_func(void *arg) {
    long start = (long)arg;
    long sum = 0;
    for (long i = start; i < start + 1000000; i++) sum += i;
    return (void *)sum;
}

int main() {
    pthread_t t1, t2;
    if (pthread_create(&t1, NULL, thread_func, (void *)0) != 0) {
        perror("pthread_create t1");
        return 1;
    }
    if (pthread_create(&t2, NULL, thread_func, (void *)1000000) != 0) {
        perror("pthread_create t2");
        return 1;
    }

    void *res1, *res2;
    pthread_join(t1, &res1);
    pthread_join(t2, &res2);

    long total = (long)res1 + (long)res2;
    printf("Total sum: %ld\n", total);

    return 0;
}
```

Compile: gcc -pthread file.c.

Threads share global/static, but locals per-thread.

Thread Attributes: Customization with pthread_attr_t

Attributes control creation behavior:
- pthread_attr_init(pthread_attr_t *attr); // Default
- pthread_attr_destroy(pthread_attr_t *attr);

Setters:
- pthread_attr_setdetachstate(attr, PTHREAD_CREATE_DETACHED/JOINABLE);
- pthread_attr_setscope(attr, PTHREAD_SCOPE_SYSTEM/PROCESS); // Linux always SYSTEM (kernel contention)
- pthread_attr_setschedpolicy(attr, SCHED_FIFO/RR/OTHER); // RT, needs cap
- pthread_attr_setschedparam(attr, const struct sched_param *param); // Priority
- pthread_attr_setstacksize(attr, size_t size); // Stack (default 8MB)
- pthread_attr_setguardsize(attr, size_t size); // Guard pages against overflow

Use in create.

Example: Detached thread:

```c
pthread_attr_t attr;
pthread_attr_init(&attr);
pthread_attr_setdetachstate(&attr, PTHREAD_CREATE_DETACHED);
pthread_create(&t, &attr, func, arg);
pthread_attr_destroy(&attr);
```

Linux: Stack size min PTHREAD_STACK_MIN (16384).

Termination and Cancellation

pthread_exit(value); from any point, runs destructors.

Cancellation: int pthread_cancel(pthread_t thread); // Request

Thread handles: pthread_setcancelstate(int state, int *old); // PTHREAD_CANCEL_ENABLE/DISABLE

pthread_setcanceltype(int type, int *old); // ASYNCHRONOUS (anytime, unsafe)/DEFERRED (at points)

Test: pthread_testcancel(); // Cancellation point if deferred.

Many funcs (sleep, read) are points.

Cleanup: pthread_cleanup_push(void (*routine)(void *), void *arg); pop(int execute);

Push/pop macro pairs, routine runs on cancel/exit.

Example:

```c
void cleanup(void *arg) { printf("Cleaned\n"); }

void *func(void *arg) {
    pthread_cleanup_push(cleanup, NULL);
    // Work
    pthread_testcancel();
    pthread_cleanup_pop(0); // 1 execute even without cancel
    return NULL;
}
```

Linux-Specific Aspects and Kernel Integration

In Linux, pthreads map 1:1 to kernel tasks (lightweight processes), scheduled independently. Futexes (kernel 2.5.7) handle contention efficiently without syscalls.

Thread-local storage (TLS): __thread int var; for per-thread globals.

gettid() (syscall): Kernel TID, differs from pthread_t.

In kernel 6.17, threading optimizes for heterogeneous cores with thread affinity hints.

6.18 rc enhances futex for vector ops, speeding sync.

Error Handling and Best Practices

Pthreads returns positive errors (no errno): EDEADLK deadlock, etc. Check !=0.

Practices:

- Sync shared data (next sections).
- Avoid cancel if possible—use flags.
- Set stack for many threads.
- Join/detach all to avoid leaks.
- Use attr for RT if needed.
- Profile with perf record -p tid.

Pitfalls: Cancel in async-unsafe; large stacks waste mem; forgetting pop.

Security: Threads share creds—drop privs process-wide.

Performance Considerations

Overhead: Creation ~10us, context switch ~1us (vs process 10-50us).

Scale: Thousands feasible, limited by mem (stack/thread).

Tune: sched_setaffinity for CPU pinning.

In multi-core, threads excel for shared data vs processes' IPC.

This interface lays threading foundation, enabling concurrency.

8.2 Thread Synchronization Primitives

Thread synchronization primitives are the building blocks for managing concurrency in multithreaded programs, ensuring that shared resources are accessed safely and efficiently without data corruption or inconsistent states. In the POSIX Threads (Pthreads) model, these primitives address the inherent challenges of threads sharing the same address space, such as race conditions—where the outcome depends on unpredictable execution order—and deadlocks, where threads wait indefinitely for each other. Synchronization is crucial for applications like parallel data processing, network servers handling multiple connections, or GUI programs updating shared state from background threads. Without proper synchronization, issues like lost updates (one thread overwrites another's changes) or inconsistent reads (partial data visibility) can lead to bugs that are notoriously hard to reproduce and debug. This section delves into the core Pthreads synchronization tools: mutexes for mutual exclusion, condition variables for signaling, semaphores for counting resources, read-write locks for asymmetric access, barriers for group coordination, and spinlocks for low-latency scenarios. We'll explore their APIs, usage patterns, error handling, performance implications, and best practices, drawing on POSIX.1-2001 standards for portability while highlighting Linux-specific implementations like futex-based efficiency in NPTL. Practical C examples will illustrate concepts, emphasizing thread-safety and deadlock avoidance. As of the stable Linux kernel 6.17 (September 2025) and the 6.18 release candidate (rc4 in November 2025), these primitives benefit from optimized futex operations for faster wakeups and better integration with real-time scheduling, enabling scalable concurrency in high-thread-count environments from mobile devices to supercomputers.

The Need for Synchronization in Multithreading

Multithreading introduces parallelism but also complexity due to shared memory. Unlike processes, threads within a process share global variables, heap allocations, and file descriptors, making uncoordinated access hazardous. A race condition occurs when two threads modify a shared variable simultaneously, leading to non-deterministic results—for instance, a counter increment (read-modify-write) might lose updates if interleaved. Synchronization primitives enforce order and exclusivity, transforming non-atomic operations into atomic ones from the threads' perspective.

POSIX defines these as portable abstractions, implemented in Linux via glibc's NPTL, which uses kernel futexes (fast userspace mutexes) for contention handling. Futexes minimize kernel involvement in uncontended cases, performing operations in user space with atomic instructions (e.g., compare-and-swap), falling back to syscalls only when waiting or waking is needed. This hybrid approach reduces latency, with uncontended mutex locks taking nanoseconds versus microseconds for kernel-mediated alternatives.

Key principles:

- **Mutual Exclusion**: Only one thread accesses a critical section at a time.
- **Condition Waiting**: Threads block until a predicate (e.g., queue not empty) is true.
- **Ordering**: Ensure happens-before relationships to avoid reordering surprises.
- **Fairness**: Prevent starvation, where a thread waits indefinitely.

Overuse can lead to serialization (reduced parallelism), so choose primitives judiciously—mutexes for short holds, semaphores for resource pools.

In kernel 6.17, futex enhancements improve multi-waiter scenarios, reducing thundering herd effects where all waiters wake unnecessarily.

Mutexes: Ensuring Mutual Exclusion

Mutexes (short for mutual exclusion) are the most basic primitive, acting as locks that protect critical sections. A thread acquires the mutex before entering the section and releases it after, blocking others during hold.

API from <pthread.h>:

- int pthread_mutex_init(pthread_mutex_t *mutex, const pthread_mutexattr_t *attr); // Initialize (attr NULL default)
- int pthread_mutex_destroy(pthread_mutex_t *mutex); // Cleanup
- int pthread_mutex_lock(pthread_mutex_t *mutex); // Acquire, block if held
- int pthread_mutex_trylock(pthread_mutex_t *mutex); // Non-block, EBUSY if held
- int pthread_mutex_timedlock(pthread_mutex_t *mutex, const struct timespec *abstime); // Timeout
- int pthread_mutex_unlock(pthread_mutex_t *mutex); // Release

Default mutex: Normal type, may deadlock if relocked by owner (undefined).

Attributes (pthread_mutexattr_init(&attr)):

- pthread_mutexattr_settype(&attr, kind): PTHREAD_MUTEX_NORMAL (basic), ERRORCHECK (detect errors like double lock), RECURSIVE (allow relock by owner, count-based), DEFAULT (normal).

- pthread_mutexattr_setrobust(&attr, PTHREAD_MUTEX_ROBUST); // If owner dies, next lock gets EOWNERDEAD, can recover with pthread_mutex_consistent().

Static init: pthread_mutex_t mutex = PTHREAD_MUTEX_INITIALIZER;

Example: Shared counter:

```c
#include <pthread.h>
#include <stdio.h>

pthread_mutex_t lock = PTHREAD_MUTEX_INITIALIZER;
int counter = 0;

void *increment(void *arg) {
    for (int i = 0; i < 1000000; i++) {
        pthread_mutex_lock(&lock);
        counter++;
        pthread_mutex_unlock(&lock);
    }
    return NULL;
}

int main() {
    pthread_t t1, t2;
    pthread_create(&t1, NULL, increment, NULL);
    pthread_create(&t2, NULL, increment, NULL);
    pthread_join(t1, NULL);
    pthread_join(t2, NULL);
    printf("Counter: %d\n", counter); // Should be 2000000
    return 0;
}
```

Without lock, counter <2000000 due to races.

Linux: Normal mutex uses futex; recursive adds count. Kernel 6.17 futex optimizes for short holds.

Errors: EDEADLK (deadlock detect in errorcheck), EINVAL (bad mutex), EOWNERDEAD (robust).

Best: Short critical sections; trylock for non-block.

Condition Variables: Signaling and Waiting

Condition variables (condvars) work with mutexes for threads to wait on predicates, signaled when true—efficient alternative to busy-waiting.

API:

- int pthread_cond_init(pthread_cond_t *cond, const pthread_condattr_t *attr);
- int pthread_cond_destroy(pthread_cond_t *cond);
- int pthread_cond_wait(pthread_cond_t *cond, pthread_mutex_t *mutex); // Release mutex, wait, reacquire on wake
- int pthread_cond_timedwait(pthread_cond_t *cond, pthread_mutex_t *mutex, const struct timespec *abstime);
- int pthread_cond_signal(pthread_cond_t *cond); // Wake one
- int pthread_cond_broadcast(pthread_cond_t *cond); // Wake all

Attr: pthread_condattr_setclock(&attr, CLOCK_MONOTONIC); for timed.

Must hold mutex before wait/signal; wait atomically releases/reacquires.

Example: Producer-consumer:

```c
pthread_mutex_t lock = PTHREAD_MUTEX_INITIALIZER;
pthread_cond_t cond = PTHREAD_COND_INITIALIZER;
int ready = 0;

void *producer(void *arg) {
    pthread_mutex_lock(&lock);
```

```c
    // Produce
    ready = 1;
    pthread_cond_signal(&cond);
    pthread_mutex_unlock(&lock);
    return NULL;
}

void *consumer(void *arg) {
    pthread_mutex_lock(&lock);
    while (!ready) {
        pthread_cond_wait(&cond, &lock);
    }
    // Consume
    printf("Data ready\n");
    pthread_mutex_unlock(&lock);
    return NULL;
}
```
While loop protects against spurious wakes (allowed by POSIX).

Linux: Condvars use futex for waits; broadcast efficient.

Errors: EINVAL, EPERM (robust mutex issues).

Best: Predicate in while; signal with mutex held.

Semaphores: Counting Resources

Semaphores are counters for resource access or signaling, supporting wait (decrement if >0, else block) and post (increment, wake if waiters).

POSIX semaphores (<semaphore.h>):

- int sem_init(sem_t *sem, int pshared, unsigned int value); // pshared 0 thread, 1 process
- int sem_destroy(sem_t *sem);
- int sem_wait(sem_t *sem); // Decrement
- int sem_trywait(sem_t *sem); // Non-block
- int sem_timedwait(sem_t *sem, const struct timespec *abs_timeout);
- int sem_post(sem_t *sem); // Increment

Binary semaphore (init 1) like mutex but no owner—can post from different thread.

Example: Limit threads:

c
```c
#include <semaphore.h>

sem_t sem;
sem_init(&sem, 0, 2); // 2 concurrent

void *worker(void *arg) {
    sem_wait(&sem);
    // Work
    sem_post(&sem);
    return NULL;
}
```
Named: sem_open(const char *name, int oflag, ...); for IPC.

Linux: Uses futex; pshared=1 maps to shared mem.

Errors: EINVAL, EAGAIN (try), ETIMEDOUT.

Best: For producer-consumer queues, thread pools.

Read-Write Locks: Asymmetric Access

rwlocks allow multiple readers or one writer, optimizing for read-heavy scenarios.

API:

- int pthread_rwlock_init(pthread_rwlock_t *rwlock, const pthread_rwlockattr_t *attr);
- int pthread_rwlock_destroy(pthread_rwlock_t *rwlock);
- int pthread_rwlock_rdlock(pthread_rwlock_t *rwlock); // Read, block if writer

- int pthread_rwlock_tryrdlock(pthread_rwlock_t *rwlock);
- int pthread_rwlock_wrlock(pthread_rwlock_t *rwlock); // Write exclusive
- int pthread_rwlock_trywrlock(pthread_rwlock_t *rwlock);
- int pthread_rwlock_unlock(pthread_rwlock_t *rwlock);

Attr: pthread_rwlockattr_setkind_np(&attr, PTHREAD_RWLOCK_PREFER_READER_NP / WRITER / WRITER_NONRECURSIVE); Linux extension.

Example: Shared data:

c

```c
pthread_rwlock_t rwlock = PTHREAD_RWLOCK_INITIALIZER;

void *reader(void *arg) {
   pthread_rwlock_rdlock(&rwlock);
   // Read
   pthread_rwlock_unlock(&rwlock);
   return NULL;
}

void *writer(void *arg) {
   pthread_rwlock_wrlock(&rwlock);
   // Write
   pthread_rwlock_unlock(&rwlock);
   return NULL;
}
```

Linux: Futex-based; prefers readers by default.

Errors: EDEADLK (recursive write), EBUSY (try).

Best: For databases, caches—readers don't block each other.

Barriers: Group Coordination

Barriers synchronize groups of threads at a point.

API:

- int pthread_barrier_init(pthread_barrier_t *barrier, const pthread_barrierattr_t *attr, unsigned int count);
- int pthread_barrier_destroy(pthread_barrier_t *barrier);
- int pthread_barrier_wait(pthread_barrier_t *barrier); // Block until count arrive, one returns PTHREAD_BARRIER_SERIAL_THREAD

Example: Parallel phases:

c

```c
pthread_barrier_t barrier;
pthread_barrier_init(&barrier, NULL, 4); // 4 threads

void *phase(void *arg) {
   // Phase 1
   pthread_barrier_wait(&barrier);
   // Phase 2
   return NULL;
}
```

All proceed after last wait.

Linux: Futex impl.

Spinlocks: Busy-Waiting for Low Latency

Spinlocks busy-wait (loop) instead of sleep, for very short holds.

API:

- int pthread_spin_init(pthread_spinlock_t *lock, int pshared);
- int pthread_spin_destroy(pthread_spinlock_t *lock);
- int pthread_spin_lock(pthread_spinlock_t *lock);
- int pthread_spin_trylock(pthread_spinlock_t *lock);
- int pthread_spin_unlock(pthread_spinlock_t *lock);

No recursive; pshared for process.

Use: High-contention short criticals, e.g., kernel but user too.

Linux: Atomic ops, no futex (busy loop).

Pros: Low latency if short. Cons: Wastes CPU if long/contended.

In 6.17, spinlocks optimize for ARM with better barriers.

Error Handling, Performance, and Best Practices

Errors: Common EAGAIN (resource), EBUSY (try), EINVAL, EDEADLK.

Performance: Sync overhead—mutex <1us uncontended, but contended syscalls. Profile with perf lock.

Practices:

- Protect all shared access.
- Minimize hold time.
- Use errorcheck/recursive judiciously.
- Condition with while for spurious.
- Destroy after use.
- Thread-safe libs (e.g., strerror_r).
- Avoid priority inversion: Use priority inheritance mutexes (pthread_mutexattr_setprotocol(&attr, PTHREAD_PRIO_INHERIT)).

Pitfalls: Deadlock (A locks X then Y, B Y then X); livelock (tryloop without backoff); starvation (unfair).

Debug: gdb thread apply all bt; valgrind --tool=helgrind for races.

In 6.18 rc, futex2 for vector waits, speeding broadcast.

These primitives enable safe concurrency, foundational for multithreading.

8.3 Thread Safety and Concurrency Issues

Thread safety and concurrency issues are central challenges in multithreaded programming, where multiple threads sharing resources can lead to subtle, non-deterministic bugs that compromise data integrity, program correctness, and system stability. Thread safety refers to the property of code that functions correctly when executed concurrently by multiple threads, without unexpected interactions or corruption of shared state. Concurrency issues arise from the interleaving of thread operations, often manifesting as race conditions, deadlocks, or visibility problems due to memory reordering. In the Pthreads model, these concerns are amplified because threads share the process's address space, making unprotected access to globals, statics, or heap data hazardous. Addressing them is essential for applications like parallel algorithms, event-driven servers, or multi-core optimizations, where failure can result in crashes, data loss, or security vulnerabilities. This subsection examines common concurrency pitfalls, strategies for achieving thread safety, reentrancy concepts, thread-safe library functions, diagnostic tools like Valgrind and ThreadSanitizer, performance trade-offs, and best practices for robust design. Building on POSIX standards, we'll highlight Linux-specific behaviors, such as memory consistency models enforced by the kernel and glibc's thread-local errno. Practical C examples will illustrate issues and fixes, emphasizing proactive detection over reactive debugging. As of the stable Linux kernel 6.17 (released on September 28, 2025, with the latest patch 6.17.7 on November 2, 2025) and the ongoing 6.18 release candidate (rc4 as of November 2, 2025), thread safety benefits from improved memory barrier optimizations in futexes and enhanced sanitizer support in glibc, facilitating safer concurrency in high-thread environments from real-time systems to data-intensive applications.

Understanding Concurrency Issues

Concurrency issues stem from the non-atomic nature of many operations and the scheduler's unpredictable interleaving of threads. The most prevalent is the **race condition**, where the outcome depends on timing—e.g., two threads incrementing a shared counter without synchronization might read the same value, compute the increment, and write back, losing one update. This is a data race if at least one access is a write without proper ordering.

Other common problems:

- **Deadlocks**: Threads hold resources while waiting for others, forming a cycle—e.g., thread A locks mutex X then Y, B locks Y then X.
- **Livelocks**: Threads react to each other in a loop, preventing progress (less common, e.g., polite backoff algorithms colliding).
- **Starvation**: A thread is perpetually denied resources due to scheduling or lock unfairness.
- **Priority Inversion**: A high-priority thread waits on a low-priority one holding a lock, effectively inheriting low priority—mitigated by priority inheritance in mutexes.

- **Memory Visibility**: Changes by one thread may not be immediately visible to others due to CPU caches or compiler reordering; barriers or volatiles ensure ordering.
- **False Sharing**: Threads accessing adjacent cache lines cause invalidations, degrading performance.

These issues are hard to reproduce, often surfacing under load or specific hardware. POSIX doesn't mandate a memory model, but Linux follows the C11/C++11 model in practice, with acquire/release semantics in primitives. In kernel 6.17, the scheduler mitigates some inversions with better priority boosting, while 6.18 rc refines memory ordering for ARM64 with improved LSE (Large System Extensions) atomics.

Achieving Thread Safety: Strategies and Patterns

Thread safety can be ensured through various strategies, balancing simplicity, performance, and correctness.

1. **Immutable Data**: Design shared structures as read-only after initialization—no sync needed.
2. **Thread-Local Storage (TLS)**: Use __thread keyword or pthread_key_create() for per-thread data, avoiding sharing.
3. **Atomic Operations**: For simple types, use <stdatomic.h> (C11) atomics like atomic_int, with atomic_load/store/fetch_add. Ensure visibility without full locks.
4. **Synchronization Primitives**: Mutexes/condvars from previous sections protect critical sections.
5. **Lock-Free Data Structures**: Use compare-and-swap (CAS) for queues/stacks, but complex to implement correctly.
6. **Reader-Writer Patterns**: rwlocks for read-heavy access.
7. **Sequential Consistency**: Volatile or memory barriers (pthread_barrier_wait implies barrier).

Reentrancy: A function is reentrant if callable by multiple threads without interference (no statics). Thread-safe implies reentrant if no global state.

Library safety: Many stdlib funcs thread-safe (e.g., malloc), but some not (strtok—use strtok_r).

Linux: glibc makes most reentrant; errno per-thread (thread-local).

Example race fix with atomic:

c
```
#include <stdatomic.h>
#include <pthread.h>
#include <stdio.h>

atomic_int counter = 0;

void *increment(void *arg) {
    for (int i = 0; i < 1000000; i++) {
        atomic_fetch_add(&counter, 1, memory_order_relaxed);
    }
    return NULL;
}

int main() {
    pthread_t t1, t2;
    pthread_create(&t1, NULL, increment, NULL);
    pthread_create(&t2, NULL, increment, NULL);
    pthread_join(t1, NULL);
    pthread_join(t2, NULL);
    printf("Counter: %d\n", counter); // Always 2000000
    return 0;
}
```

Memory order: relaxed (no ordering), seq_cst (strong), acquire/release (visibility).

Common Concurrency Patterns and Anti-Patterns

Patterns:

- **Producer-Consumer**: Mutex + condvar for queue.
- **Thread Pool**: Fixed threads, semaphore for work availability.
- **Barrier Synchronization**: pthread_barrier_wait for phases.
- **Double-Checked Locking**: Volatile + mutex for lazy init.

Anti-patterns:

- Busy-waiting: Wastes CPU—use condvars.
- Global locks: Bottlenecks—use fine-grained.
- Holding locks during I/O: Blocks others—release before slow ops.
- Nested locks: Risks deadlock—acquire in consistent order.

Deadlock avoidance: Banker's algorithm or try-locks with backoff.

Diagnostic Tools for Concurrency Issues

Detecting issues requires specialized tools:

- **Valgrind Helgrind**: valgrind --tool=helgrind ./prog detects races, lock order violations.
- **ThreadSanitizer (TSan)**: Compile with -fsanitize=thread (clang/gcc), runtime detects data races.
- **AddressSanitizer (ASan)**: -fsanitize=address for memory issues in threads.
- **gdb**: thread apply all bt for stacks; info threads.
- **perf**: perf record -e sched:sched_switch ./prog traces context switches.
- **strace -f**: Traces all threads.

Linux: /proc/<pid>/task/<tid>/ for per-thread stats.

In examples, TSan reports races with stack traces.

Performance Implications and Optimization

Sync overhead: Uncontended mutex ~10-50ns, contended ~us + context switch. Choose based on contention: spinlocks for <us holds, mutexes otherwise.

Optimization:

- Reduce shared data.
- Use lock-free (stdatomic).
- Affinity: pthread_setaffinity_np(thread, cpusetsize, &cpuset) pins to cores, reduces cache bounces.
- Profile: perf lock record ./prog; perf lock report.
- Scalability: Reader-writer over mutex for reads.

In kernel 6.17, futex_wait_multiple optimizes cond_broadcast for many waiters.

Best Practices for Thread-Safe Code

- Design immutable where possible.
- Document thread-safety (e.g., MT-Safe in man).
- Use RAII wrappers for locks (C++ std::lock_guard, C macros).
- Test under load (stress tools).
- Avoid globals; prefer TLS.
- Handle cancellation cleanly.
- Security: Sync sensitive data (e.g., creds).
- Portability: Stick to POSIX; avoid Linuxisms like futex syscall.

Pitfalls: Assuming order without barriers; double-free in cleanup; ignoring EOWNERDEAD in robust.

Advanced Topics: Memory Models and Linux Specifics

C11 memory models: seq_cst for strong, relaxed for perf. Pthreads align with this.

Linux: x86 strong model (no reorder stores), but ARM weak—use barriers.

Futex direct: syscall(__NR_futex, ...) for custom.

In 6.18 rc, futex2 for wait on multiple, reducing broadcast cost.

These practices mitigate issues, enabling reliable multithreading.

8.4 Advanced Threading Models

Advanced threading models in Linux system programming extend the foundational Pthreads interface to provide higher-level abstractions that simplify the development of concurrent applications, improve scalability, and reduce the risk of common concurrency bugs. While basic Pthreads offer low-level control over thread creation and synchronization, they require developers to manually manage thread lifecycles, load balancing, and error handling, which can lead to complex and error-prone code in large-scale systems. Advanced models address these limitations by introducing concepts like thread pools for efficient resource reuse, futures and promises for asynchronous result handling, actor-based systems for message-passing isolation, coroutines for lightweight context switching, and hybrid approaches that combine threads with processes or other concurrency primitives. These models are particularly valuable in performance-critical domains such as web servers, scientific simulations, and real-time data processing, where maximizing CPU utilization while maintaining code readability is paramount. In Linux, these models leverage kernel features like futexes for low-overhead waiting, epoll for event-driven coordination, and cgroups for thread group resource management, ensuring seamless integration with the underlying scheduler. This section explores the principles, implementations, and applications of these models, drawing on POSIX extensions where applicable and Linux-specific optimizations such as user-space scheduling hints. We'll include historical context from early threading libraries to modern frameworks, practical C examples using libraries like OpenMP and libdispatch, error handling strategies, performance analysis, and security considerations to prevent issues like thread-local storage leaks in privileged contexts. As of the stable Linux kernel 6.17 (released on September 28, 2025, with the latest patch 6.17.7 on November 2, 2025) and the ongoing 6.18 release candidate (rc4 as of November 2, 2025), advanced threading benefits from enhanced futex vector operations for faster synchronization in pooled models and improved eBPF hooks for runtime thread monitoring, enabling more dynamic and efficient concurrency in environments from multi-core desktops to distributed cloud systems.

Evolution of Advanced Threading Models

The quest for better threading abstractions began in the late 1990s as multi-core processors emerged, highlighting the inadequacies of raw Pthreads for complex applications. Early efforts included the Java threading model (1995) with executors for pooling and the Win32 thread pools (Windows NT 4.0, 1996), inspiring similar constructs in UNIX. In Linux, the transition from LinuxThreads to NPTL in kernel 2.6 (2003) provided a solid foundation, with futexes enabling user-space optimizations. Libraries like Intel's Threading Building Blocks (TBB, 2006) introduced task-based parallelism, where developers submit work items to a scheduler that dynamically assigns them to threads, abstracting away manual creation. OpenMP (Open Multi-Processing, 1997) brought directive-based parallelism to C/C++/Fortran, allowing annotations like #pragma omp parallel for to automatically thread loops. The actor model, popularized by Erlang (1986), gained traction in C with libraries like Theron (2008), emphasizing message-passing over shared memory to avoid locks entirely. Coroutines, influenced by Lua (1993) and Go's goroutines (2009), offer stackful or stackless switching for cooperative multitasking, reducing context switch overhead compared to kernel threads.

These models shift from imperative (create thread, lock mutex) to declarative (submit task, await future) programming, reducing boilerplate and errors. POSIX doesn't specify them, but standards like C11 atomics and C++11 std::thread/future provide building blocks. In Linux, glibc's NPTL ensures compatibility, with kernel support for user-mode scheduling (UMS, experimental in 3.x but evolved into eBPF schedulers).

Kernel 6.17 optimizes threading for advanced models with better group leader handling in cgroups, while 6.18 rc introduces preliminary support for user-space vector futexes, speeding up condition broadcasts in actor mailboxes.

Thread Pools: Efficient Resource Reuse

Thread pools pre-allocate a fixed or dynamic number of worker threads that consume tasks from a queue, ideal for I/O-bound or variable-load applications like HTTP servers. This model avoids the overhead of repeated pthread_create/join (~10-50µs per thread) and bounds concurrency to prevent system thrashing.

Implementation typically involves a task queue (mutex-protected array or list with condition variables for not-empty/not-full signals) and workers in infinite loops dequeuing and executing tasks. Libraries like libdispatch (Apple's Grand Central Dispatch, ported to Linux via Swift or custom) provide dispatch_queue_t for concurrent/serial queues, with dispatch_async() for submission.

Custom C example with dynamic sizing:

```c
#include <pthread.h>
#include <stdlib.h>
```

```c
#include <stdio.h>
#include <unistd.h>
#include <semaphore.h>

typedef void (*task_func)(void *);

typedef struct task {
    task_func func;
    void *arg;
    struct task *next;
} task_t;

typedef struct {
    task_t *head, *tail;
    int count;
    pthread_mutex_t mutex;
    sem_t sem;
    int shutdown;
} queue_t;

void queue_init(queue_t *q) {
    q->head = q->tail = NULL;
    q->count = 0;
    q->shutdown = 0;
    pthread_mutex_init(&q->mutex, NULL);
    sem_init(&q->sem, 0, 0);
}

void enqueue(queue_t *q, task_func func, void *arg) {
    task_t *task = malloc(sizeof(task_t));
    task->func = func;
    task->arg = arg;
    task->next = NULL;

    pthread_mutex_lock(&q->mutex);
    if (q->tail) q->tail->next = task;
    else q->head = task;
    q->tail = task;
    q->count++;
    pthread_mutex_unlock(&q->mutex);
    sem_post(&q->sem);
}

task_t *dequeue(queue_t *q) {
    sem_wait(&q->sem);
    pthread_mutex_lock(&q->mutex);
    if (q->shutdown && q->count == 0) {
        pthread_mutex_unlock(&q->mutex);
        return NULL;
    }
    task_t *task = q->head;
    q->head = task->next;
    if (!q->head) q->tail = NULL;
    q->count--;
    pthread_mutex_unlock(&q->mutex);
    return task;
```

```c
}

void *worker(void *arg) {
    queue_t *q = arg;
    while (1) {
        task_t *task = dequeue(q);
        if (!task) break;
        task->func(task->arg);
        free(task);
    }
    return NULL;
}

void sample_task(void *arg) {
    long id = (long)arg;
    printf("Task %ld in thread %lu\n", id, pthread_self());
    usleep(100000); // Simulate work
}

int main() {
    queue_t q;
    queue_init(&q);

    int num_threads = 4;
    pthread_t threads[num_threads];
    for (int i = 0; i < num_threads; i++) {
        pthread_create(&threads[i], NULL, worker, &q);
    }

    for (long i = 0; i < 20; i++) {
        enqueue(&q, sample_task, (void *)i);
    }

    // Shutdown
    for (int i = 0; i < num_threads; i++) {
        sem_post(&q.sem); // Wake to check shutdown
    }
    q.shutdown = 1;
    for (int i = 0; i < num_threads; i++) {
        pthread_join(threads[i], NULL);
    }

    return 0;
}
```

This pool uses semaphores for signaling, demonstrating dynamic task dispatch. For production, use established libraries to handle edge cases like resizing or timeouts.

Performance: Pools excel in high-task-rate scenarios, with enqueue/dequeue ~100ns uncontended. Linux's futexes ensure low-latency wakes.

Futures and Promises: Handling Asynchronous Results

Futures encapsulate pending results from asynchronous operations, allowing non-blocking computation with later retrieval. Promises fulfill futures. While C lacks built-ins, libraries like libfuture or custom implementations with condvars provide this.

Future pattern: Submit task, get future handle, block on get() or poll is_ready().

Custom example:

c

typedef struct {

```c
    void *result;
    int ready;
    int error;
    pthread_mutex_t mutex;
    pthread_cond_t cond;
} future_t;

void future_init(future_t *f) {
    f->ready = 0;
    f->error = 0;
    pthread_mutex_init(&f->mutex, NULL);
    pthread_cond_init(&f->cond, NULL);
}

void *future_get(future_t *f) {
    pthread_mutex_lock(&f->mutex);
    while (!f->ready) pthread_cond_wait(&f->cond, &f->mutex);
    void *res = f->result;
    pthread_mutex_unlock(&f->mutex);
    if (f->error) { /* handle error */ }
    return res;
}

void future_set(future_t *f, void *res) {
    pthread_mutex_lock(&f->mutex);
    f->result = res;
    f->ready = 1;
    pthread_cond_signal(&f->cond);
    pthread_mutex_unlock(&f->mutex);
}

void *async_task(void *arg) {
    future_t *f = arg;
    // Compute
    int *res = malloc(sizeof(int));
    *res = 42;
    future_set(f, res);
    return NULL;
}

int main() {
    future_t f;
    future_init(&f);
    pthread_t t;
    pthread_create(&t, NULL, async_task, &f);
    int *result = future_get(&f);
    printf("Result: %d\n", *result);
    free(result);
    pthread_join(t, NULL);
    return 0;
}
```
This blocks on get; add timedwait for timeouts.
Libraries: C++ std::future, or Pthreads-based like concurrencpp.
Linux: Condvars efficient; integrate with epoll for I/O futures.

Actor Model: Message-Passing for Isolation

The actor model treats threads as actors communicating via immutable messages, eliminating shared state and locks. Inspired by Erlang, it's implemented in C with libraries like libactor or custom mailboxes (queues + workers).

Actor benefits: Fault tolerance (supervisors restart failed actors), scalability (distributed).

Custom sketch: Actor as thread with queue, processing messages in loop.

Example:

```c
typedef struct {
    int type;
    void *data;
} message_t;

// Actor struct with queue from previous
void *actor_loop(void *arg) {
    queue_t *mailbox = arg;
    while (1) {
        message_t msg = *(message_t *)dequeue(mailbox)->arg; // Simplified
        // Process msg.type
        if (msg.type == 0) break; // Shutdown
        printf("Processed message %d\n", *(int *)msg.data);
    }
    return NULL;
}

void send_message(queue_t *mailbox, message_t msg) {
    task_t task = {NULL, &msg}; // Adapt
    enqueue(mailbox, NULL, &msg); // Custom
}
```

For full, use Akka-like frameworks ported to C.

Linux: Use io_uring for async message I/O in actors.

Coroutines and Green Threads: Lightweight Concurrency

Coroutines enable cooperative multitasking, yielding control at points without kernel switches. Stackful (ucontext, deprecated) or stackless (compiler-transformed).

libco (stackful):

```
#include <libco.h>
cothread_t main_thread, co;
void co_entry() { printf("In coroutine\n"); co_switch(main_thread); }
int main() { main_thread = co_active(); co = co_create(8192, co_entry); co_switch(co); printf("Back in main\n");
co_delete(co); return 0; }
```

Green threads: User-scheduled, like early Java. In C, simulate with coroutines.

Linux: getcontext/makecontext/swapcontext for stackful, but slow; assembly for faster.

In 6.17, userfaultfd aids stack management.

Hybrid Models: Combining Paradigms

Hybrid: Thread pools with futures (async submit, await result); actors with coroutines for intra-actor concurrency.

OpenMP + Pthreads: OpenMP for parallel regions, Pthreads for custom.

libdispatch: Queues dispatch tasks to pools, with sync/async.

In Linux, hybrids use affinity for pools, io_uring for async.

Kernel 6.18 rc enhances user sched for hybrids via eBPF.

Error Handling, Performance, and Best Practices

Errors: Model-specific; e.g., future timeout ETIMEDOUT.

Performance: Pools ~ms startup savings; coroutines ns switches vs us threads.

Practices:

- Profile contention (perf).
- Handle exceptions in tasks.
- Scale pools dynamically (monitor queue length).

- Use for appropriate granularity.
- Security: Isolate sensitive actors.
- Test with sanitizers.

Pitfalls: Pool exhaustion; coroutine recursion overflow; actor deadlocks via messages.

These models advance threading, fostering efficient concurrency.

9 Memory Management

9.1 Memory Allocation and Deallocation

Memory allocation and deallocation are core operations in Linux system programming, enabling processes to dynamically request and release memory from the kernel to manage data structures, buffers, and application state efficiently. In the context of a multitasking operating system like Linux, these mechanisms ensure that programs can scale with varying workloads while maintaining isolation and preventing resource exhaustion. Rooted in UNIX traditions, where memory was a scarce resource, Linux's memory management has evolved to support virtual memory, demand paging, and overcommitment, allowing programs to allocate more than physical RAM available through swapping and page faults. For system programmers, mastering allocation is essential for performance-critical applications, such as servers handling large datasets or embedded systems with limited RAM, where poor management can lead to fragmentation, leaks, or out-of-memory (OOM) kills. This subsection explores the standard C library functions like malloc(), free(), calloc(), realloc(), and their behaviors, POSIX extensions for aligned allocation, kernel-level interfaces via brk()/sbrk() and mmap() for advanced use, memory models including heap structure and arenas, error handling for failures, and best practices to avoid leaks using tools like Valgrind. We'll cover portability considerations under POSIX and C standards, Linux-specific optimizations like transparent huge pages (THP) and overcommit policies, practical examples in C, performance tuning, and security implications such as buffer overflows mitigated by canaries. As of the stable Linux kernel 6.17 (released on September 28, 2025, with the latest patch 6.17.7 addressing minor memory reclaim optimizations as of November 2, 2025) and the ongoing 6.18 release candidate (rc4 as of November 2, 2025), memory allocation benefits from enhanced slab allocator efficiency for small objects and better support for userfaultfd in handling page faults programmatically, enabling more resilient and high-performance applications in environments from mobile devices to supercomputers.

The Basics of Memory Management in Linux

Memory in Linux is managed through virtual addressing, where each process sees a contiguous address space divided into segments: text (code), data (initialized globals), bss (uninitialized globals), heap (dynamic allocation), and stack (local variables, function calls). The heap grows upward from the end of bss via brk() system calls, while the stack grows downward from high addresses. Allocation functions like malloc() operate on the heap, requesting memory from the kernel when needed and managing free lists internally to reuse deallocated blocks. The C standard library (glibc in Linux) provides the primary interface for user-space allocation, implementing a general-purpose allocator based on Doug Lea's dlmalloc (since glibc 2.3, 1996), which uses arenas (per-thread heaps) to reduce contention in multithreaded programs. When malloc(size) is called, it checks free bins for a fitting chunk; if none, it expands the heap with sbrk() or mmap() for large requests (>128KB by default). Free(ptr) returns the block to the free list, coalescing adjacent free chunks to combat fragmentation.

Key functions from <stdlib.h>:

- void *malloc(size_t size); // Allocates size bytes, uninitialized. Returns NULL on failure (errno ENOMEM).
- void free(void *ptr); // Deallocates, ptr from malloc/calloc/realloc or NULL (no-op).
- void *calloc(size_t nmemb, size_t size); // Allocates nmemb*size, zero-initialized.
- void *realloc(void *ptr, size_t size); // Resizes to size, copies content, frees old if moved.

Returns aligned to max_align_t (usually 16 bytes on x86-64 for SIMD).

Semantics: malloc(0) may return NULL or unique ptr; free(NULL) safe. Realloc(NULL, size) = malloc(size); realloc(ptr, 0) = free(ptr).

Linux glibc uses ptmalloc2, a dlmalloc variant with multiple arenas (up to 8*cores) for thread locality, reducing lock contention. Kernel backs with vmalloc for kernel space, but user via brk/mmap.

Example basic usage:

```c
#include <stdlib.h>
#include <stdio.h>

int main() {
    int *arr = malloc(5 * sizeof(int));
    if (!arr) { perror("malloc"); return 1; }
    for (int i = 0; i < 5; i++) arr[i] = i;
```

```c
    arr = realloc(arr, 10 * sizeof(int));
    if (!arr) { perror("realloc"); return 1; }
    for (int i = 5; i < 10; i++) arr[i] = i;

    int *zeros = calloc(5, sizeof(int)); // All 0
    free(arr);
    free(zeros);
    return 0;
}
```

Allocation Internals and Kernel Interaction

Glibc's allocator divides memory into chunks with metadata (size, prev_size, flags). Free chunks in bins by size (small, large, unsorted) for fast lookup. When heap exhausted, sbrk(increment) expands (positive) or shrinks (negative) the program break.

For large/anonymous, mmap(0, size, PROT_READ|WRITE, MAP_PRIVATE|ANONYMOUS, -1, 0) used, allowing non-contiguous allocation and easier release with munmap().

Fragmentation: External (free chunks too small) mitigated by best-fit, internal (overallocation) by rounding to powers-of-2.

Kernel view: vm_area_struct (vma) in mm_struct tracks mappings. Page faults trigger demand allocation (lazy).

Overcommit: /proc/sys/vm/overcommit_memory =1 (heuristic, default), =2 always, =0 check. Allows malloc succeed even if RAM+swap insufficient, risking OOM kill.

In kernel 6.17, mmap optimizes for THP (transparent huge pages, 2MB vs 4KB), reducing TLB misses for large allocs if vm.thp_enabled=1.

POSIX: posix_memalign(void *memptr, size_t alignment, size_t size); for aligned (power-of-2 >= sizeof(void)). valloc() (page-aligned, deprecated), memalign() (glibc).

C11 aligned_alloc(alignment, size).

Deallocation and Memory Leaks

Free coalesces adjacent free chunks, returns to bins or munmap if large/top. Double-free or invalid ptr corrupts heap (segfault or exploit).

Leaks: Unfreed memory accumulates, leading to ENOMEM or OOM. Detect with valgrind --leak-check=full ./prog.

Smart pointers in C++ (std::unique_ptr) auto-free; in C, manual or wrappers.

Realloc pitfalls: If fails, returns NULL but old ptr valid—save old before.

Error Handling and Recovery

Malloc/free don't set errno on success; malloc NULL sets ENOMEM. Check always, especially large allocs.

Recovery: Fall back to smaller sizes or error exit.

Sysconf(_SC_PAGESIZE) for page size.

Performance Optimization and Tuning

Tune glibc: mallopt(M_MMAP_THRESHOLD, 512*1024); adjusts mmap threshold.

MALLOC_CHECK_=2 aborts on corruption; MALLOC_PERTURB_=165 fills with pattern for debug.

Alternatives: jemalloc (faster, less frag for multithread), tcmalloc (Google, scalable).

Huge pages: madvise(addr, len, MADV_HUGEPAGE); for THP.

In 6.18 rc, slab allocator (small objects) optimizes for per-CPU caches, speeding malloc < page.

Security Considerations

Heap exploits: Overflow corrupts metadata (chunk size), leading to arbitrary write. Mitigations: Glibc ptmalloc safe-linking (XOR pointers), canaries in chunks, ASLR for heap base.

Use mmap for sensitive data, mprotect(PROT_NONE) guard pages.

Valgrind/ASan detect overflows/leaks.

In setuid, careful with malloc in threads.

Advanced Allocation: mmap and brk

For control, use syscall mmap/munmap (section 9.3), brk(void *addr)/sbrk(intptr_t increment).

sbrk(0) current break.

Custom allocators build on these.

POSIX: No brk/sbrk, but mmap standard.

Example manual heap expand:

c

```c
#include <unistd.h>
#include <stdio.h>
```

```
int main() {
    void *current = sbrk(0);
    printf("Current break: %p\n", current);
    void *new = sbrk(4096);
    if (new == (void *)-1) { perror("sbrk"); return 1; }
    printf("New break: %p\n", sbrk(0));
    return 0;
}
```

Practical Examples and Use Cases

Buffer management: char *buf = malloc(1024); / use */ free(buf);

Resizable array: realloc.

String concat: realloc + strcat, but calculate size first.

In servers: Pool allocators for objects.

Best Practices

- Check malloc !=NULL.
- Free all allocated.
- Avoid use-after-free (dangling ptr).
- Size calculations avoid overflow (use size_t).
- Profile with mallinfo() or mstats().
- For large, mmap anonymous.

Pitfalls: Free wrong ptr; realloc move invalidates ptrs; leak in loops.

Tools: Valgrind memcheck; electric fence for bounds.

In 6.17, OOM handler tunable via /proc/sys/vm/oom_kill_allocating_task.

This foundation prepares for advanced memory topics.

9.2 Virtual Memory Concepts

Virtual memory is a foundational concept in modern operating systems like Linux, providing an abstraction that allows processes to use more memory than physically available, isolates process address spaces for security, and enables efficient resource sharing through techniques like copy-on-write and demand paging. By mapping virtual addresses used by programs to physical RAM or disk storage, virtual memory decouples software from hardware constraints, facilitating multitasking, large applications, and system stability. Originating from the Multics project in the 1960s and adopted in UNIX Version 6 (1975), virtual memory has been integral to Linux since its inception (1991), evolving to support advanced features like huge pages and memory compression. For system programmers, understanding virtual memory is crucial for optimizing performance in memory-intensive applications, debugging issues like page faults or segmentation faults, and leveraging kernel interfaces for custom mappings. This subsection explores key virtual memory concepts, including address spaces, paging and segmentation, demand loading, swapping, overcommitment, and shared memory. We'll cover POSIX standards for portability, Linux-specific implementations like the mm_struct in the kernel's task management, practical examples using tools like pmap and /proc maps, error handling for faults, performance tuning with madvise(), and security implications such as address space layout randomization (ASLR). As of the stable Linux kernel 6.17 (released on September 28, 2025, with the latest patch 6.17.7 on November 2, 2025) and the ongoing 6.18 release candidate (rc4 as of November 2, 2025), virtual memory benefits from enhanced reclaim algorithms for low-memory scenarios and better support for userfaultfd in handling custom page faults, enabling more resilient and efficient memory usage in environments from constrained embedded systems to high-memory servers.

The Virtual Memory Abstraction

At its core, virtual memory (VM) presents each process with a private, contiguous address space, typically from 0 to a large value (e.g., 47-bit on x86-64 with 128TB limit), regardless of physical RAM. The kernel translates virtual addresses (VA) to physical addresses (PA) using hardware support like the Memory Management Unit (MMU) and page tables. This translation allows processes to operate as if they have exclusive access to memory, preventing interference and enabling features like on-demand allocation.

Key advantages:

- **Isolation**: Processes can't access others' memory, enforced by the kernel (violations cause SIGSEGV).
- **Oversubscription**: Allocate more than RAM via swapping to disk.

- **Efficiency**: Lazy loading (demand paging) defers allocation until access.
- **Sharing**: Map shared libraries or files into multiple processes.

In Linux, the kernel manages VM through the mm_struct in each task_struct, which points to a list of vm_area_struct (VMA) describing segments: text (code, read-only), data (globals), heap (brk-managed), stack (grows down), and mmap regions.

Historical note: Linux 1.0 (1994) supported basic paging on i386; 2.2 (1999) added bigmem for >1GB RAM; 2.6 (2003) introduced reverse mapping for better reclaim. POSIX defines some interfaces like mmap(), but much is OS-specific.

In kernel 6.17, VM optimizes for ARM64 with better contiguous page allocation, reducing fragmentation in deep learning workloads.

Address Spaces and Mapping

Each process has a unique virtual address space, divided into user space (low addresses) and kernel space (high, shared across processes but protected). On x86-64, user space is 47-bit (128TB), kernel 48-bit, with a gap (canonical hole).

Mappings:

- **Text Segment**: Executable code, shared, read-only, loaded from ELF binary.
- **Data/BSS**: Initialized/uninitialized globals, private.
- **Heap**: Dynamic, grown with brk()/sbrk() or mmap().
- **Stack**: Auto-grows, limited by RLIMIT_STACK (default 8MB).
- **Mmap Regions**: User-created via mmap() for files, anonymous memory, or shared.

View with /proc/<pid>/maps: start-end perm offset dev inode path
e.g., 555555554000-555555556000 r-xp 00000000 08:01 12345 /bin/bash (text)
pmap -x pid shows RSS (resident), PSS (proportional), Dirty pages.
Kernel uses page tables (multi-level on x86: PML5/4/3/2/1 for 57-bit VA in 5-level paging, enabled in 4.12).

Paging and Demand Loading

Memory divided into pages (4KB default, configurable). Paging maps VA to PA or marks invalid.
Demand Paging: Pages allocated/loded on first access (page fault). Minor fault (allocate RAM), major (disk I/O).
Fault handler: do_page_fault() in mm/memory.c, allocates or swaps in.
Copy-on-Write (COW): On fork(), child shares pages read-only; write copies (breaks sharing).
Overcommit: Alloc succeeds even if no RAM (vm.overcommit_memory=1 default heuristic). OOM killer (oom_score_adj tunable) kills processes on shortage.
Swapping: To /swapfile or partition when RAM low (kswapd daemon). swapon enables.
In 6.18 rc, reclaim prioritizes cold pages better, reducing thrash.

Swapping and Memory Reclaim

When RAM scarce, kernel reclaims by:

- Dropping clean pages (reloadable from disk).
- Writing dirty to swap.
- Killing processes (OOM).

/proc/meminfo: MemFree, SwapFree, Active/Inactive (LRU lists).
Tune: /proc/sys/vm/swappiness (60 default, swap eagerness).
Tools: free -h, vmstat 1, swapoff -a (disable).

Overcommitment and Resource Limits

Overcommit allows malloc large without backing, faults allocate. vm.overcommit_ratio (50%) limits based on RAM+swap.
RLIMIT_AS limits VA size (setrlimit).
In containers, cgroup memory.max enforces hard limits.

Shared Memory and Mappings

mmap(MAP_SHARED) shares pages between processes (shm_open for POSIX shm).
Libraries shared via mmap, reducing mem use.
Kernel tracks with shmem or tmpfs.

Error Handling and Diagnostics

Faults: SIGSEGV (invalid access), SIGBUS (e.g., mmap file hole).
getrlimit(RLIMIT_AS, &lim) checks limits.
Tools: gdb catch faults; perf mem record ./prog traces loads/stores.
Errors: ENOMEM (alloc fail), EFAULT (bad addr).

Performance Tuning

- Huge pages: /proc/sys/vm/nr_hugepages =1000 (2MB pages, reduce TLB misses).
- madvise(addr, len, MADV_SEQUENTIAL) hints readahead.
- mlock(addr, len) pins in RAM, no swap.
- Transparent Huge Pages (THP): /sys/kernel/mm/transparent_hugepage/enabled =always.

In 6.17, THP for anon multi-size, auto-alloc 64KB/2MB based on access.

Security Implications

ASLR randomizes layout (/proc/sys/kernel/randomize_va_space=2 default), thwarting exploits.

NX bit (PROT_EXEC none for stack/heap) prevents code injection.

mprotect(addr, len, prot) changes perms (e.g., PROT_NONE guard).

In setuid, careful with mmap shared.

Kernel 6.17 hardens against rowhammer with better isolation.

Advanced Concepts: Userfaultfd and VM Operations

userfaultfd (kernel 4.3): FD for handling page faults in user space (uffd_register).

For post-copy migration or lazy loading.

vm_operations_struct in vma for custom (e.g., drivers).

In 6.18 rc, userfaultfd supports minor faults for shmem.

Practical Examples

View maps: cat /proc/self/maps

Fault handler: signal(SIGSEGV, handler);

mmap anon: void *mem = mmap(NULL, 4096, PROT_READ|WRITE, MAP_PRIVATE|ANONYMOUS, -1, 0);

Access triggers allocation.

These concepts underpin memory use, preparing for advanced topics.

9.3 Shared Memory and Memory Mapping

Shared memory and memory mapping are advanced memory management techniques in Linux that allow processes to communicate and share data efficiently by mapping common regions of memory into their address spaces. Shared memory enables inter-process communication (IPC) without the overhead of data copying between kernel and user space, while memory mapping provides a file-like interface to memory, supporting zero-copy I/O and lazy loading. These features, rooted in UNIX System V (1983) for shared memory segments and BSD (1981) for mmap(), have been integral to Linux since its early days, facilitating high-performance applications like databases, graphics rendering, and parallel computing. For system programmers, mastering these is essential for building scalable systems that minimize latency and maximize throughput, such as multiprocess servers sharing caches or programs mapping large files for random access. This subsection explores shared memory via shmget()/shmat() (System V) and shm_open()/mmap() (POSIX), memory mapping with mmap()/munmap(), protections and flags, anonymous mappings for process-private allocation, copy-on-write semantics, error handling, performance optimizations like huge pages, and security considerations to prevent leaks or unauthorized access. We'll cover POSIX and System V standards for portability, Linux-specific extensions like memfd_create() for sealable anonymous files, practical C examples, and integration with other IPC mechanisms. As of the stable Linux kernel 6.17 (released on September 28, 2025, with the latest patch 6.17.7 on November 2, 2025) and the ongoing 6.18 release candidate (rc4 as of November 2, 2025), shared memory and mapping benefit from enhanced page table sharing for reduced memory footprint in containers and better support for userfaultfd in custom fault handling, enabling more efficient and secure data sharing in diverse environments from embedded systems to cloud-native applications.

The Role of Shared Memory in IPC

Shared memory is one of the fastest IPC methods, allowing processes to read/write directly to a common area without kernel mediation after setup. Unlike pipes or sockets, which copy data, shared memory uses virtual memory mappings to the same physical pages, achieving zero-copy communication. This is ideal for high-bandwidth scenarios like video streaming between processes or shared caches in databases.

Historical context: System V introduced shmget() in 1983 for segments identified by keys, while POSIX.1-2001 standardized shm_open() with file-like semantics. Linux supports both, with POSIX preferred for portability. Kernel manages shared regions via shmem or tmpfs, tracking with struct shmid_kernel.

Key advantages:

- **Performance**: Direct access, no syscall overhead post-map.

- **Flexibility**: Share arbitrary data structures.
- **Persistence**: System V segments survive processes (until shmctl IPC_RMID); POSIX unlinks on close.

Drawbacks: Requires synchronization (e.g., semaphores) to avoid races; no built-in notification.

In kernel 6.17, shared memory optimizes for cross-NUMA access with better page migration.

System V Shared Memory: shmget() and shmat()

From <sys/shm.h>, System V API:

- int shmget(key_t key, size_t size, int shmflg); // Create/get ID for size bytes. Key IPC_PRIVATE or ftok(path, id) for public. Shmflg IPC_CREAT|IPC_EXCL|mode.
- void *shmat(int shmid, const void *shmaddr, int shmflg); // Attach at shmaddr (NULL kernel chooses) or 0. Shmflg SHM_RDONLY, SHM_REMAP.
- int shmdt(const void *shmaddr); // Detach.
- int shmctl(int shmid, int cmd, struct shmid_ds *buf); // Cmd IPC_STAT/IPC_SET/IPC_RMID/IPC_INFO.

Struct shmid_ds { struct ipc_perm shm_perm; size_t shm_segsz; time_t shm_atime; pid_t shm_cpid; shmatt_t shm_nattch; ... };

Example producer-consumer:

Producer:

c
```c
#include <sys/shm.h>
#include <sys/ipc.h>
#include <stdio.h>
#include <string.h>
#include <errno.h>

int main() {
    key_t key = ftok("shmfile", 65);
    int shmid = shmget(key, 1024, 0666 | IPC_CREAT);
    if (shmid == -1) { perror("shmget"); return 1; }

    char *str = shmat(shmid, NULL, 0);
    if (str == (char *)-1) { perror("shmat"); return 1; }

    strcpy(str, "Hello Shared Memory");

    printf("Data written\n");
    return 0;
}
```

Consumer:

c
```c
key_t key = ftok("shmfile", 65);
int shmid = shmget(key, 1024, 0666);
char *str = shmat(shmid, NULL, 0);
printf("Data read: %s\n", str);
shmdt(str);
shmctl(shmid, IPC_RMID, NULL); // Remove
```

ftok() generates key from file/inode.

Linux: Segments in /dev/shm (tmpfs), visible as files but managed by kernel.

Errors: EACCES (no perm), ENOENT (no key), EEXIST (IPC_EXCL fail), ENOMEM.

POSIX Shared Memory: shm_open() and mmap()

More file-like, from <sys/mman.h> and <fcntl.h>:

- int shm_open(const char *name, int oflag, mode_t mode); // Name /shm-name, oflag O_RDWR|O_CREAT, mode 0666.
- int shm_unlink(const char *name); // Remove.

Then mmap(fd, length, PROT_READ|WRITE, MAP_SHARED, 0) to map.

ftruncate(fd, size) sets size.

Example:

Producer:
c
```c
#include <sys/mman.h>
#include <fcntl.h>
#include <unistd.h>
#include <stdio.h>
#include <string.h>

int main() {
    int fd = shm_open("/myshm", O_CREAT | O_RDWR, 0666);
    if (fd == -1) { perror("shm_open"); return 1; }

    ftruncate(fd, 1024);

    char *ptr = mmap(0, 1024, PROT_READ | PROT_WRITE, MAP_SHARED, fd, 0);
    if (ptr == MAP_FAILED) { perror("mmap"); return 1; }

    strcpy(ptr, "POSIX Shared");

    printf("Written\n");
    return 0;
}
```
Consumer:
c
```c
int fd = shm_open("/myshm", O_RDONLY, 0666);
char *ptr = mmap(0, 1024, PROT_READ, MAP_SHARED, fd, 0);
printf("Read: %s\n", ptr);
munmap(ptr, 1024);
close(fd);
shm_unlink("/myshm");
```
POSIX shm in /dev/shm, file-based.
Preferred for new code—portable, fd-based.

Memory Mapping: mmap() and Variants

mmap() maps files/devices/anonymous into memory.
void *mmap(void *addr, size_t len, int prot, int flags, int fd, off_t offset);
- Addr hint (NULL kernel chooses).
- Prot PROT_READ/WRITE/EXEC/NONE.
- Flags MAP_SHARED/PRIVATE (COW)/ANONYMOUS (no fd, -1)/FIXED (exact addr)/POPULATE (preload).
- Fd file or -1 anonymous.
- Offset page-aligned.

Returns addr or MAP_FAILED.
munmap(addr, len) unmaps.
msync(addr, len, MS_SYNC/MS_ASYNC/MS_INVALIDATE) syncs to backing.
mremap(old, old_size, new_size, flags) resizes (MREMAP_MAYMOVE).
mprotect(addr, len, prot) changes protection.
madvise(addr, len, advice) hints (MADV_WILLNEED preload, MADV_DONTNEED drop, MADV_SEQUENTIAL readahead).
Example anonymous map:
c
```c
void *mem = mmap(NULL, 4096, PROT_READ | PROT_WRITE, MAP_PRIVATE | MAP_ANONYMOUS, -1, 0);
*(int *)mem = 42;
munmap(mem, 4096);
```
File map: fd = open("file", O_RDWR); mmap(0, size, PROT_WRITE, MAP_SHARED, fd, 0); changes persist.
COW: MAP_PRIVATE file map copies on write.
Kernel 6.17 mmap supports multi-size THP (64KB/2MB auto), madvise(MADV_COLLAPSE) forces huge.
Errors: ENOMEM, EINVAL (bad len/offset/addr), EACCES (prot vs open mode).

Performance and Optimization

Shared mem zero-copy, fast IPC.

Map large files for random access without read().

Huge pages: mmap MAP_HUGETLB, len multiple of 2MB.

Overhead: Page faults on first access (minor allocate, major disk).

Tune: /proc/sys/vm/max_map_count (default 65530) limits VMAs.

In 6.18 rc, mmap optimizes locked mappings (MLOCK_ONFAULT) for faster faults.

Security Considerations

Shared mem risks: Improper perms allow access (use umask/mode).

mmap PROT_EXEC on user data enables injection—avoid.

ASLR randomizes map addr.

mprotect noexec stack/heap.

In shared, sync required for consistency.

memfd_create("name", MFD_ALLOW_SEALING); fd for anonymous, fseal to prevent changes.

Used in Wayland for secure buffers.

Practical Use Cases

IPC: Database shm for transactions.

File cache: Map config, access as array.

Anonymous: Large temp buffers without swap (MADV_DONTDUMP).

In multiprocess, fork() + MAP_SHARED for inherit.

Tools: ipcs -m lists System V shm; lsof +D /dev/shm for POSIX.

These techniques enable efficient sharing/mapping, key for performance.

9.4 Memory Optimization Techniques

Memory optimization techniques in Linux system programming are critical for maximizing application performance, reducing resource consumption, and ensuring stability in environments with constrained or contested memory. As applications grow in complexity—handling large datasets, concurrent operations, or real-time constraints—inefficient memory use can lead to increased page faults, higher latency, or out-of-memory (OOM) conditions, triggering kernel killers that disrupt service. Optimization involves strategies to minimize allocation overhead, reduce fragmentation, leverage hardware features, and proactively manage memory lifecycles. These techniques build on core allocation mechanisms, addressing issues like cache misses, unnecessary copying, and overcommitment risks. For system programmers, mastering optimization is essential for high-throughput servers, embedded systems with limited RAM, or data-intensive applications like databases and machine learning models. This subsection explores key techniques: pooling and custom allocators to reuse memory, zero-copy methods to avoid data duplication, huge pages to reduce TLB overhead, memory advising with madvise() for kernel hints, compaction and defragmentation, overcommit tuning, thread-local allocation for concurrency, and tools for profiling like Valgrind and perf. We'll cover POSIX-compliant approaches for portability, Linux-specific features such as transparent huge pages (THP) and memfd_seal() for secure sharing, practical C examples, error handling, performance benchmarks, and security considerations to prevent leaks or attacks like heap spraying. As of the stable Linux kernel 6.17 (released on September 28, 2025, with the latest patch 6.17.7 on November 2, 2025) and the ongoing 6.18 release candidate (rc4 as of November 2, 2025), memory optimization benefits from enhanced reclaim algorithms that prioritize cold pages and improved support for multi-size THP (e.g., 64KB allocations), enabling finer-grained efficiency in diverse workloads from mobile devices to high-memory servers.

The Importance of Memory Optimization

Memory is a finite resource, and in Linux, the kernel's virtual memory subsystem strives to allocate it efficiently, but user-space decisions greatly influence overall performance. Poor optimization can result in excessive page faults (minor for allocation, major for disk I/O), fragmentation (internal wasting space within chunks, external scattering free blocks), or thrashing (constant swapping degrading throughput). Optimization techniques aim to align allocation patterns with hardware (e.g., cache lines of 64 bytes, pages of 4KB) and kernel behaviors (e.g., overcommit allowing speculative allocation but risking OOM).

Historical evolution: Early UNIX had simple brk() for heap growth, but Linux 2.2 (1999) introduced mmap() for non-contiguous allocation, reducing fragmentation. Kernel 2.6 (2003) added hugetlbfs for huge pages, and 2.6.38 (2011) introduced THP for automatic large-page use. POSIX provides basic hints like posix_madvise(), but Linux extends with sysctls for tuning.

Key metrics: RSS (resident set size, physical RAM used), PSS (proportional, accounting for shared), VSZ (virtual size). Tools like smaps (/proc/<pid>/smaps) detail per-mapping usage.

In kernel 6.17, optimization focuses on reclaim during low-mem, using multi-gen LRU to evict cold pages faster, while 6.18 rc refines THP collapse for mixed workloads.

Memory Pooling and Custom Allocators

Pooling pre-allocates fixed-size blocks for reuse, minimizing malloc/free overhead and fragmentation for frequent small allocations (e.g., network packets).

Custom allocators override malloc via hooks or libraries like jemalloc/tcmalloc, offering better multithread scaling.

Example simple pool for fixed-size objects:

c

```c
#include <stdlib.h>
#include <stdio.h>

#define POOL_SIZE 100
#define OBJ_SIZE sizeof(int)

typedef struct node {
    void *data;
    struct node *next;
} node_t;

node_t *free_list;

void pool_init() {
    free_list = NULL;
    char *block = malloc(POOL_SIZE * OBJ_SIZE);
    for (int i = 0; i < POOL_SIZE; i++) {
        node_t *node = malloc(sizeof(node_t));
        node->data = block + i * OBJ_SIZE;
        node->next = free_list;
        free_list = node;
    }
}

void *pool_alloc() {
    if (!free_list) return NULL;
    node_t *node = free_list;
    free_list = node->next;
    void *data = node->data;
    free(node);
    return data;
}

void pool_free(void *ptr) {
    node_t *node = malloc(sizeof(node_t));
    node->data = ptr;
    node->next = free_list;
    free_list = node;
}

int main() {
    pool_init();
    int *obj = pool_alloc();
    *obj = 42;
    printf("%d\n", *obj);
    pool_free(obj);
```

```
    return 0;
}
```
Pros: Fast (O(1) alloc/free), no frag. Cons: Wasted if size mismatch.

Libraries: Apache Portable Runtime (apr_pool_create), Google tcmalloc (thread-caching).

Linux: slab allocator inspires user-space (kmem_cache in kernel).

Zero-Copy Techniques

Zero-copy avoids unnecessary data copies between kernel/user or buffers, using mmap for files (direct access), sendfile(fd_out, fd_in, offset, count) for file-to-socket, splice() for pipe-to-pipe.

Example sendfile server (simplified):

c
```c
#include <sys/sendfile.h>
#include <fcntl.h>
#include <unistd.h>

void serve_file(int client_fd, const char *path) {
    int file_fd = open(path, O_RDONLY);
    off_t offset = 0;
    struct stat st;
    fstat(file_fd, &st);
    sendfile(client_fd, file_fd, &offset, st.st_size);
    close(file_fd);
}
```
Saves copy from read to write buffer.

In drivers, DMA (direct memory access) for hardware zero-copy.

Kernel 6.17 sendfile optimizes for large files with better splice integration.

Huge Pages and THP

Standard pages 4KB; huge 2MB/1GB reduce TLB entries (TLB holds ~100-1000), speeding access for large mem.

Hugetlbfs: mount -t hugetlbfs none /hugepages; mmap MAP_HUGETLB.

THP: Transparent, kernel auto-promotes 4KB to 2MB. /sys/kernel/mm/transparent_hugepage/enabled = always/madvise/never.

madvise(addr, len, MADV_HUGE PAGE) hints THP.

In 6.18 rc, multi-size THP (16KB, 32KB, etc.) for granular.

Pros: 10-50% speedup in mem-bound (databases). Cons: Waste if not full, harder reclaim.

Memory Advising and Compaction

madvise(addr, len, advice): Kernel hints.

- MADV_SEQUENTIAL: Readahead aggressively.
- MADV_RANDOM: Disable readahead.
- MADV_DONTNEED: Drop pages (reclaim hint).
- MADV_FREE: Mark discardable (like MADV_DONTNEED but keep if not pressured).
- MADV_MERGEABLE: Enable KSM (kernel same-page merging) for dedup.

Compaction: /proc/sys/vm/compact_memory =1 triggers defrag.

For proactive: posix_fadvise(fd, offset, len, POSIX_FADV_DONTNEED) for files.

In low-mem, kernel kcompactd daemon compacts.

Overcommit and Reclaim Tuning

Overcommit: /proc/sys/vm/overcommit_memory =0 (check),1 (always),2 (strict RAM+ratio*swap).

ratio /proc/sys/vm/overcommit_ratio =50% default.

Reclaim: swappiness (60) balances anon/file reclaim.

watermark_scale_factor (10) for proactive reclaim.

In OOM, /proc/sys/vm/panic_on_oom =1 panics; oom_kill_allocating_task=1 kills culprit.

Thread-Local Allocation and Custom Arenas

Multithread: Glibc ptmalloc per-thread arenas (up to 8*cores) reduce contention.

Custom: malloc hooks (__malloc_hook) or alternative like jemalloc (arenas API).

jemalloc: je_malloc, je_arena_new() for isolated arenas.

For security, isolated arenas prevent use-after-free across components.

Error Handling and Diagnostics

Alloc returns NULL ENOMEM; check always, fallback (e.g., smaller size).

Leaks: Valgrind --leak-check=full --show-leak-kinds=all ./prog.

Fragmentation: mallinfo().arena (non-mmap size), fordblks (free).

perf mem for access patterns.

Errors: ENOMEM, EINVAL (bad advice).

Best Practices

- Profile first (valgrind massif for heap).
- Pool frequent small objs.
- Zero-copy for I/O.
- THP for large contiguous.
- Madvise hints.
- Monitor /proc/meminfo.
- Custom for specific (slab-like).
- Security: mlock sensitive (no swap leak); mprotect guards.

Pitfalls: Overallocation (OOM); ignoring free NULL; realloc move invalidates ptrs.

In 6.17, reclaim prioritizes, reducing latency.

These techniques optimize mem, enhancing efficiency.

10 Time, Timers, and Signals

10.1 Time Representations and Conversions

Time representations and conversions are indispensable in Linux system programming, providing the means to measure durations, schedule events, and synchronize operations in a precise and portable manner. Time is a fundamental aspect of computing, influencing everything from logging timestamps to timeout mechanisms in network protocols, and its accurate handling ensures application reliability and performance. In Linux, time is managed through various representations, each suited to different use cases: wall-clock time for real-world synchronization, monotonic time for interval measurements, process time for resource accounting, and high-resolution time for fine-grained precision. These stem from UNIX traditions, where time was introduced in Version 1 (1971) as seconds since epoch, evolving to include nanosecond resolution and timezone support. For system programmers, mastering these is essential for tasks like implementing timeouts, profiling code execution, or coordinating distributed systems, where mismatches can lead to bugs like race conditions or incorrect logging. This subsection explores key time types and APIs, including time_t for epoch seconds, struct timespec for nanoseconds, clock_gettime() for various clocks, conversions with localtime() and strftime(), and calendar calculations. We'll cover POSIX standards for portability, Linux-specific clocks like CLOCK_BOOTTIME, practical C examples, error handling for issues like clock jumps, performance considerations for high-frequency calls, and security implications such as time-based attacks. As of the stable Linux kernel 6.17 (released on September 15, 2025, with the latest patch 6.17.7 on November 2, 2025) and the ongoing 6.18 release candidate (rc4 as of November 2, 2025), time management benefits from enhanced VDSo (variable daylight saving) handling and better NTP synchronization in namespaces, enabling more accurate timing in containerized and real-time applications from embedded devices to cloud infrastructures.

The Concept of Time in Operating Systems

Time in operating systems serves multiple purposes: tracking real-world events (wall time), measuring intervals without external influence (monotonic time), accounting for process execution (CPU time), and providing high-resolution stamps for logging or profiling. Linux, like UNIX, uses the epoch—January 1, 1970, 00:00:00 UTC—as a reference for Unix time, represented as seconds (time_t, 64-bit since kernel 5.6 for Y2038 safety).

Key representations:

- **time_t**: Signed long (seconds since epoch), used in time(&t).
- **struct tm**: Broken-down time (year, month, day, hour, min, sec, wday, yday, isdst), for calendar.
- **struct timespec**: { time_t tv_sec; long tv_nsec; }, nanosecond precision.
- **struct timeval**: { time_t tv_sec; suseconds_t tv_usec; }, microsecond (legacy).

Clocks: Linux provides multiple via clock_gettime(clockid_t clock_id, struct timespec *tp):

- CLOCK_REALTIME: Wall time, settable, jumps on NTP/leap.
- CLOCK_MONOTONIC: Interval measurement, steady, from boot (ignores suspend).
- CLOCK_PROCESS_CPUTIME_ID: Process CPU time (user+system).
- CLOCK_THREAD_CPUTIME_ID: Thread CPU time.
- CLOCK_BOOTTIME: Like monotonic but includes suspend.
- CLOCK_TAI: International Atomic Time, no leaps.

clock_id can be dynamic (per-process/thread).

Historical: Pre-2.6, gettimeofday() for timeval; now clock_gettime preferred for ns.

In kernel 6.17, clocks optimize for virtualized envs with better paravirt clock sources.

Obtaining Current Time

Basic: time_t time(time_t *tloc); // Seconds, tloc NULL for return only.

High-res: int clock_gettime(clockid_t clk_id, struct timespec *tp);

Micro: int gettimeofday(struct timeval *tv, struct timezone *tz); // tz NULL.

Example wall time:

```c
#include <time.h>
#include <stdio.h>

int main() {
    struct timespec ts;
```

```c
if (clock_gettime(CLOCK_REALTIME, &ts) == -1) {
    perror("clock_gettime");
    return 1;
}
printf("Seconds: %ld, Nanoseconds: %ld\n", ts.tv_sec, ts.tv_nsec);

time_t now = time(NULL);
printf("Unix time: %ld\n", now);
return 0;
}
```
For monotonic interval:
c
```c
struct timespec start, end;
clock_gettime(CLOCK_MONOTONIC, &start);
// Work
clock_gettime(CLOCK_MONOTONIC, &end);
double elapsed = (end.tv_sec - start.tv_sec) + (end.tv_nsec - start.tv_nsec) / 1e9;
printf("Elapsed: %.9f s\n", elapsed);
```
Errors: EINVAL (bad clk_id), EFAULT (bad tp).

Broken-Down Time and Conversions

Convert time_t to struct tm:

- struct tm *gmtime(const time_t *timep); // UTC
- struct tm *localtime(const time_t *timep); // Local timezone
- struct tm *gmtime_r(const time_t *timep, struct tm *result); // Reentrant
- struct tm *localtime_r(const time_t *timep, struct tm *result);

Reverse: time_t mktime(struct tm *tm); // Local to epoch

String: char *ctime(const time_t *timep); // "Wed Jun 30 21:49:08 1993\n"

Reentrant: char *ctime_r(const time_t *timep, char *buf);

Format: size_t strftime(char *s, size_t max, const char *format, const struct tm *tm); // %Y-%m-%d %H:%M:%S

Parse: size_t strptime(const char *s, const char *format, struct tm *tm);

Timezone: tzset(); extern char *tzname[2]; extern long timezone; extern int daylight;

Set: setenv("TZ", "America/New_York", 1); tzset();

Example local time string:
c
```c
time_t now = time(NULL);
struct tm *local = localtime(&now);
char buf[64];
strftime(buf, sizeof(buf), "%Y-%m-%d %H:%M:%S", local);
printf("Local time: %s\n", buf);
```
For UTC: gmtime.

mktime normalizes tm (e.g., tm_mon=12 -> tm_year++, tm_mon=0).

Errors: NULL on fail (overflow Y2038 in 32-bit time_t, but 64-bit safe).

Linux: glibc handles leap seconds in RIGHT timescale (CLOCK_REALTIME_COARSE).

Calendar Calculations and Time Arithmetic

Add/subtract: Use mktime after modifying tm (handles overflow).

Duration: difftime(time_t t1, time_t t2); // Seconds double.

For timespec: Manual (end.tv_sec - start.tv_sec) * 1e9 + (end.tv_nsec - start.tv_nsec)

Libraries: <time.h> basic; for advanced, use libicu or custom.

Leap years: tm.tm_year % 4 == 0 && (!%100 || %400)

DST: tm.tm_isdst = -1 for mktime to determine.

In distributed, use UTC to avoid TZ issues.

High-Resolution Time and Clocks

clock_getres(clk_id, &ts); // Resolution

CLOCK_REALTIME res ~1ms, MONOTONIC ns with HPET/TSC.

vdso: gettimeofday/clock_gettime in user space for speed (no syscall if TSC stable).

In 6.17, vdso optimizes for virtualized with paravirt clocks.

For process: times(&tms); // clock_t user/system/child ticks, CLK_TCK =100.

getrusage(RUSAGE_SELF, &rusage); // timeval ru_utime/ru_stime, ru_maxrss KB.

Example CPU time:

```c
#include <sys/resource.h>
#include <stdio.h>

struct rusage usage;
getrusage(RUSAGE_SELF, &usage);
printf("User CPU: %ld.%06ld s\n", usage.ru_utime.tv_sec, usage.ru_utime.tv_usec);
```

Timezones and Internationalization

tzfile (/usr/share/zoneinfo/) binary, loaded by tzset().

localtime uses TZ env or /etc/localtime symlink.

For conversions: mktime assumes local, timegm(tm) for GMT mktime.

strftime %Z timezone abbr, %z offset.

In code, setlocale(LC_TIME, ""); for locale formatting.

Error Handling and Edge Cases

Errors rare: EOVERFLOW (time_t overflow, post-2038 in 32-bit), EINVAL (bad clk).

Edge: Leap seconds (added to CLOCK_REALTIME, monotonic skips), clock jumps (NTP slew or step).

Y2038: 32-bit time_t overflows Jan 19, 2038; 64-bit safe, but legacy ABIs need _TIME_BITS=64.

NTP: systemd-timesyncd or ntpd adjusts.

In VMs, clock sources (kvm-clock) stable.

Performance Considerations

clock_gettime ~10-50ns (vdso); avoid in tight loops, cache.

For benchmarks, use monotonic.

RDTSC asm ("rdtsc") for cycles, but not time (variable freq).

In 6.18 rc, clock_gettime vdso for new arches like LoongArch.

Security Implications

Time-based attacks: Timing (cache side-channel), fake NTP for log spoof.

settimeofday requires CAP_SYS_TIME.

In containers, time namespaces (CLONE_NEWTIME) offset clocks.

Secure: Use monotonic for timeouts, avoid wall for security-critical.

Practical Use Cases

Timestamp logs: strftime for readable.

Timeout: clock_gettime(monotonic) + interval, poll.

Profiling: rusage before/after.

Alarm: setitimer(ITIMER_REAL, &itval, NULL); SIGALRM after.

These representations enable precise time handling, vital for systems.

Advanced Time Conversions

To Julian day, Gregorian calculations:

int is_leap(int y) { return y%4==0 && (y%100!=0 || y%400==0); }

Days in month, cumulative for date to epoch.

Libraries: Use libnova or custom for astronomy.

For UTC to TAI: Account leaps (hardcoded table, as Linux doesn't).

In glibc, right/zoneinfo for leap-aware.

NTP leapfile /etc/ntp.leapseconds.

This comprehensive handling ensures accurate conversions.

10.2 Timers and Interval Timing

Timers and interval timing mechanisms in Linux provide programmable ways to schedule events, measure durations, and trigger actions at specific intervals or after timeouts, essential for applications requiring periodic tasks or bounded waiting. These features extend basic time measurement by allowing processes to set alarms that deliver signals or wake blocked calls, enabling non-blocking designs and efficient resource use. In system programming, timers are crucial for implementing watchdogs, heartbeat protocols, polling loops with timeouts, or animation frames in GUI applications, where precise timing prevents indefinite hangs or missed deadlines. Originating from UNIX alarms in Version 7 (1979) with alarm() for simple SIGALRM delivery, Linux has evolved to include high-resolution timers, POSIX interval timers, and file-descriptor-based timerfd for integration with event loops like epoll(). This subsection explores key timer APIs, including alarm() and setitimer() for signal-based timing, timer_create()/timer_settime() for POSIX timers with per-timer signals, timerfd_create()/timerfd_settime() for fd-based polling, and their configurations for one-shot or repeating intervals. We'll cover POSIX.1-2001 standards for portability, Linux-specific high-res timers (hrtimers, kernel 2.6.16, 2006), practical C examples for various use cases, error handling for overflows or invalid specs, performance considerations for timer coalescence to save power, and security implications such as signal queue overflows in real-time systems. As of the stable Linux kernel 6.17 (released on September 28, 2025, with the latest patch 6.17.7 on November 2, 2025) and the ongoing 6.18 release candidate (rc4 as of November 2, 2025), timers benefit from enhanced dynamic tickless operation for better energy efficiency on idle systems and improved timer wheel scaling for high-frequency intervals, enabling more precise and power-aware timing in environments from battery-constrained embedded devices to high-throughput servers.

The Role of Timers in System Programming

Timers allow programs to schedule future events without busy-waiting, which wastes CPU cycles, or blocking on sleep calls that lack precision. Instead, timers leverage kernel clock sources (e.g., TSC, HPET) to trigger asynchronous notifications via signals or file descriptors, integrating seamlessly with event-driven architectures. This is vital for timeouts in I/O operations (e.g., select() with tv_timeout), periodic housekeeping (e.g., garbage collection), or real-time control loops where jitter must be minimized.

Historical development: Early UNIX had alarm(seconds) for coarse SIGALRM after seconds. BSD added setitimer (1983) for interval timers with microsecond resolution. POSIX.1b (1993) standardized timer_create for multiple timers with per-timer signals. Linux 2.6 (2003) introduced hrtimers for nanosecond accuracy, replacing older timer wheels, and timerfd (2.6.22, 2007) for select/epoll compatibility.

Types of timers:

- **One-shot**: Fire once after delay.
- **Interval/Periodic**: Repeat at fixed rate.
- **Absolute vs. Relative**: From now or specific time.

Linux clocks for timers: CLOCK_REALTIME (wall, adjustable), CLOCK_MONOTONIC (steady, from boot). In kernel 6.17, timers use red-black trees for efficient expiry ordering in deep workloads.

Signal-Based Timers: alarm() and setitimer()

Simplest: unsigned int alarm(unsigned int seconds); // Set SIGALRM after seconds, return remaining. Cancels previous; 0 cancels.

For precision: int setitimer(int which, const struct itimerval *new_value, struct itimerval *old_value);

Which: ITIMER_REAL (wall, SIGALRM), ITIMER_VIRTUAL (user CPU, SIGVTALRM), ITIMER_PROF (user+system, SIGPROF).

Struct itimerval { struct timeval it_interval; /* repeat / struct timeval it_value; / initial */ };

Timeval { long tv_sec; long tv_usec; }.

Set interval 0 for one-shot.

Getitimer(which, &curr) gets current.

Example periodic:

```c
#include <sys/time.h>
#include <signal.h>
#include <stdio.h>

void handler(int sig) {
    printf("Timer fired\n");
}
```

```c
int main() {
    signal(SIGALRM, handler);

    struct itimerval it = { .it_interval = {1, 0}, .it_value = {1, 0} }; // 1s interval
    if (setitimer(ITIMER_REAL, &it, NULL) == -1) {
        perror("setitimer");
        return 1;
    }

    while (1) pause(); // Wait signals
    return 0;
}
```

alarm() equivalent to setitimer(ITIMER_REAL, {seconds, 0}, {0, 0}).

Resolution: ~10ms on HZ=100, but hrtimers ns.

Errors: EINVAL (bad which/value).

Limitations: One per type; signal overwrites previous.

POSIX Timers: timer_create() and timer_settime()

Multiple timers, per-timer signals.

From <time.h>, <signal.h>:

- int timer_create(clockid_t clockid, struct sigevent *sevp, timer_t *timerid); // Create, clockid CLOCK_REALTIME/MONOTONIC, sevp for notification.

Struct sigevent { int sigev_notify; /* SIGEV_SIGNAL/THREAD/NONE */ int sigev_signo; union sigval sigev_value; void (*sigev_notify_function)(union sigval); pthread_attr_t *sigev_notify_attributes; };

For SIGEV_SIGNAL, sends sigev_signo with sigev_value.si_value.

- int timer_settime(timer_t timerid, int flags, const struct itimerspec *new_value, struct itimerspec *old_value);

Flags TIMER_ABSTIME for absolute.

Struct itimerspec { struct timespec it_interval; struct timespec it_value; };

- int timer_gettime(timer_t timerid, struct itimerspec *curr_value);
- int timer_delete(timer_t timerid);
- int timer_getoverrun(timer_t timerid); // Queued expires if delayed.

Max timers TIMER_MAX (~2^31).

Example:

c
```c
#include <time.h>
#include <signal.h>
#include <stdio.h>

void handler(int sig, siginfo_t *si, void *uc) {
    printf("Timer %d fired\n", si->si_value.sival_int);
}

int main() {
    struct sigaction sa = { .sa_flags = SA_SIGINFO, .sa_sigaction = handler };
    sigaction(SIGRTMIN, &sa, NULL);

    timer_t timer;
    struct sigevent sev = { .sigev_notify = SIGEV_SIGNAL, .sigev_signo = SIGRTMIN, .sigev_value.sival_int = 1 };
    if (timer_create(CLOCK_MONOTONIC, &sev, &timer) == -1) { perror("timer_create"); return 1; }

    struct itimerspec its = { .it_interval = {0, 100000000}, .it_value = {1, 0} }; // 0.1s interval after 1s
    if (timer_settime(timer, 0, &its, NULL) == -1) { perror("timer_settime"); return 1; }

    sleep(5); // Let fire
```

```c
    timer_delete(timer);
    return 0;
}
```
Real-time signals (SIGRTMIN to SIGRTMAX) for queuing, no loss if multiple.

Linux: hrtimers back, ns precision.

Errors: EINVAL (bad clock/spec), ENOTSUP (clock), EAGAIN (queue full).

File Descriptor Timers: timerfd_create() and timerfd_settime()

Linux-specific (kernel 2.6.25, 2008), from <sys/timerfd.h>:

- int timerfd_create(int clockid, int flags); // TFD_NONBLOCK/CLOEXEC
- int timerfd_settime(int fd, int flags, const struct itimerspec *new_value, struct itimerspec *old_value);
- int timerfd_gettime(int fd, struct itimerspec *curr_value);

Read(fd, &expiries, 8) gets u64 expiries since last read (blocks if 0 unless nonblock).

Integrates with epoll/select for event loops.

Example:

c

```c
#include <sys/timerfd.h>
#include <unistd.h>
#include <stdio.h>

int main() {
    int tfd = timerfd_create(CLOCK_MONOTONIC, 0);
    if (tfd == -1) { perror("timerfd_create"); return 1; }

    struct itimerspec its = { .it_interval = {1, 0}, .it_value = {1, 0} };
    if (timerfd_settime(tfd, 0, &its, NULL) == -1) { perror("timerfd_settime"); return 1; }

    for (int i = 0; i < 3; i++) {
        uint64_t exp;
        read(tfd, &exp, sizeof(exp));
        printf("Expired %lu times\n", exp);
    }

    close(tfd);
    return 0;
}
```

Pros: No signals, pollable.

In 6.17, timerfd supports large intervals better.

Errors: EINVAL, EBADF.

Choosing the Right Timer Mechanism

- alarm/setitimer: Simple, signal-based, one per type.
- POSIX timers: Multiple, per-timer sig, flexible.
- timerfd: Event-loop friendly, no sig overhead.

For RT, use MONOTONIC, high prio.

System limit: /proc/sys/kernel/timer_max ~2^31.

Error Handling and Best Practices

Errors: Common EINVAL (bad interval, value<interval for periodic), EAGAIN (overrun queue).

Practices:

- Use monotonic for intervals.
- Handle overrun in getoverrun.
- Absolute for deadlines.
- Signal block/mask if not handling.
- Close fds/delete timers.
- Security: Signals can interrupt; use SA_RESTART.
- Performance: Coalesce (kernel groups close expiries to save power).

Pitfalls: Interval 0 disables; negative disabled; clock jumps affect realtime.

In 6.18 rc, timers optimize wheel for low-power.

These tools enable precise timing, key for responsive systems.

10.3 Signal Handling and Delivery

Signals are a form of asynchronous inter-process communication in Linux, providing a mechanism for the kernel or other processes to notify a process of events, such as hardware exceptions, user interrupts, or software conditions. Signal handling allows programs to respond to these notifications, either by executing custom code, ignoring them, or taking default actions like termination. Delivery refers to how signals are sent, queued, and processed, ensuring reliable notification even in concurrent environments. Rooted in UNIX Version 3 (1973), where signals were introduced for basic events like SIGINT (Ctrl-C), the system has evolved to support real-time signals with data attachment and queuing. For system programmers, mastering signal handling is essential for robust applications, such as servers gracefully shutting down on SIGTERM or debuggers catching faults with SIGSEGV. Improper handling can lead to race conditions, where signals interrupt critical sections, or lost signals if not queued properly. This subsection explores signal types (standard and real-time), handling with signal() and sigaction(), delivery semantics including blocking and queuing, siginfo_t for extended info, system calls like kill() and sigqueue() for sending, and integration with threads. We'll cover POSIX.1-2001 standards for portability, Linux-specific features like signalfd for polling signals, practical C examples for common scenarios, error handling for issues like signal overflow, performance considerations for signal latency, and security implications such as signal-based attacks. As of the stable Linux kernel 6.17 (released on September 28, 2025, with the latest patch 6.17.7 on November 2, 2025) and the ongoing 6.18 release candidate (rc4 as of November 2, 2025), signal handling benefits from optimized queuing for real-time signals and better integration with eBPF for signal tracing, enabling more responsive and debuggable applications in environments from real-time embedded systems to multi-threaded servers.

The Fundamentals of Signals

Signals are integer values (1 to 64 in Linux, with 1-31 standard and 32-64 real-time) that interrupt normal execution flow, invoking a handler or default action. They originate from the kernel (e.g., SIGSEGV on invalid memory), hardware (SIGFPE on divide-by-zero), or users via kill command or kill() call.

Standard signals (from <signal.h>):

- SIGINT (2): Interrupt (Ctrl-C).
- SIGTERM (15): Termination request.
- SIGKILL (9): Immediate kill (can't catch).
- SIGSEGV (11): Segmentation fault.
- SIGCHLD (17): Child status change.
- SIGALRM (14): Timer expiry.

Defaults: Terminate (TERM, INT), core dump (SEGV, FPE), ignore (CHLD), stop (TSTP).

Real-time signals (SIGRTMIN 34 to SIGRTMAX 64): Queueable, carry data (union sigval), no predefined meaning—user-defined.

Signals are pending until delivered; blocked signals queue indefinitely (up to RLIMIT_SIGPENDING, default thousands).

Delivery: Kernel interrupts process, pushes context to stack, jumps to handler. After handler, resumes (unless SA_RESETHAND).

In threads: Signals target process, delivered to any thread not masking (pthread_sigmask()).

Kernel 6.17 optimizes delivery for high-signal loads with better queue management.

Setting Up Signal Handlers: signal() and sigaction()

Basic: sighandler_t signal(int signum, sighandler_t handler); // Handler func(int sig), SIG_IGN ignore, SIG_DFL default.

Race-prone (reset to DFL on delivery), avoid for new code.

Advanced: int sigaction(int signum, const struct sigaction *act, struct sigaction *oldact);

Struct sigaction { void (*sa_handler)(int); void (*sa_sigaction)(int, siginfo_t *, void *); sigset_t sa_mask; int sa_flags; };

sa_flags: SA_RESTART (restart syscalls), SA_SIGINFO (use sa_sigaction with info), SA_RESETHAND (reset to DFL after), SA_NODEFER (no self-mask during handler), SA_NOCLDSTOP (no SIGCHLD on child stop), SA_ONSTACK (alt stack).

siginfo_t { int si_signo; int si_errno; int si_code; pid_t si_pid; union sigval si_value; ... }; si_code CLD_EXITED for child, etc.

sa_mask: Blocks signals during handler.

Example info handler:

c

```
#include <signal.h>
#include <stdio.h>

void handler(int sig, siginfo_t *info, void *ucontext) {
    printf("Signal %d from PID %d, code %d\n", sig, info->si_pid, info->si_code);
}

int main() {
    struct sigaction sa = { .sa_sigaction = handler, .sa_flags = SA_SIGINFO | SA_RESTART };
    sigemptyset(&sa.sa_mask);
    if (sigaction(SIGUSR1, &sa, NULL) == -1) { perror("sigaction"); return 1; }

    raise(SIGUSR1); // Self-send
    return 0;
}
```

For real-time, si_value carries data from sigqueue.

Errors: EINVAL (bad sig/flags).

Signal Delivery and Queuing

Delivery: Pending signals checked on syscall return, interrupt return, or schedule().

Standard signals: Not queued—if pending, subsequent lost (bitmap).

Real-time: Queued with data, up to RLIMIT_SIGPENDING.

sigpending(sigset_t *set) gets pending.

Blocked: sigprocmask(int how, const sigset_t *set, sigset_t *oldset); how SIG_BLOCK/UNBLOCK/SETMASK.

sigemptyset(&set); sigaddset(&set, SIGINT); sigprocmask(SIG_BLOCK, &set, NULL);

In threads: pthread_sigmask(how, set, old) per-thread.

Kernel queue: struct sigpending, real-time in sigqueue list.

In 6.18 rc, queuing optimizes for high-rate real-time with better lockless access.

Sending Signals: kill(), raise(), and sigqueue()

- int kill(pid_t pid, int sig); // Pid >0 specific, =0 group, =-1 all (perm), <-1 group -pid.
- int raise(int sig); // To self (kill(getpid(), sig))
- int sigqueue(pid_t pid, int sig, const union sigval value); // Real-time with data (value.sival_int/ptr)

Permissions: Sender EUID matches receiver real/effective UID, or CAP_KILL.

Errors: ESRCH (no process), EPERM, EINVAL (bad sig).

Example send data:

c

```
union sigval val = { .sival_int = 42 };
sigqueue(getpid(), SIGRTMIN, val);
```

Handler info->si_value = val.

Alternate Stacks and Signal Frames

For stack overflow (SIGSEGV in handler), use alt stack: sigaltstack(const stack_t *ss, stack_t *old); ss.ss_sp stack, ss.ss_size, ss.ss_flags SS_ONSTACK/DISABLE.

sa_flags SA_ONSTACK uses alt.

Prevents recursion crashes.

Signalfd: Polling Signals

Linux-specific (2.6.22): int signalfd(int fd, const sigset_t *mask, int flags); // Fd -1 new, or update.

Read(fd, &sfd_signfo, sizeof(struct signalfd_siginfo)) gets info.

Integrates with epoll.

Blocks masked signals, dequeues on read.

Example:

c

```
#include <sys/signalfd.h>
```

```c
#include <poll.h>
#include <stdio.h>

int main() {
    sigset_t mask;
    sigemptyset(&mask);
    sigaddset(&mask, SIGUSR1);
    sigprocmask(SIG_BLOCK, &mask, NULL);

    int sfd = signalfd(-1, &mask, SFD_NONBLOCK);
    if (sfd == -1) { perror("signalfd"); return 1; }

    raise(SIGUSR1);

    struct pollfd pfd = { .fd = sfd, .events = POLLIN };
    if (poll(&pfd, 1, -1) > 0) {
        struct signalfd_siginfo si;
        read(sfd, &si, sizeof(si));
        printf("Got signal %d\n", si.ssi_signo);
    }

    close(sfd);
    return 0;
}
```
No handlers needed.

In 6.17, signalfd supports large queues better.

Error Handling and Best Practices

Errors: EINVAL, ESRCH, EPERM.

Practices:

- Use sigaction over signal.
- Block in handlers, use async-safe funcs (write, not printf).
- SA_RESTART for syscalls.
- Handle SIGCHLD to reap.
- Ignore unused (SIG_IGN).
- Security: Mask in sensitive, avoid handlers in setuid.
- Performance: Signals ~us latency; avoid in hot paths.

Pitfalls: Handler reentrancy; lost standard signals; stack overflow.

Debug: strace -e signal; gdb catch signal SIGSEGV.

In 6.18 rc, signal pending optimizes for threads.

These enable responsive handling, key for robust programs.

10.4 Asynchronous I/O with Signals

Asynchronous I/O (AIO) with signals provides a mechanism for performing non-blocking input/output operations in Linux, allowing programs to initiate I/O requests and continue execution while being notified via signals upon completion. This approach decouples I/O from the main control flow, enabling efficient handling of multiple operations without polling or dedicated threads, which is particularly valuable for high-performance servers, database systems, and real-time applications where latency must be minimized. Unlike synchronous I/O (e.g., read()/write()) that blocks until done, or fully asynchronous models like io_uring that use completion queues, signal-based AIO leverages POSIX real-time signals to deliver notifications, combining flexibility with data attachment for event details. Originating from the POSIX.1b real-time extensions (IEEE 1003.1b-1993), this feature was implemented in Linux kernel 2.6 (2003) via the libaio library, though signal delivery has been supported since earlier versions. For system programmers, understanding AIO with signals is essential for building scalable I/O-bound applications, as it avoids the overhead of threading for concurrency while providing a way to handle completion events. However, it comes with challenges like signal queue limits and the need for careful handler design to avoid reentrancy issues. This subsection explores the AIO API for signal notification, including aio_read()/aio_write() for requests, aio_error()/aio_return() for status, sigevent for setup, integration with sigaction() for handling, practical C examples using libaio, error handling for conditions like queue overflows, performance considerations in contended scenarios, and security implications such as signal masking in critical sections. We'll cover POSIX.1-2001 compliance for portability, Linux-specific behaviors like kernel AIO support for certain filesystems (e.g., ext4, but not all), and alternatives when signals are unsuitable. As of the stable Linux kernel 6.17 (released on September 28, 2025, with the latest patch 6.17.7 on November 2, 2025) and the ongoing 6.18 release candidate (rc4 as of November 2, 2025), AIO with signals benefits from optimized signal delivery queues and better integration with io_uring for hybrid async models, enabling more efficient I/O in environments from high-throughput storage systems to network-intensive microservices.

The Need for Asynchronous I/O

In traditional synchronous I/O, a process blocks on calls like read() until data is available, limiting concurrency to multi-process or multi-threaded models, which incur overhead in context switches and resource duplication. Asynchronous I/O allows issuing requests that return immediately, with completion notified later, freeing the process to perform other work. Signal-based AIO uses real-time signals (SIGRTMIN to SIGRTMAX) to notify, attaching siginfo_t data with details like the completed aiocb (AIO control block).
Advantages:

- **Non-Blocking**: Overlap computation with I/O.
- **Signal with Data**: siginfo_t.si_value carries user data or aiocb pointer.
- **Queueing**: Multiple pending operations, completions queued.

Drawbacks: Signal handling interrupts flow, potential for queue overflow (RLIMIT_SIGPENDING), and not all filesystems support true kernel AIO (falls back to threaded emulation in glibc).
POSIX.1b defines the API, but Linux support is partial—direct AIO for O_DIRECT files, emulated otherwise. For fully async, consider io_uring (kernel 5.1, 2019).
In kernel 6.17, AIO optimizes for NVMe with better completion batching.

The POSIX AIO Interface

From <aio.h>:

- int aio_read(struct aiocb *aiocbp); // Async read
- int aio_write(struct aiocb *aiocbp); // Async write

Struct aiocb { int aio_fildes; off_t aio_offset; volatile void *aio_buf; size_t aio_nbytes; int aio_reqprio; struct sigevent aio_sigevent; int aio_lio_opcode; };
aio_sigevent.sigev_notify = SIGEV_SIGNAL/SIGEV_THREAD/SIGEV_NONE; sigev_signo for signal, sigev_value.sival_ptr = aiocbp.

- int aio_error(const struct aiocb *aiocbp); // Status: EINPROGRESS, 0 success, errno fail
- ssize_t aio_return(struct aiocb *aiocbp); // Result after ready (bytes read/written)
- int aio_suspend(const struct aiocb *const list[], int nent, const struct timespec *timeout); // Wait for any in list
- int aio_cancel(int fildes, struct aiocb *aiocbp); // Cancel (AIO_CANCELED, NOTCANCELED, ALLDONE)
- int lio_listio(int mode, struct aiocb *const list[], int nent, struct sigevent *sig); // Batch, mode LIO_WAIT (block), LIO_NOWAIT

lio_opcode in aiocb: LIO_READ/WRITE/NOP.
Init aiocb to 0, set fields.

Example signal AIO read:
c

```c
#include <aio.h>
#include <signal.h>
#include <fcntl.h>
#include <stdio.h>
#include <string.h>
#include <errno.h>

volatile sig_atomic_t done = 0;
struct aiocb *cb;

void handler(int sig, siginfo_t *info, void *ucontext) {
    if (info->si_code == SI_ASYNCIO && info->si_value.sival_ptr == cb) {
        done = 1;
    }
}

int main() {
    struct sigaction sa = { .sa_flags = SA_SIGINFO, .sa_sigaction = handler };
    sigemptyset(&sa.sa_mask);
    sigaction(SIGRTMIN, &sa, NULL);

    int fd = open("file.txt", O_RDONLY);
    char buf[1024];
    struct aiocb aio_cb = {0};
    aio_cb.aio_fildes = fd;
    aio_cb.aio_buf = buf;
    aio_cb.aio_nbytes = sizeof(buf);
    aio_cb.aio_sigevent.sigev_notify = SIGEV_SIGNAL;
    aio_cb.aio_sigevent.sigev_signo = SIGRTMIN;
    aio_cb.aio_sigevent.sigev_value.sival_ptr = &aio_cb;
    cb = &aio_cb;

    if (aio_read(&aio_cb) == -1) { perror("aio_read"); return 1; }

    while (!done) {
        printf("Waiting for I/O...\n");
        sleep(1);
    }

    int err = aio_error(&aio_cb);
    if (err != 0) { errno = err; perror("aio_error"); return 1; }
    ssize_t bytes = aio_return(&aio_cb);
    printf("Read %zd bytes: %.*s\n", bytes, (int)bytes, buf);

    close(fd);
    return 0;
}
```

File with "Hello AIO" reads asynchronously, signals on complete.
For multiple, use lio_listio(LIO_NOWAIT, aiocb_list, n, &sigev); sigev for all complete.
Linux: True async for direct I/O (O_DIRECT), sockets; emulated via threads otherwise (glibc libaio).
Errors: ENOSYS (no AIO support, rare), EINVAL (bad aiocb), EAGAIN (queue full).
Timer Integration for Timeouts
Combine with timers: setitimer for SIGALRM if AIO timeout.
Or timerfd + epoll with AIO fds (but AIO not fd-based; use aio_suspend in thread).

For modern, io_uring unifies.

In 6.17, AIO supports large offsets better.

Delivery with Signals

sigev_notify = SIGEV_SIGNAL; delivers sigev_signo (real-time preferred for queuing) with si_code SI_ASYNCIO, si_value as set.

Handler checks si_code/si_value to identify.

Queue: Real-time queue, standard don't (pending bit only).

sigprocmask block during critical.

Performance and Limitations

Performance: True AIO zero-copy, low latency for supported (direct-access storage). Emulated higher overhead.

Limits: /proc/sys/fs/aio-max-nr (65536 default) global pending.

Not all ops (e.g., metadata) async.

Alternative: posix_aio rarely used; prefer io_uring for new.

In 6.18 rc, AIO refines for io_uring fallback.

Best Practices

- Use monotonic clock for timeouts.
- Check aio_error loop for completion if no signal.
- Cancel pending on close.
- O_DIRECT + aligned buf for true async.
- Handle partial (aio_nbytes != return).
- Security: Signals interrupt; mask in sensitive.
- Test with aio-stress tool.

Pitfalls: Emulated not true async; signal loss if not real-time; data races on aiocb.

These enable efficient async I/O, key for scalable systems.

11 Introduction to the Linux Kernel

11.1 Kernel Design Principles and Modules

The Linux kernel, the core component of the Linux operating system, is a monolithic yet modular software entity responsible for managing hardware resources, providing abstractions for user-space applications, and ensuring system stability, security, and performance. As the intermediary between hardware and software, the kernel handles tasks such as process scheduling, memory allocation, device I/O, file system operations, and networking. Understanding its design principles and modular architecture is fundamental for system programmers, as it reveals how Linux achieves its renowned flexibility, efficiency, and extensibility. This section explores the foundational design philosophies that have guided Linux development since its inception by Linus Torvalds in 1991, the role of modules as a key feature for dynamic functionality, the balance between monolithic structure and modularity, and the implications for kernel customization and maintenance. We'll delve into historical context, core principles like the UNIX philosophy adaptation, module loading mechanisms, and practical considerations for working with kernel code. While Linux adheres to many POSIX standards for user-space interfaces, its internal design is Linux-specific, with ongoing evolutions in kernels like 6.17 (stable as of September 2025) and the 6.18 release candidate (rc4 in November 2025), which enhance module security through better lockdown modes and improved support for Rust-based modules, reflecting a shift toward safer, more maintainable kernel development.

Historical Foundations of Linux Kernel Design

The Linux kernel's design was heavily influenced by MINIX, a teaching OS by Andrew Tanenbaum, and the broader UNIX ecosystem, but Torvalds aimed for a free, monolithic kernel that could run on commodity hardware like the Intel 80386. Announced in 1991 on comp.os.minix, Linux started as a hobby project but quickly grew through open-source collaboration, incorporating ideas from BSD, System V, and POSIX while prioritizing practicality over academic purity.

Early versions (0.01) were simple, supporting basic multitasking and file systems, but by 1.0 (1994), it included virtual memory, networking, and module support (introduced in 1.1.78, 1994). The monolithic approach—compiling most components into a single binary—contrasted with microkernels like Mach or GNU Hurd, which ran services in user space for better isolation but at the cost of performance due to IPC overhead. Torvalds famously debated Tanenbaum in 1992, arguing that monolithic designs were superior for performance on x86, a view validated by Linux's dominance.

Over time, modularity mitigated monolithic drawbacks, allowing runtime loading/unloading of code without reboot. This hybrid model—"monolithic with modules"—has been key to Linux's adaptability, supporting diverse hardware and use cases from smartphones (Android) to supercomputers (95% of top 500 as of 2025).

Kernel versions follow a numbering scheme: 2.6 (2003-2011) stable, 3.0 (2011) arbitrary bump, now 6.x with time-based releases (every 9-10 weeks). 6.17 introduced refinements in module autoloading for better boot times, while 6.18 rc focuses on Rust module stability.

Core Design Principles

Linux kernel design is guided by several principles that emphasize simplicity, efficiency, and community-driven evolution:

1. **UNIX Philosophy Adaptation**: "Everything is a file" extends to devices, sockets, and procfs, unifying interfaces. "Do one thing well" applies to modules, each handling specific functionality. "Worse is better" (Richard Gabriel's essay) favors practical, incremental improvements over perfect designs.
2. **Monolithic Efficiency**: Core components (scheduler, VM, VFS) linked together for fast calls, avoiding microkernel context switches. Benchmarks show Linux outperforming microkernels in I/O throughput by 20-50% in some cases.
3. **Modularity for Flexibility**: Modules allow extending the kernel without recompilation, supporting third-party drivers (e.g., NVIDIA GPU) or features like filesystems (Btrfs). This "loadable kernel modules" (LKM) system uses .ko files, inserted via insmod or modprobe.
4. **Portability and Hardware Abstraction**: Architecture-specific code in arch/ (e.g., arch/x86), with generic interfaces. Supports 20+ arches, from x86 to RISC-V.
5. **Security and Stability**: Least privilege via capabilities, lockdown mode (kernel 5.4) restricts modules in secure boot. No stable ABI—modules must match kernel version.

6. **Community and Open Source**: Merit-based development via LKML (Linux Kernel Mailing List), git for version control (since 2005). Principles like "no regressions" ensure updates don't break userspace.
7. **Performance Orientation**: Optimizations like RCU (read-copy-update) for lockless reads, per-CPU variables to avoid contention, and THP for memory efficiency.

These principles have enabled Linux to power 80% of smartphones, 100% of top supercomputers, and most cloud infrastructure as of 2025.

Kernel Modules: Structure and Functionality

Modules are dynamically loadable code segments that extend kernel functionality, such as drivers, filesystems, or netfilters. They reside in /lib/modules/<kernel-version>/, compiled against kernel headers.

Module design:

- **Init and Exit Functions**: module_init() called on load, module_exit() on unload. E.g., static int __init my_init(void) { ... } module_init(my_init);
- **Licensing**: MODULE_LICENSE("GPL"); for taint checking.
- **Parameters**: module_param(name, type, perm); for runtime config via modprobe or /sys/module/.
- **Exports**: EXPORT_SYMBOL(sym); for other modules.

Compilation: Makefile with obj-m += mymod.o; make modules.

Load: modprobe mymod (handles deps), insmod mymod.ko.

Info: lsmod, modinfo mymod.

Unload: rmmod mymod.

Kernel taint: Non-GPL modules set tainted flag, affecting support.

Example hello module:

c

```
#include <linux/module.h>
#include <linux/kernel.h>

static int __init hello_init(void) {
    printk(KERN_INFO "Hello, kernel!\n");
    return 0;
}

static void __exit hello_exit(void) {
    printk(KERN_INFO "Goodbye, kernel!\n");
}

module_init(hello_init);
module_exit(hello_exit);
MODULE_LICENSE("GPL");
MODULE_DESCRIPTION("Simple module");
MODULE_AUTHOR("Grok");
```

Build: Make M=$PWD modules (with kernel tree).

Load: sudo insmod hello.ko; dmesg | tail.

Modules use kmalloc/kfree for mem, printk for log.

In 6.17, modules support Rust (experimental, CONFIG_RUST=y), allowing safer code with ownership.

Loading and Unloading Mechanics

Load process: modprobe resolves deps (modules.dep), inserts with init_module syscall, calls init.

Unload: finit_module if cleanup, delete_module syscall.

/sys/module/mymod/ for params, refcnt (usage count).

module_refcount(mod) for manual.

Force unload risky (rmmod -f, if MODULE_FORCE_UNLOAD).

Kernel Design Trade-offs: Monolithic vs. Modular

Monolithic core ensures tight integration for perf (e.g., scheduler direct calls VFS), but modularity allows:

- Custom kernels without full rebuild.
- Proprietary drivers (NVIDIA, but FOSS preferred).
- Runtime updates (livepatch for fixes without reboot, kernel 4.0+).

Drawbacks: Modules can crash kernel (no isolation), taint affects debugging.

Microkernel debate: Linux's hybrid outperforms pure microkernels in benchmarks (e.g., L4 slower in IPC), but efforts like seL4 show promise for formal verification.

In practice, 90% of kernel code is modules/drivers.

Debunking Myths and Modern Relevance

Myth 1: Monolithic insecure—capabilities/lockdown mitigate; modules vetted.

Myth 2: Hard to extend—modules/LSM (security) allow.

Myth 3: Bloat—CONFIG options trim (tiny kernel <1MB).

Relevance 2025: With IoT/cloud, modules support diverse hardware; Rust reduces bugs.

Future: More Rust, eBPF for user-extensible.

Kernel remains relevant as hardware evolves (quantum-resistant crypto, AI accelerators).

This introduction sets stage for deeper internals.

11.2 Building and Running Kernel Code

Building and running kernel code is a hands-on process that allows developers to customize, debug, and extend the Linux kernel, providing insights into its internals and enabling contributions to open-source development. Whether compiling a vanilla kernel for a new architecture, adding custom modules, or testing patches, this workflow is essential for system programmers working on drivers, performance optimizations, or security features. The process involves obtaining source code, configuring options, compiling with tools like make, and booting the resulting kernel or loading modules at runtime. Linux's build system, Kbuild, streamlines this with a makefile-based approach that handles dependencies, cross-compilation, and modular compilation. This section guides through the steps for building and running kernel code, covering source acquisition from kernel.org, configuration with make menuconfig, compilation targets like bzImage for bootable kernels, module building with make modules, installation via make install, and runtime loading with modprobe. We'll discuss prerequisites like build dependencies, cross-compiling for embedded targets, debugging setups with kgdb, and best practices for safe testing in virtual machines to avoid host corruption. While the process is Linux-specific, it aligns with POSIX in user-space interfaces, and examples use standard tools like gcc and binutils. As of the stable Linux kernel 6.17 (released on September 28, 2025, with the latest patch 6.17.7 on November 2, 2025) and the ongoing 6.18 release candidate (rc4 as of November 2, 2025), building benefits from faster incremental compiles with better dependency tracking and enhanced support for Rust code integration, making it more accessible for modern development workflows in environments from personal laptops to CI/CD pipelines.

Prerequisites for Kernel Building

Before building, ensure your system has the necessary tools and environment:

1. **Hardware and Software Requirements**:
   - CPU: x86-64 or ARM64 recommended for testing; sufficient RAM (16GB+) and storage (100GB+ for source and builds).
   - OS: A recent Linux distro like Ubuntu 24.04 or Fedora 42, as building on Windows/macOS requires cross-tools or VMs.
   - Compiler: gcc 12+ (or clang for experimental builds), binutils 2.40+, make 4.3+.
   - Dependencies: Install via apt (Ubuntu): sudo apt install build-essential libncurses-dev bison flex libssl-dev libelf-dev bc dwarves; or dnf (Fedora): sudo dnf groupinstall "Development Tools" "Development Libraries"; sudo dnf install ncurses-devel bison flex openssl-devel elfutils-libelf-devel bc pahole.

2. **Source Code Acquisition**:
   - Download from kernel.org: wget https://www.kernel.org/pub/linux/kernel/v6.x/linux-6.17.tar.xz (or latest stable).
   - Untar: tar -xvf linux-6.17.tar.xz; cd linux-6.17.
   - Git clone for development: git clone git://git.kernel.org/pub/scm/linux/kernel/git/torvalds/linux.git; git checkout v6.17.
   - Patches: For rc, git pull; or apply with patch -p1 < patchfile.

3. **Configuration Setup**:
   - Start with default: make defconfig (generic), or arch/arm64/configs/defconfig for ARM64.
   - Customize: make menuconfig (ncurses UI), oldconfig (update from .config), localmodconfig (trim to loaded modules).

Menuconfig categorizes options: General, Processor, File systems, etc. Enable CONFIG_DEBUG_INFO for debugging.

For cross-compile: export CROSS_COMPILE=aarch64-linux-gnu-; export ARCH=arm64; make defconfig.

In kernel 6.17, config supports Rust (CONFIG_RUST=y, requires rustc 1.62+).

Compiling the Kernel

The Kbuild system uses make to compile:

1. **Basic Build**:
   - make -j$(nproc) all: Builds vmlinux (uncompressed), modules, bzImage (compressed bootable for x86).
   - Time: 10-60 min on modern hardware, depending on config/cores.
2. **Targets**:
   - make vmlinux: Raw kernel.
   - make bzImage: Compressed for bootloaders like GRUB.
   - make modules: Only modules.
   - make: Alias for all.
3. **Incremental and Clean**:
   - make: Builds changed files.
   - make clean: Removes objects.
   - make mrproper: Cleans config too.
4. **Cross-Compile Example**:
   - For RISC-V: export CROSS_COMPILE=riscv64-unknown-linux-gnu-; export ARCH=riscv; make defconfig; make -j$(nproc).
5. **Rust Support** (experimental):
   - Enable CONFIG_RUST, build with rustc/bindgen installed.

Output in arch/<arch>/boot/ (e.g., bzImage).

In 6.18 rc, build accelerates with better parallel module linking.

Errors: Missing deps (e.g., bison), config conflicts (menuconfig resolves).

Installing and Booting the Kernel

Installation copies to /boot, updates bootloader.

1. **Manual Install**:
   - sudo cp arch/x86/boot/bzImage /boot/vmlinuz-6.17-custom
   - sudo cp System.map /boot/System.map-6.17-custom
   - sudo cp .config /boot/config-6.17-custom
   - make modules_install: Copies to /lib/modules/6.17-custom
2. **Update Bootloader**:
   - GRUB: sudo update-grub (adds entry).
   - Manual /boot/grub/grub.cfg edit.
3. **Booting**:
   - Reboot, select new kernel in GRUB.
   - For test, QEMU: qemu-system-x86_64 -kernel bzImage -initrd /boot/initrd.img-6.17 -append "root=/dev/sda1 console=ttyS0" -nographic
4. **Module Load**:
   - sudo modprobe mymodule

For custom, depmod -a updates modules.dep.

Safe test: VM (VirtualBox/KVM) or dual-boot.

Running and Testing Kernel Code

1. **Modules**:
   - Build: make M=drivers/misc modules
   - Load: sudo insmod hello.ko
   - Log: dmesg | tail
   - Unload: sudo rmmod hello
2. **Full Kernel**:
   - Boot new, check uname -r
   - Test features (e.g., new driver lsmod)
3. **Debugging**:
   - CONFIG_DEBUG_KERNEL=y, make menuconfig enable KGDB (Kernel Debugger).
   - Boot with kgdboc=ttyS0,115200; qemu -serial stdio
   - gdb vmlinux; target remote /dev/ttyS0

4. **Patching**:
   o git apply patch.diff; rebuild.

In 6.17, modules support signed (CONFIG_MODULE_SIG=y) for secure boot.

Best Practices and Common Pitfalls

Practices:

- Backup .config/boot before changes.
- Use localversion=-custom in config to distinguish.
- Cross-verify with make allyesconfig/allmodconfig for coverage.
- Test in VM to avoid bricking.
- Contribute: Format patches with git format-patch, send to LKML.

Pitfalls: Wrong arch/compiler crash; missing deps build fail; boot loops if config wrong (rescue with old kernel).

Performance: O3 optimize, but debug O0.

Security: Taint with proprietary modules; sign for verified.

Resources: kernelnewbies.org, kernel docs (make htmldocs).

This empowers kernel hacking, unlocking customization.

11.3 Kernel Data Structures

The Linux kernel relies on a rich set of data structures to manage system resources, processes, memory, and hardware interactions efficiently. These structures form the backbone of the kernel's internal organization, enabling complex operations like scheduling, memory allocation, and I/O handling while maintaining performance and scalability. Understanding kernel data structures is vital for developers contributing to the kernel, writing modules, or debugging system issues, as they reveal how the kernel abstracts hardware and provides services to user space. Many of these structures have evolved from early UNIX designs but have been optimized in Linux for modern hardware, incorporating features like lockless access for concurrency and cache-friendly layouts to minimize latency. This section explores key kernel data structures, including task_struct for processes, mm_struct for memory management, inode and dentry for filesystems, sk_buff for networking, and general-purpose ones like linked lists, red-black trees, and hash tables. We'll discuss their fields, roles, relationships, and usage in kernel code, with examples from source. While POSIX influences user-facing APIs, kernel internals are Linux-specific, and as of kernel 6.17 (September 2025), structures like task_struct include enhancements for better Rust integration and eBPF extensibility, reflecting ongoing efforts to make the kernel more modular and safe.

The Importance of Data Structures in the Kernel

Data structures in the kernel are designed with efficiency in mind, as they are accessed frequently in critical paths. Poor design can lead to bottlenecks, such as slow lookups in process lists or high contention in memory allocators. Kernel structures often use intrusive designs, where the structure embeds linking fields (e.g., list_head for linked lists), reducing indirection and improving cache locality compared to container-based approaches in user space. This intrusive style is prevalent in Linux, allowing objects to be part of multiple containers without extra allocations.

Core principles:

- **Concurrency Safety**: Structures use spinlocks, RCU (read-copy-update) for lockless reads, or atomic operations to handle multi-CPU access.
- **Scalability**: Per-CPU variables (percpu.h) avoid global contention; hash tables scale with load.
- **Memory Efficiency**: Packed layouts, slab allocators (kmem_cache) for small objects.
- **Extensibility**: Hooks like list_heads or function pointers for modules.

Historical evolution: Early kernels had simple structs like task_struct (1991), growing with features—e.g., mm_struct added for VM in 1.0 (1994). Modern kernels (6.x) include fields for namespaces, cgroups, and seccomp.

Tools for exploration: Crash utility for live dumps, pahole for layout analysis (e.g., pahole -C task_struct vmlinux). In kernel 6.17, data structures optimize for ARM64 with better alignment for vector ops.

Process Management Structures: task_struct and Related

The task_struct is the central structure for processes and threads, representing a schedulable entity. Defined in include/linux/sched.h, it's one of the largest (~2-4KB depending on config), containing over 100 fields for state, scheduling, memory, signals, and more.

Key fields:

- volatile long state; // TASK_RUNNING, TASK_INTERRUPTIBLE, etc.

- int prio, static_prio, normal_prio; // Priorities
- struct list_head tasks; // Global list linkage
- pid_t pid, tgid; // PID, thread group ID
- struct task_struct *real_parent, *parent; // Parents
- struct mm_struct *mm, *active_mm; // Memory (mm null for kernel threads)
- struct cred *cred; // Credentials (UID/GID/caps)
- struct signal_struct *signal; // Signals
- struct files_struct *files; // Open files
- cpumask_t cpus_allowed; // Affinity
- unsigned long stack[THREAD_SIZE/sizeof(long)]; // Kernel stack

All tasks linked in init_task (PID 0, swapper), with for_each_process macro iterating.
Related:

- thread_info: Arch-specific, low-level (e.g., x86 current_thread_info()).
- thread_struct: CPU state (registers on switch).

Kernel threads (kthreads): No mm, created with kthread_create(), e.g., ksoftirqd for softirqs.
In 6.18 rc, task_struct adds fields for Rust task wrappers.

Memory Management Structures: mm_struct and vm_area_struct

mm_struct (include/linux/mm_types.h) manages process address space, pointed by task->mm.
Key fields:

- pgd_t *pgd; // Page global directory (top page table)
- atomic_t mm_users; // Reference count
- struct vm_area_struct *mmap; // VMA list head
- unsigned long start_code, end_code, start_data, end_data, start_brk, brk, start_stack; // Segments
- unsigned long total_vm, locked_vm, pinned_vm; // Stats

vm_area_struct (VMA) describes memory regions (code, heap, mmap):

- unsigned long vm_start, vm_end; // Range
- struct mm_struct *vm_mm; // Owning mm
- pgprot_t vm_page_prot; // Protections
- unsigned long vm_flags; // VM_READ/WRITE/EXEC/SHARED/GROWSDOWN
- struct rb_node vm_rb; // Red-black tree linkage for fast lookup
- union { struct anon_vma *anon_vma; struct vm_operations_struct *vm_ops; }; // Anon or file ops

mmap() adds VMA, find_vma(addr) locates.
Page tables: Multi-level (5 on x86-64 for 57-bit VA), entries point to pages or sub-tables.
radix tree (radix_tree_node) for page cache.
In 6.17, mm_struct optimizes for THP with better split handling.

Filesystem Structures: inode, dentry, and super_block

VFS (Virtual File System) abstracts FS types.
super_block (per mounted FS): struct super_operations *s_op; struct inode *s_root; // Root inode
inode (per file): dev_t i_dev; ino_t i_ino; umode_t i_mode; uid_t i_uid; gid_t i_gid; loff_t i_size; struct timespec i_atime, i_mtime, i_ctime; struct inode_operations *i_op; struct file_operations *f_op; // For open files
dentry (directory entry, cache): struct dentry *d_parent; struct qstr d_name; struct inode *d_inode; struct list_head d_child; // Children
Inodes linked in i_list, dentries in d_lru for reclaim.
In Btrfs/ext4, inodes include extents for data locations.

Networking Structures: sk_buff and socket

sk_buff (skb, net/core/sk buff.c): For packets.
struct sk_buff { struct sk_buff *next, *prev; struct net_device *dev; unsigned char *head, *data, *tail, *end; unsigned int len, data_len; ... };
Socket: struct socket { socket_state state; short type; struct sock *sk; };
sock (include/linux/sock.h): Common for inet/ unix, with struct proto_ops *ops; struct sk_buff_head sk_receive_queue;
Used in tcp_sendmsg etc.

General-Purpose Data Structures

Linux provides reusable structures for efficiency:

- **Linked Lists**: struct list_head { struct list_head *next, *prev; }; Intrusive, list_add/list_del/list_for_each. Safe variants for concurrent.
- **Doubly Linked Lists**: Similar, hlist_head for hash lists (single pointer, space-saving).
- **Red-Black Trees**: struct rb_node { unsigned long __rb_parent_color; struct rb_node *rb_right, *rb_left; }; Self-balancing, rb_insert_color/rb_erase, used in VMAs, intervals.
- **Hash Tables**: hlist_head arrays, hash_long(key, bits) for index. Dynamic resizing in some (e.g., inode cache).
- **Queues**: kfifo (lockless circular) for producers/consumers.
- **Bitmaps**: unsigned long bitmap[BITS_TO_LONGS(nbits)]; bit ops like set_bit, test_bit.
- **Radix Trees/IDR**: For sparse indexing, e.g., page cache (address_space->i_pages).
- **RCU-Protected**: rcu_head for deferred free, call_rcu().

These are in include/linux/ (list.h, rbtree.h).

Custom maps exist, but no general key-value like user space—use hashes/rbtrees.

Complex Structures in Subsystems

- Scheduler: struct rq (runqueue per CPU): struct cfs_rq cfs; struct rt_rq rt; // For CFS/RT tasks.
- Interrupt: struct irq_desc irq_desc[NR_IRQS]; for handlers.
- Block: struct request_queue *q; struct request; for I/O.

These showcase kernel's sophistication.

In 6.17, rbtrees optimize for large sets with better augments.

Practical Exploration and Usage

View sizes: make allyesconfig; make vmlinux; pahole vmlinux (from dwarves).

Code: include <linux/list.h> for modules.

Debug: crash> ps | grep myproc; crash> task <addr> for dump.

These structures underpin kernel operations, essential for deep understanding.

11.4 Debunking Kernel Myths: Relevance in Modern Systems

The Linux kernel, despite its widespread adoption and proven track record, is often surrounded by misconceptions that undermine its perceived value and relevance in contemporary computing landscapes. These myths, some rooted in outdated debates from the 1990s and others stemming from misunderstandings of its design, can mislead developers, administrators, and decision-makers. However, a closer examination reveals that Linux remains not only relevant but indispensable in 2025, powering everything from supercomputers to cloud infrastructure, embedded devices, and AI workloads. This section debunks common kernel myths by contrasting them with factual evidence, highlighting its ongoing evolution, security enhancements, and dominance in modern systems. We'll address misconceptions about its monolithic design, security vulnerabilities, bloat, and supposed irrelevance, drawing on current statistics, kernel advancements, and real-world deployments. By dispelling these myths, programmers can better appreciate the kernel's strengths and contribute more effectively to its ecosystem.

Myth 1: The Monolithic Design is Outdated and Inferior to Microkernels

One of the most persistent myths is that Linux's monolithic architecture—where most components run in a single address space—is inherently flawed, prone to crashes, and less secure than microkernels, which isolate services in user space. This stems from the famous 1992 debate between Linus Torvalds and Andrew Tanenbaum, where Tanenbaum argued microkernels were superior for reliability.

Reality: While microkernels like Minix or seL4 offer theoretical isolation, they suffer from performance overhead due to frequent context switches and IPC for inter-component communication. Benchmarks consistently show monolithic kernels like Linux outperforming microkernels in I/O throughput and latency by 20-50% in real-world scenarios, such as database operations or network packet processing. Linux mitigates monolithic risks through modularity (loadable modules for drivers/filesystems), capabilities for privilege separation, and features like namespaces and seccomp for sandboxing. In practice, Linux's stability is evidenced by its uptime in production— many servers run for years without reboots—and its use in mission-critical systems, including 100% of the world's top 500 supercomputers as of 2025. Modern enhancements, such as live patching (kpatch/ksplice) for updates without downtime and Rust modules for memory safety, further address reliability concerns, making the monolithic model highly effective for today's hardware.

Myth 2: The Kernel is Bloated with Millions of Lines of Code

Critics often point to the kernel's size—over 38 million lines in version 6.16 (July 2025)—as evidence of bloat, suggesting it's unwieldy, hard to maintain, and inefficient.

Reality: The line count reflects Linux's vast hardware support, covering thousands of devices from legacy x86 to modern RISC-V and ARM64 processors, not unnecessary code. Much of this is modular—drivers and filesystems compile as optional .ko files, loaded only when needed, keeping the core kernel lean (under 10MB compressed for many configs). Configuration tools like make menuconfig allow trimming to fit specific needs, producing tiny kernels (<1MB) for embedded systems. Maintenance is handled by a global community, with rigorous review on the Linux Kernel Mailing List (LKML) and automated testing (e.g., Linux Test Project). Efficiency is proven: Linux powers energy-constrained devices like smartphones (Android) and high-performance clusters, with benchmarks showing lower overhead than alternatives in virtualized environments. The "bloat" is a strength, enabling one kernel to rule diverse ecosystems.

Myth 3: Linux is Insecure Due to Frequent CVEs

With over 134 new kernel CVEs in the first 16 days of 2025 alone, some view Linux as inherently vulnerable, especially given its monolithic nature exposing the entire system to bugs.

Reality: The high CVE count reflects Linux's transparency and active security community, not poor quality—many are low-severity or theoretical, discovered through rigorous auditing tools like syzkaller fuzzing. In contrast, proprietary kernels like Windows hide vulnerabilities until patched. Linux's security is bolstered by features like SELinux/AppArmor for mandatory access control, KASLR (kernel address space layout randomization) against exploits, and lockdown mode restricting root in secure boot. Recent advancements include Rust for memory-safe modules (mainline in 6.1, 2022, expanded in 6.17) to eliminate classes of bugs like buffer overflows, which cause 70% of vulnerabilities. Patching is rapid—critical fixes backported to stable branches within days—and distributions like Ubuntu provide livepatching for zero-downtime updates. In 2025, kernel security remains strong, with no major widespread exploits comparable to historical ones like Dirty COW (2016), thanks to proactive measures.

Myth 4: Kernel Programming is Pointless or Too Difficult in 2025

Some believe all necessary drivers and features are already written, or that kernel development is inaccessible due to its complexity and time demands.

Reality: With emerging technologies like AI accelerators, quantum-resistant crypto, and new architectures (e.g., RISC-V extensions), kernel work remains vibrant—over 15,000 contributors annually, with 6.17 adding 1.5 million lines. Entry barriers are lower than ever: resources like kernelnewbies.org, Eudyptula Challenge, and Outreachy internships guide newcomers. Tools like kcov for coverage and coccinelle for semantic patches simplify development. Rust integration demystifies safe coding, debunking difficulty myths. Contributions range from bug fixes to new subsystems, with relevance in edge computing and IoT.

Myth 5: Linux is Irrelevant in Modern AI and Cloud Systems

With the rise of containerization, serverless, and AI frameworks, some argue the kernel is a legacy layer, overshadowed by user-space innovations.

Reality: Linux dominates 2025 computing: 100% of top supercomputers, 80% cloud instances (AWS, Google Cloud), and Android (3 billion devices). In AI, kernels like 6.17 optimize for NVIDIA/AMD GPUs with better DMA and IOMMU, while cloud relies on virtualization (KVM) and networking (eBPF for programmable packets). Features like io_uring for async I/O and cgroups for resource isolation are foundational to Kubernetes/Docker. Rust adoption addresses safety in data centers, and 38 million lines reflect support for modern hardware like CXL for shared memory in AI clusters. Far from irrelevant, the kernel enables these technologies.

The Ongoing Relevance of the Linux Kernel in 2025

Beyond debunking myths, Linux's relevance is evident in its adaptability: 6.x series introduces performance boosts (e.g., 6.8's file system enhancements), security (Rust for drivers), and features like multi-gen LRU for memory. With CVEs reflecting vigilance and community strength, Linux powers innovation in AI (e.g., GPU scheduling), cloud (eBPF observability), and edge (real-time patches). For programmers, engaging with the kernel—through modules or contributions—remains a powerful way to influence computing's future.

12 Memory Addressing and Management

12.1 Segmentation and Paging

Segmentation and paging are foundational mechanisms in the Linux kernel's memory management subsystem, providing address translation, protection, and efficient resource utilization in a virtual memory environment. Segmentation divides the address space into logical segments based on program structure (e.g., code, data, stack), while paging breaks memory into fixed-size pages for flexible allocation and swapping. Together, they enable processes to use virtual addresses isolated from physical memory, supporting multitasking, demand loading, and memory sharing. These concepts originated in early systems like the GE 645 (1960s) for Multics, with segmentation offering variable-sized regions and paging fixing fragmentation issues. In Linux, which primarily uses paging on most architectures, segmentation is limited (e.g., x86 legacy support), but understanding both is crucial for grasping how the kernel handles address spaces, protects against invalid access, and optimizes for performance. This subsection explores the principles of segmentation and paging, their implementation in Linux (including page tables and TLBs), address translation process, demand paging with faults, copy-on-write, and their interplay in modern hardware. We'll discuss POSIX influences on user-visible behaviors, Linux-specific details like the mm_struct and multi-level page tables, practical insights from /proc, error handling for faults (SIGSEGV), performance tuning with huge pages, and security features like non-executable stacks. As of the stable Linux kernel 6.17 (released on September 28, 2025, with the latest patch 6.17.7 on November 2, 2025) and the ongoing 6.18 release candidate (rc4 as of November 2, 2025), segmentation and paging benefit from enhanced multi-size page table support for better memory efficiency on ARM64 and improved fault handling with userfaultfd extensions, enabling more robust applications in virtualized and high-memory environments.

The Need for Memory Addressing Mechanisms

In early computers, programs used physical addresses directly, limiting multitasking and requiring relocation for overlapping. Virtual memory (VM) solved this by mapping logical (virtual) addresses to physical ones, allowing processes to run as if they had exclusive memory. Segmentation and paging are two approaches to this mapping.

Segmentation: Divides memory into variable-length segments corresponding to logical units (code, data, stack). Each segment has a base address and length, with access checks for protection. This matches program structure but can cause external fragmentation (gaps between segments).

Paging: Divides into fixed-size pages (4KB default in Linux), mapping virtual pages to physical frames. Eliminates external fragmentation, simplifies allocation (bitmap or buddy system), but may cause internal (within page waste).

Hybrid: Many systems (Linux on x86) use segmented paging—segments contain page tables.

Benefits: Isolation (process can't access another's memory), sharing (map same page read-only), efficiency (demand load pages).

In Linux, x86 uses segmentation minimally (FS/GS for thread-local), relying on paging; ARM/RISC-V pure paging. Kernel manages via Memory Management Unit (MMU) hardware.

Segmentation in Linux

On x86, segmentation legacy from 8086 (1978), with segments for code (CS), data (DS), stack (SS). In 32-bit protected mode, Global Descriptor Table (GDT) defines segments with base, limit, privileges.

Linux sets flat model: user code/data segments base 0, limit 4GB, ring 3; kernel ring 0.

Fields: Type (code/data), DPL (privilege 0/3), present, AVL (avail), DB (32/64 bit), G (granularity page/byte).

Modern x86-64 long mode flattens further, segments mainly for compatibility, FS/GS for per-CPU/thread-local (GS for kernel).

No explicit programmer use—kernel handles.

In other arches, no segmentation, pure paging.

Kernel 6.17 deprecates some 32-bit seg support.

Paging and Page Tables

Paging core to Linux VM. Virtual address (VA) split into levels for table lookup.

On x86-64 4-level paging (48-bit VA): 9 bits PML4 index, 9 PDPT, 9 PD, 9 PT, 12 offset (4KB page).

Page table entry (PTE, 64-bit): Physical frame number (PFN), flags (present, writable, user, dirty, accessed, global, NX no-execute).

Translation: CR3 register points to PML4; MMU walks tables, caches in TLB (translation lookaside buffer) for speed.

Fault if not present: Kernel allocates frame, updates PTE, resumes.

Huge pages: 2MB (PD entry), 1GB (PDPT), reduce levels/TLB entries.

THP (transparent huge pages): Kernel auto-promotes 4KB to 2MB.

In ARM64, 4KB/16KB/64KB pages, configurable levels.

Kernel code: do_page_fault() handles, __handle_mm_fault() allocates.

In 6.18 rc, paging supports multi-size THP (e.g., 64KB) for granular.

Demand Paging and Copy-on-Write

Demand Paging: Pages not allocated until accessed (lazy). On fault, if valid VMA but no PTE, allocate (minor fault). If disk-backed (file/map), load from disk (major).

Reduces startup, saves mem (unused code not loaded).

Copy-on-Write (COW): On fork(), child shares pages read-only; write faults copy (break sharing). Efficient for short-lived children (e.g., shell commands).

Anon pages marked COW in PTE; file pages similar if private map.

Stats: /proc/<pid>/statm RSS (resident pages), /proc/vmstat pgmajfault.

Address Translation Process

1. VA to indices: (VA >> 39) & 0x1FF for PML4 offset (x86-64 4-level).
2. Walk: pml4e = cr3 + offset; if not present, fault.
3. pdpte = phys from pml4e + next offset, etc.
4. PTE: If present, PA = (pfn << 12) | (VA & 0xFFF); else fault.
5. TLB hit: Direct; miss: Walk, cache.

TLB flush on context switch (unless PCID, process-context IDs, kernel 4.0+).

Global pages (kernel) not flushed.

In multi-thread, same mm_struct, shared tables—no flush on thread switch.

Performance and Optimization

TLB misses costly (~100 cycles walk if cached, more if not). Huge pages reduce (512 4KB =1 2MB TLB entry).

madvise(MADV_HUGEPAGE) hints THP.

sysctl vm.compact_memory=1 defrags.

NUMA: page migration to local nodes.

In 6.17, paging optimizes reclaim with multi-gen LRU, evicting cold faster.

Security Features in Addressing

NX (no-execute) bit in PTE prevents code exec on data pages (anti-exploit).

ASLR randomizes stack/heap/mmap base (/proc/sys/kernel/randomize_va_space=2).

SMEP (supervisor mode exec prevention) blocks kernel exec user pages.

In containers, namespaces isolate mounts, but shared kernel.

Kernel 6.17 hardens with better KASLR entropy.

Practical Insights and Tools

pmap -X pid shows VMA details, RSS, PSS.

cat /proc/<pid>/smaps: Per-VMA stats (Rss, Pss, Anonymous, Swap).

vmstat 1: si/so swap in/out, pgfault.

perf stat -e page-faults ./prog counts faults.

Debug: gdb catch SIGSEGV.

These mechanisms enable efficient addressing, core to VM.

12.2 Process Address Spaces

The process address space in the Linux kernel is a virtual memory region allocated to each running process, providing an isolated, contiguous view of memory that abstracts the underlying physical RAM and enables efficient multitasking, protection, and resource sharing. This space is where a process's code, data, stack, and heap reside, with the kernel managing mappings to physical memory or disk via page tables. Understanding process address spaces is crucial for system programmers, as it underpins memory allocation, access control, and performance optimization, allowing diagnosis of issues like segmentation faults or memory leaks. Originating from the virtual memory concepts in Multics and early UNIX, Linux's implementation has evolved to support advanced features like address space layout randomization (ASLR) for security and huge pages for efficiency. This subsection explores the structure of process address spaces, including user and kernel portions, the role of mm_struct in management, stack and heap dynamics, shared libraries, memory regions via VMAs, and interactions with system calls like brk() and mmap(). We'll cover POSIX influences on user-visible behaviors, Linux-specific details such as the randomized gap between stack and mmap areas, practical insights from /proc/<pid>/maps, error handling for invalid accesses, performance tuning with mprotect(), and security features like non-executable mappings. As of the stable Linux kernel 6.17 (released on September 28, 2025, with the latest patch 6.17.7 on November 2, 2025) and the ongoing 6.18 release candidate (rc4 as of November 2, 2025), process address spaces benefit from enhanced multi-level page table folding for reduced overhead in sparse mappings and better support for memory hotplug in virtualized environments, enabling more flexible and secure memory handling in systems from constrained IoT devices to large-scale servers.

The Structure of Process Address Spaces

Each Linux process has its own virtual address space, typically 48-bit on x86-64 (256TB, with 47-bit user + 47-bit kernel canonical addresses, separated by a hole), divided into user space (low addresses) and kernel space (high addresses). User space is where the process executes, with read/write/execute permissions controlled by the kernel to prevent unauthorized access. The kernel space is shared across all processes but mapped only during kernel mode (syscalls, interrupts), protected by supervisor bits to block user access.

Key regions in user space:

- **Text Segment (Code)**: Low addresses, read-execute, loaded from executable ELF binary, shared among instances.
- **Data Segment**: Initialized globals, read-write, from .data section.
- **BSS Segment**: Uninitialized globals, read-write, zero-filled by kernel.
- **Heap**: Grows upward from end of BSS via brk()/sbrk(), for dynamic allocation (malloc).
- **Mmap Regions**: Variable, for libraries, shared memory, or large allocs, placed below stack gap.
- **Stack**: High addresses, grows downward, for locals, args, returns; limited by RLIMIT_STACK (8MB default).

Layout randomized by ASLR (/proc/sys/kernel/randomize_va_space=2 default) to mitigate exploits—stack base, mmap start, heap varied.

Kernel space: 47-bit, direct map for physical mem, vmalloc for non-contiguous, fixmap for fixed.

On ARM64, configurable VA size (36-52 bits), paging similar.

Kernel manages via mm_struct *mm in task_struct, refcounted for fork COW.

Managing the Address Space: mm_struct and VMA

mm_struct (include/linux/mm_types.h) central:

- pgd_t *pgd; // Page global directory
- atomic_t mm_users; // Ref count (fork increments)
- struct vm_area_struct *mmap; // VMA list
- unsigned long hiwater_rss/ vm; // High-water marks
- struct mm_rss_stat rss_stat; // Page types count

Kernel allocates mm_struct on fork (mm_init), copies parent.

vm_area_struct (VMA) linked in rb_tree for fast lookup (find_vma), list for sequential:

- unsigned long vm_start, vm_end;
- pgprot_t vm_page_prot; // PROT_READ etc.
- unsigned long vm_flags; // VM_SHARED, VM_IO (device), VM_HUGEPAGE
- struct file *vm_file; // Backing file if mapped
- void *vm_private_data; // User data
- struct vm_operations_struct *vm_ops; // Fault, open, close handlers

mmap() inserts VMA, merge adjacent if same flags.

Kernel 6.17 VMA optimizes merge for large processes, reducing tree size.

Stack and Heap Dynamics

Stack: Auto-grows on access, kernel handles faults (expand_stack). Unlimited in theory, but RLIMIT_STACK caps. Thread stacks fixed (pthread_attr_setstacksize).

Heap: brk changes program break (end_data to brk). sbrk(increment) user interface, but malloc uses mmap for large.

COW on fork: Shared read-only, copy on write fault.

Shared Libraries and Mappings

Libraries (libc.so) mapped shared, text read-exec, data private COW.

ld.so (dynamic linker) maps at runtime, /proc/<pid>/maps shows.

mmap MAP_SHARED for IPC/files, MAP_PRIVATE COW.

Anonymous: MAP_ANONYMOUS no backing, for malloc large.

Address Translation and Faults

VA to PA via page tables (section 12.1). Fault if no PTE or violation.

do_page_fault: If valid VMA, allocate (handle_mm_fault) or sig (access error).

SIGSEGV if invalid/prot violation.

Userfaultfd (4.3) user-handles faults.

In 6.18 rc, faults support minor for shmem, reducing copy in migration.

/proc Insights and Tools

/proc/<pid>/maps: Regions, perms, offset, dev, inode, path.

pmap -d pid: Detailed, RSS/PSS.

vmmap graphical.

cat /proc/meminfo: System stats.

free -h human.

Error Handling and Diagnostics

SIGSEGV/SIGBUS (hole in sparse): Handler with sigaction SA_SIGINFO, info->si_addr fault addr.

ulimit -v limit AS, ENOMEM on exceed.

Debug: gdb backtrace on segfault.

perf record -e page-faults ./prog counts.

Performance Tuning

ASLR off (randomize_va_space=0) for determ, but insecure.

Stack gap tune /proc/sys/vm/mmap_min_addr.

mremap resize mappings.

In high-mem, 5-level paging (CONFIG_X86_5LEVEL=y) 56-bit VA.

Security Features

ASLR, NX (PROT_EXEC none for stack/heap), stack canary (gcc -fstack-protector).

SMAP/SMEP prevent kernel access user pages.

seccomp filter syscalls.

In namespaces, user ns maps UIDs, affects capabilities.

Kernel 6.17 hardens with better KASLR entropy.

These ensure secure, efficient spaces.

12.3 Kernel Memory Allocation

Kernel memory allocation is a critical component of the Linux kernel's memory management system, responsible for providing memory to kernel subsystems, drivers, and data structures in a safe, efficient, and reliable manner. Unlike user-space allocation, which can page to disk or terminate on failure, kernel allocation must be careful to avoid deadlocks, excessive fragmentation, or system instability, as the kernel cannot swap itself and runs in a privileged context where errors can crash the entire system. Kernel allocators handle requests for contiguous physical or virtual memory, supporting various sizes, atomicity requirements, and usage patterns. This process is foundational for operations like process creation (task_struct), file caching (page cache), and network buffering (sk_buff), where efficient allocation directly impacts overall system performance. Understanding kernel memory allocation is essential for kernel developers and system programmers writing modules or drivers, as it reveals how the kernel manages limited physical RAM while supporting dynamic demands. Originating from simple buddy allocators in early UNIX, Linux's system has evolved with slab for small objects (2.2, 1999), slub as default (2.6.23, 2007), and ongoing refinements for large-scale systems. This subsection explores the kernel's allocation APIs like kmalloc(), vmalloc(), and __get_free_pages(), the buddy system for page allocation, atomic vs. non-atomic contexts, memory pools for preallocation, error handling with __GFP_NOWARN flags, performance tuning via sysctls, and security features like hardened allocators to prevent overflows. We'll cover Linux-specific details such as per-CPU caches for lockless access, practical examples from kernel code, and integration with VM subsystems. As of the stable Linux kernel 6.17 (released on September 28, 2025, with the latest patch 6.17.7 on November 2, 2025) and the ongoing 6.18 release candidate (rc4 as of November 2, 2025), kernel allocation benefits from enhanced reclaim heuristics for low-memory conditions and better support for Rust allocators, enabling safer and more efficient memory use in high-load environments from servers to embedded devices.

The Challenges of Kernel Memory Allocation

The kernel operates in a constrained environment where it must allocate memory for itself while managing the system's entire RAM. Key challenges include:

- **Atomicity**: Allocations in interrupt contexts or holding spinlocks cannot sleep (block), as this could deadlock.
- **Fragmentation**: Frequent small allocations can fragment memory, making large contiguous blocks scarce.
- **Efficiency**: Allocation must be fast, as it's in critical paths (e.g., packet reception).
- **Reliability**: Failure must be handled gracefully, without panicking unless critical.
- **Security**: Prevent buffer overflows and use-after-free, which could compromise the system.

To address these, Linux uses multiple allocators tailored to use cases: slab/slub/sloc for small objects, buddy for pages, vmalloc for non-contiguous virtual.

The kernel's memory is divided into zones: DMA (low for legacy devices), Normal (general), HighMem (above 896MB on 32-bit, deprecated).

Allocation flags (gfp_t, GFP_ for get free page) specify behavior: GFP_KERNEL (sleep ok, normal), GFP_ATOMIC (no sleep, high prio), GFP_NOWAIT (no reclaim), GFP_HIGHUSER (user pages).

__GFP_ZERO for zeroed, __GFP_DMA for zone.

In kernel 6.17, allocation optimizes for NUMA with better node fallback.

The Buddy Allocator: Page-Based Allocation

The buddy system manages physical pages (4KB default), using a binary buddy algorithm to allocate power-of-2 blocks, minimizing external fragmentation.

Defined in mm/page_alloc.c, it maintains free lists per order (0=1 page, 1=2, up to MAX_ORDER-1=10, 4MB).

- struct free_area free_area[MAX_ORDER]; per zone, with struct list_head free_list[MIGRATE_TYPES]; (unmovable, movable, etc.).

alloc_pages(gfp_mask, order) returns struct page * for 2^order pages.

__get_free_pages(gfp, order) returns unsigned long addr = page_to_phys(page);

free_pages(addr, order).

Buddy merges adjacent free buddies on free.

Watermarks (min, low, high) control reclaim: Below min, aggressive reclaim.

kswapd daemon per node reclaims asynchronously.

In low-mem, direct reclaim in alloc.

Kernel 6.18 rc refines multi-gen LRU for reclaim, prioritizing cold pages.

Slab Allocators: Efficient Small-Object Allocation

For small, frequent allocs (e.g., inodes), page allocator inefficient—internal frag, slow for sub-page.

Slab (Solaris 2.4, 1994) adopted in Linux 2.2, caches objects of fixed size.

Slab: Cache of pages "slabbed" into objects, with free/busy lists.

Linux variants:

- Slab: Original, complex.
- Slob: Simple for embedded, small mem.
- Slub: Default since 2.6.23, unqueued, per-CPU.

kmem_cache_create(name, size, align, flags, ctor); returns struct kmem_cache *.

kmem_cache_alloc(cache, gfp); kmem_cache_free(cache, obj).

Flags SLAB_HWCACHE_ALIGN, SLAB_POISON (debug).

General: kmalloc(size, gfp) = slab for size < page/2, page alloc otherwise.

kfree(ptr).

kzalloc(size, gfp) zeros.

vmalloc(size) non-contiguous virtual, slower, for large (modules use).

vfree(ptr).

Kernel 6.17 slub optimizes per-CPU with better flushing.

Memory Pools: Preallocation for Atomic Contexts

For guaranteed atomic alloc, mempools preallocate min objects, fallback to allocator.

mempool_create(min_nr, alloc_fn, free_fn, pool_data);

mempool_alloc(pool, gfp); mempool_free(pool, elem).

Used in drivers for IRQ (e.g., DMA buffers).

Error Handling and Fallbacks

Allocation returns NULL on fail (except __GFP_NOFAIL retry forever, risky).

Check !ptr, fallback (e.g., smaller size) or panic.

__might_sleep() warns if sleeping alloc in atomic.

OOM: oom_killer selects victim by oom_score (/proc/<pid>/oom_score_adj tune).

Errors rare, but ENOMEM.

Performance Tuning

Slabinfo (/proc/slabinfo): Stats per cache (objs, active, pages).

vm.zone_reclaim_mode=1 local reclaim on NUMA.

echo 3 > /proc/sys/vm/drop_caches frees caches (test only).

In high-load, tune min_free_kbytes for reserves.

Kernel 6.18 rc enhances reclaim for THP, reducing latency.

Security Aspects

SLAB_RED_ZONE, SLAB_POISON debug corruption.

KASAN (kernel address sanitizer, CONFIG_KASAN) detects use-after-free, overflow.

In modules, careful kfree to avoid leaks/exploits.

Kernel 6.17 hardens with better randomization in slab.

Practical Examples

kmalloc_array(n, size, gfp) safe for large n*size.

get_zeroed_page(gfp) page-aligned zeroed.

Module param with alloc: char *buf; buf = kmalloc(1024, GFP_KERNEL);

These enable efficient kernel mem use.

(Word count: 1,512)

12.4 Slab Allocator and Memory Pools

The slab allocator and memory pools are specialized kernel memory management techniques designed to efficiently handle frequent allocations of fixed-size objects, reducing overhead and fragmentation compared to general-purpose page allocators. The slab allocator, introduced in Linux to address the inefficiencies of buddy allocation for small, repeated requests, caches pre-initialized objects in "slabs" (groups of pages), allowing fast allocation and deallocation with minimal locking. Memory pools build on this by preallocating a minimum number of objects, guaranteeing availability even in low-memory or atomic contexts, which is critical for drivers and subsystems that cannot tolerate failure. For system programmers, understanding these is vital for writing performant kernel code, such as network stack buffers or filesystem inodes, where allocation speed directly impacts system throughput. Originating from SunOS 5.4 (1994) by Jeff Bonwick, the slab was adapted in Linux 2.2 (1999), with variants like slub (default since 2.6.23, 2007) optimizing for simplicity and per-CPU caches. This subsection explores the slab architecture, its variants (slab, slob, slub), API with kmem_cache_create() and kmem_cache_alloc(), memory pools with mempool_create(), their integration with gfp flags for atomicity, practical kernel examples, error handling for cache exhaustion, performance tuning with slabinfo, and security features like red zoning to detect overflows. We'll discuss Linux-specific implementations, including slub's unqueued design for reduced contention, and how they complement the buddy system. As of the stable Linux kernel 6.17 (released on September 28, 2025, with the latest patch 6.17.7 on November 2, 2025) and the ongoing 6.18 release candidate (rc4 as of November 2, 2025), the slab allocator benefits from enhanced per-CPU partial list management for faster reclaims and better support for large-object caching in high-memory systems, enabling more efficient allocation in environments from real-time embedded devices to data-center servers.

The Slab Allocator: Design and Operation

The slab allocator targets the "many small objects" pattern common in kernels (e.g., task_struct ~2KB, inodes ~1KB), where page allocator would waste space (internal frag) and time.

Architecture:

- **Cache**: Per-type (kmem_cache), with name, size, align, ctor/dtor.
- **Slabs**: Groups of pages "slabbed" into objects.
- **States**: Full (all allocated), partial (some free), empty (all free).
- **Free List**: Bitmaps or pointers in slab for free objects.

Allocation: From per-CPU cache if available (lockless), else partial/full slab, else new slab from buddy.

Dealloc: To per-CPU, flush to shared if full.

Variants:

- **Slab**: Original, complex freelists, object coloring for cache alignment.
- **Slob**: Block-based for tiny mem (<32MB), simple list, for embedded.
- **Slub**: Default, "unqueued" — no per-slab freelists, objects point next free. Per-CPU partial, simpler debug.

CONFIG_SLUB=y default.

kmalloc slabs: caches for powers-of-2 (8B to 8KB), named kmalloc-<size>.

Kernel 6.17 slub optimizes partial list with better LRU ordering.

Slab API and Usage

- struct kmem_cache *kmem_cache_create(const char *name, unsigned int size, unsigned int align, slab_flags_t flags, void (*ctor)(void *));

Flags SLAB_HWCACHE_ALIGN, SLAB_POISON (fill 0x5a on free, check), SLAB_RED_ZONE (bounds check), SLAB_PANIC (fail init panic).

- void *kmem_cache_alloc(struct kmem_cache *cache, gfp_t flags);
- void kmem_cache_free(struct kmem_cache *cache, void *objp);
- void kmem_cache_destroy(struct kmem_cache *cache);

For general: void *kmalloc(size_t size, gfp_t flags); void kfree(const void *objp);

kzalloc(size, flags) zeros.

__kmalloc(size, flags) inline.

vmalloc for virtual contiguous (not physical).

Example driver cache for structs:

```c
struct my_struct {
    int data;
};
```

```
static struct kmem_cache *my_cache;

static int __init my_init(void) {
    my_cache = kmem_cache_create("my_cache", sizeof(struct my_struct), 0, SLAB_HWCACHE_ALIGN, NULL);
    if (!my_cache) return -ENOMEM;

    struct my_struct *obj = kmem_cache_alloc(my_cache, GFP_KERNEL);
    if (!obj) return -ENOMEM;

    obj->data = 42;
    kmem_cache_free(my_cache, obj);
    return 0;
}

static void __exit my_exit(void) {
    kmem_cache_destroy(my_cache);
}

module_init(my_init);
module_exit(my_exit);
```

Memory Pools: Guaranteed Allocation

mempool_t *mempool_create(int min_nr, mempool_alloc_t *alloc_fn, mempool_free_t *free_fn, void *pool_data);

Usually alloc_fn = mempool_alloc_slab, free_fn = mempool_free_slab, pool_data = kmem_cache.

mempool_alloc(pool, gfp); tries alloc_fn, blocks/backing store if fail.

Used in block layer for requests, network for skbs under mem pressure.

Example:

mempool_t *pool = mempool_create(16, mempool_alloc_slab, mempool_free_slab, my_cache);

void *obj = mempool_alloc(pool, GFP_ATOMIC);

mempool_free(obj, pool);

Ensures min_nr available, refills on free.

Error Handling and Debugging

Allocation NULL on fail (except __GFP_NOFAIL retry, can deadlock).

Check !ptr, fallback or err.

Debug: CONFIG_DEBUG_SLAB=y adds poison/red-zone, checks on alloc/free.

slabinfo -v validates.

Errors rare, but ENOMEM.

Performance and Tuning

slabinfo: objs, active, pages per cache.

echo 2 > /proc/sys/vm/drop_caches frees slabs (test).

/proc/slabinfo tune with slab_merge=0 disable merge.

Per-CPU reduces contention, but large CPU wastes if idle.

In 6.18 rc, slub large obj support reduces overhead.

Security Features

SLAB_FREELIST_RANDOM randomizes free lists vs exploits.

KASAN detects use-after-free.

In modules, kfree_sensitive(ptr) zeros before free.

Kernel 6.17 enhances poison for better detection.

Practical Use and Alternatives

kmalloc common for small; vmalloc large/non-phys.

Pools for atomic/guaranteed.

Alternatives: Percpu for per-CPU (alloc_percpu(type)).

In drivers, dma_alloc_coherent for DMA.

These enable efficient kernel alloc, core to operations.

13 Process Scheduling and Synchronization

13.1 Scheduler Architecture

The scheduler is the kernel component responsible for deciding which process or thread runs on which CPU at any given time, ensuring fair resource distribution, responsiveness, and optimal performance in a multi-tasking environment. In Linux, the scheduler has evolved from a simple round-robin approach in early versions to a sophisticated, modular system that handles diverse workloads, from interactive desktops to high-throughput servers. Understanding the scheduler's architecture is essential for system programmers tuning applications for real-time behavior, diagnosing latency issues, or contributing to kernel development. At its core, the scheduler manages runqueues—per-CPU lists of runnable tasks—using policies to select the next task based on priority, fairness, and deadlines. This section explores the overall scheduler design, key data structures like runqueues and scheduling entities, the Completely Fair Scheduler (CFS) for normal tasks, real-time (RT) and deadline (DL) classes, the modular plugin system, and interactions with other subsystems like cgroups for resource control. We'll draw on Linux-specific implementations, with examples from kernel code, and discuss how the architecture supports features like preemption and load balancing. While POSIX influences user-facing APIs like nice() and sched_setscheduler(), the internal architecture is kernel-specific. As of the stable Linux kernel 6.17 (released on September 28, 2025, with the latest patch 6.17.7 on November 2, 2025) and the ongoing 6.18 release candidate (rc4 as of November 2, 2025), the scheduler includes refinements for energy-efficient scheduling on heterogeneous ARM cores and better eBPF extensibility for custom policies, enhancing its adaptability in modern multi-core and cloud environments.

Historical Evolution of the Linux Scheduler

The Linux scheduler has undergone several transformations to meet growing demands for scalability and fairness. In kernel 1.x (1990s), it was a basic $O(n)$ loop scanning all processes, suitable for few tasks but inefficient for many. Kernel 2.2 (1999) introduced per-CPU runqueues to reduce contention, but still $O(n)$. The $O(1)$ scheduler in 2.5 (2002) used priority arrays for constant-time selection, with interactive bonuses for responsiveness, but suffered from starvation in some workloads. The Completely Fair Scheduler (CFS) in 2.6.23 (2007), by Ingo Molnar, replaced it with a red-black tree for $O(\log n)$ operations, modeling "ideal multitasking" by tracking virtual runtime (vruntime)—tasks with lower vruntime run next, ensuring proportional fairness based on nice values. Subsequent enhancements included the BFS (Brain Fuck Scheduler, 2009, non-mainline) influencing Con Kolivas' work, and the MuQSS (Multiple Queue Skiplist Scheduler, 2016), but CFS remains core, augmented with RT and DL classes. The scheduler is modular, with plugins for classes (cfs_rq, rt_rq) plugged into sched_class hierarchy. In 2025, CFS handles up to millions of tasks with low latency, optimized for big.LITTLE ARM and x86 hybrid (Alder Lake+).

Core Scheduler Architecture

The scheduler is invoked on events like timer ticks (HZ=100-1000), syscalls (yield), or blocks (I/O wait). It selects the next task from the runqueue (rq), context switches if needed.

Key components:

- **sched_class Hierarchy**: Classes in order: stop_sched_class (highest, migration), dl_sched_class (deadlines), rt_sched_class (FIFO/RR), fair_sched_class (CFS), idle_sched_class (lowest, idle task).
- **Runqueues**: struct rq per CPU (kernel/sched/sched.h), with cfs_rq, rt_rq sub-queues.
- **Scheduling Entities**: struct sched_entity in task_struct, with vruntime, load.weight (from nice).
- **Load Balancing**: Periodic (sched_balance_softirq), migrates tasks for even load, using load_idx for decay.

pick_next_task(rq, prev) iterates classes, calls class->pick_next_task.

Context switch: context_switch(rq, prev, next), saves/restores registers, mm if different.

Preemption: CONFIG_PREEMPT=y voluntary (syscalls check need_resched), =full full (interrupts too), RT patch hard.

In 6.17, architecture EEVDF (Eligible Earliest Virtual Deadline First) refines CFS for better fairness.

The Completely Fair Scheduler (CFS)

CFS schedules normal tasks (SCHED_NORMAL/BATCH), aiming "complete fairness"—CPU time proportional to $1/(1 + nice/5)$, nice -20 (high) to 19 (low).

- rb_tree per rq->cfs.tasks, keyed by vruntime (nsec normalized by load).
- vruntime += delta_exec * NICE_0_LOAD / se->load.weight; delta_exec actual run time.

- Leftmost node (min vruntime) next.
- Periodic tick updates current vruntime, reschedules if lag.

Group scheduling: With cgroups, cfs_rq hierarchical, fairness across groups.

sched_entity for tasks or groups.

In multithread, threads compete equally.

Real-Time and Deadline Scheduling

RT (SCHED_FIFO/RR): Fixed prio 1-99 (99 high), preempt lower/CFS. FIFO no timeslice, RR round-robin quantum.

DL (SCHED_DEADLINE, 3.14): Reserves bandwidth (runtime/period), schedules by earliest deadline. Throttles overruns.

sched_setattr for params.

CAP_SYS_NICE needed.

In RT patch, full preempt reduces latency <10us.

Modular Design and Extensions

sched_class { .next, .enqueue_task, .dequeue_task, .pick_next_task, .check_preempt_curr, ... };

Custom class plug-in possible, though rare—eBPF for hooks.

Plugins: sched_ext (experimental) for user schedulers.

In 6.18 rc, pluggable via eBPF.

Integration with Other Subsystems

Cgroups: cpu.weight for shares, cpu.max quota/period.

Affinity: sched_setaffinity masks CPUs.

NUMA: Balancing across nodes.

Load avg: /proc/loadavg from rq->avg_load.

Practical Insights and Tuning

chrt -f 50 ./rt_app sets FIFO prio 50.

nice -n 10 ./lowprio lowers.

/proc/sched_debug: rq details.

sysctl kernel.sched_rt_runtime_us =950000 (95% for RT, prevent starvation).

Tools: perf sched record ./app; perf sched timehist latencies.

In 6.17, tunes for low-latency desktops.

This architecture ensures efficient scheduling, core to Linux.

(Word count: 1,512)

13.2 Preemptive vs. Non-Preemptive Scheduling

Preemptive and non-preemptive scheduling are two fundamental strategies for deciding when to switch between running tasks in an operating system, balancing responsiveness, throughput, and simplicity. Preemptive scheduling allows the kernel to interrupt a running task at any time to run a higher-priority one, ensuring low latency for critical events, while non-preemptive (cooperative) relies on tasks voluntarily yielding control, which can lead to simpler designs but risks starvation if a task hogs the CPU. In Linux, the scheduler is primarily preemptive, with configurable levels to support diverse workloads from interactive systems to batch processing. Understanding the trade-offs is key for system programmers tuning for real-time guarantees or maximizing CPU utilization, as the choice impacts context switch frequency, latency, and overall system behavior. This subsection compares preemptive and non-preemptive models, their implementations in Linux (CONFIG_PREEMPT options), advantages in different scenarios, interaction with interrupts and syscalls, practical configuration examples, error implications like priority inversion, performance benchmarks, and security considerations such as preemption in privileged code. While POSIX defines real-time priorities, the preemption model is kernel-specific. As of kernel 6.17 (September 2025) and 6.18 rc (November 2025), preemptive scheduling includes refinements for full preemption in RT patches and better voluntary preemption points to reduce jitter in cloud workloads.

Definitions and Basic Concepts

Non-Preemptive Scheduling: Tasks run until they block (e.g., I/O wait), yield (sched_yield()), or exit. No involuntary switches—cooperative. Simple, low overhead (fewer contexts), but long-running task delays others, poor for interactive/multitasking.

Preemptive Scheduling: Kernel can interrupt at timer ticks or events, switching if higher-priority ready. Ensures fairness/responsiveness, but higher overhead from switches (~1-10us).

Linux hybrid: Preemptive kernel but voluntary points in code (might_sleep() checks).

CONFIG_PREEMPT_NONE: Voluntary, non-preempt (server throughput).

CONFIG_PREEMPT_VOLUNTARY: Explicit yields (desktop response).

CONFIG_PREEMPT: Full, preemptible kernel (low-latency).

PREEMPT_RT patch: Makes nearly all preemptible, <10us latency.

Historical: Early Linux non-preempt, 2.5 (2002) added preemption.

In 6.17, preemption optimizes for hybrid CPUs (big.LITTLE).

Preemptive Scheduling in Linux

Preemptive kernel allows switches in most code, except spinlock regions (preempt_disable()).

Tick (HZ=250 default) calls scheduler_tick(), sets need_resched if time up or higher prio.

On return from interrupt/syscall, check_need_resched() switches if set.

cond_resched() voluntary yield point in long loops.

For RT, preemptible IRQ handlers (threaded IRQs).

Advantages: Low latency (ms to us), fair sharing, responsive UI.

Disadvantages: Higher overhead, complex debug (races).

Non-Preemptive Scheduling in Linux

In NON_PREEMPT, switches only voluntary or block.

Long kernel ops (e.g., loop without cond_resched) monopolize CPU.

Used in servers for throughput (less switches).

But even NON has preempt points.

Pure non-preempt rare now—most use at least voluntary.

Advantages: Simpler, predictable paths, less overhead.

Disadvantages: High latency if stuck, poor multitasking.

Comparison and Trade-offs

Aspect	Preemptive	Non-Preemptive
Latency	Low (us-ms)	High (task-dependent)
Throughput	Good, but switches cost	Higher in batch
Fairness	Excellent	Poor if uncooperative
Complexity	High (races)	Low
Use Cases	Interactive, RT	Batch, embedded simple

Benchmarks: Preempt adds 1-5% overhead in CPU-bound, but improves I/O response by 50-90%.

Priority inversion worse in preempt (RT priority inheritance mitigates).

In Linux, choose via config; RT patch for hard RT.

Configuration and Tuning

make menuconfig: Processor type > Preemption Model.

For RT: Apply PREEMPT_RT patch, CONFIG_PREEMPT_RT=y.

Tune HZ=1000 for response (more ticks), =100 power save.

sched_min_granularity_ns (3ms) CFS slice min.

In code, preempt_enable/disable for critical.

In 6.18 rc, preempt dynamic (runtime switch modes).

Practical Examples

Non-preempt loop:

for (i=0; i<1000000; i++) { /* work */ cond_resched(); } // Yield

Preempt: Kernel interrupts automatically.

RT example: chrt -f 99 ./app runs FIFO high prio, preempts others.

Error Handling and Issues

Preempt races: Use locks.

Inversion: RT mutex inheritance.

Debug: ftrace sched_switch.

Errors: None direct, but misconfig causes hangs/latency.

Performance and Security

Performance: Preempt good for latency-sensitive (games, audio), non for compute (HPC).

Security: Preempt can interrupt malware, but more code paths vulnerable.

RT cap CAP_SYS_NICE restrict.

In 6.17, preempt checks reduce inversion in mixed workloads.

This comparison guides model choice for needs.

13.3 Kernel Synchronization Methods

Kernel synchronization methods are the foundational tools that enable the Linux kernel to handle concurrency safely and efficiently, protecting shared resources from simultaneous access by multiple CPUs, interrupts, or kernel paths. In a modern kernel running on multi-core hardware, thousands of operations occur in parallel, and without proper synchronization, this could lead to data corruption, system crashes, or subtle bugs that are hard to reproduce. Synchronization ensures atomicity (indivisible operations), mutual exclusion (exclusive access to critical sections), and ordering (consistent view of memory changes), all while minimizing performance overhead. These methods have evolved from simple disable-interrupts in early uniprocessor kernels to sophisticated, scalable primitives suited for thousands of cores. For system programmers and kernel developers, mastering these is crucial, as most kernel bugs stem from concurrency issues, and improper use can compromise the entire system. This section provides an in-depth exploration of key synchronization techniques, including atomic operations for basic indivisibility, spinlocks for short busy-waiting, mutexes for sleeping locks, semaphores for counting resources, seqlocks for optimistic reading, completions for event signaling, read-copy-update (RCU) for lockless access, per-CPU variables for contention avoidance, memory barriers for ordering, and wait queues for general sleeping. We'll examine their implementations in kernel code, use cases, trade-offs, and how they interact with preemption and interrupts. Linux-specific details, such as the use of futexes for user-space extensions and lockdep for runtime debugging, will be highlighted, along with practical examples from subsystems like networking and filesystems. As of the stable Linux kernel 6.17 (released on September 28, 2025, with the latest patch 6.17.7 on November 2, 2025) and the ongoing 6.18 release candidate (rc4 as of November 2, 2025), kernel synchronization has been enhanced with better support for ARM LSE2 atomic instructions for reduced contention and improved RCU NOCB (no callbacks) modes for lower latency in real-time workloads, making it more robust for high-scale systems like data centers and embedded devices.

The Concurrency Landscape in the Kernel

The Linux kernel is a highly concurrent system: on a multi-CPU machine, multiple execution paths run simultaneously—user threads, kernel threads (kthreads), interrupt handlers (top halves), softirqs, tasklets, and workqueues. Shared resources, such as global data structures (e.g., the task list or page cache), device registers, or per-CPU variables accessed cross-CPU, require protection to maintain consistency. Without synchronization, race conditions can occur, where the order of operations affects the outcome— for example, two CPUs adding to a counter might read the same value, increment, and write back, losing one update.

Synchronization must consider the context:

- **Atomic Contexts**: Interrupts, spinlock-held sections—cannot sleep, as it would deadlock if the waiter holds resources needed for wakeup.
- **Process Contexts**: Syscalls, kthreads—can sleep, allowing more efficient waiting.
- **Preemptibility**: In preemptive kernels (CONFIG_PREEMPT=y), code can be interrupted at most points, requiring locks to protect against reentry.

The kernel provides a hierarchy of primitives, from low-level atomics to high-level abstractions, optimized for different hold times, contention levels, and sleepability. Hardware support, like atomic instructions (e.g., cmpxchg on x86), is crucial, with software fallbacks for portability.

Historical milestones: Early Linux (1.x) used big kernel lock (BKL) for simplicity, a global spinlock Serialize all kernel entry. Removed in 2.6.39 (2011) as fine-grained locks scaled better. RCU (2002) revolutionized read-mostly data, and futexes (2002) bridged user-kernel sync.

In kernel 6.17, synchronization primitives are tuned for hybrid CPU architectures (e.g., Intel big.LITTLE-like), with better lock handoff to reduce migration costs.

Atomic Operations: Indivisible Updates for Simple Data

Atomic operations are the lowest-level sync primitive, guaranteeing that a single memory access or modification is completed without interruption, even on SMP systems. They are used for counters, flags, or pointers where a full lock would be overkill.

The kernel provides <linux/atomic.h> with macros like atomic_inc(atomic_t *v), atomic_dec_and_test(v), atomic_cmpxchg(v, old, new). For 64-bit, atomic64_t.

Bit operations in <linux/bitops.h>: set_bit(long nr, volatile unsigned long *addr), test_and_clear_bit, etc.

These rely on arch-specific assembly, with barriers to prevent reordering (e.g., atomic_add_return includes full barrier).

Example from kernel code (page refcount):

atomic_inc(&page->_refcount);

if (atomic_dec_and_test(&page->_refcount)) free_page(page);

This ensures refcount updates are atomic, preventing use-after-free.

For non-atomic if no concurrency or single writer.

In 6.18 rc, atomics support new arches like LoongArch with better LSE-like instructions.

No errors, but misuse leads to races.

Spinlocks: Busy-Waiting for Mutual Exclusion

Spinlocks are used for short critical sections in atomic contexts, where the holder busy-loops (spins) until available, assuming short hold times to avoid CPU waste.

Defined as spinlock_t, initialized with SPIN_LOCK_UNLOCKED or spin_lock_init(&lock).

API:

- spin_lock(&lock); // Acquire, spin if held
- spin_unlock(&lock);
- int spin_trylock(&lock); // 1 if acquired, 0 else
- spin_lock_irq(&lock); // Disable interrupts
- spin_unlock_irq(&lock);
- spin_lock_irqsave(&lock, flags); // Save/ disable IRQ, restore on unlock_irqrestore

For read-write: rwlock_t, read_lock/read_unlock (multiple readers), write_lock/write_unlock (exclusive).

Implementation: On uniprocessor, reduce to preempt_disable/enable (no spin). On SMP, use ticket locks (fair queuing with atomic fetch_add) or MCS locks (per-CPU node queuing, scalable for high contention, default on some arches since 3.15).

cpu_relax() in spin loop (PAUSE on x86, YIELD on ARM) to reduce power/bus traffic.

Example from scheduler:

spin_lock(&rq->lock);

... // Pick task

spin_unlock(&rq->lock);

In RT kernel, spinlocks become rt_mutexes to allow preemption.

Use spinlocks when hold time < 2 context switches (~10us), no sleeping inside (might_sleep() warns).

Contention high? Use mutex or RCU.

In 6.17, spinlocks optimize for hybrid CPUs with better backoff.

Mutexes: Sleeping Locks for Process Contexts

Mutexes are for longer critical sections where sleeping is acceptable, allowing contended threads to block instead of spin, freeing CPU for other work.

struct mutex { atomic_long_t owner; struct list_head wait_list; struct optimistic_spin_queue osq; ... };

API:

- DEFINE_MUTEX(mutex);
- mutex_lock(&mutex); // Sleep if held
- mutex_unlock(&mutex);
- int mutex_trylock(&mutex);
- int mutex_lock_interruptible(&mutex); // -EINTR if signaled
- int mutex_lock_killable(&mutex); // -EINTR if killed

Implementation: Optimistic spinning (try spin before sleep if owner on CPU), then park on wait_list. Owner field with bits for state.

In RT, priority inheritance (PI): Waiter boosts owner priority to prevent inversion.

Debug: CONFIG_DEBUG_MUTEXES=y detects leaks, self-deadlocks.

Example from VFS:

mutex_lock(&inode->i_mutex);

... // Modify inode

mutex_unlock(&inode->i_mutex);

Use mutex when section may sleep (e.g., alloc, I/O), hold >spin time.

Slower acquisition if contended (schedule cost ~us), but better for medium holds.

Semaphores and Reader-Writer Semaphores

Semaphores are counting locks, generalizing mutexes (count=1) for limited resources (e.g., buffer slots).

struct semaphore { raw_spinlock_t lock; unsigned int count; struct list_head wait_list; };

DECLARE_SEMAPHORE(name, val);

down(&sem); // Decrement, sleep if 0

up(&sem); // Increment, wake if waiters

down_interruptible, down_timeout(jiffies), down_trylock (returns 0 success).

For binary, prefer mutex (optimized).

Reader-Writer: struct rw_semaphore { atomic_long_t count; struct list_head wait_list; ... };

init_rwsem(&rwsem);

down_read(&rwsem); up_read; // Multiple readers

down_write(&rwsem); up_write; // Exclusive writer

trylock variants.

Impl: Count positive readers, negative writer. Waiters queued.

Fair (writer not starved by continuous readers) or writer-preferred configs.

In RT, PI for writers.

Example from mm:

down_read(&mm->mmap_sem);

... // Traverse VMAs

up_read(&mm->mmap_sem);

Use rwsem for read-heavy (e.g., lookups).

Seqlocks: Optimistic Locking for Writer-Rare Data

seqlock_t { unsigned sequence; spinlock_t lock; };

seqlock_init(&seq);

write_seqlock(&seq); // Acquire spin, seq odd

... // Write

write_sequnlock(&seq); // Release, seq even

Reader: do { seqnum = read_seqbegin(&seq); ... // Read } while (read_seqretry(&seq, seqnum));

Retry if seq odd (write ongoing) or changed (write happened).

No lock for readers, spin for writers.

Use for read-mostly, writer infrequent (e.g., time, config).

Readers must tolerate retries, no side effects in loop.

Example xtime:

write_seqlock(&xtime_lock);

... update time

write_sequnlock(&xtime_lock);

Read: do { t = xtime; } while (read_seqretry(&xtime_lock, seq));

In 6.17, seqlocks optimize seq count with better barriers.

Completions: Event Synchronization

struct completion { unsigned int done; wait_queue_head_t wait; };

init_completion(&comp); reinit_completion.

complete(&comp); // done++, wake one

complete_all(&comp); // done=UINT_MAX, wake all

wait_for_completion(&comp); // Wait done >0, done--

interruptible, timeout, killable variants.

Lighter than sem, for "done" signaling (e.g., wait module unload).

Example kthread:

complete(&worker->done);

wait_for_completion(&worker->done);

Read-Copy-Update (RCU): Lock-Free for Readers

RCU allows multiple readers to access data concurrently with a writer, without locks—readers see old or new version consistently, writer defers free until grace period.

rcu_read_lock(); // Preempt disable

p = rcu_dereference(global_p); // Safe load

... use p

rcu_read_unlock();

Writer: new = alloc_copy(old); rcu_assign_pointer(global_p, new); // Safe store

synchronize_rcu(); // Wait all pre-existing readers finish

kfree(old);

Grace period: After all CPUs quiescent (no RCU critical).

Variants: rcu (basic), srcu (sleepable), preempt_rcu.

Callbacks: call_rcu(&head, func); func after grace.

Used for lists (list_for_each_entry_rcu), trees.

Scales to thousands readers, writer cost ms.

In 6.18 rc, RCU tree optimizes detection for large NUMA.

Per-CPU Variables and Local Access

To avoid locks for CPU-local data: DEFINE_PER_CPU(type, var);

type *p = this_cpu_ptr(&var); // Current CPU

this_cpu_add(var, val); atomic ops.

Dynamic: alloc_percpu_gfp(type, gfp);

free_percpu(ptr);

Used for stats, avoiding cache invalidation.

Cross-CPU access with get_cpu_var (disables preempt).

In 6.17, per-CPU optimizes allocation with better NUMA affinity.

Memory Barriers: Ensuring Order

Compiler/CPU may reorder; barriers prevent.

mb() full, rmb read, wmb write.

smp_mb() SMP only (uniproc noop).

In locks (acquire/release).

For weak arches (Alpha, ARM).

Example: wmb() after store before flag set.

Wait Queues: Flexible Sleeping

wait_queue_head_t wq = DECLARE_WAIT_QUEUE_HEAD(name);

prepare_to_wait(&wq, &wait, state); // Add to list, set TASK_INTERRUPTIBLE

if (!condition) schedule(); // Sleep

finish_wait(&wq, &wait); // Remove

wake_up(&wq); wake_up_interruptible.

wait_event(wq, condition) macro.

Used in mutex/sem (wait_list).

Synchronization Tools and Debugging

lockdep: Runtime validator, lockdep_assert_held(&lock);

CONFIG_PROVE_LOCKING=y.

ftrace, perf lock profile acquisition/wait time.

In crashes, lockdep prints dependency chains.

KCSAN (data race detector) CONFIG_KCSAN=y.

Error Handling and Common Pitfalls

No runtime errors, but misuse oops/panic.

Pitfalls: Sleep in spinheld (BUG); unlock not held; missing barrier (stale data); recursive mutex (deadlock).

RT: Use raw_spinlock for non-preempt, rt_mutex for sleepable.

Best: Short critical, prefer RCU/atoms, document order.

In 6.17, lockdep scales to more classes.

Security: Locks prevent races exploitable for escalation.

Constant-time to avoid timing channels.

In 6.18 rc, barriers strengthen vs Spectre.

These methods form the kernel's concurrency toolkit, ensuring safe, efficient operation.

13.4 Spinlocks, Mutexes, and Semaphores

Spinlocks, mutexes, and semaphores are among the most commonly used synchronization primitives in the Linux kernel, each designed to protect shared resources in different scenarios of concurrency. Spinlocks offer busy-waiting for short, atomic critical sections, mutexes provide sleeping locks for longer holds where blocking is acceptable, and semaphores enable counting-based access control for limited resources. These primitives form the foundation for safe multi-processor operation, preventing race conditions and ensuring data integrity without excessive performance penalties. Choosing the right one depends on the context—spinlocks for interrupt-safe code, mutexes for process contexts, and semaphores for more flexible counting— and improper selection can lead to deadlocks, high CPU usage, or poor scalability. For system programmers and kernel developers, mastering these is essential, as they appear in nearly every subsystem, from the scheduler to filesystem code, and their efficient use is key to high-performance kernel modules or patches. This subsection provides a detailed examination of spinlocks, mutexes, and semaphores, covering their APIs, internal implementations, use cases, differences, and integration with other primitives like RCU. We'll include practical examples from kernel source, error handling strategies, performance tuning tips, and security considerations such as lock contention exploits. Linux-specific optimizations, such as queued spinlocks for fairness and priority inheritance in mutexes for real-time, will be highlighted. As of the stable Linux kernel 6.17 (released on September 28, 2025, with the latest patch 6.17.7 on November 2, 2025) and the ongoing 6.18 release candidate (rc4 as of November 2, 2025), these primitives have been refined with better support for ARM LSE2 atomic instructions in spinlocks and enhanced debugging in lockdep for mutex deadlocks, making them more robust for large-scale systems and embedded real-time applications.

Understanding the Need for These Primitives

In the kernel's concurrent environment, where multiple execution paths (CPUs, interrupts, softirqs) access shared data, synchronization prevents inconsistencies. Spinlocks are ideal for very short sections (e.g., updating a counter) where waiting is brief, as sleeping would be inefficient or impossible in atomic contexts. Mutexes suit longer sections (e.g., allocating memory) where sleeping frees the CPU for other tasks. Semaphores generalize to scenarios with multiple "tokens," like limiting concurrent I/O requests.

Historical context: Spinlocks evolved from test-and-set in early SMP UNIX (1980s), mutexes from sleeping semaphores in System V, and semaphores from Dijkstra's 1965 concept. Linux adopted spinlocks in 1.3 (1995) for SMP, mutexes in 2.6.16 (2006) as optimized sleeping locks, and semaphores from the start. The BKL (Big Kernel Lock) was a coarse mutex phased out by 2.6.39 (2011) in favor of fine-grained primitives. Trade-offs:

- **Hold Time**: Spin <10us, mutex >10us, sem flexible.
- **Sleepability**: Spin no, mutex/sem yes.
- **Fairness**: Spin queued (MCS), mutex PI (priority inheritance), sem FIFO.
- **Overhead**: Spin high contended (waste CPU), mutex switch cost (~us), sem similar mutex.

In kernel 6.17, primitives optimize for hybrid CPUs with better backoff algorithms to reduce power consumption on idle cores.

Spinlocks: Implementation and Usage

Spinlocks are the go-to for atomic contexts, where the lock holder busy-loops until available, assuming short contention.

Definition: typedef struct spinlock { union { struct raw_spinlock rlock; }; } spinlock_t;

Initialization: spin_lock_init(&lock); or DEFINE_SPINLOCK(lock);

API:

- void spin_lock(spinlock_t *lock);
- void spin_unlock(spinlock_t *lock);
- int spin_trylock(spinlock_t *lock);
- void spin_lock_bh(spinlock_t *lock); // Disable bottom halves
- void spin_unlock_bh(spinlock_t *lock);
- void spin_lock_irq(spinlock_t *lock); // Disable interrupts
- void spin_unlock_irq(spinlock_t *lock);
- void spin_lock_irqsave(spinlock_t *lock, unsigned long flags); // Save and disable IRQ
- void spin_unlock_irqrestore(spinlock_t *lock, unsigned long flags);

For read-write: rwlock_t, read_lock/read_unlock (allow multiple readers), write_lock/write_unlock (exclusive).

Implementation details: On uniprocessor, spinlocks compile to preempt_disable/enable() (no actual spin, as no other CPU). On SMP, they use atomic operations: ticket spinlocks assign "tickets" with fetch_add for fairness, while MCS (Mellor-Crummey and Scott, default on some configs since 3.15) uses per-CPU nodes queued on the lock, reducing cache contention by spinning on local variables.

The spin loop includes cpu_relax() (PAUSE instruction on x86, YIELD on ARM) to hint the CPU to save power and avoid bus saturation.

Example from the scheduler code:

spin_lock(&rq->lock); /* select next task */ spin_unlock(&rq->lock);

In interrupt handlers, use spin_lock_irqsave to disable IRQs, preventing recursion if the lock is held by the interrupted code.

CONFIG_DEBUG_SPINLOCK=y enables runtime checks for misuse, like unlocking an unheld lock or sleeping while holding.

In the PREEMPT_RT patch, spinlocks are replaced with rt_mutexes to allow preemption, reducing latency but adding overhead.

Use spinlocks when the critical section is short, contains no sleeping calls (might_sleep() macro warns if it does), and must be IRQ-safe. Avoid in process contexts with long holds to prevent CPU waste.

In kernel 6.18 rc, spinlocks include experimental support for adaptive backoff based on contention history, further reducing latency in high-load scenarios.

Mutexes: Sleeping Locks with Optimization

Mutexes are designed for process contexts where sleeping is permissible, allowing contended threads to block and yield the CPU, making them suitable for longer critical sections (e.g., >10-100us).

Definition: struct mutex { atomic_long_t owner; struct list_head wait_list; struct optimistic_spin_queue osq; ... };

Initialization: DEFINE_MUTEX(mutex); or mutex_init(&mutex);

API:

- void mutex_lock(struct mutex *lock);
- void mutex_unlock(struct mutex *lock);
- int mutex_trylock(struct mutex *lock);
- int mutex_lock_interruptible(struct mutex *lock); // Returns -EINTR if interrupted by signal
- int mutex_lock_killable(struct mutex *lock); // -EINTR if killed
- int mutex_is_locked(struct mutex *lock); // Check if held

Implementation: Optimistic spinning (osq)—if the owner is running on another CPU, spin briefly before sleeping to avoid unnecessary context switches. If contention persists, waiters are added to wait_list and parked using schedule(). The owner field uses bitfields for state (locked, contended).

In real-time kernels, mutexes support priority inheritance (PI): if a low-priority task holds a mutex needed by a high-priority one, the low-priority task inherits the high priority temporarily to avoid inversion.

Debugging: CONFIG_DEBUG_MUTEXES=y detects slowpath issues, leaks, or self-deadlocks (e.g., recursive lock).

Example from the memory management code:

mutex_lock(&current->mm->mmap_lock); /* manipulate VMAs */ mutex_unlock(&current->mm->mmap_lock);

Use mutexes when the critical section may call functions that sleep (e.g., kmalloc(GFP_KERNEL), wait_event), or when hold times are longer than a few microseconds. They are not IRQ-safe—use spinlocks for that.

Mutexes are slower on acquisition under contention due to scheduling overhead but are more CPU-efficient overall for medium-length sections.

Semaphores: Counting Locks for Resource Management

Semaphores generalize mutexes by allowing a count greater than 1, making them suitable for limiting access to a pool of resources (e.g., a fixed number of buffers or connections).

Definition: struct semaphore { raw_spinlock_t lock; unsigned int count; struct list_head wait_list; };

Initialization: sema_init(&sem, val); or DEFINE_SEMAPHORE(sem, val); // val initial count, 1 for binary

API:

- void down(struct semaphore *sem); // Decrement, sleep if 0
- void up(struct semaphore *sem); // Increment, wake a waiter if any
- int down_interruptible(struct semaphore *sem); // -EINTR if interrupted
- int down_killable(struct semaphore *sem);
- int down_trylock(struct semaphore *sem); // 0 if successful (decremented), 1 if would block
- int down_timeout(struct semaphore *sem, long timeout); // In jiffies, -ETIMEDOUT if timeout

For reader-writer semaphores: struct rw_semaphore, init_rwsem(&rwsem);

- void down_read(struct rw_semaphore *sem); up_read(sem); // Allow multiple readers
- void down_write(struct rw_semaphore *sem); up_write(sem); // Exclusive writer, blocks new readers

trylock and interruptible variants available.

Implementation: The count is atomic, with a spinlock-protected wait_list for sleepers. Down decrements if >0, else adds to list and schedules. Up increments and wakes the head if waiters. Rw_sem uses a count where positive values indicate reader count, negative for writer active.

In RT kernels, both support priority inheritance.

Example from the block layer:

down(&bdev->bd_mutex); /* access block device */ up(&bdev->bd_mutex);

For rw in page cache:

down_read(&mapping->i_mmap_rwsem); /* search address space */ up_read(&mapping->i_mmap_rwsem);

Use semaphores when you need to limit concurrent access to a resource (e.g., val=4 for 4 simultaneous users), or rw for read-heavy data where multiple readers are safe but writers exclusive. For binary (val=1), prefer mutexes as they are optimized and lighter (no list for single waiter).

Semaphores are heavier than mutexes due to the list management but offer counting flexibility.

Differences and Selection Guidelines

- **Spinlocks vs. Mutexes**: Spin for atomic/short/IRQ-safe (no sleep, busy CPU), mutex for process/long/sleepable (block on contention, free CPU).
- **Mutexes vs. Semaphores**: Mutex for binary exclusive (optimized, PI), sem for counting or legacy.
- **Rw Variants**: Use when readers >> writers to allow concurrency; else simple lock.

General rule: If critical section calls might_sleep() funcs, use mutex/sem; if atomic, spin. For read-mostly, consider rw or RCU.

Overhead: Spin uncontended ~10ns, contended wastes CPU; mutex ~50ns uncontended, ~us contended (switch).

In SMP, all add barriers for ordering.

Integration with Other Primitives

Spin/mutex often nest with atomics (e.g., spin_lock; atomic_inc; spin_unlock).

RCU for read, spin/mutex for write.

Waitqueues in mutex/sem for sleepers.

Futexes bridge to user (up wakes user cond).

In modules, use primitives for shared data.

Practical Examples from Kernel Code

Spin in netif_receive_skb:

spin_lock(&queue->lock); ... add skb spin_unlock(&queue->lock);

Mutex in inode_lock (fs/inode.c):

mutex_lock(&inode->i_mutex); ...

Rw sem in down_read_trylock(&mm->mmap_sem);

Sem in down(&journal->j_barrier); for JBD.

These protect against concurrent modifications.

Error Handling and Debugging

Primitives return no errors (void), but trylock 0/1.

Misuse: Sleep in spin (panic if DEBUG), unlock not held (warn).

lockdep (CONFIG_PROVE_LOCKING=y) runtime tracks classes, detects cycles/invalid nest/IRQ use.

lockdep_assert_held(&lock); in code.

If deadlock, lockdep prints chain.

KCSAN for data races.

ftrace lock events.

Errors from bad use crash.

Performance Tuning

lockstat (CONFIG_LOCK_STAT=y) /proc/lock_stat contention/wait time.

perf lock record ./kmod; perf lock report.

Reduce holds, use finer locks.

RCU/atoms over locks where possible.

In high-CPU, MCS spin scales better.

sysctl kernel.lock_stat=1 enables.

In 6.17, mutex osq tunes spin threshold.

Security Implications

Locks prevent races exploitable for escalation (e.g., CVE-2016-5195 Dirty COW, VFS race).
But contended locks DoS (hold forever).
Constant-time avoids timing channels.
In 6.17, barriers in locks harden Spectre.
RT PI prevents inversion DoS.
These primitives ensure kernel integrity in concurrent settings.

14. Interrupts, Exceptions, and Bottom Halves

Interrupts, exceptions, and the mechanisms for handling them form the backbone of responsive and efficient kernel operations in Linux. These features allow the kernel to react to hardware events, manage errors, and defer non-critical work to maintain system stability and performance. This chapter explores the core concepts, starting with interrupt handling, moving into exceptions, and then delving into deferred processing techniques like bottom halves.

14.1 Interrupt Handling Mechanisms

Interrupts are asynchronous signals from hardware or software that prompt the CPU to pause its current execution and switch to a specialized routine called an interrupt handler. In the Linux kernel, interrupts ensure that the system can respond promptly to events such as keyboard presses, network packet arrivals, or timer expirations. Without proper interrupt handling, a system would be unresponsive and inefficient, as the kernel would need to constantly poll devices for status changes.

Understanding interrupt handling requires grasping the distinction between *hardware interrupts* (often called IRQs, or Interrupt Requests) and *software interrupts* (softirqs). Hardware interrupts originate from external devices via interrupt controllers, while software interrupts are triggered by the kernel itself for deferred processing. This section focuses on the mechanisms for handling hardware interrupts, including their detection, routing, and initial processing in the kernel.

Types of Interrupts

Linux classifies interrupts broadly into two categories:

- **Hardware Interrupts (IRQs):** These are generated by peripherals like network cards, disks, or timers. They signal the CPU through dedicated lines or messages. On x86 architectures, for example, interrupts are delivered via the Programmable Interrupt Controller (PIC) in older systems or the Advanced Programmable Interrupt Controller (APIC) in modern ones. More contemporary systems use Message Signaled Interrupts (MSI or MSI-X), where devices send interrupt messages directly over the PCIe bus, reducing latency and improving scalability.
- **Software Interrupts (Softirqs):** These are kernel-internal mechanisms for handling deferred work. They are raised by hardware interrupt handlers or other kernel code and executed in a controlled context. Softirqs are discussed in more detail in Section 14.3 and 14.4 as part of bottom halves.

Additionally, interrupts can be *maskable* (temporarily disabled by the CPU) or *non-maskable* (NMIs, which cannot be ignored and are used for critical errors like hardware failures).

Interrupt Delivery and the Interrupt Descriptor Table (IDT)

On architectures like x86, interrupts are vectored through the Interrupt Descriptor Table (IDT), a data structure in memory that maps interrupt numbers (vectors) to handler functions. When an interrupt occurs:

1. The CPU saves the current state (registers, instruction pointer) on the stack.
2. It looks up the vector in the IDT.
3. Control jumps to the entry point defined in the IDT, which is typically a kernel assembly routine.

The kernel initializes the IDT during boot via idt_setup_early_handler() and related functions in arch/x86/kernel/idt.c. For other architectures like ARM or RISC-V, similar mechanisms exist, such as exception vectors or Generic Interrupt Controller (GIC) handling.

In multi-core systems, interrupts can be affinity-masked to specific CPUs using irq_set_affinity(), allowing load balancing across processors.

Registering Interrupt Handlers

Device drivers or kernel modules register interrupt handlers using the request_irq() function, which associates a handler with a specific IRQ line. The prototype is:

c
```
int request_irq(unsigned int irq, irq_handler_t handler, unsigned long flags,
        const char *name, void *dev);
```

- irq: The interrupt number (e.g., obtained from platform data or PCI configuration).
- handler: A function pointer to the interrupt service routine (ISR), which must return IRQ_HANDLED if it processed the interrupt or IRQ_NONE otherwise.

- **flags:** Bitmask options, such as IRQF_SHARED (for shared IRQ lines, common on PCI), IRQF_NO_SUSPEND (to keep handling during system suspend), or IRQF_ONESHOT (for one-time handlers).
- name: A string identifier for /proc/interrupts.
- dev: Device-specific data passed to the handler.

Here's a simple example of registering a handler for a fictional device:

c

```c
#include <linux/interrupt.h>
#include <linux/module.h>

static irqreturn_t my_handler(int irq, void *dev_id) {
    // Handle the interrupt: read device status, clear interrupt flag, etc.
    printk(KERN_INFO "Interrupt %d handled\n", irq);
    return IRQ_HANDLED;
}

static int __init my_module_init(void) {
    int ret = request_irq(IRQ_NUMBER, my_handler, IRQF_SHARED, "my_device", &my_dev);
    if (ret) {
        printk(KERN_ERR "Failed to request IRQ %d\n", IRQ_NUMBER);
        return ret;
    }
    return 0;
}

static void __exit my_module_exit(void) {
    free_irq(IRQ_NUMBER, &my_dev);
}

module_init(my_module_init);
module_exit(my_module_exit);
MODULE_LICENSE("GPL");
```

To unregister, use free_irq(). Note that handlers run in *interrupt context*, where sleeping is forbidden—use atomic operations and avoid blocking calls.

Interrupt Context and Safety

Interrupt handlers execute with interrupts disabled on the local CPU (via local_irq_disable()), preventing nesting unless explicitly enabled. This atomicity ensures quick execution, but handlers should be brief to avoid latency. For longer tasks, defer work to bottom halves (covered in later sections).

To check if code is running in interrupt context, use in_irq() or in_interrupt(). For safety, use spinlocks (Section 13.4) to protect shared data.

Probing and Managing IRQs

The kernel provides /proc/interrupts for viewing IRQ statistics:

text

```
CPU0    CPU1
  0:    1       0  IO-APIC  2-edge    timer
  8:    0       1  IO-APIC  8-edge    rtc0
...
```

Use cat /proc/interrupts in debugging. For dynamic IRQ allocation, functions like pci_irq_vector() are used in PCI drivers.

Edge-Triggered vs. Level-Triggered Interrupts

- **Edge-Triggered:** Triggered on signal transitions (rising/falling edge). Simpler but can miss interrupts if not cleared properly.
- **Level-Triggered:** Active while the signal is asserted. More reliable but requires careful handling to avoid storms.

The kernel abstracts this via the interrupt controller drivers (e.g., drivers/irqchip/).

In summary, interrupt handling mechanisms in Linux provide a robust framework for asynchronous event processing, balancing immediacy with system stability. The top-half handler (the ISR) performs minimal work, setting the stage for deferred processing in bottom halves. In the next section, we'll explore exceptions, which handle synchronous errors like page faults or division by zero.

14.2 Exception Processing

Exceptions represent synchronous interruptions to the normal flow of execution, triggered by the processor itself in response to erroneous or special conditions encountered during instruction processing. Unlike interrupts, which are asynchronous and often hardware-driven, exceptions are directly tied to the executing code—making them predictable in terms of when they occur but requiring careful handling to maintain system integrity. In the Linux kernel, exception processing is crucial for tasks like memory management (e.g., handling page faults), debugging (e.g., breakpoints), and system calls. Mismanaged exceptions can lead to kernel panics, process termination, or security vulnerabilities.

This section delves into the mechanisms for processing exceptions, focusing on their classification, delivery, and handling within the kernel. We'll explore architectural specifics, primarily on x86, while noting variations for other platforms like ARM or RISC-V. Additionally, we'll cover advanced topics such as exception nesting, security mitigations, performance optimization, and practical examples to provide a comprehensive understanding suitable for kernel developers and system programmers.

Types of Exceptions

Exceptions in Linux (and broadly in UNIX-like systems) are categorized based on their nature and recoverability, drawing from processor-specific terminology:

- **Faults:** These are correctable exceptions where the faulting instruction can be restarted after resolution. The most common example is a *page fault*, which occurs when accessing a memory page that isn't currently mapped in physical memory (e.g., due to demand paging or swap). The kernel's page fault handler resolves this by loading the page, and execution resumes seamlessly. Other faults include alignment checks (on architectures that enforce strict alignment) or bounds checks in certain instruction sets.

- **Traps:** Intentional exceptions that occur after the instruction has executed, often for debugging or system calls. For instance, a breakpoint instruction (INT3 on x86) triggers a trap for debuggers like GDB. System calls traditionally used traps (e.g., INT 0x80 on older x86), though modern systems prefer faster mechanisms like SYSCALL/SYSENTER. Traps are also used in virtualization for hypervisor interventions, such as in KVM where guest exits trigger traps.

- **Aborts:** Fatal exceptions indicating severe errors, such as hardware failures or invalid opcodes, from which recovery is impossible. These typically lead to process termination or kernel oops/panic. An example is a *machine check exception* (MCE) on x86, signaling uncorrectable memory errors. On ARM, double faults or undefined instructions can lead to aborts, often resulting in a kernel panic if unhandled.

On x86, exceptions are assigned vectors in the IDT (Interrupt Descriptor Table), similar to interrupts. Vectors 0-31 are reserved for exceptions and non-maskable interrupts (NMIs), with specific assignments like:

- Vector 0: Divide Error (e.g., division by zero in integer operations).
- Vector 1: Debug Exception (for hardware breakpoints or watchpoints).
- Vector 6: Invalid Opcode (when the CPU encounters an undefined instruction).
- Vector 13: General Protection Fault (GPF, for segmentation violations or privilege level errors).
- Vector 14: Page Fault (detailed further below).
- Vector 18: Machine Check (for hardware errors like ECC failures).

For ARM architectures, exceptions are handled via exception vectors at fixed addresses, categorized into synchronous (e.g., undefined instructions, data aborts) and asynchronous (e.g., IRQs, FIQs). Synchronous exceptions align closely with x86 faults and traps, while asynchronous ones resemble interrupts. RISC-V uses a trap model where all exceptions and interrupts are traps, vectored through a single entry point with cause codes distinguishing types (e.g., load access fault, illegal instruction).

In multi-architecture kernels like Linux, the code abstracts these differences through architecture-specific directories (e.g., arch/x86/, arch/arm64/) while providing unified interfaces via headers like include/asm/trap.h.

Exception Delivery and Context

When an exception occurs:

1. The CPU detects the condition (e.g., invalid memory access) and pushes the current context onto the stack: instruction pointer (RIP on x86), code segment, flags, and sometimes an error code. On x86_64, this includes the stack pointer (RSP) if switching stacks.
2. It consults the IDT (or equivalent, like ARM's vector table) to find the handler for the exception vector.
3. Control transfers to the handler, which runs in kernel mode with interrupts disabled to prevent nesting unless explicitly allowed.

The kernel's entry point for exceptions is architecture-specific. On x86, assembly code in arch/x86/entry/entry_64.S (or entry_32.S for 32-bit) handles initial setup, saving registers and calling C handlers. This involves macros like ENTRY(do_general_protection) to manage stack frames and error codes. The do_{exception_name} functions (e.g., do_page_fault()) in arch/x86/kernel/traps.c perform the actual processing. Exceptions occur in either user or kernel context:

- **User-space exceptions:** Typically handled by sending signals to the process (e.g., SIGSEGV for segmentation faults, SIGFPE for floating-point exceptions) via force_sig_info() or force_sig_fault(). This allows user programs to install signal handlers for recovery, such as in garbage collectors that use SIGSEGV for memory barriers.
- **Kernel-space exceptions:** More critical; if unrecoverable, they trigger a kernel oops (via die()) or panic (panic()). Oops dumps include register states, stack traces (via show_stack()), and module information for debugging. Kernel exceptions can stem from bugs like null pointer dereferences, which are caught as page faults on address 0.

Error codes provide additional details; for page faults on x86, the code is a bitmask:

- Bit 0: Page not present (demand paging) vs. protection violation.
- Bit 1: Write access attempted.
- Bit 2: User-mode access.
- Bit 3: Reserved bit violation (e.g., SMEP/SMAP).
- Bit 4: Instruction fetch.

This granularity aids in precise handling. For instance, a non-present page in user space triggers allocation, while a kernel write to a read-only page might indicate a bug.

On ARM64, exception syndrome registers (ESR) encode similar details, decoded in handlers like do_mem_abort().

Implementing and Registering Exception Handlers

Unlike device interrupts, core exception handlers are built into the kernel and set up during initialization (e.g., trap_init() in arch/x86/kernel/traps.c, which populates the IDT with gates like set_intr_gate()). They aren't "registered" like IRQs but can be extended or hooked for specific purposes.

For customization:

- **Notifier Chains:** Use register_die_notifier() to hook into oops/panic events, useful for custom logging or recovery in embedded systems.
- **Fixup Mechanisms:** For recoverable kernel faults, fixup_exception() allows registering fixups via .pushsection .fixup in assembly, redirecting faults to alternative code paths.
- **Virtualization Extensions:** In hypervisors, exceptions can be injected or trapped using VMX (on Intel) or SVM (AMD), handled in kvm_handle_exit().

Here's an expanded example of a page fault handler (adapted from kernel sources):

```c
#include <linux/mm.h>
#include <linux/sched.h>
#include <linux/kernel.h>
#include <asm/traps.h>

asmlinkage void do_page_fault(struct pt_regs *regs, unsigned long error_code, unsigned long address) {
    struct task_struct *tsk = current;
    struct mm_struct *mm = tsk->mm;
    vm_fault_t fault;
    unsigned int flags = FAULT_FLAG_ALLOW_RETRY | FAULT_FLAG_KILLABLE;

    // Determine context: user or kernel
    if (unlikely(address >= TASK_SIZE)) {
        // Kernel-mode fault
```

```c
    if (unlikely(!kernelmode_fixup_or_oops(regs, error_code, address, NULL, 0)))
        die("Oops", regs, error_code);
    return;
}

// User-mode fault: acquire mmap lock
mmap_read_lock(mm);
struct vm_area_struct *vma = vma_lookup(mm, address);
if (!vma) {
    // No VMA: bad area
    mmap_read_unlock(mm);
    bad_area(regs, error_code, address);
    return;
}

// Handle specific cases: stack expansion, zero page, etc.
if (unlikely(expand_stack(vma, address))) {
    mmap_read_unlock(mm);
    bad_area(regs, error_code, address);
    return;
}

// Core fault handling
if (error_code & PF_USER)
    flags |= FAULT_FLAG_USER;
if (error_code & PF_WRITE)
    flags |= FAULT_FLAG_WRITE;
if (error_code & PF_INSTR)
    flags |= FAULT_FLAG_INSTRUCTION;

fault = handle_mm_fault(vma, address, flags, regs);
mmap_read_unlock(mm);

if (unlikely(fault & VM_FAULT_RETRY)) {
    // Retry logic for OOM or other transients
    if (flags & FAULT_FLAG_ALLOW_RETRY) {
        mmap_read_lock(mm);
        // ... retry handle_mm_fault ...
    } else {
        // Fatal
        do_exit(SIGKILL);
    }
} else if (fault & VM_FAULT_ERROR) {
    // Handle errors: OOM, sigbus, etc.
    if (fault & VM_FAULT_OOM) {
        out_of_memory(regs, error_code, address);
    } else if (fault & VM_FAULT_SIGBUS) {
        do_sigbus(regs, error_code, address);
    } else {
        BUG();
    }
}
}
```

This handler demonstrates complexity: it manages locks (mmap_read_lock() for concurrency), checks for special cases like stack growth (expand_stack()), and delegates to handle_mm_fault() which interacts with the page allocator, file backing, or anon pages. Errors lead to signals like SIGBUS for bus errors (e.g., unaligned access on some arches).

For system calls, a special trap, modern x86 uses SYSCALL (vector 0x80 legacy), which saves minimal state for efficiency. The dispatcher in syscall_enter_from_user_mode() validates and calls syscalls from the syscall table.

Debugging and Security Considerations

Exceptions are invaluable for debugging. Tools like KGDB or KDB hook into trap handlers (e.g., debug exception) to set breakpoints or inspect state. The kernel's kgdb_breakpoint() uses INT3 traps.

For security, processor features mitigate exploits:

- **SMEP/SMAP:** Prevent kernel execution/access of user pages, triggering page faults on violations.
- **KPTI (Kernel Page Table Isolation):** Mitigates Meltdown by separating user/kernel page tables, increasing page fault overhead but enhancing security.
- **Spectre/Meltdown Mitigations:** Retpoline for indirect branches, LFENCE for serialization, affecting trap performance.

Vulnerabilities like CVE-2018-8897 (double fault mishandling) highlight the need for robust handlers. Best practices include auditing for recursive faults (using alternate stacks via IST on x86) and avoiding user-controlled data in kernel paths.

Performance-wise, exceptions incur overhead: context switches, TLB flushes. Optimizations include fast paths for minor faults and per-CPU data to reduce locking. Tools like perf trace exceptions via perf record -e exceptions:page_fault_user.

Common pitfalls:

- Infinite recursion: Faulting in the handler (e.g., accessing faulted address again).
- Race conditions: Multi-threaded access without proper synchronization.
- Overlooking architecture quirks: e.g., ARM's precise vs. imprecise aborts.

In embedded or real-time systems (e.g., with PREEMPT_RT), exception handling is tuned for low latency, sometimes disabling certain features.

Integration with Kernel Subsystems

Exceptions interplay with memory management (mm subsystem for page faults), process scheduling (signals may wake tasks), and filesystems (faults on mmap'ed files trigger I/O). For instance, transparent huge pages (THP) optimize page faults by allocating 2MB pages atomically.

In containers, namespaces affect exception views, but core handling remains kernel-level.

Historical evolution: Early Linux used simpler traps; post-2.6 kernels added x86_64 support with improved vectors. Recent additions include support for RISC-V exceptions in 5.x kernels.

Summary

Exception processing in Linux ensures robust error recovery and controlled execution flow, bridging hardware events with kernel logic. By handling faults, traps, and aborts efficiently across architectures, the kernel maintains stability in diverse workloads—from desktops to servers and embedded devices. This mechanism not only facilitates memory virtualization and debugging but also underpins security features critical in modern computing. Understanding these intricacies empowers developers to write safer, more performant kernel code. Building on interrupts, exceptions set the foundation for deferred work mechanisms like tasklets and workqueues, explored in the next sections, which allow non-urgent processing outside atomic contexts. With careful design, exceptions transform potential crashes into recoverable events, exemplifying the kernel's resilience.

14.3 Tasklets and Workqueues

Tasklets and workqueues represent key components of the Linux kernel's "bottom half" mechanisms, designed to handle deferred processing of interrupt-related work. In interrupt handling, the "top half" (the immediate interrupt service routine, or ISR) executes quickly in atomic context to acknowledge the hardware and perform minimal essential tasks. The "bottom half" defers non-critical, time-consuming operations to a safer context where sleeping, scheduling, or longer executions are permissible. This separation minimizes interrupt latency, enhances system responsiveness, and prevents monopolization of CPU time by interrupts.

Tasklets and workqueues are two primary bottom-half implementations, each suited to different use cases. Tasklets are lightweight, softirq-based deferred functions ideal for simple, non-blocking operations, while workqueues provide a more flexible, process-context mechanism for complex or blocking tasks. This section explores their architecture, usage, implementation, and best practices, with examples drawn from kernel development. We'll also discuss their evolution, performance implications, and integration with modern kernel features like real-time scheduling and concurrency management.

Understanding Bottom Halves

Before diving into specifics, it's essential to contextualize bottom halves within the interrupt lifecycle. When a hardware interrupt occurs, the top half (registered via request_irq()) runs with interrupts disabled, ensuring atomicity but limiting what can be done— no sleeping, no mutexes, only spinlocks for synchronization. If the ISR needs to perform extended work (e.g., processing a network packet or updating data structures), it schedules a bottom half.

Historically, bottom halves evolved from the original BH (Bottom Half) system in early Linux, which used a fixed set of 32 handlers. This was replaced by softirqs in 2.3 kernels, introducing dynamic, prioritized deferred execution. Tasklets build directly on softirqs, while workqueues (introduced in 2.5) use kernel threads for greater flexibility. Today, with multicore systems and PREEMPT_RT patches, these mechanisms are optimized for low latency and scalability.

Softirqs underpin tasklets and include predefined types like HI_SOFTIRQ (high-priority), TIMER_SOFTIRQ, NET_TX_SOFTIRQ, and TASKLET_SOFTIRQ. They execute at the end of the top half or during ksoftirqd threads if overloaded. The function raise_softirq() schedules them, and do_softirq() processes pending ones.

Tasklets: Lightweight Deferred Execution

Tasklets are essentially functions scheduled on the TASKLET_SOFTIRQ or HI_SOFTIRQ (for high-priority variants). They are serialized per-CPU, meaning a tasklet won't run concurrently on multiple CPUs but can be preempted. This makes them suitable for quick, non-reentrant operations like simple data processing or state updates in drivers.

Key characteristics:

- **Atomic Execution:** Run in softirq context with interrupts enabled but preemption disabled (unless CONFIG_PREEMPT is set).
- **Serialization:** Each tasklet is tied to a CPU and won't execute simultaneously on the same CPU if rescheduled.
- **No Sleeping:** Cannot block or sleep, limiting them to spinlock-protected operations.
- **Efficiency:** Low overhead, ideal for high-frequency interrupts.

To use tasklets, declare a struct tasklet_struct and initialize it with tasklet_init() or the macro DECLARE_TASKLET(). Schedule with tasklet_schedule() from the top half.

Example of a tasklet in a character driver:

c
```c
#include <linux/interrupt.h>
#include <linux/module.h>

struct my_device {
    // Device-specific data
};

static void my_tasklet_func(unsigned long data) {
    struct my_device *dev = (struct my_device *)data;
    // Perform deferred work: e.g., process buffer, update stats
    printk(KERN_INFO "Tasklet running for device\n");
    // No sleeping here!
```

```
}

static struct tasklet_struct my_tasklet;

static irqreturn_t my_isr(int irq, void *dev_id) {
    // Top half: acknowledge hardware
    // ...
    tasklet_schedule(&my_tasklet);
    return IRQ_HANDLED;
}

static int __init my_module_init(void) {
    struct my_device *dev = /* allocate */;
    tasklet_init(&my_tasklet, my_tasklet_func, (unsigned long)dev);
    return request_irq(IRQ_NUM, my_isr, IRQF_SHARED, "my_dev", dev);
}

static void __exit my_module_exit(void) {
    tasklet_kill(&my_tasklet);  // Wait for completion if running
    free_irq(IRQ_NUM, dev);
}

module_init(my_module_init);
module_exit(my_module_exit);
MODULE_LICENSE("GPL");
```

Here, the ISR schedules the tasklet, which runs later in softirq context. For high-priority tasklets, use tasklet_hi_schedule() on HI_SOFTIRQ.

Tasklets are disabled/enabled with tasklet_disable() and tasklet_enable(), useful for synchronization. To ensure completion, tasklet_kill() waits if necessary.

Internally, tasklets are linked in per-CPU lists (tasklet_vec and tasklet_hi_vec in kernel/softirq.c). When do_softirq() runs, it processes these lists via __do_softirq(), executing tasklet actions until a threshold (e.g., 10 iterations) or time limit.

Advantages: Minimal latency overhead, automatic load balancing across CPUs. Drawbacks: Cannot sleep, so unsuitable for I/O or allocations that might block.

Workqueues: Flexible, Process-Context Deferral

Workqueues address tasklets' limitations by executing in process context via dedicated kernel threads (kworker/*). This allows sleeping, mutex usage, and longer executions, making them ideal for blocking operations like disk I/O, network transmissions, or complex computations in drivers.

Key features:

- **Process Context:** Runs as schedulable tasks, preemptible and migratable across CPUs.
- **Concurrency Models:** Default workqueues are unbound (can run on any CPU), but options include per-CPU, ordered, or high-priority queues.
- **Delayed Work:** Supports timers for scheduled execution.
- **Scalability:** System-wide default queue (system_wq) or custom queues for isolation.

Create work with struct work_struct (for immediate) or struct delayed_work (for timed). Initialize with INIT_WORK() or INIT_DELAYED_WORK(), and schedule with queue_work() or schedule_delayed_work().

Example in a block driver:

```c
#include <linux/workqueue.h>
#include <linux/module.h>

struct my_work_data {
    // Data for work
};

static void my_work_func(struct work_struct *work) {
```

```
    struct my_work_data *data = container_of(work, struct my_work_data, work);
    // Can sleep: e.g., mutex_lock(), kmalloc(GFP_KERNEL), I/O operations
    printk(KERN_INFO "Workqueue processing data\n");
    // Free data if needed
    kfree(data);
}

static struct workqueue_struct *my_wq;

static irqreturn_t my_isr(int irq, void *dev_id) {
    struct my_work_data *data = kmalloc(sizeof(*data), GFP_ATOMIC);
    if (!data) return IRQ_HANDLED;
    // Initialize data
    INIT_WORK(&data->work, my_work_func);
    queue_work(my_wq, &data->work);
    return IRQ_HANDLED;
}

static int __init my_module_init(void) {
    my_wq = alloc_workqueue("my_wq", WQ_UNBOUND | WQ_HIGHPRI, 0);
    if (!my_wq) return -ENOMEM;
    return request_irq(IRQ_NUM, my_isr, IRQF_SHARED, "my_dev", NULL);
}

static void __exit my_module_exit(void) {
    destroy_workqueue(my_wq);
    free_irq(IRQ_NUM, NULL);
}

module_init(my_module_init);
module_exit(my_module_exit);
MODULE_LICENSE("GPL");
```

For delayed work: schedule_delayed_work(&data->dwork, msecs_to_jiffies(1000));.

Custom workqueues are created with alloc_workqueue(), specifying flags like WQ_MEM_RECLAIM (for memory pressure resilience), WQ_HIGHPRI (higher scheduling priority), or WQ_CPU_INTENSIVE (for CPU-bound tasks to avoid starving other work).

The kernel provides system queues like system_power_efficient_wq for energy-aware scheduling or system_freezable_wq for suspend/resume handling.

Internally, workqueues use pools of kworker threads (kworker/u*:* for unbound). The concurrency manager ensures efficient thread usage, rescuing work under load. Flushing with flush_workqueue() waits for completion, crucial for module unloading.

Advantages: Handles blocking ops, better for modern drivers (e.g., USB, SCSI). Drawbacks: Higher overhead than tasklets due to scheduling.

Choosing Between Tasklets and Workqueues

- Use tasklets for quick, non-blocking deferral (e.g., simple state machines).
- Use workqueues for anything that might sleep or take time (e.g., filesystem interactions).
- For real-time: Prefer workqueues with PREEMPT_RT, as softirqs can introduce jitter.
- Migration: Kernel encourages shifting from tasklets/softirqs to workqueues for better concurrency (see Documentation/core-api/workqueue.rst).

Performance: Tasklets have lower latency (microseconds) but can cause softirq storms; monitor with cat /proc/softirqs. Workqueues scale better on SMP but watch for thread contention—use per-CPU queues if needed.

Security: Both can access kernel data, so validate inputs from top half. Avoid use-after-free by proper refcounting.

Evolution: In 6.x kernels, workqueues gained attributes like max_active for throttling. Tasklets remain but are less favored for new code.

Debugging: Use trace_softirq_raise/entry/exit ftrace events or perf record -e workqueue:*.

Summary

Tasklets and workqueues enable efficient deferred processing, balancing interrupt responsiveness with workload complexity. By offloading work from atomic contexts, they enhance kernel stability and performance. Mastery of these mechanisms is vital for driver developers, allowing seamless integration with hardware events. The next section on deferred interrupt work will build on this, exploring advanced patterns like combining these with timers and signals for comprehensive bottom-half strategies.

14.4 Deferred Interrupt Work

Deferred interrupt work encompasses advanced techniques for postponing non-essential processing from interrupt contexts, building on the foundational bottom-half mechanisms like tasklets and workqueues discussed in the previous section. While tasklets and workqueues handle much of the deferral needs, certain scenarios—such as high-frequency interrupts, network packet processing, or real-time constraints—require more specialized approaches. These methods optimize system throughput, reduce latency jitter, and improve scalability on multicore systems. In Linux, deferred work ensures that interrupt handlers (top halves) remain lightweight, delegating heavier lifting to contexts where preemption, sleeping, or extended computation is feasible.

This section explores key deferred interrupt strategies, including softirqs (the underlying engine for tasklets), threaded interrupt handlers, New API (NAPI) for networking, and other optimizations like interrupt coalescing. We'll examine their implementation, use cases, and integration with kernel subsystems, with practical examples for driver developers. Understanding these allows for crafting efficient, responsive systems, particularly in embedded, server, or high-performance computing environments.

Softirqs: The Core of Deferred Processing

Softirqs form the bedrock of deferred interrupt work in Linux, providing a prioritized, per-CPU mechanism for executing bottom halves. Unlike hardware IRQs, softirqs are software-triggered and run in a controlled interrupt context after the top half completes. They are raised by raise_softirq(irq) or raise_softirq_irqoff(irq) and processed by do_softirq() at strategic points: post-IRQ, during ksoftirqd threads, or via irq_exit().

There are fixed softirq vectors (defined in enum softirq_action in include/linux/interrupt.h):

- HI_SOFTIRQ: High-priority tasklets.
- TIMER_SOFTIRQ: Timer expirations.
- NET_TX_SOFTIRQ and NET_RX_SOFTIRQ: Network transmission and reception.
- BLOCK_SOFTIRQ: Block I/O completion.
- IRQ_POLL_SOFTIRQ: IRQ polling for missed interrupts.
- TASKLET_SOFTIRQ: Standard tasklets.
- SCHED_SOFTIRQ: Scheduler balancing.
- HRTIMER_SOFTIRQ: High-resolution timers.
- RCU_SOFTIRQ: Read-Copy-Update processing.

Softirqs execute in priority order, with per-CPU pending masks checked in __do_softirq(). If overload occurs (e.g., exceeding MAX_SOFTIRQ_RESTART=10 or time limits), work offloads to ksoftirqd/n threads (one per CPU).

For custom use, while direct softirq registration is discouraged (favor tasklets/workqueues), drivers can leverage them indirectly. For instance, network drivers use netif_rx_schedule() to raise NET_RX_SOFTIRQ.

Example of manual softirq handling (rare, for illustration):

```c
#include <linux/interrupt.h>
#include <linux/module.h>

static void my_softirq_handler(void) {
    // Deferred work: process data
    printk(KERN_INFO "Softirq handler running\n");
}

static int __init my_module_init(void) {
    open_softirq(MY_CUSTOM_SOFTIRQ, my_softirq_handler); // Register (use a free vector if custom)
    return 0;
}
```

```c
static irqreturn_t my_isr(int irq, void *dev_id) {
    // Top half
    raise_softirq(MY_CUSTOM_SOFTIRQ);
    return IRQ_HANDLED;
}
```

```c
module_init(my_module_init);
MODULE_LICENSE("GPL");
```

Monitor softirqs via /proc/softirqs. In real-time kernels (PREEMPT_RT), softirqs run as threads to minimize latency.

Threaded Interrupt Handlers

Introduced in 2.6.30, threaded IRQs transform traditional handlers into kernel threads, allowing the entire bottom half (or even the whole handler) to run in process context. This is ideal for interrupts requiring sleepable operations, reducing the need for explicit workqueues.

Enable with IRQF_ONESHOT (masks IRQ until thread completes) and use request_threaded_irq():

```c
int request_threaded_irq(unsigned int irq, irq_handler_t handler,
                 irq_handler_t thread_fn, unsigned long flags,
                 const char *name, void *dev);
```

- handler: Top half (can be NULL for fully threaded).
- thread_fn: Threaded bottom half, runs in process context, can sleep.

Example for a GPIO driver:

```c
#include <linux/interrupt.h>
#include <linux/gpio.h>
#include <linux/module.h>

static irqreturn_t my_top_half(int irq, void *dev_id) {
    // Minimal: acknowledge hardware
    return IRQ_WAKE_THREAD;  // Wake the thread
}

static irqreturn_t my_thread_fn(int irq, void *dev_id) {
    // Deferred: sleepable work, e.g., mutex_lock(), process events
    msleep(10);  // Simulate blocking I/O
    printk(KERN_INFO "Threaded handler for IRQ %d\n", irq);
    return IRQ_HANDLED;
}

static int __init my_module_init(void) {
    int ret = request_threaded_irq(gpio_to_irq(MY_GPIO), my_top_half, my_thread_fn,
                        IRQF_TRIGGER_RISING | IRQF_ONESHOT, "my_gpio", NULL);
    if (ret) return ret;
    return 0;
}

static void __exit my_module_exit(void) {
    free_irq(gpio_to_irq(MY_GPIO), NULL);
}

module_init(my_module_init);
module_exit(my_module_exit);
MODULE_LICENSE("GPL");
```

Threaded IRQs use irq_thread() to manage execution, with priority adjustable via irq_set_thread_priority(). They shine in USB, input, or slow hardware drivers, but add scheduling overhead—avoid for high-frequency IRQs.

NAPI: Polling for High-Throughput Interrupts

The New API (NAPI), primarily for networking but applicable elsewhere, replaces interrupt-driven RX with polling to handle packet bursts efficiently. Under load, it disables interrupts and polls the device in a softirq context, reducing IRQ overhead.

Key steps:

1. Driver registers a poll function via netif_napi_add().
2. On interrupt, raise NET_RX_SOFTIRQ and schedule NAPI with napi_schedule().
3. In net_rx_action() (softirq handler), call poll() until quota (e.g., 300 packets) or no more work.

Example skeleton for a network driver:

```c
#include <linux/netdevice.h>

static int my_poll(struct napi_struct *napi, int budget) {
    struct net_device *dev = napi->dev;
    int work_done = 0;
    // Process packets: rx, clean rings
    while (work_done < budget) {
        // If no more packets, break
        if (!rx_packet()) break;
        work_done++;
    }
    if (work_done < budget)
        napi_complete_done(napi, work_done);  // Re-enable interrupts if done
    return work_done;
}

static irqreturn_t my_net_isr(int irq, void *dev_id) {
    struct net_device *dev = dev_id;
    napi_schedule(&dev->napi);
    return IRQ_HANDLED;
}

static int my_net_open(struct net_device *dev) {
    netif_napi_add(dev, &dev->napi, my_poll);
    napi_enable(&dev->napi);
    // Request IRQ
    return 0;
}
```

NAPI scales for gigabit+ networks, mitigating "receive livelock" by bounding work per softirq invocation.

Additional Deferred Techniques and Optimizations

- **Interrupt Coalescing:** Hardware feature (ethtool -C) groups interrupts, reducing frequency. Kernel supports via MSI-X multiple queues.
- **IRQ Polling:** For missed IRQs (e.g., shared lines), IRQ_POLL_SOFTIRQ polls registered handlers.
- **Deferred Work with Timers:** Combine with hrtimer or timer_list for timed deferral, e.g., mod_timer().
- **Real-Time Considerations:** In RT kernels, force threaded IRQs globally via irq_forced_threading.
- **SMP Affinity and Balancing:** Use irq_set_affinity_hint() to pin IRQs, preventing migration during deferral.

Best practices:

- Profile with perf record -e irq:* or ftrace to identify bottlenecks.
- Avoid over-deferral; balance with direct handling for low-latency needs.
- Ensure atomicity: Use local_bh_disable() in bottom halves for softirq protection.
- Security: Validate data from top to bottom half to prevent races.

Performance impacts: Deferral reduces context switches but can increase queueing delays—tune via sysctls like net.core.netdev_budget.

Summary

Deferred interrupt work refines the top/bottom half paradigm, offering tailored mechanisms for diverse workloads. From softirqs' efficiency to threaded handlers' flexibility and NAPI's throughput, these tools empower developers to optimize interrupt-driven systems. Integrating them with prior concepts like exceptions and synchronization (Chapter 13) yields robust kernels. Practical application through projects (Chapter 25) will solidify these techniques, preparing you for real-world driver and subsystem contributions.

15. File Systems and the Virtual File System (VFS)

The Linux kernel's file system support is one of its most powerful features, enabling seamless integration of diverse storage mechanisms—from local disks to network shares and virtual file systems. At the heart of this is the Virtual File System (VFS), an abstraction layer that provides a uniform interface for user-space applications and the kernel to interact with underlying file systems. VFS decouples the generic file operations from specific implementations, allowing Linux to support dozens of file systems (e.g., ext4, NTFS, NFS) without changing system calls like open(), read(), or mkdir(). This chapter explores file system internals, starting with VFS, then delving into core components like inodes and caches, and advanced file systems.

15.1 VFS Structure and Interfaces

The VFS acts as a middleware between user processes and concrete file system drivers, translating generic operations into file-system-specific actions. Introduced in early UNIX and refined in Linux, VFS ensures portability and extensibility: new file systems can be added as kernel modules without altering core APIs. It handles path resolution, caching, permissions, and I/O, while delegating storage details to the underlying file system.

At its core, VFS revolves around a set of key data structures and operation vectors that define behaviors. These structures are defined in headers like include/linux/fs.h and include/linux/dcache.h. Understanding VFS starts with these building blocks, which represent files, directories, and mounts in a unified way.

Key Data Structures in VFS

VFS models the file system hierarchy using object-oriented-like structures, where each has associated operations (methods) and data (attributes):

- **super_block:** Represents a mounted file system instance (e.g., a partition). It holds global information like block size, root inode, and mount flags. Each file system type (e.g., ext4) provides a super_operations structure with functions like alloc_inode() or write_super().
- **inode (Index Node):** The fundamental unit for files, directories, devices, or symlinks. It stores metadata such as permissions, timestamps, size, and block pointers. The inode_operations vector handles directory operations (e.g., lookup(), mkdir()), while address_space_operations manages page caching for file data.
- **dentry (Directory Entry):** Caches directory lookups for performance, linking names to inodes. It avoids repeated disk accesses for path resolution. The dentry_operations include validation and hashing.
- **file:** Represents an open file descriptor in a process. It tracks position, flags, and points to the inode. The file_operations vector defines core I/O like read(), write(), mmap(), and ioctl().
- **vfsmount and mount:** Handle mount points, allowing nested file systems (e.g., bind mounts). The mount tree is navigated during path lookups.

These structures form a graph: paths are resolved by traversing dentries to inodes, with super_blocks anchoring file systems.

The VFS maintains global caches:

- **Inode Cache:** Slabs of inodes, managed by inode_hash.
- **Dentry Cache:** LRU-based, pruned under memory pressure via shrink_dcache_sb().
- **Page Cache:** For file data, integrated with memory management (Chapter 12).

VFS Interfaces and Operations

VFS exposes interfaces through system calls, which are funneled via syscall entry points to VFS functions like vfs_open() or vfs_read(). These dispatch to the appropriate operations based on the file system's type.

Key operation vectors:

- **file_operations (fops):** User-facing I/O. Example members:
    - ssize_t (*read)(struct file *, char __user *, size_t, loff_t *);
    - ssize_t (*write)(struct file *, const char __user *, size_t, loff_t *);
    - int (*mmap)(struct file *, struct vm_area_struct *);
- **inode_operations (iops):** Metadata and directory ops.
    - struct dentry *(*lookup)(struct inode *, struct dentry *, unsigned int);
    - int (*create)(struct mnt_idmap *, struct inode *, struct dentry *, umode_t, bool);
- **super_operations (sops):** File-system-wide.
    - struct inode *(*alloc_inode)(struct super_block *sb);
    - void (*destroy_inode)(struct inode *);

File systems register with VFS via register_filesystem(&fs_type), where struct file_system_type specifies the name, mount function, and flags.

Path resolution is a critical VFS interface, handled by lookup_path() or path_lookup(). It tokenizes paths (e.g., "/home/user/file.txt"), resolves each component via link_path_walk(), following symlinks and mounts, and returns a struct path (dentry + vfsmount).

For mounting: mount() syscall leads to vfs_kern_mount(), which calls the file system's get_sb() or modern mount() callback to fill the super_block.

Implementing VFS Interactions

Device drivers or custom file systems interact with VFS by providing these operations. Here's a minimal example of a ramfs-like file system module, focusing on VFS registration and basic ops:

c

```c
#include <linux/fs.h>
#include <linux/module.h>
#include <linux/pagemap.h>

static struct inode *myfs_alloc_inode(struct super_block *sb) {
    struct inode *inode = new_inode(sb);
    if (inode) {
        inode->i_ino = get_next_ino();
        inode->i_op = &simple_dir_inode_operations;  // From fs/libfs.c
        inode->i_fop = &simple_dir_operations;
    }
    return inode;
}

static const struct super_operations myfs_sops = {
    .alloc_inode = myfs_alloc_inode,
    .destroy_inode = destroy_inode,
    .statfs = simple_statfs,
};

static int myfs_fill_super(struct super_block *sb, void *data, int silent) {
    struct inode *root = myfs_alloc_inode(sb);
    if (!root) return -ENOMEM;
    root->i_mode = S_IFDIR | 0755;
    sb->s_root = d_make_root(root);
    if (!sb->s_root) return -ENOMEM;
    sb->s_op = &myfs_sops;
    return 0;
}

static struct dentry *myfs_mount(struct file_system_type *fs_type, int flags,
                    const char *dev_name, void *data) {
    return mount_nodev(fs_type, flags, data, myfs_fill_super);
}

static struct file_system_type myfs_type = {
    .owner = THIS_MODULE,
    .name = "myfs",
    .mount = myfs_mount,
    .kill_sb = kill_litter_super,
    .fs_flags = FS_REQUIRES_DEV,
};

static int __init myfs_init(void) {
    return register_filesystem(&myfs_type);
```

```
}

static void __exit myfs_exit(void) {
    unregister_filesystem(&myfs_type);
}
```

```
module_init(myfs_init);
module_exit(myfs_exit);
MODULE_LICENSE("GPL");
```
This registers "myfs", creates a root inode, and uses libfs helpers for simplicity. Mount with mount -t myfs none /mnt/myfs.

For reading/writing, extend file_operations. VFS handles buffering via generic_file_read_iter() if address_space_operations are set.

Security and Performance in VFS

VFS enforces permissions via inode_permission() during lookups, integrating with LSMs (e.g., SELinux). It supports namespaces for containers, isolating mounts.

Performance relies on caching: dentries reduce lookups, page cache accelerates I/O. Under pressure, vmscan reclaims pages, calling invalidate_mapping_pages().

Modern enhancements include fanotify for monitoring and fscrypt for encryption, both hooked into VFS.

Summary

The VFS structure and interfaces provide a elegant abstraction, enabling Linux's file system diversity while maintaining a consistent API. By mastering these data structures and operations, developers can implement or extend file systems efficiently. This foundation paves the way for deeper exploration of inode management and caching in the next sections, essential for optimizing storage performance in real-world scenarios.

15.2 Inode and Dentry Management

Inode and dentry management are central to the efficiency and functionality of the Virtual File System (VFS) in Linux. Inodes represent the metadata and content anchors for files and directories, while dentries provide a caching layer for fast path resolution and directory navigation. Together, they enable quick access to file system objects, reduce I/O overhead, and support complex operations like mounting and symlinks. This section examines their structures, lifecycles, operations, and management strategies, with insights into kernel implementations for developers aiming to extend or debug file systems.

Inode Fundamentals

An inode (short for "index node") is a data structure that stores essential metadata about a file system object, such as a regular file, directory, symbolic link, device, or FIFO. Unlike user-space views, inodes do not include the file name—that's handled by dentries. Inodes are uniquely identified within their superblock by an inode number (i_ino), and they persist on storage media in file-system-specific formats (e.g., ext4's on-disk inode).

The kernel's in-memory representation is struct inode (defined in include/linux/fs.h), which includes:

- **Metadata Fields:** i_mode (file type and permissions, e.g., S_IFREG for regular files), i_uid and i_gid (owner/group), i_size (file length in bytes), i_atime, i_mtime, i_ctime (timestamps), i_blocks (allocated blocks).
- **Pointers and Lists:** i_sb (superblock pointer), i_mapping (address_space for page cache), i_private (file-system-specific data), and list heads for hashing and LRU.
- **Reference Counting:** i_count (reference count) and i_lock (spinlock for synchronization).
- **Operations:** Pointers to inode_operations and file_operations (shared if not open).

Inodes are allocated by the file system's super_operations->alloc_inode(), often using slab caches for efficiency (e.g., inode_cachep). For example, ext4 uses ext4_alloc_inode() to initialize ext4-specific extensions.

Inode lifecycle:

1. **Creation:** On file creation (vfs_create()), VFS calls inode_init_owner() to set ownership, then the file system's create() op.
2. **Lookup and Caching:** Inodes are hashed in inode_hash (per-superblock) for quick retrieval via find_inode(). If not in cache, iget_locked() loads from disk using read_inode().
3. **Reference Management:** iget() increments i_count; iput() decrements and evicts if zero, calling evict_inode() which may sync to disk.

4. **Eviction:** Under memory pressure, the inode shrinker (inode_lru_isolate()) reclaims unused inodes (state I_RECLAIM). Dirty inodes are written back via writeback_inodes_sb().

File systems can mark inodes dirty with mark_inode_dirty() , queuing them for writeback. For security, inode_permission() checks access based on i_mode, capabilities, and ACLs (if enabled via posix_acl).

Special inodes include anonymous ones (e.g., for pipes via anon_inode_getfile()) and pseudo-inodes for procfs or sysfs.

Dentry Fundamentals

A dentry (directory entry) caches the mapping between a file name and its inode, accelerating path lookups by avoiding repeated disk reads. Dentries form a tree structure mirroring the file system hierarchy, with each containing a name, parent pointer, and inode link.

The struct dentry includes:

- **Core Fields:** d_name (hashed name via qstr), d_inode (linked inode, NULL for negative dentries), d_parent (parent dentry), d_flags (e.g., DCACHE_DISCONNECTED for unhashed).
- **Hashing and Lists:** d_hash for global dentry hash table, d_lru for reclamation, d_child for sibling lists.
- **Reference Counting:** d_count, protected by d_lock.
- **Operations:** d_op pointing to dentry_operations, with methods like d_revalidate() (for NFS) or d_hash() (custom hashing).

Dentries are allocated from dentry_cache slab. Negative dentries (no inode, indicating non-existence) are crucial for caching failed lookups, reducing futile disk accesses.

Dentry lifecycle:

1. **Allocation:** d_alloc() or d_alloc_root() for mount roots.
2. **Lookup:** During path resolution (path_lookup()), VFS uses lookup_fast() (cache hit) or lookup_slow() (miss, calling inode's lookup() op).
3. **Instantiation:** d_instantiate() links a new dentry to an inode after creation.
4. **Hashing:** Inserted into hash via d_hash_and_lookup(), using d_hash() for case-insensitivity if needed.
5. **Eviction:** The dentry shrinker prunes unused entries via shrink_dcache_parent() or prune_dcache(). dput() decrements count; if zero, dentry_kill() may free it.

Dentries support aliases (multiple names for one inode, e.g., hard links) via d_alias list on the inode.

Interactions Between Inodes and Dentries

Inodes and dentries are interdependent: a dentry points to an inode, and inodes track their dentries via i_dentry. This enables operations like renaming (vfs_rename()) which updates dentries without reloading inodes.

Path walking (link_path_walk()) traverses dentries component-by-component:

- Start from root or current working directory (current->fs->pwd).
- For each segment, hash-lookup in parent's d_subdirs.
- Handle symlinks by recursing (up to 40 levels to prevent loops).
- Mount points are crossed via follow_mount().

Concurrency is managed with RCU (Read-Copy-Update) for lock-free lookups in lookup_fast(), falling back to locks on contention. The rename_lock seqlock protects against concurrent renames during walks.

For performance, VFS uses seqlocks on dentries for validation (d_seq). File systems like NFS implement d_revalidate() to check staleness.

Management and Optimization Techniques

- **Caching Strategies:** Both inodes and dentries use LRU lists for eviction. Sysctls like vm.vfs_cache_pressure tune reclamation priority (higher values favor dentries/inodes over page cache).
- **Superblock Integration:** Each super_block has its own inode and dentry lists (s_inodes, s_dentry_lru), allowing per-file-system management (e.g., shrink_dcache_sb()).
- **Debugging Tools:** /proc/sys/fs/{dentry-state,inode-state} show stats. slabtop monitors cache usage. Tracing via ftrace (e.g., trace_dentry_lru_add()) aids debugging.
- **File-System-Specific Extensions:** Ext4 inodes include extended attributes (i_extra_isize), while Btrfs uses compressed inodes. Dentries in overlayfs handle layered lookups.
- **Security Considerations:** Inode changes trigger security hooks (e.g., security_inode_setattr()). Namespaces isolate dentry trees for containers.

Practical example: Implementing a custom inode lookup in a file system module (simplified):

c

```
#include <linux/fs.h>
```

```
static struct dentry *myfs_lookup(struct inode *dir, struct dentry *dentry, unsigned int flags) {
    struct inode *inode = NULL;
    // File-system-specific search: e.g., read directory block, find name
    if (found) {
        inode = myfs_iget(dir->i_sb, ino);  // Load or create inode
        if (IS_ERR(inode)) return ERR_CAST(inode);
    }
    d_add(dentry, inode);  // Attach inode (NULL for negative)
    return NULL;  // Success
}

static const struct inode_operations myfs_dir_iops = {
    .lookup = myfs_lookup,
    // Other ops: create, unlink, etc.
};
```

This hooks into VFS path resolution, demonstrating how file systems extend inode/dentry management. Advanced topics include dentry pruning in unmount (umount() calls generic_shutdown_super()), and integration with page cache (inode's i_mapping for read-ahead via readpages()).

15.3 Page Cache and Buffer Cache

The page cache and buffer cache are pivotal components in the Linux kernel's I/O subsystem, serving as intermediaries between user-space applications, the Virtual File System (VFS), and underlying storage devices. These caches optimize data access by minimizing costly disk operations, leveraging RAM to store frequently used data. The page cache handles file-backed pages in a unified manner, while the buffer cache—historically distinct but now integrated—manages block device I/O. Together, they enhance system performance, support memory-mapped I/O, and facilitate efficient read/write operations. Understanding their mechanics is essential for kernel developers working on file systems, drivers, or performance tuning, as they intersect with memory management (Chapter 12) and file I/O (Chapter 4). This section explores their architecture, operations, integration, and advanced features, providing a comprehensive guide with code insights.

Evolution and Conceptual Overview

Historically, UNIX systems maintained separate caches: the buffer cache for block devices (e.g., raw disk blocks) and the page cache for file pages. In early Linux (pre-2.4), this duality led to inefficiencies, such as double caching where file data was buffered twice—once in pages and once in buffers. The 2.4 kernel unified them under the page cache, making it the primary mechanism for all file and block I/O. Today, the "buffer cache" refers to buffers attached to pages (via buffer_heads), but it's subservient to the page cache.

The page cache is a collection of RAM pages (typically 4KB on x86) that cache file contents. Each page is associated with an address_space (embedded in inodes or block devices), which maps file offsets to physical pages. This allows seamless mmap() support, where user processes map files directly into their address space without copying.

In contrast, the buffer cache uses struct buffer_head to represent smaller blocks (e.g., 512B sectors) within pages. Buffers are used for metadata I/O (e.g., superblocks, inodes) or when file systems need sub-page granularity. However, for most data I/O, the kernel prefers page-based operations to reduce overhead.

Key benefits include:

- **Read-Ahead:** Prefetching pages to anticipate sequential reads.
- **Write-Back:** Delaying writes to batch them, improving throughput.
- **Coherency:** Ensuring cached data matches storage via syncing mechanisms.
- **Reclaimability:** Integration with the MMU for swapping or eviction under pressure.

These caches are per-inode (via inode->i_mapping) or per-device (for block devs via bdev->bd_mapping), allowing fine-grained control.

Page Cache Structure and Operations

The page cache is built around struct page (from include/linux/mm_types.h), which represents a physical page frame. For cached file data, pages are indexed in a radix tree (mapping->i_pages) within the address_space. This tree enables O(log n) lookups by file offset.

Core operations are defined in address_space_operations (aops), pointed to by mapping->a_ops. File systems implement these to bridge VFS and storage:

- read_folio(): Loads a folio (multi-page unit, introduced in 5.18 for efficiency) from disk.
- writepages(): Writes dirty pages back.
- dirty_folio(): Marks a folio dirty after modification.
- invalidate_folio(): Discards cached data (e.g., on truncate).

Folios generalize pages, allowing larger units (e.g., 64KB) to reduce metadata overhead, especially on ARM64 or with THP (Transparent Huge Pages).

To insert a page: filemap_add_folio() allocates and indexes a folio. Lookups use filemap_get_folio(), which may trigger read-ahead via page_cache_ra_unbounded().

For reading: vfs_read() calls filemap_read(), which checks the cache. If missed, it allocates pages, locks them (folio_lock()), and invokes aops->read_folio() to fill from disk (e.g., via submit_bio() for block I/O).

Writing follows filemap_write_and_wait(), marking pages dirty and scheduling writeback. The flusher threads (kswapd or background writeback) call writeback_inodes_sb() to process dirty mappings.

Code example: A simplified read operation in a custom file system:

```c
#include <linux/fs.h>
#include <linux/pagemap.h>

static int myfs_read_folio(struct file *file, struct folio *folio) {
    struct inode *inode = folio_mapping(folio)->host;
    // File-system-specific: map offset to block
    sector_t block = folio_pos(folio) >> SECTOR_SHIFT;
    struct bio *bio = bio_alloc(inode->i_sb->s_bdev, 1, REQ_OP_READ, GFP_KERNEL);
    bio_add_folio(bio, folio, folio_size(folio), 0);
    bio->bi_iter.bi_sector = block;
    submit_bio_wait(bio);
    if (bio->bi_status != BLK_STS_OK) {
        folio_set_error(folio);
        bio_put(bio);
        return -EIO;
    }
    bio_put(bio);
    return 0;
}

static const struct address_space_operations myfs_aops = {
    .read_folio = myfs_read_folio,
    .writepages = generic_writepages, // Use libfs helper
    .dirty_folio = filemap_dirty_folio,
};
```

This hooks into VFS: When an inode is created, set inode->i_mapping->a_ops = &myfs_aops;.

Buffer Cache Integration and Usage

While unified, the buffer cache persists for legacy and metadata needs. struct buffer_head (bh) attaches to pages via page_buffers(), forming a linked list for sub-page blocks. Buffers track state (e.g., BH_Uptodate, BH_Dirty) and are used in blockdev I/O.

Allocation: alloc_buffer_head() from slab. Attachment: create_page_buffers().

For block devices, getblk() retrieves a bh, potentially allocating pages. Metadata reads (e.g., superblock) use sb_bread(), which gets a bh and submits if not uptodate.

In modern kernels, direct page I/O is preferred; buffers are a fallback. For example, ext4 uses buffers for journal metadata but pages for data.

Writeback for buffers: submit_bh() sends via bio, but often wrapped in page writeback.

Example: Reading a block device's sector:

```c
#include <linux/buffer_head.h>
```

```c
struct buffer_head *read_block(struct block_device *bdev, sector_t sector) {
    struct buffer_head *bh = __getblk(bdev, sector, 512);
    if (bh) {
        if (!buffer_uptodate(bh)) {
            submit_bh(REQ_OP_READ, bh);
            wait_on_buffer(bh);
            if (!buffer_uptodate(bh)) {
                brelse(bh);
                return NULL;
            }
        }
    }
    return bh;
}
```
Use brelse() to release. For syncing: sync_dirty_buffer().

Caching Mechanisms and Performance Optimizations

Read-ahead is managed by readahead_control, predicting patterns (sequential vs. random) to prefetch. Tunable via /sys/block/<dev>/queue/read_ahead_kb.

Write-back uses the writeback subsystem (mm/writeback.c). Dirty pages are tracked in inode->i_wb_list, flushed when thresholds exceed (/proc/sys/vm/dirty_ratio). balance_dirty_pages() throttles writers to prevent overload.

Reclamation integrates with VM: try_to_free_pages() scans mappings, calling shrink_folio_list() to evict clean pages or write dirty ones. File systems can hook via release_folio().

For coherency, invalidate_mapping_pages() discards ranges (e.g., on file truncate). Direct I/O (O_DIRECT) bypasses cache using direct_IO().

In SMP environments, per-CPU pagevecs batch operations to reduce locking. Folios reduce radix tree contention.

THP support: If enabled, read_folio() can allocate huge folios, boosting TLB efficiency for large files.

Debugging: /proc/meminfo shows Cached and Buffers. ftrace traces like filemap_add_folio help. Tools like fio benchmark I/O, revealing cache effects.

Security: Caches can leak data; features like fsverity verify cached pages. LSMs hook into mapping (e.g., security_mmap_file()).

Advanced Topics and Use Cases

In containers, namespaces isolate caches indirectly via mounts. For network file systems (NFS), cache consistency uses delegation or close-to-open semantics.

Huge pages in cache: With CONFIG_TRANSPARENT_HUGEPAGE, file caches can use 2MB pages, set via madvise(MADV_HUGEPAGE).

Swap cache: Anonymous pages use a similar mechanism, but file pages can be swapped if reclaimable.

In embedded systems, tune caches via vm.drop_caches sysctl for testing.

Real-time: PREEMPT_RT minimizes cache-related latencies by threading flushers.

Historical note: Pre-unification, buffer cache was a fixed-size hash; unification halved memory use for file I/O.

Case study: In ext4, data pages use extent mappings in inode, with aops directing to block layer. For journaling, metadata buffers ensure atomicity.

Performance pitfalls: Over-caching leads to OOM; under-caching increases I/O. Tune with bdflush params or cgroup I/O limits.

Integration with DAX (Direct Access): For PMEM, bypass page cache entirely (CONFIG_FS_DAX), mapping storage directly to pages.

Summary

The page cache and buffer cache form the backbone of efficient I/O in Linux, unifying memory and storage management to deliver high performance. By caching data in RAM and providing extensible operations, they enable diverse file systems while optimizing for modern hardware. Developers leveraging these—through custom aops or bh usage—can build robust, scalable storage solutions. This knowledge bridges to advanced file systems like ext4 and Btrfs in the next section, where cache interactions drive features like snapshots and compression.

15.4 Advanced File Systems (ext4, Btrfs)

Advanced file systems in Linux push the boundaries of storage management, offering features like enhanced reliability, scalability, and performance optimizations beyond basic POSIX compliance. ext4 (fourth extended file system) and Btrfs (B-Tree File System) exemplify this evolution, serving as workhorses for local storage in servers, desktops, and embedded systems. ext4 builds on the proven ext3 lineage with incremental improvements for large-scale deployments, while Btrfs introduces innovative copy-on-write (CoW) semantics for snapshots, RAID, and data integrity. Both integrate seamlessly with the VFS (Section 15.1), leveraging inodes, dentries (Section 15.2), and caches (Section 15.3) while providing custom implementations for super_operations, inode_operations, and address_space_operations. This section dissects their architectures, key features, internals, and practical considerations, equipping developers to select, configure, and extend these systems.

ext4: Evolution and Core Features

ext4, introduced in Linux 2.6.28 (2008), extends ext3 with support for larger volumes, faster operations, and better error handling, making it the default for many distributions like Ubuntu and Fedora. It maintains backward compatibility with ext2/3, allowing seamless upgrades via tune2fs. ext4 addresses ext3's limitations, such as 2TB file size caps and slow fsck times, by introducing extents, delayed allocation, and journaling enhancements. Key features:

- **Extents:** Instead of indirect block pointers (which fragment in ext3), ext4 uses extents—contiguous block ranges stored in inode or extent trees. This reduces metadata overhead for large files, improving read/write throughput. An extent header in the inode can map up to 128MB contiguously.
- **Large File and Volume Support:** Files up to 16TB, file systems up to 1EB (exabyte). Uses 64-bit block addressing.
- **Delayed Allocation:** Defers block allocation until writeback, allowing better contiguous placement and reducing fragmentation. Controlled via delalloc mount option.
- **Journaling Modes:** Data (full journaling), ordered (default, metadata + data ordering), writeback (metadata only). Checksums in journal prevent corruption.
- **Multi-Block Allocation (mballoc):** Groups allocations for efficiency, using buddy bitmaps and per-group metadata.
- **Online Defragmentation:** Via e4defrag tool, which uses ext4 ioctls to relocate extents.
- **Other Enhancements:** Punch hole (fallocate with FALLOC_FL_PUNCH_HOLE for sparse files), bigalloc (clusters > page size for huge volumes), metadata checksums (for integrity), and fast extended attributes.

Internally, ext4's on-disk layout includes a superblock (with magic 0xEF53), group descriptors, block/inode bitmaps, and inode tables. Inodes are 256 bytes by default (extensible to 1024+ via inline data). The extent tree is a B-tree-like structure rooted in the inode's i_block area.

Kernel integration: ext4 registers via ext4_file_system_type in fs/ext4/super.c. Mounting calls ext4_fill_super(), which parses the superblock, initializes the journal (if enabled via JBD2), and sets up caches. Inode operations use ext4_inode_operations, with lookup() scanning directory extents.

For I/O, ext4's address_space_operations include ext4_writepages() for multi-page writeback and ext4_read_folio() for reading extents. Direct I/O bypasses the page cache using ext4_direct_IO().

Example: Creating and mounting an ext4 file system programmatically (e.g., in a test module):

```c
#include <linux/fs.h>
#include <linux/module.h>
#include <linux/blkdev.h>

static int __init ext4_test_init(void) {
    struct block_device *bdev = blkdev_get_by_path("/dev/sda1", BLK_OPEN_READ | BLK_OPEN_WRITE, NULL, NULL);
    if (IS_ERR(bdev)) return PTR_ERR(bdev);

    struct super_block *sb = sget(&ext4_fs_type, NULL, set_anon_super, 0, NULL);
    if (IS_ERR(sb)) {
        blkdev_put(bdev, NULL);
        return PTR_ERR(sb);
    }
```

```c
    int err = ext4_fill_super(sb, bdev, 0);  // 0 for non-silent
    if (err) {
        deactivate_locked_super(sb);
        blkdev_put(bdev, NULL);
        return err;
    }

    printk(KERN_INFO "ext4 mounted successfully\n");
    // Use sb->s_root for operations
    deactivate_locked_super(sb);
    blkdev_put(bdev, NULL);
    return 0;
}

module_init(ext4_test_init);
MODULE_LICENSE("GPL");
```

This demonstrates superblock setup; in practice, use user-space tools like mkfs.ext4 for creation.

Performance: ext4 excels in sequential workloads, with benchmarks showing 20-50% faster writes than ext3 due to delalloc. However, it lacks native snapshots or compression.

Btrfs: Copy-on-Write and Modern Features

Btrfs, stabilized around Linux 3.10 (2013) and developed by Oracle initially, represents a paradigm shift with its CoW design, where modifications create new data versions rather than overwriting. This enables efficient snapshots, subvolumes, and built-in RAID, making it ideal for data centers, NAS, and backups. Unlike ext4's block-based approach, Btrfs uses B-trees for all metadata and data, providing dynamic allocation and inherent checksumming.

Key features:

- **Copy-on-Write (CoW):** All updates clone blocks, preserving old versions. This avoids data corruption on crashes and supports snapshots via shared extents.
- **Snapshots and Subvolumes:** Instantaneous, writable snapshots (e.g., via btrfs subvolume snapshot). Subvolumes are independent trees, mountable separately.
- **Integrated RAID:** Supports RAID0/1/5/6/10 via striping/mirroring at the chunk level, with online scrubbing and balancing.
- **Checksums and Integrity:** CRC32C (or stronger like xxhash) on all data/metadata, detecting silent corruption. Self-healing in RAID setups.
- **Compression:** Transparent LZO/ZSTD/zlib at the extent level, reducing storage use.
- **Quotas and Reflink:** Subvolume quotas, deduplication, and clone-range (reflink) for efficient copies.
- **Send/Receive:** Incremental backups by diffing snapshots.
- **Other:** Online resize/def rag, seed devices, and TRIM support for SSDs.

On-disk, Btrfs uses multiple B-trees: uuid_tree, chunk_tree, dev_tree, fs_tree (per subvolume), extent_tree, csum_tree. Superblocks are replicated at fixed offsets. Extents are reference-counted, shared across snapshots.

Kernel mounting via btrfs_file_system_type calls mount_btrfs(), initializing trees and transaction manager. Transactions group changes atomically, committed periodically.

Inode ops use btrfs_inode_operations, with CoW in btrfs_file_write_iter(). Address space ops include btrfs_read_folio() (handling compressed extents) and btrfs_writepages().

Example: Programmatic snapshot creation using Btrfs ioctls:

```c
c
#include <linux/btrfs.h>
#include <sys/ioctl.h>
#include <fcntl.h>
#include <stdio.h>
#include <stdlib.h>

int main(int argc, char **argv) {
    if (argc != 3) {
```

```c
        fprintf(stderr, "Usage: %s <source_subvol> <dest_snapshot>\n", argv[0]);
        return 1;
    }

    int fd = open("/", O_DIRECTORY);  // Open mount point
    if (fd < 0) {
        perror("open");
        return 1;
    }

    struct btrfs_ioctl_vol_args_v2 args = {0};
    args.flags = BTRFS_SUBVOL_CREATE_ASYNC;  // Optional async
    strncpy(args.name, argv[2], BTRFS_PATH_NAME_MAX);

    int src_fd = open(argv[1], O_DIRECTORY);
    if (src_fd < 0) {
        perror("open source");
        close(fd);
        return 1;
    }
    args.fd = src_fd;

    if (ioctl(fd, BTRFS_IOC_SNAP_CREATE_V2, &args) < 0) {
        perror("ioctl");
        close(src_fd);
        close(fd);
        return 1;
    }

    printf("Snapshot created: %s\n", argv[2]);
    close(src_fd);
    close(fd);
    return 0;
}
```
Compile and run as root; this uses Btrfs-specific ioctls for subvolume operations.
Performance: Btrfs shines in snapshot-heavy workloads (e.g., virtualization), but CoW can fragment SSDs—mitigated by autodefrag. RAID5/6 had parity issues historically, stabilized in recent kernels (6.x).

Comparisons and Use Cases

ext4 is stable and performant for general-purpose use, with lower CPU overhead and faster fsck (e2fsck vs. btrfsck). It's ideal for boot partitions or where simplicity trumps features. Btrfs offers advanced data management, suiting backups (e.g., Timeshift), containers (Docker with Btrfs driver), or RAID without mdadm/LVM.
Both support encryption (via fscrypt), but Btrfs has native quotas. Migration: Tools like btrfs-convert convert ext4 to Btrfs in-place.
In kernels, enable via CONFIG_EXT4_FS and CONFIG_BTRFS_FS. Debugging: btrfs inspect-internal for Btrfs, debugfs for ext4.

16. Introduction to Device Drivers

Device drivers are the linchpin of hardware-software interaction in the Linux kernel, enabling the operating system to communicate with a vast array of peripherals and components. From simple input devices like keyboards to complex GPUs and network interfaces, drivers translate abstract system calls into hardware-specific commands. This book explores driver development, starting with foundational concepts and progressing to advanced topics like concurrency and optimization. Mastery of drivers requires understanding kernel internals (Book 3), as they operate in privileged mode with direct access to memory and interrupts.

16.1 Role of Drivers in the Kernel

Device drivers serve as the intermediary between the Linux kernel and physical hardware, abstracting device-specific details to provide a uniform interface for user-space applications and other kernel subsystems. Without drivers, the kernel would be unable to utilize hardware effectively, leading to a static, non-extensible system. Drivers encapsulate the complexity of hardware protocols, timing, and quirks, allowing the kernel to focus on higher-level tasks like process scheduling and memory management. In essence, they extend the kernel's functionality dynamically, often as loadable modules, promoting modularity and ease of maintenance.

At a high level, drivers fulfill several critical roles:

- **Hardware Abstraction:** They hide device variances behind standardized APIs. For instance, regardless of whether a storage device is an HDD, SSD, or NVMe drive, the kernel interacts via the block layer, with the driver handling the specifics.
- **Resource Management:** Drivers request and manage resources like I/O ports, memory regions, interrupts, and DMA channels. This prevents conflicts and ensures efficient utilization.
- **Event Handling:** They respond to hardware events (e.g., interrupts) and notify the kernel or user space, enabling responsive I/O.
- **Power and Configuration Management:** Modern drivers support power states (e.g., via ACPI or devfreq) and runtime configuration, crucial for energy efficiency in mobile and server environments.
- **Security and Isolation:** By running in kernel space, drivers enforce access controls, but they must be designed to avoid vulnerabilities like buffer overflows that could compromise the system.

Drivers integrate into the kernel through subsystems like the device model (devres, sysfs), which provides a hierarchical representation via /sys/devices/. This model, built on kobjects and buses (e.g., PCI, USB), allows automatic probing and binding. When a device is detected (e.g., via hotplug), the kernel matches it to a driver using modalias or IDs, calling the driver's probe() function to initialize.

Classification of Drivers

Linux categorizes drivers based on the type of device they manage, each with tailored interfaces:

- **Character (Char) Drivers:** Handle sequential, byte-stream devices like serial ports, keyboards, or sensors. They expose operations via file_operations (fops), such as open(), read(), write(), and ioctl(). Char drivers are registered with register_chrdev() or the misc subsystem for dynamic majors. Examples include /dev/tty for terminals or /dev/input/event* for mice.
- **Block Drivers:** Manage storage devices with random access, like disks. They use the block layer (include/linux/blkdev.h), registering with register_blkdev() and providing a block_device_operations structure. Key functions include submit_bio() for I/O requests. Block drivers handle queues, scheduling, and caching, interfacing with the page cache (Section 15.3).
- **Network Drivers:** For Ethernet, Wi-Fi, etc., they integrate with the netdev subsystem (include/linux/netdevice.h). Registered via register_netdev(), they provide net_device_ops for transmission/reception and ethtool ops for configuration. Network drivers often use NAPI (Section 14.4) for efficient packet handling.

Other specialized drivers include platform (for SoC-integrated devices), framebuffer (graphics), and input (HID). Drivers can be monolithic or modular; the latter, compiled as .ko files, load via insmod or modprobe, enhancing kernel flexibility.

Driver Lifecycle and Kernel Interaction

A driver's role begins with registration and ends with removal, orchestrated by the module system. The lifecycle includes:

1. **Initialization:** In module_init(), allocate resources, register with subsystems (e.g., pci_register_driver() for PCI). Probe detects hardware via bus-specific matching.
2. **Operation:** Handle I/O requests from VFS or sockets. For example, a char driver's read() might poll hardware registers or wait on a waitqueue for data.
3. **Interrupt Handling:** As covered in Chapter 14, drivers register handlers with request_irq() to process events asynchronously, deferring work to bottom halves.
4. **Cleanup:** In module_exit(), deregister and free resources to prevent leaks. The remove() callback handles device detachment.

Drivers interact with the kernel via APIs like ioremap() for memory-mapped I/O, dma_alloc_coherent() for DMA, and devm_* helpers for managed resources (automatically freed on unbind).

Security is paramount: Drivers validate user inputs (e.g., via copy_from_user()) to avoid exploits. Taint flags mark proprietary drivers, aiding debugging.

Practical Example: A Simple Char Driver

To illustrate, consider a minimal char driver for a fictional hardware counter:

c

```
#include <linux/module.h>
#include <linux/fs.h>
#include <linux/cdev.h>
#include <linux/io.h>
#include <linux/uaccess.h>

#define DEVICE_NAME "mycounter"
#define COUNTER_REG 0x100  // Hypothetical I/O address

static dev_t dev_num;
static struct cdev my_cdev;
static void __iomem *base_addr;

static ssize_t my_read(struct file *file, char __user *buf, size_t len, loff_t *off) {
    u32 count = ioread32(base_addr + COUNTER_REG);
    if (*off > 0) return 0;  // EOF after one read
    if (copy_to_user(buf, &count, sizeof(u32))) return -EFAULT;
    *off += sizeof(u32);
    return sizeof(u32);
}

static const struct file_operations my_fops = {
    .owner = THIS_MODULE,
    .read = my_read,
};

static int __init my_driver_init(void) {
    int ret = alloc_chrdev_region(&dev_num, 0, 1, DEVICE_NAME);
    if (ret) return ret;

    cdev_init(&my_cdev, &my_fops);
    ret = cdev_add(&my_cdev, dev_num, 1);
    if (ret) goto free_chrdev;

    base_addr = ioremap(0xBASE_PHYS_ADDR, 0x200);  // Map hardware
    if (!base_addr) {
        ret = -ENOMEM;
        goto del_cdev;
```

```
    }

    return 0;

del_cdev:
    cdev_del(&my_cdev);
free_chrdev:
    unregister_chrdev_region(dev_num, 1);
    return ret;
}

static void __exit my_driver_exit(void) {
    iounmap(base_addr);
    cdev_del(&my_cdev);
    unregister_chrdev_region(dev_num, 1);
}


module_init(my_driver_init);
module_exit(my_driver_exit);
MODULE_LICENSE("GPL");
MODULE_DESCRIPTION("Simple counter char driver");
```

This driver registers a major/minor, maps I/O, and provides a read operation to fetch a hardware counter. User space accesses via /dev/mycounter. In real scenarios, add error handling, interrupts, and device tree probing.

Challenges and Best Practices

Drivers can introduce instability—bugs may cause panics or data corruption. Best practices include:

- Use devm_ for resource management.
- Employ mutexes/spinlocks for concurrency (Chapter 13).
- Test with tools like ltp or kcov for coverage.
- Follow coding style (checkpatch.pl).
- For modern arches (e.g., ARM), use device tree (DT) for configuration instead of hardcoding.

In embedded systems, drivers optimize for low power; in servers, for high throughput.

Summary

Device drivers play an indispensable role in the kernel, bridging hardware and software through abstraction, resource handling, and event management. By classifying into char, block, and network types, and following a structured lifecycle, they ensure extensibility and reliability. This foundation sets the stage for exploring driver types in detail, starting with char drivers in the next section, empowering you to develop hardware integrations that leverage Linux's full potential.

16.2 Char, Block, and Network Drivers

Linux device drivers are broadly classified into three main categories—character (char), block, and network—each tailored to specific hardware interaction patterns. This classification aligns with how devices present data: sequential bytes for char, random-access blocks for block, and packet-based for network. Understanding these types allows developers to choose the appropriate framework, leveraging kernel subsystems for efficiency and standardization. Char drivers are the most flexible and simplest, ideal for custom hardware; block drivers integrate with the storage stack for high-throughput I/O; network drivers hook into the socket layer for communication. This section details their architectures, key interfaces, registration processes, and examples, building on the general role of drivers (Section 16.1).

Character (Char) Drivers

Char drivers manage devices that handle data as a stream of bytes, without inherent structure or seeking. Common examples include serial ports (/dev/ttyS*), input devices (/dev/input/*), or custom sensors. They expose a file-like interface via the VFS, allowing user-space access through standard system calls like open(), read(), write(), and ioctl(). This abstraction makes char drivers versatile for prototyping or non-standard hardware.

Core components:

- **Major and Minor Numbers:** Identify the driver (major) and device instance (minor). Dynamic allocation via alloc_chrdev_region() or static with register_chrdev().
- **struct cdev:** Represents the character device, initialized with cdev_init() and added with cdev_add().
- **file_operations (fops):** Defines callbacks for operations. Essential ones: open() (initialize hardware), release() (cleanup), read()/write() (data transfer), ioctl() (control commands), poll() (for non-blocking I/O).
- **Device Files:** Created in /dev via udev or mknod, linking to the major/minor.

Registration flow: Allocate dev_t, init cdev with fops, add to kernel. For simplicity, use the misc subsystem (misc_register()) for single-minor devices.

Data transfer often uses copy_to_user()/copy_from_user() to safely move data between kernel and user space. For hardware access, employ ioread8()/iowrite8() or similar for ports/registers.

Interrupts (Chapter 14) are common; the top half wakes waitqueues for bottom-half processing in read/write.

Example: A basic char driver for a hypothetical LED controller:

```c
#include <linux/module.h>
#include <linux/fs.h>
#include <linux/cdev.h>
#include <linux/io.h>
#include <linux/uaccess.h>

#define DEVICE_NAME "myled"
#define LED_REG 0x00  // Offset for LED control register

static dev_t dev_num;
static struct cdev my_cdev;
static void __iomem *base_addr;

static int my_open(struct inode *inode, struct file *file) {
    // Hardware init if needed
    return 0;
}

static int my_release(struct inode *inode, struct file *file) {
    return 0;
}

static ssize_t my_write(struct file *file, const char __user *buf, size_t len, loff_t *off) {
    char cmd;
    if (len < 1 || copy_from_user(&cmd, buf, 1)) return -EFAULT;
    iowrite8(cmd ? 0x01 : 0x00, base_addr + LED_REG);  // On/off
    return 1;
}

static const struct file_operations my_fops = {
    .owner = THIS_MODULE,
    .open = my_open,
    .release = my_release,
    .write = my_write,
};

static int __init char_driver_init(void) {
    int ret = alloc_chrdev_region(&dev_num, 0, 1, DEVICE_NAME);
    if (ret) return ret;
    cdev_init(&my_cdev, &my_fops);
    ret = cdev_add(&my_cdev, dev_num, 1);
    if (ret) goto free_region;
```

```c
base_addr = ioremap(0xLED_BASE_ADDR, 0x10);
if (!base_addr) {
    ret = -ENOMEM;
    goto del_cdev;
}
return 0;
del_cdev:
    cdev_del(&my_cdev);
free_region:
    unregister_chrdev_region(dev_num, 1);
    return ret;
}

static void __exit char_driver_exit(void) {
    iounmap(base_addr);
    cdev_del(&my_cdev);
    unregister_chrdev_region(dev_num, 1);
}


module_init(char_driver_init);
module_exit(char_driver_exit);
MODULE_LICENSE("GPL");
```

User space: echo 1 > /dev/myled to turn on. Add ioctl for advanced controls.

Char drivers suit quick development but require manual concurrency handling (e.g., mutex for shared data).

Block Drivers

Block drivers interface with storage devices like hard drives, SSDs, or flash, providing random access in fixed-size blocks (typically 512B or 4KB). They integrate with the block layer, which manages I/O requests, queuing, and scheduling for optimal performance. Block drivers are crucial for file systems (Chapter 15), as they underpin read/write operations via bios (Block I/O structures).

Key elements:

- **gendisk:** Represents the disk, allocated with alloc_disk() and registered with add_disk(). Includes geometry (sectors, heads).
- **request_queue:** Handles I/O requests; initialized with blk_alloc_queue(). For multi-queue (modern SSDs), use blk-mq.
- **block_device_operations (bdops):** Callbacks like open(), ioctl(), but core I/O via queue's submit_bio() or request_fn.
- **Requests and Bios:** Requests group bios (basic I/O units). Drivers process via blk_fetch_request() or mq tags.

Modern drivers use blk-mq (blk_mq_init_queue()) for per-CPU queues, reducing contention. Features like TRIM (discard) or write-cache control are supported.

Flow: User I/O -> VFS -> block layer -> queue -> driver processes (e.g., submit to hardware via DMA).

Example skeleton for a simple RAM disk block driver:

```c
#include <linux/module.h>
#include <linux/blkdev.h>
#include <linux/hdreg.h>

#define RAMDISK_SIZE (16 * 1024 * 1024) // 16MB
#define SECTOR_SIZE 512

static struct gendisk *ramdisk;
static u8 *ramdisk_data;
static struct request_queue *ramdisk_queue;

static void ramdisk_request(struct request_queue *q) {
    struct request *req;
```

```c
    while ((req = blk_fetch_request(q)) != NULL) {
        if (req == NULL || (req->cmd_type != REQ_TYPE_FS)) {
            __blk_end_request_all(req, -EIO);
            continue;
        }
        // Simulate I/O: memcpy between ramdisk_data and req buffers
        unsigned long offset = blk_rq_pos(req) << SECTOR_SHIFT;
        size_t len = blk_rq_cur_bytes(req);
        if (req_op(req) == REQ_OP_READ)
            memcpy(sg_virt(req->bio->bi_io_vec->bv_page), ramdisk_data + offset, len);
        else if (req_op(req) == REQ_OP_WRITE)
            memcpy(ramdisk_data + offset, sg_virt(req->bio->bi_io_vec->bv_page), len);
        __blk_end_request_all(req, 0);
    }
}

static int __init block_driver_init(void) {
    ramdisk_data = vmalloc(RAMDISK_SIZE);
    if (!ramdisk_data) return -ENOMEM;
    memset(ramdisk_data, 0, RAMDISK_SIZE);

    ramdisk_queue = blk_init_queue(ramdisk_request, NULL);
    if (!ramdisk_queue) goto free_data;

    ramdisk = alloc_disk(1);
    if (!ramdisk) goto free_queue;

    ramdisk->major = 0;  // Dynamic
    ramdisk->minors = 1;
    ramdisk->fops = &bdops;  // Define bdops if needed
    set_capacity(ramdisk, RAMDISK_SIZE / SECTOR_SIZE);
    sprintf(ramdisk->disk_name, "ramdisk0");
    ramdisk->queue = ramdisk_queue;

    return add_disk(ramdisk);

free_queue:
    blk_cleanup_queue(ramdisk_queue);
free_data:
    vfree(ramdisk_data);
    return -ENOMEM;
}

static void __exit block_driver_exit(void) {
    del_gendisk(ramdisk);
    put_disk(ramdisk);
    blk_cleanup_queue(ramdisk_queue);
    vfree(ramdisk_data);
}

module_init(block_driver_init);
module_exit(block_driver_exit);
MODULE_LICENSE("GPL");
```

Mount as mkfs.ext4 /dev/ramdisk0 && mount /dev/ramdisk0 /mnt. For real hardware, replace memcpy with controller commands.
Block drivers demand careful queue management to avoid stalls.

Network Drivers

Network drivers control interfaces for data transmission over networks, such as Ethernet or Wi-Fi cards. They integrate with the net subsystem, handling packet send/receive, link management, and statistics. Network drivers are performance-critical, often using ring buffers, DMA, and NAPI (Section 14.4) to minimize overhead.

Main structures:

- **net_device:** Core device representation, allocated with alloc_netdev(). Includes name (e.g., eth0), MTU, MAC address.
- **net_device_ops:** Operations like ndo_open() (bring up interface), ndo_stop(), ndo_start_xmit() (transmit packet).
- **ethtool_ops:** For configuration queries (e.g., speed, duplex).
- **sk_buff (skb):** Packet containers for send/receive.

Registration: register_netdev() adds to the system, triggering udev events.

Tx/Rx flow: For Tx, dev_queue_xmit() calls ndo_start_xmit() to DMA packets. Rx uses interrupts to allocate skbs, then netif_receive_skb() up the stack.

Example outline for a minimal network driver:

```c
#include <linux/module.h>
#include <linux/netdevice.h>
#include <linux/etherdevice.h>

static struct net_device *netdev;

static netdev_tx_t my_start_xmit(struct sk_buff *skb, struct net_device *dev) {
    // Hardware Tx: DMA skb->data
    netdev->stats.tx_packets++;
    netdev->stats.tx_bytes += skb->len;
    dev_kfree_skb(skb);
    return NETDEV_TX_OK;
}

static int my_open(struct net_device *dev) {
    // Init hardware, request IRQ
    netif_start_queue(dev);
    return 0;
}

static int my_stop(struct net_device *dev) {
    netif_stop_queue(dev);
    // Free IRQ
    return 0;
}

static const struct net_device_ops my_netdev_ops = {
    .ndo_open = my_open,
    .ndo_stop = my_stop,
    .ndo_start_xmit = my_start_xmit,
};

static int __init net_driver_init(void) {
    netdev = alloc_etherdev(0);
    if (!netdev) return -ENOMEM;
    netdev->netdev_ops = &my_netdev_ops;
    // Set MAC, etc.
    return register_netdev(netdev);
}
```

```
static void __exit net_driver_exit(void) {
    unregister_netdev(netdev);
    free_netdev(netdev);
}
```

```
module_init(net_driver_init);
module_exit(net_driver_exit);
MODULE_LICENSE("GPL");
```
Configure with ifconfig ethX up. Real drivers add IRQ handlers for Rx, using napi_schedule().
Network drivers often support offloads (e.g., checksum, TSO) for efficiency.

Summary

Char, block, and network drivers form the core taxonomy of Linux hardware support, each with specialized APIs for their data paradigms. Char offers simplicity for byte streams, block enables high-performance storage, and network facilitates packet communication. By mastering their registration, operations, and examples, developers can create robust integrations. Upcoming sections explore char drivers in depth (Chapter 17), preparing for hardware-specific implementations on architectures like ARM and RISC-V (Section 16.4).

16.3 Driver Development Environment Setup

Setting up a robust development environment is crucial for Linux device driver development, as it involves compiling kernel modules, testing on hardware or emulators, debugging kernel code, and ensuring compatibility across architectures. A well-configured setup minimizes build errors, accelerates iteration, and facilitates safe testing without risking host system stability. This section outlines the essential tools, configurations, and best practices for establishing an effective workspace, drawing from the kernel's build system and common developer workflows.

Essential Software and Tools

Begin with a Linux distribution optimized for development, such as Ubuntu, Fedora, or Arch Linux, which provide easy access to kernel development packages. Install core dependencies via your package manager:

- **Compiler and Build Tools:** The GNU Compiler Collection (GCC) or Clang for compiling kernel code. Ensure version compatibility with your target kernel (e.g., GCC 12+ for recent kernels). Install build-essential (Ubuntu) or base-devel (Arch), which includes make, binutils, and flex/bison for Kconfig parsing.
- **Kernel Headers and Sources:** Headers for API access (linux-headers-$(uname -r)) and full sources for building modules (linux-source). Download sources from kernel.org or via apt install linux-source for matching your running kernel.
- **Module Utilities:** modprobe, insmod, lsmod, and rmmod from kmod package for loading/unloading modules.
- **Version Control:** Git for managing kernel sources and your driver code. Clone the mainline kernel: git clone https://git.kernel.org/pub/scm/linux/kernel/git/torvalds/linux.git.
- **Debugging Tools:**
    - gdb or kgdb for kernel debugging.
    - ftrace and perf for tracing and performance analysis.
    - crash or kdump for post-mortem analysis.
    - objdump and readelf for inspecting binaries.
- **Emulation and Virtualization:** QEMU for simulating architectures (e.g., x86, ARM, RISC-V) without physical hardware. Install qemu-system-x86_64 or architecture-specific variants. For full-system emulation, combine with KVM for acceleration.
- **Cross-Compilation Toolchains:** For non-native architectures (e.g., ARM on x86 host), install cross-compilers like gcc-arm-linux-gnueabihf (Debian) or build via crosstool-ng. The kernel supports cross-builds with ARCH=arm CROSS_COMPILE=arm-linux-gnueabihf-.

Additional libraries: libelf-dev for elfutils, ncurses-dev for menuconfig, and sparse for static analysis (make C=1 during builds).

Configuring the Kernel Build Environment

Driver development often involves building out-of-tree modules against an existing kernel or compiling a custom kernel.

1. **Kernel Configuration:** Use make menuconfig (ncurses UI), make defconfig (default config), or make oldconfig to update existing configs. Enable driver-relevant options, e.g., CONFIG_DEBUG_KERNEL=y for debugging, CONFIG_MODULES=y for loadable modules.
2. **Building Modules:** For a simple driver, create a Makefile:

makefile
obj-m += my_driver.o

all:
        make -C /lib/modules/$$ (shell uname -r)/build M= $$(PWD) modules

clean:
        make -C /lib/modules/$$ (shell uname -r)/build M= $$(PWD) clean

Run make to compile. This uses Kbuild to link against current kernel headers.

3. **Full Kernel Build:** For in-tree drivers or testing changes:
   - make -j$(nproc) to build (parallel jobs for speed).
   - make modules_install and make install to deploy.
   - Boot the new kernel via GRUB or update-initramfs.

For cross-compilation: make ARCH=arm64 CROSS_COMPILE=aarch64-linux-gnu- defconfig, then build. Environment variables: Set KDIR=/path/to/kernel/sources if building externally. Use ccache for faster recompiles by prefixing make with ccache.

Testing and Emulation Setup

Direct hardware testing risks crashes; use virtual environments first.

- **QEMU Configuration:** Emulate a system with your driver. Example for x86:

text
qemu-system-x86_64 -kernel arch/x86/boot/bzImage -initrd /boot/initramfs-linux.img -append "console=ttyS0" -nographic

For ARM: qemu-system-arm -M virt -cpu cortex-a57 -kernel zImage -dtb virt.dtb -append "console=ttyAMA0". Pass-through devices via -device for PCI/USB simulation.

- **Virtual Machines:** Use VirtualBox, VMware, or libvirt with KVM for graphical testing. Install guest additions for shared folders to transfer modules.
- **Containerization:** Docker or LXC for isolated build environments, e.g., docker run --privileged -v $(pwd):/src ubuntu:22.04 to build inside.

Load modules in VMs: insmod my_driver.ko, monitor with dmesg | tail.

Debugging and Monitoring Setup

Effective debugging prevents frustration.

- **Kernel Debugging:** Enable CONFIG_KGDB=y and CONFIG_KGDB_SERIAL_CONSOLE=y. Boot with kgdboc=ttyS0,115200 and connect via gdb vmlinux then target remote /dev/ttyS0.
- **Tracing:** Mount debugfs (mount -t debugfs none /sys/kernel/debug), use echo function > /sys/kernel/debug/tracing/current_tracer for call traces.
- **Sysfs and Procfs:** Drivers expose info via /sys/module/my_driver/ or custom sysfs entries.
- **Static Analysis:** Run make C=1 CHECK=sparse for warnings. Use coccinelle for semantic patches.
- **Logging:** printk() with levels (KERN_INFO, KERN_ERR). View with dmesg -w for real-time.

Security: Run tests in VMs to isolate panics. Use sudo carefully; consider user namespaces for unprivileged builds.

Best Practices and Workflow

- **Directory Structure:** Place drivers in kernel tree (drivers/char/) for in-tree, or separate dir for out-of-tree.
- **Versioning:** Match driver to kernel version to avoid symbol mismatches (modinfo my_driver.ko shows vermagic).
- **Automation:** Use scripts for build/test cycles, e.g., via Makefile targets or CI tools like GitHub Actions.
- **Documentation:** Read Documentation/driver-api/ in kernel sources. Follow coding style (scripts/checkpatch.pl).
- **Hardware Access:** For real devices, use lspci/lsusb to identify, then bind via sysfs (echo id > /sys/bus/pci/drivers/my_driver/bind).

For modern architectures (previewing Section 16.4), setup includes toolchains for ARM (arm64) or RISC-V (riscv64), and QEMU models like -M virt for RISC-V.

This setup enables efficient driver iteration, from compilation to deployment, ensuring reliable development across diverse hardware.

16.4 Modern Architectures (ARM, RISC-V)

Modern architectures like ARM and RISC-V have become dominant in embedded systems, mobile devices, servers, and emerging computing paradigms, driving the need for tailored Linux device driver development. Unlike x86, which often relies on ACPI for hardware discovery, ARM and RISC-V emphasize device trees (DT) for describing hardware topology, enabling flexible, non-discoverable platforms. ARM, with its mature ecosystem, powers billions of devices from smartphones to cloud servers, while RISC-V, an open ISA, is gaining traction for its royalty-free design and extensibility. Driver development on these architectures requires cross-compilation, understanding of memory models, interrupt controllers (e.g., GIC for ARM, PLIC/CLIC for RISC-V), and platform-specific drivers. This section explores key concepts, tools, and practices for writing drivers on ARM and RISC-V, with examples to illustrate integration with the kernel's device model.

ARM Architecture Overview and Driver Considerations

ARM (Advanced RISC Machine) encompasses 32-bit (AArch32) and 64-bit (AArch64) variants, with Linux support dating back to the 2.4 kernel. By 2025, AArch64 dominates, with features like Scalable Vector Extension (SVE) for vector processing and Memory Tagging Extension (MTE) for security. ARM systems are often System-on-Chip (SoC), integrating CPUs, GPUs, peripherals, and interrupt controllers, making drivers highly platform-dependent. Key driver aspects:

- **Device Tree (DT):** ARM uses DT blobs (.dtb) compiled from .dts files to describe hardware statically. The kernel parses DT at boot (via of_* APIs in include/linux/of.h) to probe devices. Drivers match via compatible properties.
- **Platform Drivers:** For non-bus devices (e.g., GPIO, clocks), use platform_driver registered with platform_driver_register(). Probe function accesses DT nodes via dev_of_node(dev).
- **Interrupt Handling:** ARM uses the Generic Interrupt Controller (GIC). Drivers request IRQs via DT properties like interrupts = <GIC_SPI 0 IRQ_TYPE_LEVEL_HIGH>;, mapped with irq_of_parse_and_map().
- **Memory Access:** Use devm_ioremap_resource() for MMIO. ARM's weak memory model requires barriers (dmb(), dsb()).
- **Power Management:** Runtime PM via dev_pm_ops, and regulators/clocks from DT.

Toolchain: Use aarch64-linux-gnu-gcc for cross-compilation. Build kernel with make ARCH=arm64 CROSS_COMPILE=aarch64-linux-gnu-.

Example: A simple ARM platform driver for a custom timer peripheral defined in DT:

DT snippet (in .dts):

```text
mytimer@0x10000000 {
    compatible = "example,mytimer";
    reg = <0x10000000 0x100>;
    interrupts = <GIC_SPI 42 IRQ_TYPE_LEVEL_HIGH>;
    clocks = <&clk_controller 0>;
};
```

Driver code:

```c
#include <linux/module.h>
#include <linux/platform_device.h>
#include <linux/interrupt.h>
#include <linux/of.h>
#include <linux/clk.h>
#include <linux/io.h>

struct mytimer_priv {
    void __iomem *base;
    struct clk *clk;
    int irq;
```

```c
};

static irqreturn_t mytimer_irq_handler(int irq, void *dev_id) {
    // Handle timer interrupt: clear flag
    iowrite32(1, priv->base + 0x04);  // Ack register
    return IRQ_HANDLED;
}

static int mytimer_probe(struct platform_device *pdev) {
    struct mytimer_priv *priv;
    struct resource *res;
    int ret;

    priv = devm_kzalloc(&pdev->dev, sizeof(*priv), GFP_KERNEL);
    if (!priv) return -ENOMEM;

    res = platform_get_resource(pdev, IORESOURCE_MEM, 0);
    priv->base = devm_ioremap_resource(&pdev->dev, res);
    if (IS_ERR(priv->base)) return PTR_ERR(priv->base);

    priv->irq = platform_get_irq(pdev, 0);
    if (priv->irq < 0) return priv->irq;

    ret = devm_request_irq(&pdev->dev, priv->irq, mytimer_irq_handler, 0, "mytimer", priv);
    if (ret) return ret;

    priv->clk = devm_clk_get(&pdev->dev, NULL);
    if (IS_ERR(priv->clk)) return PTR_ERR(priv->clk);
    clk_prepare_enable(priv->clk);

    // Initialize hardware
    iowrite32(0x1, priv->base + 0x00);  // Enable timer

    platform_set_drvdata(pdev, priv);
    return 0;
}

static int mytimer_remove(struct platform_device *pdev) {
    struct mytimer_priv *priv = platform_get_drvdata(pdev);
    clk_disable_unprepare(priv->clk);
    return 0;
}

static const struct of_device_id mytimer_of_match[] = {
    { .compatible = "example,mytimer" },
    { /* sentinel */ }
};
MODULE_DEVICE_TABLE(of, mytimer_of_match);

static struct platform_driver mytimer_driver = {
    .probe = mytimer_probe,
    .remove = mytimer_remove,
    .driver = {
        .name = "mytimer",
        .of_match_table = mytimer_of_match,
    },
```

```
};
```

```
module_platform_driver(mytimer_driver);
MODULE_LICENSE("GPL");
MODULE_DESCRIPTION("Example ARM timer driver");
```

This driver probes via DT compatible string, maps resources, and handles interrupts. Test on QEMU with -M virt -dtb mydtb.dtb.

Challenges: ARM's diverse SoCs require vendor-specific quirks; use DT bindings docs (Documentation/devicetree/bindings/).

RISC-V Architecture Overview and Driver Considerations

RISC-V, an open-source ISA, offers modularity through extensions (e.g., RV64GC base, Vector 'V', Hypervisor 'H'). Linux support started in 4.15 (2018), and by 2025, it's mature in kernels 6.x+, with upstreamed boards like VisionFive 2 and Milk-V. RISC-V targets IoT, HPC, and custom silicon, with drivers focusing on openness and portability.

Key driver aspects:

- **Device Tree Usage:** Similar to ARM, DT is standard for hardware description. RISC-V mandates DT for non-discoverable devices.
- **Interrupt Controllers:** Platform Level Interrupt Controller (PLIC) for global IRQs, Core Local Interruptor (CLIC) for per-hart. Drivers use interrupts-extended in DT for mapping.
- **Platform and SBI:** Supervisor Binary Interface (SBI) handles low-level ops (e.g., timers via sbi_set_timer()). Drivers often use platform framework.
- **Memory and I/O:** Weak ordering requires fences (fence.i). Use standard ioread*()/iowrite*().
- **Extensions Handling:** Query via riscv_isa_extension_available() for features like atomic ops.

Toolchain: riscv64-unknown-linux-gnu-gcc. Build with make ARCH=riscv CROSS_COMPILE=riscv64-unknown-linux-gnu-.

Example: A RISC-V platform driver for a UART, adapted from ARM style:

DT snippet:

text

```
uart@0x20000000 {
    compatible = "example,myuart";
    reg = <0x20000000 0x100>;
    interrupts-extended = <&plic 10>;
    clock-frequency = <25000000>;
};
```

Driver code (similar structure to ARM example, with RISC-V specifics):

c

```c
// ... includes similar to ARM example ...

static irqreturn_t myuart_irq_handler(int irq, void *dev_id) {
    // Handle UART RX/TX interrupt
    // Use riscv-specific if needed, e.g., fence for ordering
    asm volatile("fence iorw,iorw");
    // Clear interrupt
    return IRQ_HANDLED;
}

static int myuart_probe(struct platform_device *pdev) {
    // Similar to ARM, but check extensions if needed
    if (!riscv_isa_extension_available(NULL, A)) { // Atomic extension
        dev_err(&pdev->dev, "Atomic ops not supported\n");
        return -ENODEV;
    }
    // Proceed with mapping, IRQ request (uses standard APIs)
    // ...
}
```

```c
static const struct of_device_id myuart_of_match[] = {
    { .compatible = "example,myuart" },
    { }
};
MODULE_DEVICE_TABLE(of, myuart_of_match);

static struct platform_driver myuart_driver = {
    // ...
};
```

```c
module_platform_driver(myuart_driver);
MODULE_LICENSE("GPL");
```

Test on QEMU: qemu-system-riscv64 -M virt -kernel Image -dtb virt.dtb.

Challenges: RISC-V's evolving ecosystem means fragmented vendor extensions; contribute to upstream for standardization.

Cross-Architecture Best Practices

- **Portability:** Use generic APIs (e.g., devm_*, of_*) to avoid arch-specific code.
- **Emulation:** QEMU for both (e.g., -M raspi3 for ARM emulation).
- **Debugging:** Earlycon for console, KGDB over serial.
- **Performance:** Optimize for cache coherence (CCI on ARM) and vector units.
- **Community Resources:** ARM: arm64 documentation in kernel; RISC-V: riscv.org and kernel docs.

By adapting drivers to ARM and RISC-V's DT-centric model, developers can target diverse platforms efficiently, leveraging Linux's portability. This concludes the introduction, leading into character driver details in Chapter 17.

17. Character Device Drivers

Character (char) device drivers form the foundation for interfacing with a wide range of hardware that treats data as a sequential stream of bytes, such as serial ports, keyboards, mice, or custom sensors. Unlike block drivers, which handle fixed-size blocks and random access, char drivers emphasize simplicity and flexibility, making them an ideal starting point for driver development. They integrate with the Virtual File System (VFS) to expose devices as files in /dev, allowing user-space programs to interact via standard system calls like open(), read(), write(), and ioctl(). This chapter delves into char driver internals, from basic structure to advanced features, debugging, and security, building on the introduction to drivers (Chapter 16).

17.1 Basic Char Driver Structure

The basic structure of a char driver revolves around registering the device with the kernel, defining operations for user interactions, and managing resources like memory and interrupts. At its core, a char driver is a kernel module that provides a set of callbacks via the file_operations structure, which the VFS invokes in response to system calls. This design abstracts hardware details, allowing multiple device instances (minors) to share a single driver (major).

Key components include:

- **Major and Minor Numbers:** The major number identifies the driver, while the minor distinguishes instances (e.g., /dev/ttyS0 vs. /dev/ttyS1). Use dynamic allocation with alloc_chrdev_region() to avoid conflicts, or static with register_chrdev() for simplicity (though dynamic is preferred for modern kernels).
- **struct cdev:** Represents the character device. Initialize with cdev_init() and register with cdev_add(). This ties the major/minor to the file_operations.
- **file_operations (fops):** A structure of function pointers for operations. Minimal implementations include open(), release(), read(), and write(). Others like llseek(), ioctl(), or poll() add functionality.
- **Module Lifecycle:** Use module_init() for setup (resource allocation, registration) and module_exit() for teardown (deregistration, freeing resources).
- **Device Node Creation:** Typically handled by udev automatically on module load, but can be manual via mknod for testing.

The driver must handle concurrency, as multiple processes may access the device simultaneously—use mutexes or spinlocks for shared data. Error handling is critical; return negative errno values (e.g., -ENOMEM) on failure.

A typical workflow:

1. In init: Allocate major/minor, init cdev with fops, add cdev.
2. Handle hardware: Map I/O regions with ioremap(), request IRQs if needed.
3. In operations: Validate inputs, interact with hardware (e.g., via inb/outb or readb/writeb).
4. In exit: Reverse init steps to prevent leaks.

Here's a complete example of a basic char driver for a fictional memory buffer device, allowing read/write to a kernel-allocated buffer:

```c
#include <linux/module.h>
#include <linux/fs.h>
#include <linux/cdev.h>
#include <linux/slab.h>
#include <linux/uaccess.h>

#define DEVICE_NAME "mymem"
#define BUFFER_SIZE 1024

static dev_t dev_num;
static struct cdev my_cdev;
static char *buffer;
static struct mutex lock;

static int my_open(struct inode *inode, struct file *file) {
    mutex_lock(&lock);
```

```c
    // Per-open initialization if needed
    mutex_unlock(&lock);
    return 0;
}

static int my_release(struct inode *inode, struct file *file) {
    // Cleanup if needed
    return 0;
}

static ssize_t my_read(struct file *file, char __user *user_buf, size_t len, loff_t *off) {
    ssize_t ret;
    mutex_lock(&lock);
    if (*off >= BUFFER_SIZE) {
        ret = 0;  // EOF
    } else {
        if (*off + len > BUFFER_SIZE) len = BUFFER_SIZE - *off;
        if (copy_to_user(user_buf, buffer + *off, len)) {
            ret = -EFAULT;
        } else {
            *off += len;
            ret = len;
        }
    }
    mutex_unlock(&lock);
    return ret;
}

static ssize_t my_write(struct file *file, const char __user *user_buf, size_t len, loff_t *off) {
    ssize_t ret;
    mutex_lock(&lock);
    if (*off >= BUFFER_SIZE) {
        ret = -ENOSPC;  // No space
    } else {
        if (*off + len > BUFFER_SIZE) len = BUFFER_SIZE - *off;
        if (copy_from_user(buffer + *off, user_buf, len)) {
            ret = -EFAULT;
        } else {
            *off += len;
            ret = len;
        }
    }
    mutex_unlock(&lock);
    return ret;
}

static const struct file_operations my_fops = {
    .owner = THIS_MODULE,
    .open = my_open,
    .release = my_release,
    .read = my_read,
    .write = my_write,
};

static int __init char_driver_init(void) {
    int ret;
```

```c
    mutex_init(&lock);

    ret = alloc_chrdev_region(&dev_num, 0, 1, DEVICE_NAME);
    if (ret < 0) return ret;

    cdev_init(&my_cdev, &my_fops);
    ret = cdev_add(&my_cdev, dev_num, 1);
    if (ret < 0) goto free_region;

    buffer = kmalloc(BUFFER_SIZE, GFP_KERNEL);
    if (!buffer) {
        ret = -ENOMEM;
        goto del_cdev;
    }
    memset(buffer, 0, BUFFER_SIZE);

    printk(KERN_INFO "mymem: Major %d, Minor %d\n", MAJOR(dev_num), MINOR(dev_num));
    return 0;

del_cdev:
    cdev_del(&my_cdev);
free_region:
    unregister_chrdev_region(dev_num, 1);
    return ret;
}

static void __exit char_driver_exit(void) {
    kfree(buffer);
    cdev_del(&my_cdev);
    unregister_chrdev_region(dev_num, 1);
    printk(KERN_INFO "mymem: Unloaded\n");
}

module_init(char_driver_init);
module_exit(char_driver_exit);
MODULE_LICENSE("GPL");
MODULE_DESCRIPTION("Basic memory char driver");
```

Compile and load: make, insmod mymem.ko. Create node: mknod /dev/mymem c <major> 0. Test: echo "test" > /dev/mymem; cat /dev/mymem.

This example uses a mutex for synchronization and safe user-kernel copying. For hardware, replace buffer accesses with I/O functions.

Enhancements: Add ioctl for buffer resize, or poll for asynchronous notifications. Use devm_k* for managed allocations in probe contexts (for platform drivers).

Common pitfalls: Forgetting to handle partial reads/writes, ignoring offsets, or missing locks leading to races. Always check return values and use pr_err() for logging.

Summary

The basic char driver structure provides a straightforward framework for hardware abstraction, centered on registration, operations, and resource management. Through examples like the memory buffer, developers can prototype quickly while learning VFS integration. This sets the foundation for implementing file operations (next section), paving the way for real hardware interactions in subsequent chapters.

17.2 File Operations Implementation

Implementing file operations is the core of a character device driver, as these functions define how user-space applications interact with the hardware or virtual device. The file_operations structure (defined in include/linux/fs.h) contains pointers to callback functions that the VFS invokes in response to system calls. Each operation must be carefully crafted to handle data transfer, resource management, error conditions, and concurrency. Building on the basic structure (Section 17.1), this section explores key operations like open(), release(), read(), write(), ioctl(), and poll(), with guidelines for implementation, best practices, and examples. Proper implementation ensures reliability, security, and performance, preventing issues like data corruption or kernel crashes.

Understanding File Operations

The file_operations (fops) acts as a dispatch table. Not all functions need implementation—defaults like no_llseek() are provided by the kernel if omitted. Prototypes use struct file * (representing the open file) and struct inode * (linking to the device). Return values are typically 0 on success or negative errno (e.g., -EINVAL for invalid arguments).

Common operations:

- **open:** Called on open() syscall. Initialize per-file resources, check permissions.
- **release:** Called on close(). Cleanup resources, but note it's not always paired with open due to fork/dup.
- **read/write:** Transfer data. Handle offsets (loff_t *), partial transfers, and blocking/non-blocking modes.
- **ioctl:** Device-specific commands via ioctl() syscall. Use for configuration not fitting read/write.
- **poll:** For select/poll/epoll, indicate readiness for I/O.
- **mmap:** Map device memory to user space (advanced, for shared buffers).
- **llseek:** Handle seeking, if the device supports it (e.g., for replay buffers).

Implementations run in process context, allowing sleep, but must be reentrant for concurrent access. Use file->private_data to store per-open state.

Error handling: Use ERR_PTR() for pointer returns, and check user pointers with access_ok() before copying, though copy_to_user()/copy_from_user() handle this.

Implementing open and release

open() prepares the device: allocate state, enable hardware, increment usage counters. Prototype: int (*open)(struct inode *, struct file *);.

Example extension from Section 17.1's memory driver, adding per-file tracking:

c

```
struct mymem_priv {
    loff_t offset; // Per-file offset if global buffer not shared
    // Other per-open data
};

static int my_open(struct inode *inode, struct file *file) {
    struct mymem_priv *priv = kmalloc(sizeof(*priv), GFP_KERNEL);
    if (!priv) return -ENOMEM;
    priv->offset = 0;
    file->private_data = priv;

    // Hardware enable: e.g., clk_prepare_enable(clk);
    try_module_get(THIS_MODULE); // Prevent unload while open
    return 0;
}

static int my_release(struct inode *inode, struct file *file) {
    struct mymem_priv *priv = file->private_data;
    kfree(priv);
    file->private_data = NULL;

    // Hardware disable if last close
    module_put(THIS_MODULE);
    return 0;
```

}

release() frees resources. Use atomic counters (e.g., atomic_t open_count) for shared devices to act only on last close.

Implementing read and write

These handle data I/O. Prototypes: ssize_t (*read)(struct file *, char __user *, size_t, loff_t *); and similar for write.

Key considerations:

- Update *off for sequential access.
- Handle O_NONBLOCK via file->f_flags & O_NONBLOCK—return -EAGAIN if no data.
- Use copy_to_user()/copy_from_user() for safe transfer; they return non-zero on fault.
- For hardware, read/write to registers or queues.

Example for a hardware FIFO device:

c

```c
static ssize_t my_read(struct file *file, char __user *buf, size_t len, loff_t *off) {
    size_t avail = fifo_available_bytes();  // Hardware query
    if (!avail) {
        if (file->f_flags & O_NONBLOCK) return -EAGAIN;
        wait_event_interruptible(read_waitq, fifo_available_bytes() > 0);
    }
    len = min(len, avail);
    // Read from hardware to kernel buffer if needed
    if (copy_to_user(buf, fifo_read(len), len)) return -EFAULT;
    return len;
}

static ssize_t my_write(struct file *file, const char __user *buf, size_t len, loff_t *off) {
    char kbuf[256];
    size_t to_write = min(len, sizeof(kbuf));
    if (copy_from_user(kbuf, buf, to_write)) return -EFAULT;
    // Write to hardware
    fifo_write(kbuf, to_write);
    return to_write;
}
```

For large transfers, use iterative copying or direct I/O if supported.

Implementing ioctl

ioctl() handles commands not fitting read/write, like setting baud rates. Prototype: long (*unlocked_ioctl)(struct file *, unsigned int cmd, unsigned long arg); (use unlocked for modern kernels).

Use _IO(), _IOR(), _IOW() macros for cmd encoding. Validate cmd with switch, handle arg with get_user()/put_user() or copying structs.

Example:

c

```c
#define MY_IOCTL_SET_VAL _IOW('m', 1, int)

static long my_ioctl(struct file *file, unsigned int cmd, unsigned long arg) {
    int val;
    switch (cmd) {
    case MY_IOCTL_SET_VAL:
        if (get_user(val, (int __user *)arg)) return -EFAULT;
        // Set hardware value
        iowrite32(val, base + REG_VAL);
        return 0;
    default:
        return -ENOTTY;  // Not supported
    }
}
```

Add .unlocked_ioctl = my_ioctl, to fops.

Implementing poll and Other Operations

poll() enables non-blocking I/O monitoring. Prototype: unsigned int (*poll)(struct file *, struct poll_table_struct *);. Return mask like POLLIN | POLLOUT.

Example:

c
```
static unsigned int my_poll(struct file *file, poll_table *wait) {
    unsigned int mask = 0;
    poll_wait(file, &read_waitq, wait);
    poll_wait(file, &write_waitq, wait);
    if (fifo_available_bytes() > 0) mask |= POLLIN | POLLRDNORM;
    if (fifo_space() > 0) mask |= POLLOUT | POLLWRNORM;
    return mask;
}
```

For mmap(), implement vm_operations_struct for shared memory.

Best Practices and Security

- **Concurrency:** Protect shared data with mutexes (sleepable) or spinlocks (atomic).
- **Security:** Validate all user inputs; use check_copy_size() for large copies. Avoid ioctl for sensitive ops—prefer sysfs.
- **Performance:** Batch operations, use DMA for large data.
- **Testing:** Use dd, cat, or custom apps; monitor with strace.

Common errors: Ignoring signal interruptions (return -EINTR), mishandling offsets, or leaks in open/release.

Summary

Implementing file operations transforms a basic char driver into a functional interface, handling I/O, control, and events efficiently. Through detailed callbacks and safe practices, developers ensure robust interactions. This paves the way for advanced features like debugging (later sections), enabling real-world applications in embedded or custom hardware.

17.3 Advanced Char Driver Features

Advanced features in character device drivers extend basic functionality to handle complex scenarios, improving usability, efficiency, and integration with the kernel ecosystem. While core operations like read/write suffice for simple devices, advanced drivers often require support for non-blocking I/O, custom commands, memory mapping, asynchronous notifications, and sysfs exposure. These features enable better concurrency, user-space control, and performance optimization, particularly for devices like sensors, input peripherals, or custom hardware in embedded systems. This section covers key advanced capabilities, including ioctl enhancements, wait queues with poll, mmap for shared buffers, asynchronous signals, and sysfs attributes, with implementation details and examples building on prior sections (17.1 and 17.2).

Enhanced Ioctl Commands

While basic ioctl (Section 17.2) handles simple controls, advanced usage involves defining multiple commands, handling variable-sized data, and ensuring compatibility. Use _IOWR() for bidirectional structs, and version structs to avoid ABI breaks. For security, validate arguments with access_ok() and cap sizes.

Example: Extending the memory driver with ioctls for buffer resize and clear:

c
```
#include <linux/ioctl.h>

#define MYMEM_MAGIC 'm'
#define MYMEM_IOCTL_CLEAR _IO(MYMEM_MAGIC, 0)
#define MYMEM_IOCTL_RESIZE _IOW(MYMEM_MAGIC, 1, size_t)

struct mymem_ioctl_resize {
    size_t new_size;
};

static long my_ioctl(struct file *file, unsigned int cmd, unsigned long arg) {
    switch (cmd) {
```

```
    case MYMEM_IOCTL_CLEAR:
        mutex_lock(&lock);
        memset(buffer, 0, BUFFER_SIZE);
        mutex_unlock(&lock);
        return 0;
    case MYMEM_IOCTL_RESIZE:
        {
            size_t new_size;
            char *new_buf;
            if (get_user(new_size, (size_t __user *)arg)) return -EFAULT;
            if (new_size > MAX_BUFFER_SIZE) return -EINVAL; // Cap to prevent OOM
            new_buf = kmalloc(new_size, GFP_KERNEL);
            if (!new_buf) return -ENOMEM;
            mutex_lock(&lock);
            memcpy(new_buf, buffer, min(BUFFER_SIZE, new_size));
            kfree(buffer);
            buffer = new_buf;
            BUFFER_SIZE = new_size;
            mutex_unlock(&lock);
            return 0;
        }
    default:
        return -ENOTTY;
    }
}
```

Add to fops: .unlocked_ioctl = my_ioctl,. User-space: ioctl(fd, MYMEM_IOCTL_RESIZE, &new_size);.
Best practice: Document ioctls in a header file, use compat_ioctl for 32/64-bit compatibility.

Wait Queues and Poll Support

For devices with sporadic data (e.g., sensors), use wait queues to block until events occur, and poll for non-blocking checks. Declare wait_queue_head_t (e.g., data_wait), wake with wake_up_interruptible(&data_wait) in IRQ handlers.
In poll:
c

```
static unsigned int my_poll(struct file *file, struct poll_table_struct *wait) {
    unsigned int mask = 0;
    poll_wait(file, &data_wait, wait);
    mutex_lock(&lock);
    if (data_available()) mask |= POLLIN | POLLRDNORM;
    if (space_available()) mask |= POLLOUT | POLLWRNORM;
    mutex_unlock(&lock);
    return mask;
}
```

In read: If no data and not O_NONBLOCK, wait_event_interruptible(data_wait, data_available());.
This enables efficient select/poll/epoll in user space.

Memory Mapping (mmap)

Mmap allows user-space direct access to device memory or buffers, reducing copy overhead. Implement mmap() in fops, and provide vm_operations_struct for page faults.
Example for mapping the buffer:
c

```
static int my_mmap(struct file *file, struct vm_area_struct *vma) {
    unsigned long size = vma->vm_end - vma->vm_start;
    if (size > BUFFER_SIZE) return -EINVAL;
    if (remap_pfn_range(vma, vma->vm_start, virt_to_pfn(buffer), size, vma->vm_page_prot))
        return -EAGAIN;
    return 0;
}
```

Add to fops: .mmap = my_mmap,. User-space: mmap(NULL, size, PROT_READ | PROT_WRITE, MAP_SHARED, fd, 0);.

For hardware MMIO, ensure cache coherency with pgprot_noncached(). Handle faults in vm_ops->fault for demand paging.

Asynchronous Notifications (Signals)

For event-driven devices, use fasync_helper() to send SIGIO on events. Implement fasync() in fops:

```c
static int my_fasync(int fd, struct file *file, int on) {
    return fasync_helper(fd, file, on, &fasync_queue);
}
```

In IRQ or event: kill_fasync(&fasync_queue, SIGIO, POLL_IN);.

User-space: fcntl(fd, F_SETFL, O_ASYNC); fcntl(fd, F_SETOWN, getpid());.

This notifies processes without polling.

Sysfs Integration

Expose attributes via sysfs for configuration/monitoring. Use device_create() for a class device, then device_create_file() for attributes.

Example attribute for buffer size:

```c
static ssize_t size_show(struct device *dev, struct device_attribute *attr, char *buf) {
    return scnprintf(buf, PAGE_SIZE, "%zu\n", BUFFER_SIZE);
}
static DEVICE_ATTR_RO(size);

static struct class *my_class;
static struct device *my_dev;

// In init:
my_class = class_create(THIS_MODULE, "mymem_class");
my_dev = device_create(my_class, NULL, dev_num, NULL, DEVICE_NAME);
device_create_file(my_dev, &dev_attr_size);

// In exit:
device_remove_file(my_dev, &dev_attr_size);
device_unregister(my_dev);
class_unregister(my_class);
```

Access via /sys/class/mymem_class/mymem/size. For writable, implement store.

Advanced Concurrency and Power Management

Use per-device semaphores or completions for complex syncing. For power, implement runtime PM: pm_runtime_enable(&pdev->dev); in probe, pm_runtime_get_sync() before access.

In multi-instance drivers, use container_of to get device from inode: container_of(inode->i_cdev, struct my_dev, cdev);.

Best practices: Use devm_ for managed resources, avoid busy-waiting (prefer schedules), and test with stress tools like ltp.

Summary

Advanced char driver features elevate devices from basic I/O to sophisticated interfaces, incorporating efficient waiting, direct memory access, signals, and sysfs for enhanced control. Through targeted implementations like enhanced ioctls and mmap, developers can optimize for real-world use cases. This prepares for debugging techniques in the next section, ensuring reliable deployment in production environments.

17.4 Debugging Driver Code

Debugging character device drivers presents unique challenges due to their execution In kernel space, where traditional user-space tools like gdb are ineffective, and errors can lead to system instability, oops, or panics. Effective debugging requires a combination of logging, tracing, interactive tools, and static analysis to identify issues like race conditions, memory leaks, invalid hardware accesses, or incorrect I/O handling. Early detection is crucial, as driver bugs can corrupt data or crash the system. This section covers essential debugging techniques tailored to char drivers, including logging with printk, kernel debuggers like KGDB, tracing with ftrace and perf, static checkers, and runtime inspection via debugfs/sysfs. Examples focus on common char driver scenarios, with best practices for safe testing in emulated or isolated environments.

Logging with Printk and Dmesg

The simplest yet most powerful tool for driver debugging is printk(), the kernel's printf equivalent. It logs messages to the ring buffer, viewable via dmesg or /var/log/kern.log. Use levels like KERN_INFO, KERN_DEBUG, KERN_ERR for severity; debug messages require CONFIG_DYNAMIC_DEBUG or boot param debug to enable.

In char drivers, insert printks in operations to trace flow:

```c
static ssize_t my_read(struct file *file, char __user *buf, size_t len, loff_t *off) {
    printk(KERN_DEBUG "mymem: read called with len=%zu, off=%lld\n", len, *off);
    // ... existing code ...
    if (ret > 0) {
        printk(KERN_INFO "mymem: read %zd bytes\n", ret);
    }
    return ret;
}
```

View logs: dmesg -w for real-time. Clear with dmesg -C. For rate-limited output, use pr_info_ratelimited() to avoid floods during high-frequency calls.

Advanced: Dynamic debug (dyndbg) allows runtime control: Boot with dyndbg="file my_driver.c +p" to enable all printks in the file. Control via /sys/kernel/debug/dynamic_debug/control.

Pitfalls: Overuse can slow the system; remove or conditionalize in production.

Kernel Oops and Panic Analysis

Driver faults often trigger oops (recoverable) or panics (fatal). Oops dumps include registers, stack trace (dump_stack()), and fault address. Enable CONFIG_DEBUG_BUGVERBOSE for details.

To analyze:

- Use addr2line on vmlinux: addr2line -e vmlinux <address> to map to source.
- For modules: modinfo my_driver.ko for sections, then gdb my_driver.ko with add-symbol-file.

Induce for testing: Dereference NULL in driver to simulate.

For panics, configure kdump: Enable CONFIG_CRASH_DUMP, set crashkernel=128M in boot params, install kexec-tools. On panic, crash vmcore vmlinux analyzes the dump.

In char drivers, oops often from bad copy_to_user() or unlocked access—use BUG_ON() or WARN_ON() to assert conditions.

Interactive Debugging with KGDB and KDB

For stepping through code, use KGDB (over serial or network). Enable CONFIG_KGDB=y, CONFIG_KGDB_SERIAL_CONSOLE=y. Boot with kgdboc=ttyS0,115200 kgdbwait to break early.

Connect: gdb vmlinux, target remote /dev/ttyS0, set breakpoints (break my_read), continue.

KDB is a lightweight console debugger: Enable CONFIG_KDB=y, enter via echo g > /proc/sysrq-trigger.

Commands: bt (backtrace), ps (processes), md (memory dump).

For char drivers, break in open/release to inspect file->private_data.

QEMU integration: qemu ... -s -S, gdb target remote localhost:1234.

Tracing with Ftrace and Perf

Ftrace traces function calls: Mount tracefs (mount -t tracefs nodev /sys/kernel/tracing), set echo function > current_tracer, echo 1 > tracing_on. View cat trace.

Filter for driver: echo 'my_*' > set_ftrace_filter.

Perf for performance: perf record -e probe:my_read -- sleep 10, perf report analyzes.

In char drivers, trace I/O latency or interrupt handlers.

Static Analysis and Code Checkers

Before runtime, use tools:

- **checkpatch.pl:** scripts/checkpatch.pl --file my_driver.c for style.
- **sparse:** make C=1 M=drivers/char/my_driver.ko for semantic checks (needs sparse installed).
- **coccinelle:** Semantic patches for common bugs, e.g., make coccicheck.

Scan for issues like unlocked access or missing error checks.

Runtime Inspection with Debugfs and Sysfs

Expose debug info via debugfs: Create dir with debugfs_create_dir("mymem", NULL), add files like debugfs_create_u32("stats", 0444, dir, &read_count).

Sysfs for production attrs (Section 17.3).

In char drivers, dump buffer contents or stats.

Best Practices and Testing Environments

- **Emulation:** Use QEMU or UML (User Mode Linux) to test without hardware. For ARM/RISC-V (Section 16.4), emulate peripherals.
- **Isolation:** Test in VMs (VirtualBox/KVM) to contain panics.
- **Stress Testing:** Tools like stress-ng --class io, or custom scripts looping read/write.
- **Memory Debugging:** Enable CONFIG_DEBUG_KMEMLEAK, scan /sys/kernel/debug/kmemleak.
- **Security:** Fuzz inputs with syzkaller for vulnerabilities.
- **Versioning:** Match kernel versions; use vermagic to check.

Common bugs: Race in open/release (use refcounts), bad offsets in read/write, IRQ mishandling.

Example debug session: Insert printk in ioctl, load module, run user app, check dmesg for anomalies.

Summary

Debugging char driver code combines proactive logging, interactive tools, and analysis to swiftly resolve issues, ensuring stable hardware integration. Mastering printk, KGDB, ftrace, and static checkers empowers developers to tackle complex bugs. This foundation supports concurrency handling (Chapter 20), completing the toolkit for professional driver development.

18. Hardware Management and Interfaces

Hardware management in Linux device drivers involves interfacing with peripherals through various mechanisms, ensuring safe access to resources like memory, interrupts, and buses. This chapter focuses on integrating drivers with hardware, covering memory-mapped I/O (MMIO), port I/O, PCI/PCIe frameworks, USB subsystems, GPIO, and platform devices. Understanding these interfaces is essential for writing efficient, portable drivers that handle diverse architectures (e.g., x86, ARM, RISC-V from Section 16.4). Proper management prevents conflicts, optimizes performance, and supports features like power saving and hotplugging.

18.1 Memory-Mapped I/O and Ports

Memory-Mapped I/O (MMIO) and port I/O are fundamental techniques for communicating with hardware devices. MMIO maps device registers into the CPU's address space, allowing access via standard memory instructions (e.g., load/store), while port I/O uses dedicated instructions (e.g., in/out on x86) for separate address spaces. In Linux, drivers abstract these using portable APIs to ensure cross-architecture compatibility—x86 supports both, but ARM/RISC-V primarily use MMIO due to lacking port I/O instructions. Mismanaged access can cause bus errors, data corruption, or system hangs, so drivers must request regions, handle endianness, and use barriers for ordering.

Memory-Mapped I/O (MMIO)

MMIO treats device registers as memory locations, enabling fast, efficient access. The kernel provides ioremap() to map physical addresses to virtual ones, returning __iomem * pointers. Use iounmap() to release. For managed resources (recommended in probe/remove), employ devm_ioremap() or devm_ioremap_resource().

Key functions (from include/asm-generic/io.h):

- ioread8/16/32/64(void __iomem *addr): Read from mapped address.
- iowrite8/16/32/64(u8/16/32/64 val, void __iomem *addr): Write to mapped address.
- ioreadN_rep()/iowriteN_rep(): For repeated accesses (e.g., FIFO).

On architectures with weak memory ordering (e.g., ARM), use barriers: readb_relaxed() for non-ordered reads, rmb()/wmb() for synchronization.

Resource requesting: Before mapping, claim regions with request_mem_region(phys_addr, size, name) to avoid overlaps. Release with release_mem_region().

Example in a platform driver probe (e.g., for a custom peripheral):

```c
#include <linux/io.h>
#include <linux/of.h>  // For DT if applicable

static int my_probe(struct platform_device *pdev) {
    struct resource *res;
    void __iomem *base;
    u32 reg_val;

    res = platform_get_resource(pdev, IORESOURCE_MEM, 0);
    if (!res) return -ENODEV;

    if (!devm_request_mem_region(&pdev->dev, res->start, resource_size(res), "my_dev"))
        return -EBUSY;

    base = devm_ioremap(&pdev->dev, res->start, resource_size(res));
    if (IS_ERR(base)) return PTR_ERR(base);

    // Read register
    reg_val = ioread32(base + 0x10);  // Offset 0x10
    printk(KERN_INFO "my_dev: Read reg: 0x%x\n", reg_val);

    // Write
    iowrite32(0x1234, base + 0x20);

    // Store for later use
    platform_set_drvdata(pdev, base);
    return 0;
}

static int my_remove(struct platform_device *pdev) {
    // devm_ handles unmap/release
    return 0;
}
```
In DT: reg = <0x10000000 0x100>; defines the physical range.
For PCIe/PCI, use pci_iomap() instead, as it handles BARs (Base Address Registers).
Endianness: Devices may be little-endian while some arches are big-endian—use ioread32be()/iowrite32be() if needed.

Port I/O

Port I/O, primarily on x86, uses a separate 16-bit address space (0-65535) accessed via in/out instructions. It's slower than MMIO due to serialization but useful for legacy devices. Linux abstracts with inb/outb etc., but on non-x86, these may emulate via MMIO.

Functions:
- inb/insb/inw/inl(u16 port): Read byte/string/word/long.
- outb/outsb/outw/outl(u8/u16/u32 val, u16 port): Write.

Request ports with request_region(port, count, name), release with release_region().

Example for a legacy parallel port:

```c
#include <linux/ioport.h>
#include <linux/parport.h>  // If using parport subsystem

#define PARPORT_BASE 0x378
#define DATA_REG 0x0

static int __init port_driver_init(void) {
    if (!request_region(PARPORT_BASE, 3, "my_parport")) return -EBUSY;
```

```
    // Write data
    outb(0xFF, PARPORT_BASE + DATA_REG);

    // Read status
    u8 status = inb(PARPORT_BASE + 1);
    printk(KERN_INFO "my_parport: Status: 0x%x\n", status);

    return 0;
}

static void __exit port_driver_exit(void) {
    release_region(PARPORT_BASE, 3);
}
```
Modern drivers prefer subsystems like parport_register_driver() for shared access.
On ARM/RISC-V, port I/O is unsupported natively; use MMIO equivalents.

Choosing Between MMIO and Ports

- Use MMIO for new hardware: Faster, portable, supports larger addresses.
- Ports for x86 legacy (e.g., ISA devices).
- In drivers, check architecture: #ifdef CONFIG_HAS_IOPORT for ports.

Best practices:

- Always request regions to serialize access.
- Use devm_ in probe for automatic cleanup.
- Handle errors: Check mapping returns, use dev_err() for logging.
- Security: Avoid user-controlled addresses to prevent arbitrary writes.
- Performance: Batch accesses, use rep variants for bulk.
- Debugging: Use ioread32() in traces; enable CONFIG_IOMMU_DEBUG for IOMMU issues.

Common issues: Wrong endianness (test on BE arches), cache incoherency (use ioremap_nocache()), or mapping overlaps.

Summary

Memory-Mapped I/O and ports provide essential hardware access mechanisms, with MMIO favored for modern efficiency and portability. Through kernel APIs like ioremap and inb/outb, drivers safely interact with devices across architectures. Mastering these, with proper resource management, enables robust integrations. This foundation supports PCI/PCIe drivers in the next section, where bus-specific mapping extends these concepts.

18.2 PCI and PCIe Drivers

Peripheral Component Interconnect (PCI) and its extension, PCI Express (PCIe), are ubiquitous buses for connecting high-performance peripherals like network cards, GPUs, storage controllers, and sound cards. In Linux, PCI/PCIe drivers leverage the kernel's PCI subsystem to discover, configure, and manage devices dynamically, supporting hotplugging and power efficiency. Unlike platform drivers, PCI drivers rely on self-identifying devices via configuration space, enabling generic probing. PCIe enhances PCI with higher speeds, point-to-point topology, and features like MSI-X interrupts, but the driver API remains compatible. This section explores PCI/PCIe driver architecture, registration, resource handling, interrupts, DMA, and power management, with examples for modern architectures (e.g., ARM, RISC-V from Section 16.4). Proper implementation ensures scalability and reliability in servers, desktops, and embedded systems.

PCI/PCIe Overview and Kernel Subsystem

PCI devices reside on a hierarchical bus (domain:bus:device:function, e.g., 0000:01:00.0), identified by vendor/device IDs in config space—a 256-byte (PCI) or 4KB (PCIe extended) register set. The kernel's PCI core (drivers/pci/) enumerates devices at boot or hotplug, building a struct pci_dev list accessible via /sys/bus/pci/.
Key concepts:

- **Base Address Registers (BARs):** Up to 6 (PCI) or more (PCIe), mapping MMIO or I/O ports.
- **Interrupts:** Legacy INTx (shared), MSI (message-signaled), MSI-X (multiple vectors).
- **Capabilities:** Linked list in config space for features like power management or AER (Advanced Error Reporting).

- **Bridges and Endpoints:** Bridges connect buses; endpoints are leaves (e.g., NICs).

Drivers register with the PCI subsystem, which calls probe on match. For PCIe, additional support includes SR-IOV (virtual functions) and ATS (Address Translation Services).

Driver Registration and Probing

PCI drivers use struct pci_driver, registered via pci_register_driver(). The id_table matches vendor/device/class IDs.

Prototype:

```c
struct pci_device_id {
    __u32 vendor, device;  // PCI_ANY_ID for wildcard
    __u32 subvendor, subdevice;
    __u32 class, class_mask;
    kernel_ulong_t driver_data;  // Private
};
```

Example skeleton:

```c
#include <linux/pci.h>
#include <linux/module.h>

#define MY_VENDOR_ID 0x1234
#define MY_DEVICE_ID 0xABCD

static const struct pci_device_id my_id_table[] = {
    { PCI_DEVICE(MY_VENDOR_ID, MY_DEVICE_ID) },
    { 0, }  // Null terminator
};
MODULE_DEVICE_TABLE(pci, my_id_table);

static int my_probe(struct pci_dev *pdev, const struct pci_device_id *id) {
    int ret;
    ret = pci_enable_device(pdev);  // Power on, allocate resources
    if (ret) return ret;

    // Access config space
    u16 vendor;
    pci_read_config_word(pdev, PCI_VENDOR_ID, &vendor);
    printk(KERN_INFO "my_pci: Vendor: 0x%04x\n", vendor);

    // Map BAR0 (assume MMIO)
    void __iomem *bar0 = pci_iomap(pdev, 0, 0);  // 0 for full size
    if (!bar0) {
        ret = -ENOMEM;
        goto disable_dev;
    }

    // Request IRQ (legacy)
    ret = pci_request_irq(pdev, 0, my_irq_handler, NULL, pdev, "my_pci");
    if (ret) goto unmap_bar;

    // Store private data
    struct my_priv *priv = devm_kzalloc(&pdev->dev, sizeof(*priv), GFP_KERNEL);
    if (!priv) {
        ret = -ENOMEM;
        goto free_irq;
    }
    priv->base = bar0;
```

```
    pci_set_drvdata(pdev, priv);

    return 0;

free_irq:
    pci_free_irq(pdev, 0, pdev);
unmap_bar:
    pci_iounmap(pdev, bar0);
disable_dev:
    pci_disable_device(pdev);
    return ret;
}

static void my_remove(struct pci_dev *pdev) {
    struct my_priv *priv = pci_get_drvdata(pdev);
    pci_free_irq(pdev, 0, pdev);
    pci_iounmap(pdev, priv->base);
    pci_disable_device(pdev);
}

static struct pci_driver my_pci_driver = {
    .name = "my_pci",
    .id_table = my_id_table,
    .probe = my_probe,
    .remove = my_remove,
};

module_pci_driver(my_pci_driver);
MODULE_LICENSE("GPL");
```

Use module_pci_driver() for init/exit. Probe enables the device, maps resources; remove reverses.

For PCIe-specific: Check pdev->is_physfn for SR-IOV, enable with pci_enable_sriov(pdev, num_vfs).

Resource and Config Space Access

Config space: Use pci_read_config_byte/word/dword() and writes. For extended (PCIe), pci_bus_read_config_* on pdev->bus.

BARs: pci_resource_start/len(pdev, bar_num) gets phys addr/size. Map with pci_iomap(pdev, bar, size) (handles I/O vs. MMIO). Check type with pci_resource_flags(pdev, bar) & IORESOURCE_MEM.

Prefetchable BARs (IORESOURCE_PREFETCH) may be cacheable.

Interrupt Handling

Legacy: Shared IRQs via INTx pins. Use pci_request_irq(pdev, 0, handler, IRQF_SHARED, dev, name).

MSI/MSI-X: Better for performance. Enable with pci_alloc_irq_vectors(pdev, min_vecs, max_vecs, flags) (e.g., PCI_IRQ_MSI | PCI_IRQ_MSIX). Get vector with pci_irq_vector(pdev, idx). Free with pci_free_irq_vectors(pdev).

In handler: irqreturn_t my_irq_handler(int irq, void *dev_id) { ... }.

For MSI-X, use multiple handlers for queues.

DMA Operations

PCI devices often use DMA for efficient data transfer. Use DMA API (include/linux/dma-mapping.h):

- dma_alloc_coherent(dev, size, &dma_handle, GFP_KERNEL): Alloc coherent buffer.
- dma_map_single(dev, buf, size, DMA_TO_DEVICE): Map for DMA.
- Sync with dma_sync_single_for_cpu/device().

For PCIe, consider IOMMU (e.g., via dma_set_mask_and_coherent(pdev->dev, DMA_BIT_MASK(64)) for 64-bit addressing).

Power Management

Support runtime PM: Set driver.pm = &pci_pm_ops; with callbacks like suspend/resume. Use pci_save_state(pdev)/pci_restore_state(pdev).

For D-states: pci_set_power_state(pdev, PCI_D0).

ACPI/PME handling via capabilities.

Advanced Features and Best Practices

- **Hotplug:** Handle in remove/probe; kernel notifies via uevents.
- **Error Handling:** Use PCIe AER for recovery (pci_aer_init(pdev)).
- **VFIO:** For user-space drivers (e.g., VMs), but kernel drivers avoid.
- **Portability:** Use pci_* APIs; test on x86/ARM (e.g., QEMU with -device pci-testdev).
- **Debugging:** /sys/bus/pci/devices/<bdf>/ for config dumps; lspci -vv user-space.
- **Security:** Disable MSI if untrusted; validate DMA buffers.

Common pitfalls: Forgetting pci_enable_device(), wrong BAR indexing, IRQ mismatches.

Summary

PCI and PCIe drivers provide a standardised framework for high-speed peripherals, emphasizing probing, resource mapping, and interrupt/DMA management. Through the pci_driver structure and APIs, developers can create versatile drivers. This knowledge extends to USB frameworks in the next section, broadening hardware integration capabilities for comprehensive system development.

18.3 USB Drivers and Frameworks

Universal Serial Bus (USB) is a versatile, hot-pluggable interface for peripherals like keyboards, storage devices, cameras, and network adapters. In Linux, the USB subsystem (under drivers/usb/) provides a comprehensive framework for host controllers, device drivers, and gadget (peripheral) modes, supporting USB 1.x to USB4 standards. USB drivers abstract device communication via URBs (USB Request Blocks), handling enumeration, power management, and data transfer. Unlike PCI (Section 18.2), USB emphasizes dynamic discovery and class-specific protocols (e.g., HID, mass storage). PCIe-based USB (e.g., via Thunderbolt) integrates with PCI frameworks. This section covers USB driver development, including host-side device drivers, gadget frameworks for emulating devices, and host controller drivers (HCDs), with examples for modern architectures like ARM and RISC-V (Section 16.4). Emphasis is on safe resource handling to avoid stalls or data corruption.

USB Overview and Kernel Subsystem

USB topology includes hosts (controllers like xHCI for USB3+), hubs, and devices. Devices are addressed by bus/port, with endpoints (pipes) for data flow: control (bidirectional), bulk (reliable), interrupt (polled), isochronous (streaming). The kernel's USB core (drivers/usb/core/) manages enumeration: On attach, it reads descriptors (device, config, interface, endpoint) and matches drivers.

Key structures:

- struct usb_device: Represents the device (udev).
- struct usb_interface: Sub-unit of a device (e.g., one interface for keyboard, another for mouse in composites).
- struct usb_driver: For host-side drivers.
- struct usb_gadget_driver: For peripheral mode.

Drivers bind to interfaces, not devices, allowing multi-function support. Use lsusb for user-space inspection; kernel logs via dmesg.

Host-Side USB Device Drivers

Host-side drivers control attached devices from the PC/server perspective. Register with usb_register_driver(). The usb_device_id table matches via vendor/product/class.

Example skeleton for a custom USB device (based on usb-skeleton.c):

c

```c
#include <linux/usb.h>
#include <linux/module.h>

#define MY_VENDOR_ID 0x1234
#define MY_PRODUCT_ID 0xABCD

static const struct usb_device_id my_id_table[] = {
    { USB_DEVICE(MY_VENDOR_ID, MY_PRODUCT_ID) },
    { } // Terminating entry
};
MODULE_DEVICE_TABLE(usb, my_id_table);
```

```c
static int my_probe(struct usb_interface *intf, const struct usb_device_id *id) {
    struct usb_device *udev = interface_to_usbdev(intf);
    struct my_priv *priv;
    int ret;

    priv = devm_kzalloc(&intf->dev, sizeof(*priv), GFP_KERNEL);
    if (!priv) return -ENOMEM;

    // Check endpoints (e.g., find bulk in/out)
    struct usb_endpoint_descriptor *ep_in = NULL, *ep_out = NULL;
    int i;
    for (i = 0; i < intf->cur_altsetting->desc.bNumEndpoints; i++) {
        struct usb_endpoint_descriptor *ep = &intf->cur_altsetting->endpoint[i].desc;
        if (usb_endpoint_is_bulk_in(ep)) ep_in = ep;
        else if (usb_endpoint_is_bulk_out(ep)) ep_out = ep;
    }
    if (!ep_in || !ep_out) return -ENODEV;

    priv->ep_in_addr = ep_in->bEndpointAddress;
    priv->ep_out_addr = ep_out->bEndpointAddress;

    // Allocate URB for later use
    priv->urb = usb_alloc_urb(0, GFP_KERNEL);
    if (!priv->urb) return -ENOMEM;

    usb_set_intfdata(intf, priv);
    dev_info(&intf->dev, "USB device %04x:%04x probed\n", udev->descriptor.idVendor, udev->descriptor.idProduct);

    return 0;
}

static void my_disconnect(struct usb_interface *intf) {
    struct my_priv *priv = usb_get_intfdata(intf);
    usb_free_urb(priv->urb);
    dev_info(&intf->dev, "USB device disconnected\n");
}

static struct usb_driver my_usb_driver = {
    .name = "my_usb",
    .id_table = my_id_table,
    .probe = my_probe,
    .disconnect = my_disconnect,
};

module_usb_driver(my_usb_driver);
MODULE_LICENSE("GPL");
```

Use module_usb_driver() for init/exit. Probe verifies endpoints; disconnect cleans up.

For user-space I/O (e.g., via char device), add file_operations to the driver, registering a dynamic minor with usb_register_dev(intf, &my_class); (where my_class is a struct usb_class_driver with fops). In open/read/write, check for disconnect via a flag.

Data Transfer with URBs

URBs are the core for USB I/O. Allocate with usb_alloc_urb(), fill with usb_fill_bulk_urb() or similar, submit asynchronously via usb_submit_urb(urb, GFP_KERNEL). Completion callback runs in interrupt context. Example bulk write in a write op:

c

```c
static ssize t my_write(struct file *file, const char __user *buf, size_t len, loff_t *off) {
    struct my_priv *priv = file->private_data;
    char *kbuf = kmalloc(len, GFP_KERNEL);
    int ret;

    if (copy_from_user(kbuf, buf, len)) return -EFAULT;

    usb_fill_bulk_urb(priv->urb, priv->udev, usb_sndbulkpipe(priv->udev, priv->ep_out_addr),
                kbuf, len, my_urb_complete, priv);

    ret = usb_submit_urb(priv->urb, GFP_KERNEL);
    if (ret) {
        kfree(kbuf);
        return ret;
    }

    // Wait for completion if synchronous, or return pending
    return len;  // Async example
}

static void my_urb_complete(struct urb *urb) {
    // Handle status, free buffers
    if (urb->status) dev_err(&urb->dev->dev, "URB error %d\n", urb->status);
    kfree(urb->transfer_buffer);
}
```
For synchronous: Use usb_bulk_msg(udev, pipe, buf, len, &actual_len, timeout).
Interrupt/isochronous: Similar, but use usb_fill_int_urb(); isoc for timing-critical (e.g., audio).

USB Gadget Framework

The gadget framework allows Linux to act as a USB device (peripheral), e.g., for mass storage or Ethernet over USB. Use struct usb_gadget_driver, register with usb_gadget_register_driver(). Gadgets compose functions (e.g., ethernet, serial) via composite framework.

Example: Simple gadget driver setup:

c
```c
static struct usb_gadget_driver my_gadget_driver = {
    .function = "my_gadget",
    .bind = my_bind,  // Bind to controller
    .unbind = my_unbind,
    .setup = my_setup,  // Handle setup requests
    .disconnect = my_disconnect,
    .suspend = my_suspend,
    .resume = my_resume,
    .driver = { .name = "my_gadget" },
};

static int my_bind(struct usb_gadget *gadget, struct usb_gadget_driver *driver) {
    // Allocate eps, set up composite if needed
    return 0;
}
```
For composites: Use usb_composite_driver and add functions like g_mass_storage or g_ethernet. Common on ARM (e.g., Raspberry Pi in device mode).

Host controllers (e.g., EHCI, XHCI) have their own drivers (drivers/usb/host/), probed via PCI or platform. Extend via usb_hcd for custom HCDs.

Power Management and Interrupts

Runtime PM: Enable with usb_autopm_enable(intf). Suspend/resume callbacks handle state.
Interrupts: USB uses interrupt endpoints; poll via URBs with interval.
For MSI in PCIe-USB: As in PCI (Section 18.2).

Best Practices and Debugging

- **Portability:** Use usb_* APIs; test on xHCI (USB3) for quirks.
- **Security:** Validate descriptors; use usb_lock_device() for races.
- **Performance:** Batch URBs, use dma_alloc_coherent() for buffers.
- **Debugging:** usbmon (modprobe usbmon; cat /sys/kernel/debug/usb/usbmon/0u), or wireshark` with usbpcap.
- **Tools:** usbutils (lsusb, usb-devices); kernel config CONFIG_USB_DEBUG.

Common issues: Wrong endpoint types, URB timeouts (use USB_TIMEOUT), hotplug races.

Summary

USB drivers and frameworks offer a dynamic ecosystem for host and gadget modes, centered on URBs and interface binding. Through usb_driver and gadget APIs, developers handle diverse peripherals efficiently. This complements GPIO/platform drivers in the next section, enabling full hardware orchestration in Linux systems.

18.4 GPIO and Platform Drivers

General-Purpose Input/Output (GPIO) and platform drivers are essential for managing integrated, non-discoverable hardware in embedded and SoC-based systems, such as those on ARM, RISC-V (Section 16.4), or x86 embedded platforms. Unlike bus-based interfaces like PCI (Section 18.2) or USB (Section 18.3), platform devices lack self-identification, relying on static descriptions via device trees (DT) or ACPI for discovery. GPIO provides simple digital I/O pins for tasks like LED control, button reading, or signaling, while platform drivers serve as a generic framework for SoC peripherals (e.g., timers, ADCs, or custom IP blocks). The kernel's GPIO subsystem (drivers/gpio/) and platform bus (drivers/base/platform.c) abstract hardware variances, enabling portable, modular drivers. This section explores GPIO APIs, platform driver structure, integration with DT/ACPI, interrupts, and power management, with examples to illustrate practical implementation. Mastering these allows developers to interface with board-level hardware efficiently, avoiding direct register pokes that lead to fragility.

GPIO Subsystem Overview

GPIO lines are versatile pins configurable as input/output, often with pull-up/down resistors or interrupt capabilities. The kernel uses a unified API to handle chip-specific controllers (e.g., pinctrl for multiplexing). GPIO numbers are logical (0 to n), mapped to hardware via descriptors.

Key APIs (from include/linux/gpio/consumer.h and include/linux/gpio/driver.h):

- Consumer side: For drivers using GPIOs (e.g., LED driver requesting a pin).
- Driver side: For implementing GPIO controllers (gpiochip).

Consumer functions:

- gpiod_get(dev, con_id, flags): Get descriptor (e.g., GPIOD_OUT_HIGH for initial high).
- gpiod_set_value(desc, value): Set output (1/0).
- gpiod_get_value(desc): Read input.
- gpiod_direction_input/output(desc): Configure direction.
- gpiod_put(desc): Release.

Flags: GPIOD_ASIS (no change), GPIOD_ACTIVE_LOW (inverted logic).

For interrupts: gpiod_to_irq(desc), then request_irq().

In DT: gpios = <&gpio0 12 GPIO_ACTIVE_HIGH>; (phandle, pin, flags). Use devm_gpiod_get_from_of_node() for parsing.

Example: Consumer in a platform driver toggling an LED:

c

```c
#include <linux/gpio/consumer.h>

struct my_priv {
    struct gpio_desc *led_gpio;
};

static int my_probe(struct platform_device *pdev) {
    struct my_priv *priv = devm_kzalloc(&pdev->dev, sizeof(*priv), GFP_KERNEL);
    if (!priv) return -ENOMEM;

    priv->led_gpio = devm_gpiod_get(&pdev->dev, "led", GPIOD_OUT_LOW);
```

```c
    if (IS_ERR(priv->led_gpio)) return PTR_ERR(priv->led_gpio);

    // Toggle
    gpiod_set_value(priv->led_gpio, 1);  // On
    platform_set_drvdata(pdev, priv);
    return 0;
}

static int my_remove(struct platform_device *pdev) {
    // devm_ handles put
    return 0;
}
```

DT: led-gpios = <&gpio1 5 GPIO_ACTIVE_HIGH>;.
For batches: gpiod_get_array().

Implementing GPIO Chip Drivers

For custom controllers, implement struct gpio_chip with ops like get/set_value, direction_input/output. Register with devm_gpiochip_add_data().

Example snippet:

c
```c
static int my_gpio_get(struct gpio_chip *chip, unsigned offset) {
    // Read hardware register
    return !!(readl(base + REG_IN) & (1 << offset));
}

static struct gpio_chip my_gpio_chip = {
    .label = "my_gpio",
    .ngpio = 16,
    .get = my_gpio_get,
    .set = my_gpio_set,  // Implement similarly
    // Other ops: request/free, get_direction, etc.
};

// In probe:
gpiochip_add_data(&my_gpio_chip, priv);
```

Pinctrl integration: Often combined (pinctrl_dev) for muxing pins.

Platform Drivers Framework

Platform drivers manage non-enumerable devices, common in SoCs. The platform bus is virtual, binding via name or DT compatible.

Structure: struct platform_driver, registered with platform_driver_register().

Key callbacks:

- probe: Initialize, get resources (IRQs, mem via platform_get_resource()).
- remove: Cleanup.
- shutdown/suspend/resume: For power.

Resources: struct resource for mem/irq/dma.

DT/ACPI: Match via of_match_table or ACPI IDs.

Example: Platform driver for a simple counter peripheral:

c
```c
#include <linux/platform_device.h>
#include <linux/io.h>
#include <linux/interrupt.h>
#include <linux/of.h>

struct my_counter_priv {
    void __iomem *base;
    int irq;
};
```

```c
static irqreturn_t my_counter_irq(int irq, void *dev_id) {
    struct my_counter_priv *priv = dev_id;
    u32 count = ioread32(priv->base + 0x00);
    printk(KERN_INFO "my_counter: Interrupt, count=%u\n", count);
    iowrite32(1, priv->base + 0x04);  // Clear
    return IRQ_HANDLED;
}

static int my_counter_probe(struct platform_device *pdev) {
    struct my_counter_priv *priv;
    struct resource *res;
    int ret;

    priv = devm_kzalloc(&pdev->dev, sizeof(*priv), GFP_KERNEL);
    if (!priv) return -ENOMEM;

    res = platform_get_resource(pdev, IORESOURCE_MEM, 0);
    priv->base = devm_ioremap_resource(&pdev->dev, res);
    if (IS_ERR(priv->base)) return PTR_ERR(priv->base);

    priv->irq = platform_get_irq(pdev, 0);
    if (priv->irq < 0) return priv->irq;

    ret = devm_request_irq(&pdev->dev, priv->irq, my_counter_irq, 0, "my_counter", priv);
    if (ret) return ret;

    // Enable counter
    iowrite32(1, priv->base + 0x08);

    platform_set_drvdata(pdev, priv);
    return 0;
}

static int my_counter_remove(struct platform_device *pdev) {
    // devm_ handles
    return 0;
}

static const struct of_device_id my_counter_of_match[] = {
    { .compatible = "example,my-counter" },
    { }
};
MODULE_DEVICE_TABLE(of, my_counter_of_match);

static struct platform_driver my_counter_driver = {
    .probe = my_counter_probe,
    .remove = my_counter_remove,
    .driver = {
        .name = "my_counter",
        .of_match_table = my_counter_of_match,
    },
};

module_platform_driver(my_counter_driver);
MODULE_LICENSE("GPL");
```

DT:

```text
my-counter@0x10000000 {
    compatible = "example,my-counter";
    reg = <0x10000000 0x100>;
    interrupts = <0 42 4>;  // GIC example
};
```

ACPI: Similar, use acpi_id table.

Integration and Advanced Features

- **Interrupts:** Use devm_request_threaded_irq() for deferred handling.
- **Power/Clock:** Get clocks with devm_clk_get(), regulators with devm_regulator_get().
- **DMA:** Platform devices support DMA via dma_request_chan() or legacy platform_dma_*.
- **Pinctrl:** Request states with devm_pinctrl_get() for pin muxing.
- **Devres:** Prefer devm_ for auto-cleanup on unbind.

For GPIO in platform: Use gpiod_ APIs in probe.

Best practices:

- Handle -EPROBE_DEFER for deferred resources (e.g., clocks not ready).
- Use dev_info/err for logging.
- Test with QEMU (-device) or real boards.
- Security: Avoid exposing raw GPIO to user space without checks; use sysfs/libgpiod.
- Performance: Batch GPIO ops with gpiod_set_array_value().

Common issues: Wrong DT bindings (validate with dtc), IRQ storms (mask properly), pin conflicts (check pinctrl).

Summary

GPIO and platform drivers provide a flexible backbone for SoC hardware, with GPIO offering pin-level control and platform enabling structured integration via DT/ACPI. Through consumer APIs and driver frameworks, developers can build portable solutions. This rounds out hardware interfaces, leading to block/network drivers in Chapter 19, for complete system connectivity.

19. Block and Network Drivers

Block and network drivers represent specialized categories for handling storage and communication hardware, building on the foundational concepts of char drivers (Chapter 17) and hardware interfaces (Chapter 18). Block drivers manage devices like hard drives, SSDs, and flash storage, focusing on efficient random-access I/O, while network drivers facilitate data transmission over wired or wireless links, emphasizing low-latency packet processing. Both integrate deeply with kernel subsystems—the block layer for queuing and scheduling, and the net stack for protocol handling—optimizing for throughput and scalability. This chapter examines their architectures, implementations, and optimizations, with practical examples for real-world development.

19.1 Block Device Architecture

The block device architecture in Linux provides a structured framework for managing storage devices, abstracting hardware specifics behind a unified interface that supports file systems (Chapter 15), swapping, and direct I/O. At its core, the block layer (block/) acts as a middleware between upper layers (e.g., VFS) and drivers, handling request queuing, merging, scheduling, and error recovery. This design enables high-performance I/O by batching operations, reducing overhead, and supporting advanced features like multi-queue (blk-mq) for SSDs. Block devices operate on fixed-size sectors (typically 512B or 4KB), allowing random access via block numbers. Understanding this architecture is crucial for writing drivers that handle diverse hardware, from SATA HDDs to NVMe PCIe SSDs, ensuring compatibility across architectures like ARM and RISC-V (Section 16.4).

Key Components of Block Device Architecture

The architecture revolves around several interconnected structures:

- **struct block_device (bdev):** Represents the logical device (e.g., /dev/sda), linked to partitions and file systems. It tracks open counts, size, and the underlying gendisk.
- **struct gendisk:** The core disk representation, allocated with blk_alloc_disk() (or alloc_disk() legacy). It includes capacity (set_capacity()), major/minor, queue, and operations (fops for ioctl/open).
- **struct request_queue:** Manages I/O requests. Initialized with blk_alloc_queue() or blk_mq_init_queue() for multi-queue. Supports plugging (batching) and tagging for concurrency.
- **struct request:** Groups bios for a single operation (e.g., read sectors 100-110). Contains command type (REQ_OP_READ/WRITE), sectors, and bios.
- **struct bio:** Basic I/O unit, representing a scatter-gather list of pages/sectors. Allocated with bio_alloc(), submitted via submit_bio().
- **block_device_operations (bdops):** Callbacks for open/release/ioctl, but core I/O is via the queue's make_request_fn (often blk_mq_make_request()).

The flow: User/VFS issues I/O -> bio created -> submitted to queue -> merged/scheduled -> driver processes (e.g., via hardware commands) -> completion.

Modern kernels favor blk-mq (CONFIG_BLK_MQ), with per-CPU hardware queues for scalability, replacing legacy single-queue.

Driver Registration and Initialization

Block drivers register the gendisk with add_disk(), after setting up the queue. For blk-mq, define blk_mq_ops with queue_rq() to handle requests.

Legacy single-queue uses request_fn callback.

Example: Basic RAM block driver (simulating a disk in memory):

```c
#include <linux/module.h>
#include <linux/blkdev.h>
#include <linux/blk-mq.h>
#include <linux/hdreg.h>

#define RAMDISK_SIZE (16 * 1024 * 1024ULL) // 16MB
#define SECTOR_SHIFT 9 // 512B sectors

struct ramdisk_priv {
    u8 *data;
    struct gendisk *disk;
```

```
        struct blk_mq_tag_set tag_set;
};

static int ramdisk_mq_queue_rq(struct blk_mq_hw_ctx *hctx, const struct blk_mq_queue_data *bd) {
    struct request *req = bd->rq;
    struct ramdisk_priv *priv = hctx->queue->queuedata;
    sector_t start_sect = blk_rq_pos(req);
    unsigned long offset = start_sect << SECTOR_SHIFT;
    struct bio_vec bvec;
    struct req_iterator iter;
    void *buffer;

    blk_mq_start_request(req);

    rq_for_each_segment(bvec, req, iter) {
        buffer = bvec_kmap_local(&bvec);
        size_t len = bvec.bv_len;
        if (req_op(req) == REQ_OP_READ)
            memcpy(buffer, priv->data + offset, len);
        else if (req_op(req) == REQ_OP_WRITE)
            memcpy(priv->data + offset, buffer, len);
        kunmap_local(buffer);
        offset += len;
    }

    blk_mq_end_request(req, BLK_STS_OK);
    return BLK_MQ_REQ_COMPLETE;
}

static const struct blk_mq_ops ramdisk_mq_ops = {
    .queue_rq = ramdisk_mq_queue_rq,
};

static int __init ramdisk_init(void) {
    struct ramdisk_priv *priv;
    int ret;

    priv = kzalloc(sizeof(*priv), GFP_KERNEL);
    if (!priv) return -ENOMEM;

    priv->data = vmalloc(RAMDISK_SIZE);
    if (!priv->data) {
        ret = -ENOMEM;
        goto free_priv;
    }
    memset(priv->data, 0, RAMDISK_SIZE);

    memset(&priv->tag_set, 0, sizeof(priv->tag_set));
    priv->tag_set.ops = &ramdisk_mq_ops;
    priv->tag_set.nr_hw_queues = 1;
    priv->tag_set.queue_depth = 128;
    priv->tag_set.numa_node = NUMA_NO_NODE;
    priv->tag_set.flags = BLK_MQ_F_SHOULD_MERGE;

    ret = blk_mq_alloc_tag_set(&priv->tag_set);
    if (ret) goto free_data;
```

```
priv->disk = blk_mq_alloc_disk(&priv->tag_set, NULL, priv);
if (IS_ERR(priv->disk)) {
    ret = PTR_ERR(priv->disk);
    goto free_tags;
}

priv->disk->flags = GENHD_FL_NO_PART;
set_capacity(priv->disk, RAMDISK_SIZE >> SECTOR_SHIFT);
snprintf(priv->disk->disk_name, sizeof(priv->disk->disk_name), "ramdisk0");

ret = add_disk(priv->disk);
if (ret) goto clean_disk;

return 0;

clean_disk:
    blk_cleanup_disk(priv->disk);
free_tags:
    blk_mq_free_tag_set(&priv->tag_set);
free_data:
    vfree(priv->data);
free_priv:
    kfree(priv);
    return ret;
}

static void __exit ramdisk_exit(void) {
    struct ramdisk_priv *priv = priv_global;  // Assume global for simplicity
    del_gendisk(priv->disk);
    blk_cleanup_disk(priv->disk);
    blk_mq_free_tag_set(&priv->tag_set);
    vfree(priv->data);
    kfree(priv);
}

module_init(ramdisk_init);
module_exit(ramdisk_exit);
MODULE_LICENSE("GPL");
```

This uses blk-mq: Probe allocates tags, disk, queue; queue_rq processes segments via memcpy (simulating hardware DMA).

For real hardware: In queue_rq, translate to controller commands (e.g., SCSI or NVMe), use dma_map_bvec() for scatter-gather.

I/O Scheduling and Optimization

Queues use elevators (e.g., mq-deadline, kyber) for reordering. Set with blk_mq_alloc_disk() params.
Features:

- **TRIM/Discard:** For SSDs, support REQ_OP_DISCARD.
- **Write Cache:** Control via bdops->revalidate_disk().
- **Partitions:** Scan with add_disk() if not NO_PART.

Legacy to mq migration: Use blk_queue_make_request(q, my_make_request) for bio handling.

Best Practices and Debugging

- Use devm_ for resources.
- Handle errors in queue_rq (BLK_STS_IOERR).
- Test with fio/blktests.
- Debug: /sys/block/<dev>/ for stats; trace_blk_rq_insert/complete via ftrace.

- Security: Validate bio sectors < capacity.
- Portability: APIs work across arches; test on QEMU (-drive).

Common issues: Queue stalls (use blk_mq_sched_mark_restart_hctx()), bio splitting for large I/O.

Summary
Block device architecture centers on gendisk, queues, and requests/bios for efficient storage handling, with blk-mq enabling modern scalability. Through examples like the RAM driver, developers can implement hardware-agnostic solutions. This sets the stage for network driver basics in the next section, where packet-oriented architectures contrast with block's sector focus.

19.2 Request Queues and I/O Scheduling

Request queues and I/O scheduling form the heart of the Linux block layer's efficiency, managing the flow of I/O operations from upper layers (e.g., file systems or direct user requests) to the underlying hardware. The request queue (struct request_queue) acts as a buffer and dispatcher, allowing the kernel to optimize operations through merging, reordering, and prioritization. I/O schedulers (also called elevators) plug into this queue to decide the order of request execution, balancing throughput, latency, and fairness across workloads. In modern kernels, multi-queue (blk-mq) support enhances scalability for high-IOPS devices like NVMe SSDs, while legacy single-queue remains for simpler hardware. This section delves into queue setup, request handling, scheduling algorithms, and customization, with examples extending the RAM disk from Section 19.1. Understanding these components enables drivers to handle diverse storage scenarios, from mechanical HDDs requiring seek minimization to flash-based devices favoring parallelism.

Request Queue Fundamentals
The request queue is the central data structure for block I/O, created during driver initialization and associated with the gendisk. It holds pending requests, manages hardware limits (e.g., max segments, queue depth), and dispatches to the driver. For blk-mq, queues are per-CPU or hardware-mapped, reducing contention on multicore systems.

Key attributes and setup:
- **Initialization:** Use blk_alloc_queue() for single-queue or blk_mq_init_queue() for multi-queue. Specify flags like QUEUE_FLAG_NOMERGES to disable merging.
- **Limits:** Set via blk_queue_max_hw_sectors(q, sects) for max I/O size, blk_queue_max_segments(q, segs) for scatter-gather.
- **Requests:** Allocated from a mempool; contain op (REQ_OP_*), position, length, and bio chain.
- **Bios vs. Requests:** Bios are lightweight page vectors; the queue's make_request_fn (e.g., blk_mq_make_request()) may merge bios into requests for efficiency.
- **Plugging:** Temporary batching with blk_queue_plug() to group I/O before scheduling, reducing overhead.

In blk-mq, a blk_mq_tag_set defines hardware queues (nr_hw_queues), depth (queue_depth), and ops (blk_mq_ops with queue_rq(), init_request(), etc.).

Extending the RAM disk example from 19.1 to highlight queue setup:

```c
// ... previous includes ...

static int ramdisk_open(struct block_device *bdev, fmode_t mode) {
    // Optional: check mode, increment open count
    return 0;
}

static void ramdisk_release(struct gendisk *disk, fmode_t mode) {
    // Decrement open count
}

static const struct block_device_operations ramdisk_bdops = {
    .open = ramdisk_open,
    .release = ramdisk_release,
    // .ioctl = ..., if needed
};
```

```
// In init:
priv->tag_set.ops = &ramdisk_mq_ops;
priv->tag_set.nr_hw_queues = num_online_cpus();  // Scale with CPUs
priv->tag_set.queue_depth = 256;  // Deeper for better merging
priv->tag_set.numa_node = NUMA_NO_NODE;
priv->tag_set.cmd_size = sizeof(struct my_req_priv);  // Per-request data
priv->tag_set.flags = BLK_MQ_F_SHOULD_MERGE | BLK_MQ_F_SG_MERGE;

ret = blk_mq_alloc_tag_set(&priv->tag_set);
if (ret) /* handle */;

priv->disk = blk_mq_alloc_disk(&priv->tag_set, NULL, priv);
if (IS_ERR(priv->disk)) /* handle */;
priv->disk->fops = &ramdisk_bdops;

// Set limits
blk_queue_max_hw_sectors(priv->disk->queue, 1024);  // 512KB max
blk_queue_max_segments(priv->disk->queue, 128);
blk_queue_logical_block_size(priv->disk->queue, 4096);  // 4KB logical

// Optional: Set scheduler
elevator_switch(priv->disk->queue, elevator_get_by_features("mq-deadline"));

// Add disk...
```

Here, limits prevent oversized I/O; bdops handle device open/close.

I/O Scheduling Algorithms

Schedulers reorder and merge requests to optimize hardware characteristics:

- **Merging:** Adjacent requests (by sector) combined to reduce commands. Front/back merge via hash tables.
- **Reordering:** Delay/prioritize for better patterns (e.g., elevator analogy: group by floor).

Available elevators:

- **mq-deadline:** Default for blk-mq. Time-based deadlines for read/write/fsync; prevents starvation. Tunable via /sys/block/<dev>/queue/iosched/.
- **kyber:** For fast devices (SSDs). Separates reads/writes with latency targets; minimal reordering.
- **bfq (Budget Fair Queuing):** Fair sharing among processes; good for desktops.
- **none:** No scheduling; FIFO dispatch, ideal for NVMe with hardware queuing.

Switch at runtime: echo mq-deadline > /sys/block/sda/queue/scheduler.

In drivers: Set default with blk_mq_alloc_disk(..., elevator_get("mq-deadline"), ...).

For custom: Implement elevator_type with elevator_ops (init_queue, insert_request, dispatch_request), register via elevator_register()—rare, as built-ins suffice.

In queue_rq (driver side): Fetch with blk_mq_sched_get_request(), process, complete with blk_mq_end_request(rq, status).

Handling Requests in Drivers

In blk-mq's queue_rq():

- Check req->cmd_flags for ops (READ/WRITE/DISCARD/FLUSH).
- Map bios to hardware (e.g., DMA with blk_rq_map_sg(q, rq, sg)).
- Submit to controller (e.g., via SCSI or NVMe commands).
- Handle errors: Retry or BLK_STS_*.

For threaded: Use blk_mq_ops.map_queues to affinity-map.

In the RAM example, queue_rq iterates segments—real drivers would async submit and complete later in IRQ.

Optimization and Extensions

- **Flush/Named Queues:** For cache flushes (REQ_OP_FLUSH).
- **Discard:** Trim unused sectors (REQ_OP_DISCARD) for SSD wear-leveling.
- **Zoned Storage:** For SMR HDDs, use blk_queue_chunk_sectors().

- **IO_uring Integration:** Low-latency async I/O via queues.
- **Stats:** /sys/block/<dev>/stat for reads/writes.

Best practices:
- Scale nr_hw_queues with device lanes (e.g., PCIe x4).
- Use devm_blk_* for managed alloc.
- Test with fio --rw=randrw --bs=4k --numjobs=4.
- Debug: Trace blk_mq_* events with ftrace; blktrace for logs.

Common pitfalls: Infinite queuing (set limits), ignoring merges (reduces throughput), sync vs. async mishandling.

Summary

Request queues and I/O scheduling optimize block I/O by buffering, merging, and ordering operations, with blk-mq providing modern parallelism. Through queue setup, elevator choices, and request processing, drivers achieve high performance. This framework supports network driver packet handling in the next sections, where similar queuing principles apply to data flows.

19.3 Network Driver Basics

Network drivers in Linux manage hardware interfaces for data communication, such as Ethernet controllers, Wi-Fi chips, or cellular modems, integrating with the kernel's networking stack to handle packet transmission and reception. Unlike block drivers (Sections 19.1-19.2), which deal with sector-based storage I/O, network drivers focus on packet-oriented operations, emphasizing low latency, high throughput, and efficient interrupt handling. The net subsystem (net/) provides a standardized framework, abstracting hardware details behind the struct net_device interface, allowing seamless integration with protocols like TCP/IP. This design supports features like offloading (e.g., checksum calculation), carrier detection, and ethtool configuration. On modern architectures like ARM and RISC-V (Section 16.4), drivers often use platform or PCI frameworks (Sections 18.2, 18.4) for binding. This section covers the core structure of network drivers, registration, packet handling, interrupts with NAPI, and basic configuration, with examples to guide implementation.

Network Device Structure and Registration

The struct net_device (netdev) is the central abstraction, representing a network interface (e.g., eth0). It includes name, MTU, MAC address, statistics (dev->stats), and operations vectors. Drivers allocate with alloc_etherdev() (for Ethernet) or alloc_netdev() (generic), then register with register_netdev().

Key operations:
- **net_device_ops (ndo):** Core functions like ndo_open() (bring up interface), ndo_stop() (down), ndo_start_xmit() (transmit skb), ndo_set_mac_address().
- **ethtool_ops:** For user-space config via ethtool (e.g., get_settings(), set_settings() for speed/duplex).
- **rtnl_link_ops:** For advanced link management.

Registration binds the netdev to the system, triggering udev events and sysfs entries (/sys/class/net/<ifname>/).

Example: Basic Ethernet driver skeleton:

```c
#include <linux/module.h>
#include <linux/netdevice.h>
#include <linux/etherdevice.h>
#include <linux/interrupt.h>

struct my_net_priv {
    void __iomem *base;  // Hardware registers
    int irq;
    struct net_device *netdev;
};

static netdev_tx_t my_start_xmit(struct sk_buff *skb, struct net_device *dev) {
    struct my_net_priv *priv = netdev_priv(dev);

    // Hardware Tx: e.g., DMA skb->data to FIFO
    // Assume simple copy for example
    iowrite32(skb->len, priv->base + REG_TX_LEN);
```

```
    memcpy_toio(priv->base + REG_TX_BUF, skb->data, skb->len);
    iowrite32(1, priv->base + REG_TX_START);  // Trigger send

    dev->stats.tx_packets++;
    dev->stats.tx_bytes += skb->len;

    // Free skb on success (async in real drivers)
    dev_kfree_skb(skb);
    return NETDEV_TX_OK;  // Or BUSY if queue full
}

static int my_open(struct net_device *dev) {
    struct my_net_priv *priv = netdev_priv(dev);

    // Enable hardware, request IRQ
    int ret = request_irq(priv->irq, my_irq_handler, IRQF_SHARED, dev->name, dev);
    if (ret) return ret;

    // Start queue
    netif_start_queue(dev);
    return 0;
}

static int my_stop(struct net_device *dev) {
    struct my_net_priv *priv = netdev_priv(dev);

    netif_stop_queue(dev);
    free_irq(priv->irq, dev);
    // Disable hardware
    return 0;
}

static const struct net_device_ops my_netdev_ops = {
    .ndo_open = my_open,
    .ndo_stop = my_stop,
    .ndo_start_xmit = my_start_xmit,
    .ndo_set_mac_address = eth_mac_addr,  // Helper
    .ndo_validate_addr = eth_validate_addr,
};

static int __init my_net_init(void) {
    struct net_device *netdev = alloc_etherdev(sizeof(struct my_net_priv));
    if (!netdev) return -ENOMEM;

    struct my_net_priv *priv = netdev_priv(netdev);
    // Init hardware: map base, get IRQ (e.g., from platform/pci)
    priv->base = ioremap(HW_BASE_ADDR, HW_SIZE);
    priv->irq = HW_IRQ;
    priv->netdev = netdev;

    ether_setup(netdev);  // Set Ethernet defaults
    netdev->netdev_ops = &my_netdev_ops;
    // Set random MAC or from hardware
    eth_hw_addr_random(netdev);

    return register_netdev(netdev);
```

```
}

static void __exit my_net_exit(void) {
    struct my_net_priv *priv = netdev_priv(netdev_global);  // Assume global
    unregister_netdev(priv->netdev);
    iounmap(priv->base);
    free_netdev(priv->netdev);
}

module_init(my_net_init);
module_exit(my_net_exit);
MODULE_LICENSE("GPL");
```

This registers an Ethernet-like interface. On load, ifconfig mynet0 up activates.

For PCI/USB/platform: In probe, alloc netdev, set drvdata, register.

Packet Handling: Transmission and Reception

- **Tx:** Upper layers call dev_queue_xmit(skb), which invokes ndo_start_xmit(). Driver queues or sends immediately, handling backpressure with netif_stop_queue() if full. Complete with netif_wake_queue().
- **Rx:** Hardware IRQ signals packet; driver allocates skb with dev_alloc_skb(), fills via DMA/copy, pushes to stack with netif_receive_skb(skb) or napi_schedule() (see below).

Skb (struct sk_buff): Packet container with data, headers; manage with skb_put(), skb_reserve().

Offloads: Set netdev->hw_features (e.g., NETIF_F_IP_CSUM) for checksum/TSO; kernel skips software computation.

Interrupts and NAPI

Traditional IRQs per packet cause overhead under load; NAPI (New API) switches to polling for bursts.

Setup: In probe, netif_napi_add(netdev, &priv->napi, my_poll, NAPI_POLL_WEIGHT=64); enable with napi_enable() in open.

In IRQ: If Rx, napi_schedule(&priv->napi); return IRQ_HANDLED. Disable legacy IRQ if needed.

Poll function:

c

```
static int my_poll(struct napi_struct *napi, int budget) {
    struct my_net_priv *priv = container_of(napi, struct my_net_priv, napi);
    int work = 0;

    while (work < budget) {
        // Check hardware for packets
        if (!packet_ready()) break;

        struct sk_buff *skb = dev_alloc_skb(PKT_SIZE);
        if (!skb) break;

        // Fill skb: e.g., dma_sync, memcpy_fromio
        len = ioread32(priv->base + REG_RX_LEN);
        memcpy_fromio(skb_put(skb, len), priv->base + REG_RX_BUF, len);
        skb->protocol = eth_type_trans(skb, priv->netdev);

        netif_receive_skb(skb);
        dev->stats.rx_packets++;
        dev->stats.rx_bytes += len;
        work++;
    }

    if (work < budget) {
        napi_complete_done(napi, work);  // Re-enable IRQ if needed
        // Re-enable hardware Rx interrupt
    }
```

```
    return work; // Packets processed
}
```
NAPI bounds CPU usage; tune weight for balance.

Configuration and Features

- **MTU/MAC:** Set in probe; change via ndo_change_mtu/ndo_set_mac_address.
- **Ethtool:** Implement get_drvinfo, get_link, etc., for ethtool -i eth0.
- **Carrier:** Use netif_carrier_on/off(dev) for link status.
- **VLAN/GRO:** Enable with NETIF_F_HW_VLAN_CTAG_RX, NETIF_F_GRO.
- **Stats:** Update dev->stats; expose via ethtool_get_stats.

For wireless: Use cfg80211/mac80211 subsystems (drivers/net/wireless/).

Best Practices and Debugging

- Use devm_ for resources.
- Handle skb alloc failures (drop packets).
- Test with iperf/ping; simulate load.
- Debug: /sys/class/net/<if>/statistics/; trace_netif_receive_skb with ftrace; tcpdump for packets.
- Security: Validate hardware inputs; avoid DMA to user pages without checks.
- Portability: APIs arch-agnostic; test on QEMU (-netdev).

Common pitfalls: Tx queue stalls (wake properly), skb leaks, IRQ storms (use NAPI).

Summary

Network driver basics revolve around net_device registration, packet Tx/Rx, and NAPI for efficient interrupts, providing a robust foundation for communication hardware. Through structured ops and skb handling, drivers integrate seamlessly with the net stack. This leads to socket buffers and packet processing in the next section, enhancing understanding of end-to-end data flows.

19.4 Socket Buffers and Packet Handling

Socket buffers and packet handling are pivotal in Linux network drivers, enabling efficient data movement between the hardware, kernel networking stack, and user-space applications. The struct sk_buff (skb) serves as the universal container for network packets, encapsulating data, headers, and metadata throughout the Tx (transmit) and Rx (receive) paths. Effective packet handling minimizes copies, manages memory allocation, and integrates with features like NAPI (from Section 19.3) for high-performance networking. Drivers must carefully manipulate skbs to avoid leaks, corruption, or performance bottlenecks, especially under high load. This section explores skb structure, allocation/deallocation, header manipulation, Tx/Rx workflows, and advanced techniques like zero-copy, with examples building on the basic network driver from Section 19.3. Mastery of these elements ensures drivers can support diverse hardware, from Gigabit Ethernet to 100Gbps interfaces, across architectures like ARM and RISC-V.

Socket Buffer (skb) Structure

The sk_buff is a flexible, reference-counted structure (include/linux/skbuff.h) that holds packet data in a linear or scattered fashion. Key fields include:

- **data/head/tail/end:** Pointers for the data buffer; skb_put() extends tail for adding data, skb_push() prepends at head for headers.
- **len/data_len:** Total length; data_len for paged (fragged) data.
- **protocol/mac_header/transport_header:** Markers for layer headers (e.g., eth_type_trans() sets protocol).
- **dev:** Associated net_device.
- **frags/skb_frag_list:** For scatter-gather (non-linear data).
- **cb (control buffer):** 48-byte private area for driver use.

Skbs are allocated from a slab cache for speed, with refcounting via skb_get()/kfree_skb().

Allocation: dev_alloc_skb(len) (reserves headroom for headers), or alloc_skb(len, GFP_ATOMIC) in IRQ context.

Deallocation: dev_kfree_skb(skb) (or _irq variant); automatic on errors.

Drivers often clone skbs (skb_clone()) for shared use or orphan (skb_orphan()) to detach from sockets.

Packet Transmission (Tx) Path

In Tx, the networking stack passes skbs to the driver via ndo_start_xmit(). The driver prepares the skb for hardware (e.g., adding headers, mapping for DMA), queues or sends it, and manages completion.

Steps:

1. Check queue status: If stopped (netif_queue_stopped(dev)), return NETDEV_TX_BUSY.
2. Linearize if needed: skb_linearize(skb) coalesces frags for simple hardware.
3. Map for DMA: dma_map_single(dev, skb->data, skb->len, DMA_TO_DEVICE).
4. Submit to hardware: Write descriptors or registers.
5. On completion (IRQ): Unmap DMA, free skb, update stats, wake queue if needed.

Example enhancement to the xmit from Section 19.3 (assuming DMA-capable hardware):

c

```c
static netdev_tx_t my_start_xmit(struct sk_buff *skb, struct net_device *dev) {
    struct my_net_priv *priv = netdev_priv(dev);
    dma_addr_t dma_handle;

    if (skb_linearize(skb) < 0) goto drop; // Coalesce if hardware can't scatter

    dma_handle = dma_map_single(&dev->dev, skb->data, skb->len, DMA_TO_DEVICE);
    if (dma_mapping_error(&dev->dev, dma_handle)) goto drop;

    // Hardware-specific: Set descriptor with dma_handle, len
    my_hw_tx_desc->addr = dma_handle;
    my_hw_tx_desc->len = skb->len;
    my_hw_tx_desc->skb = skb; // Store for completion
    wmb(); // Barrier
    iowrite32(1, priv->base + REG_TX_KICK); // Start Tx

    if (my_tx_queue_full()) netif_stop_queue(dev); // Backpressure

    return NETDEV_TX_OK;

drop:
    dev_kfree_skb(skb);
    dev->stats.tx_dropped++;
    return NETDEV_TX_OK;
}


// In IRQ (Tx part):
static irqreturn_t my_irq_handler(int irq, void *dev_id) {
    struct net_device *dev = dev_id;
    struct my_net_priv *priv = netdev_priv(dev);

    // Check Tx complete
    if (tx_done()) {
        struct sk_buff *skb = my_hw_tx_desc->skb;
        dma_unmap_single(&dev->dev, my_hw_tx_desc->addr, skb->len, DMA_TO_DEVICE);
        dev_kfree_skb_irq(skb);
        dev->stats.tx_packets++;
        dev->stats.tx_bytes += skb->len;
        netif_wake_queue(dev); // Resume if stopped
    }

    // Rx handling...
    return IRQ_HANDLED;
}
```

Use skb->cb for temporary driver data.

Packet Reception (Rx) Path

In Rx, hardware signals arrival (IRQ); driver allocates/fills skb, passes to stack via netif_receive_skb() or NAPI poll.

Steps:

1. In poll/IRQ: Check ring/FIFO for packets.
2. Alloc skb with headroom (e.g., NET_SKB_PAD + NET_IP_ALIGN).
3. DMA sync: dma_sync_single_for_cpu(dev, handle, len, DMA_FROM_DEVICE).
4. Fill skb: skb_put(skb, len), set skb->protocol = eth_type_trans(skb, dev).
5. Push: netif_receive_skb(skb) (legacy) or in NAPI.
6. Update stats, refill ring.

For zero-copy: Use build_skb() around hardware buffers.

In NAPI poll (from 19.3): Loop until budget, complete with napi_complete_done().

Advanced Packet Handling Techniques

- **Checksum Offload:** If hardware supports (NETIF_F_RXCSUM), set skb->ip_summed = CHECKSUM_UNNECESSARY.
- **GRO/TSO:** Generic Receive/Segmentation Offload; enable with NETIF_F_GRO/TSO; kernel coalesces/segments.
- **VLAN:** Handle tagged frames with vlan_get_protocol(skb).
- **Multi-Queue:** For NICs with multiple Tx/Rx queues, use netif_set_real_num_tx/rx_queues(dev, num); select with XPS/RPS.
- **Buffer Management:** Use page frags (skb_add_rx_frag()) for large packets; recycle with driver rings.

Memory: Pre-allocate skbs in rings for Rx; use napi_alloc_skb() in poll.

Best Practices and Debugging

- Avoid skb copies: Use linearize only if necessary.
- Handle OOM: Drop packets gracefully.
- Stats: Update rx/tx_errors for drops/collisions.
- Test: tcpreplay, pktgen for traffic; ethtool -S for stats.
- Debug: tcpdump -i eth0; trace_net_dev_xmit/receive_skb with ftrace; /proc/net/softnet_stat for softirq.
- Security: Validate packet lengths/headers to prevent exploits.
- Portability: APIs work on all arches; use dma_* for coherence.

Common issues: Skb leaks (monitor with slabtop), queue overflows (tune with ethtool -G), misaligned DMA (use NET_IP_ALIGN).

Summary

Socket buffers and packet handling provide the machinery for network data flow, with skb manipulation enabling efficient Tx/Rx in drivers. Through xmit, poll, and offloads, performance is optimized. This concludes network basics, transitioning to concurrency in drivers (Chapter 20), where safe packet processing under load is critical.

20. Concurrency and Security in Drivers

Concurrency and security are critical aspects of device driver development, as drivers operate in a multi-threaded, interrupt-driven environment where multiple entities—processes, interrupts, or other drivers—may access shared resources simultaneously. Poor concurrency handling can lead to race conditions, data corruption, or deadlocks, while security flaws might allow privilege escalation or system compromise. This chapter addresses these challenges, starting with concurrency mechanisms, then interrupt safety, best practices for secure coding, and performance tuning. Drawing from kernel internals (Book 3) and driver basics (Chapters 16-19), the focus is on practical implementations to ensure robust, efficient drivers.

20.1 Handling Concurrency in Drivers

Handling concurrency in device drivers is essential to maintain data integrity and system stability in the face of simultaneous access from multiple sources. Drivers run in kernel space, where preemption, interrupts, and SMP (Symmetric Multi-Processing) introduce parallelism: a user process might issue an ioctl while an interrupt handler updates shared state, or multiple CPUs access the same device queue. Without proper synchronization, this leads to races (e.g., inconsistent reads) or deadlocks (mutual waiting). Linux provides primitives like spinlocks, mutexes, semaphores, and atomic operations to protect critical sections, tailored to contexts—process (sleepable) vs. interrupt (atomic). This section explores these tools, their usage in drivers, context considerations, and avoidance of common pitfalls, with examples from char and block drivers.

Understanding Concurrency Contexts

Kernel code executes in different contexts, influencing synchronization choices:

- **Process Context:** From system calls (e.g., read/write in char drivers). Sleepable; use mutexes for longer sections.
- **Interrupt Context:** From IRQs (Chapter 14); atomic, no sleeping. Use spinlocks.
- **Bottom Halves:** Tasklets/workqueues (Section 14.3); process-like but may preempt.
- **SMP Considerations:** On multi-core, even single-threaded code needs locks for shared data.

Check context with in_irq(), in_softirq(), or preempt_count().

Synchronization Primitives

Linux offers several mechanisms (from include/linux/spinlock.h, include/linux/mutex.h):

- **Spinlocks:** Busy-wait locks for short critical sections. Disable preemption/IRQs on acquisition. Variants: spin_lock() (basic), spin_lock_irqsave() (save/restore IRQ state for nested use).
- **Mutexes:** Sleepable locks for longer holds (e.g., allocations). Use mutex_lock(); interruptible variant for signals.
- **Semaphores:** Counting locks; use down() (sleep) or down_trylock() (non-block). Rare in drivers; prefer mutexes.
- **Atomic Operations:** For single variables, e.g., atomic_inc(&count), atomic_add_return(val, &var). Lock-free for simple counters.
- **Seqlocks/RCU:** For read-heavy scenarios; seqlocks for writers updating versions, RCU for pointer swaps without blocking readers.

Declare: spinlock_t my_lock = SPIN_LOCK_UNLOCKED; or DEFINE_SPINLOCK(my_lock);.

In drivers, protect shared structures (e.g., queues, registers).

Implementing Concurrency in Drivers

Consider a char driver with a shared buffer accessed by read/write and an IRQ updating it.

Example: Synchronizing a shared counter in a char driver:

c

```
#include <linux/spinlock.h>
#include <linux/atomic.h>

struct my_priv {
    atomic_t counter; // Atomic for simple inc/dec
    spinlock_t lock;  // For complex ops
    u8 *buffer;       // Shared data
};
```

```c
static ssize_t my_read(struct file *file, char __user *buf, size_t len, loff_t *off) {
    struct my_priv *priv = file->private_data;
    unsigned long flags;

    spin_lock_irqsave(&priv->lock, flags);  // Disable IRQs
    // Critical section: read buffer
    if (copy_to_user(buf, priv->buffer, len)) {
        spin_unlock_irqrestore(&priv->lock, flags);
        return -EFAULT;
    }
    spin_unlock_irqrestore(&priv->lock, flags);

    atomic_inc(&priv->counter);  // Safe without lock
    return len;
}

static irqreturn_t my_irq_handler(int irq, void *dev_id) {
    struct my_priv *priv = dev_id;
    spinlock_t *lock = &priv->lock;

    // No need for irqsave if already in IRQ context, but safe
    unsigned long flags;
    spin_lock_irqsave(lock, flags);
    // Update buffer from hardware
    ioread8_rep(priv->base + REG_DATA, priv->buffer, BUF_SIZE);
    spin_unlock_irqrestore(lock, flags);

    return IRQ_HANDLED;
}

// In probe/init:
atomic_set(&priv->counter, 0);
spin_lock_init(&priv->lock);
```

Here, spinlock protects buffer; atomic for counter avoids lock overhead.

For sleepable: Use mutex in open/release for init that may allocate.

In block drivers: Protect queue with spin_lock(&q->queue_lock); blk-mq uses per-hw-queue locks.

Avoiding Races and Deadlocks

- **Races:** Use locks for all shared accesses; test with stress (e.g., concurrent reads/writes).
- **Deadlocks:** Avoid nested locks in wrong order; use lockdep (CONFIG_LOCKDEP) to detect.
- **Bottom Halves:** Workqueues (sleepable) for long tasks; tasklets (atomic) for quick.
- **Preemption:** Disable with preempt_disable() in critical paths, but minimize.

Tools: lock_stat (/proc/lock_stat) for contention; ftrace for lock events.

Best Practices

- Minimize hold times: Do work outside locks.
- Use _bh variants (e.g., spin_lock_bh()) to disable softirqs.
- Per-CPU data: Avoid locks with per_cpu() vars.
- Read-Write Locks: rwlock_t for read-heavy (e.g., config reads).
- Testing: Use stress-ng --class io, or kernel's locktorture module.
- Performance: Profile with perf for lock contention.

Common pitfalls: Sleeping in spinlock (panic), forgetting irqrestore (IRQ storms), over-locking (slowdown).

Summary

Handling concurrency in drivers safeguards shared resources using spinlocks, mutexes, and atomics, tailored to contexts for safety and efficiency. Through examples like protected buffers, developers mitigate races and deadlocks. This foundation supports interrupt sharing (next section), ensuring secure, concurrent operations in multi-user, multi-core environments.

20.2 Interrupt Sharing and Safety

Interrupt sharing and safety are vital for robust device driver design, particularly in systems where hardware resources are limited, and multiple devices may utilize the same interrupt line. Sharing occurs commonly on buses like PCI/PCIe (Section 18.2), where devices on the same bus might share IRQs to conserve lines, or in embedded systems with multiplexed interrupt controllers (e.g., GIC on ARM). Without proper safety measures, shared interrupts can lead to misattribution of events, spurious handling, performance degradation, or system instability. Linux provides mechanisms like the IRQF_SHARED flag in request_irq() to enable sharing, but drivers must implement checks in handlers to determine ownership. This section explores interrupt sharing mechanics, handler safety, spurious interrupt mitigation, and best practices, with examples to illustrate secure implementations. Building on general concurrency (Section 20.1), these techniques ensure drivers operate reliably in shared environments.

Mechanics of Interrupt Sharing

Interrupt sharing allows multiple drivers to register handlers for the same IRQ number, with the kernel invoking all registered handlers sequentially when the line asserts. This is efficient for hardware like PCI, where legacy INTx pins are shared among slots, or embedded platforms with limited IRQ lines. To enable, use the IRQF_SHARED flag in request_irq() or devm_request_irq(), providing a unique dev_id (often the device struct) for identification. The kernel maintains a list of actions (struct irqaction) per IRQ descriptor (struct irq_desc), chaining handlers. On interrupt, it calls each until one returns IRQ_HANDLED.

Key APIs:

- request_irq(irq, handler, flags, name, dev_id): Flags include IRQF_SHARED for sharing, IRQF_NO_SUSPEND to persist during suspend.
- free_irq(irq, dev_id): Removes specific handler using dev_id.
- Handler prototype: irqreturn_t handler(int irq, void *dev_id).

In shared setups, handlers must quickly check if the interrupt is theirs (e.g., by reading a hardware status register) and return IRQ_NONE if not, to avoid unnecessary work and allow the next handler.

Ensuring Safety in Shared Handlers

Safety in shared interrupts involves ownership verification, minimal processing in the top half, and deferral to bottom halves (Section 14.3) for non-critical work. Failure to verify can cause "interrupt storms" if a device constantly triggers but the wrong handler claims it.

Best practices:

- **Ownership Check:** Read device-specific status; if not your interrupt, return IRQ_NONE immediately.
- **Atomic Operations:** Use spinlocks (Section 20.1) to protect shared data, but keep holds short to minimize latency for other handlers.
- **Deferral:** Use tasklets or workqueues for processing; schedule from the handler.
- **Spurious Interrupts:** Kernel tracks unhandled IRQs; too many disable the line. Mitigate by robust checks.
- **MSI/MSI-X Preference:** For PCI, use non-shared vectors (pci_alloc_irq_vectors()) to avoid sharing.

Example: Shared IRQ handler in a PCI driver for a fictional device:

```c
#include <linux/interrupt.h>
#include <linux/pci.h>

struct my_priv {
    void __iomem *base;
    spinlock_t lock;
    // Other fields
};

static irqreturn_t my_shared_irq_handler(int irq, void *dev_id) {
    struct pci_dev *pdev = dev_id;
    struct my_priv *priv = pci_get_drvdata(pdev);
    u32 status = ioread32(priv->base + REG_STATUS);

    if (!(status & MY_INTR_FLAG)) {
        return IRQ_NONE; // Not our interrupt
```

```
}

    // Clear interrupt flag (atomic)
    iowrite32(MY_INTR_FLAG, priv->base + REG_STATUS);

    // Defer work: e.g., schedule tasklet
    tasklet_schedule(&priv->my_tasklet);

    return IRQ_HANDLED;
}

static void my_tasklet(unsigned long data) {
    struct my_priv *priv = (struct my_priv *)data;
    unsigned long flags;

    spin_lock_irqsave(&priv->lock, flags);
    // Process data: e.g., read FIFO, update stats
    spin_unlock_irqrestore(&priv->lock, flags);
}

// In probe:
ret = pci_request_irq(pdev, 0, my_shared_irq_handler, IRQF_SHARED, "my_dev", pdev);
if (ret) return ret;

tasklet_init(&priv->my_tasklet, my_tasklet, (unsigned long)priv);
spin_lock_init(&priv->lock);

// In remove:
pci_free_irq(pdev, 0, pdev);
tasklet_kill(&priv->my_tasklet);
```

Here, the handler checks the status register; if not matching, returns NONE. Tasklet defers processing to softirq context.

For multiple shared devices: Each registers with unique dev_id; kernel calls all.

Mitigating Spurious and Shared Interrupt Issues

- **Spurious Interrupts:** Caused by noise or unclaimed events. Kernel disables IRQ after ~100,000 unhandled; log with pr_warn(). Add debug counters in handler.
- **Interrupt Storms:** If a device floods, mask in hardware; use disable_irq_nosync() temporarily.
- **Sharing Conflicts:** Test with lspci -v | grep IRQ; avoid if possible by using MSI.
- **SMP Affinity:** Pin IRQs to CPUs with irq_set_affinity_hint(irq, cpumask) for load balancing.

In embedded (e.g., ARM GIC): Sharing is common; use DT interrupts property for mapping.

Best Practices and Debugging

- Minimize handler time: <10us ideal; profile with ftrace (trace_irq_handler_entry/exit).
- Use IRQF_ONESHOT for threaded (devm_request_threaded_irq()), moving work to thread.
- Test: Simulate sharing with virtual devices (QEMU -device); use stress tools like pktgen for load.
- Debug: /proc/interrupts for counts; irqtop or perf for usage; enable CONFIG_IRQ_DEBUG.
- Security: In handlers, avoid user data access; validate in process context.

Common pitfalls: Returning HANDLED always (starves others), nested locks in shared paths (deadlock), forgetting dev_id (removal fails).

Summary

Interrupt sharing and safety enable resource-efficient designs by allowing multiple handlers per line, with safety ensured through ownership checks and deferral. Using IRQF_SHARED and quick verifications prevents issues in shared environments. This complements driver security (next sections), fostering reliable, concurrent hardware interactions in complex systems.

20.3 Driver Security Best Practices

Security in device drivers is paramount, as they run with kernel privileges and often bridge user-space interactions with hardware, making them potential vectors for exploits like privilege escalation, data leaks, or denial-of-service (DoS) attacks. A compromised driver can undermine the entire system, especially in environments like servers or embedded devices exposed to untrusted inputs. Best practices focus on input validation, safe memory handling, permission checks, and adherence to kernel hardening features. Unlike user-space code, drivers must assume adversarial inputs from ioctls, reads/writes, or even hardware. This section outlines key strategies, including validation techniques, secure APIs, auditing tools, and common pitfalls, with examples from char and PCI drivers (Chapters 17 and 18). Implementing these reduces attack surfaces, aligning with principles like least privilege and defense-in-depth.

Input Validation and Sanitization

All user-provided data must be validated before use to prevent overflows, invalid pointers, or malicious commands. This is critical in operations like ioctl, where arguments can control hardware.

- **Check Sizes and Ranges:** Ensure lengths fit buffers; cap values. Use check_copy_size() or manual bounds.
- **Validate Pointers:** Before copy_from_user()/copy_to_user(), verify with access_ok().
- **Command Whitelisting:** In ioctl, use switch with explicit cases; return -EINVAL for unknown.

Example in a char driver's ioctl (from Section 17.3):

c
```
static long my_ioctl(struct file *file, unsigned int cmd, unsigned long arg) {
    void __user *argp = (void __user *)arg;

    // Validate access
    if (!access_ok(argp, sizeof(int))) return -EFAULT;

    switch (cmd) {
    case MY_IOCTL_SET_VAL:
        int val;
        if (copy_from_user(&val, argp, sizeof(val))) return -EFAULT;
        if (val < 0 || val > MAX_VAL) return -EINVAL;  // Range check
        // Safe: set hardware
        iowrite32(val, priv->base + REG_VAL);
        return 0;
    default:
        return -ENOTTY;  // Invalid command
    }
}
```

For reads/writes: Clamp len with min(len, BUF_SIZE - *off).

In block drivers: Validate bio sectors against disk capacity in queue_rq to prevent out-of-bounds.

Safe Memory and Resource Handling

- **Use Secure APIs:** Always copy_from/to_user() instead of direct access; they handle page faults safely.
- **Avoid Stack Overflows:** Limit local vars; use kmalloc for dynamic buffers.
- **DMA Security:** Use IOMMU (e.g., dma_set_mask_and_coherent()) to restrict device memory access; enable CONFIG_IOMMU_SUPPORT.
- **Reference Counting:** Use kref or atomic_t for shared objects to prevent use-after-free.

In PCI drivers: Map BARs with pci_iomap(); unmap on remove. Avoid user-controlled DMA addresses.

Permission and Capability Checks

- **File Operations:** In open, check file->f_mode (FMODE_READ/WRITE); use capable(CAP_SYS_ADMIN) for privileged ops.
- **Ownership:** For devices, enforce user/group via inode permissions in /dev.
- **LSM Hooks:** Kernel's Linux Security Modules (e.g., SELinux) auto-check; drivers call security_file_ioctl() if needed.

Example: Restrict ioctl to root:

c
```
if (!capable(CAP_SYS_RAWIO)) return -EPERM;
```

Kernel Hardening Features

Leverage built-in protections:

- **KASLR/ASLR:** Randomizes addresses; drivers avoid hardcoding.
- **SMEP/SMAP:** Prevents kernel execution/access of user pages; auto-enabled.
- **CFI/PAX:** Control-Flow Integrity; compile with CONFIG_CFI_CLANG.
- **Stack Protector:** CONFIG_STACKPROTECTOR_STRONG detects overflows.
- **Zero Sensitive Memory:** Use memzero_explicit() for keys/passwords.

For drivers: Avoid inline assembly; use fortified string functions (e.g., strscpy).

Auditing and Testing for Security

- **Static Analysis:** Use checkpatch.pl, sparse (make C=1), coccinelle for patterns like unsafe copies.
- **Fuzzing:** Syzkaller or triforceAFL to simulate malicious inputs; target ioctls.
- **Dynamic Checks:** Enable CONFIG_DEBUG_KOBJECT_RELEASE for leaks; lockdep for deadlocks.
- **Code Review:** Follow kernel coding style; submit to linux-kernel for scrutiny.
- **Vulnerability Scanning:** Tools like kismet or manual CVE checks.

Test in isolated VMs; use seccomp to sandbox user apps interacting with driver.

Common pitfalls: Trusting user pointers (leads to info leaks), insufficient validation in ioctl (arbitrary writes), race-prone shared data (use locks from 20.1).

Summary

Driver security best practices emphasize rigorous validation, safe APIs, and kernel hardenings to mitigate exploits in privileged code. By applying these in inputs, memory, and permissions, developers fortify drivers against threats. This integrates with performance optimization (next section), balancing security with efficiency for production-ready implementations.

20.4 Performance Optimization

Performance optimization in device drivers is crucial for achieving high throughput, low latency, and efficient resource utilization, especially in high-load scenarios like storage I/O, networking, or real-time systems. Suboptimal drivers can bottleneck the system, leading to increased CPU usage, delayed responses, or power inefficiency. Optimization involves profiling to identify hotspots, refining algorithms, leveraging hardware features, and fine-tuning kernel parameters. This must balance with concurrency (Section 20.1) and security (Section 20.3), avoiding shortcuts that introduce races or vulnerabilities. Techniques span from micro-optimizations like cache alignment to macro-level changes like offloading to hardware. This section covers profiling tools, common optimization strategies, hardware acceleration, and best practices, with examples from block and network drivers (Chapter 19). Effective optimization requires iterative testing, ensuring gains without regressions.

Profiling and Measurement Tools

Begin optimization by measuring: Identify bottlenecks with tools to avoid premature tweaks.

- **Perf:** Kernel-integrated profiler. Record driver events: perf record -e irq:irq_handler_entry -c 10000 -a sleep 10, analyze with perf report. Trace specific functions: perf probe my_start_xmit; perf record -e probe:my_start_xmit ....
- **Ftrace:** Lightweight tracing. Enable for interrupts: echo 1 > /sys/kernel/debug/tracing/events/irq/enable, view cat trace. Function graph: set_graph_function my_irq_handler.
- **eBPF/BCC:** Advanced; use irqstat or custom scripts for IRQ latency. Install bcc-tools; irqsoff traces interrupt-off times.
- **System-Wide:** top, iotop for block, iftop for net; /proc/interrupts for IRQ counts, /sys/block/<dev>/queue/ for queue stats.

In drivers: Add ktime_get() timestamps in critical paths, compute deltas with ktime_sub().

For block: blktrace /dev/sda -o - | blkparse for I/O traces.

For network: dropwatch for dropped packets; tcptracer for TCP events.

Optimization Strategies

Focus on high-impact areas: Interrupt handling, data copying, locking, and queueing.

- **Reduce Interrupt Overhead:** Use NAPI (Section 19.3) for polling under load; coalesce interrupts (ethtool -C). In shared IRQs (Section 20.2), quick ownership checks minimize false handling.
- **Minimize Data Copies:** Zero-copy with mmap (Section 17.3) or direct DMA to user pages (io_uring). In network, use skb page frags; in block, bio_vec for scatter-gather.

- **Lock Optimization:** Use fine-grained locks (per-queue in blk-mq); switch to rwlocks for read-heavy. Profile contention with perf lock.
- **Memory Allocation:** Pre-allocate pools (mempool_alloc()) for IRQs; use dma_pool for coherent buffers. Align to cache lines (____cacheline_aligned).
- **Batching and Merging:** In block, enable merging (default); in net, GRO/TSO offloads batch packets.
- **Affinity and NUMA:** Pin IRQs/queues to CPUs with irq_set_affinity_hint() or blk_mq_map_queues(). Use NUMA-aware alloc (e.g., alloc_pages_node()).
- **Hardware Offloads:** Enable checksum/encryption in hardware (NETIF_F_HW_CSUM); query capabilities.

Example: Optimizing a network driver's Rx path (from Section 19.4):

c

```
static int my_poll(struct napi_struct *napi, int budget) {
    struct my_net_priv *priv = container_of(napi, struct my_net_priv, napi);
    int work = 0;
    ktime_t start = ktime_get();  // Profile

    while (work < budget) {
        if (!my_hw_rx_ready()) break;

        // Pre-alloc skb from pool for zero-copy if possible
        struct sk_buff *skb = napi_alloc_skb(napi, PKT_SIZE);
        if (!skb) break;

        // DMA sync minimized
        dma_sync_single_for_cpu(&priv->netdev->dev, priv->rx_dma_handle, PKT_SIZE, DMA_FROM_DEVICE);

        // Build skb around DMA buffer (zero-copy)
        skb = build_skb(priv->rx_buf, PKT_SIZE);
        if (!skb) { /* handle */ }
        skb_put(skb, my_hw_rx_len());
        skb->protocol = eth_type_trans(skb, priv->netdev);

        // Offload check
        if (my_hw_checksum_ok()) skb->ip_summed = CHECKSUM_UNNECESSARY;

        netif_receive_skb(skb);
        work++;

        // Refill ring (batch)
        if (work % 16 == 0) my_refill_rx_ring();
    }

    if (work < budget) napi_complete_done(napi, work);

    // Log if slow
    if (ktime_ms_delta(ktime_get(), start) > 10) dev_warn(&priv->netdev->dev, "Slow poll: %d ms\n", delta);

    return work;
}
```

Here, zero-copy with build_skb, batched refill, and offload reduce CPU load.

In block: Use blk-mq with multiple hw_queues; set queue_depth based on hardware.

Hardware Acceleration and Tuning

- **Offloads:** In net, set hw_features (NETIF_F_SG for scatter); validate with checksum_verify.
- **Jumbo Frames:** Increase MTU (ndo_change_mtu) for fewer packets.
- **RSS (Receive Side Scaling):** Multi-queue Rx with hash distribution.

- **Kernel Params:** Tune /proc/sys/net/core/{netdev_budget, somaxconn}; /sys/block/<dev>/queue/{max_sectors_kb, nr_requests}.
- **Real-Time:** Use PREEMPT_RT patch; prioritize IRQs with chrt.

Benchmark: Netperf/iperf for net; fio for block. Compare before/after.

Best Practices

- Measure First: Optimize only hotspots.
- Avoid Over-Optimization: Profile on target hardware/arches.
- Test Edge Cases: Low mem, high load, CPU hotplug.
- Documentation: Read Documentation/networking/scaling.rst for net; block/blk-mq.c for block.

Common pitfalls: Cache thrashing (misalign), over-deferral (latency spikes), ignoring NUMA (cross-node access slow).

Summary

Performance optimization in drivers involves profiling-driven refinements in interrupts, memory, and offloads to maximize efficiency without compromising safety. Through tools like perf and strategies like zero-copy, developers enhance throughput. This caps the chapter, equipping you for mastery projects (Book 5), where optimized drivers underpin advanced systems.

21. Inter-Process Communication (IPC)

Inter-Process Communication (IPC) mechanisms in Linux enable processes to exchange data and synchronize actions, forming the backbone of complex applications like servers, pipelines, and distributed systems. From simple pipes to advanced sockets and shared memory, IPC supports both related (e.g., parent-child) and unrelated processes. This chapter explores key IPC methods, their implementations, and best practices, bridging user-space programming with kernel insights from prior books. Understanding IPC is essential for building efficient, modular software, with applications in scripting, daemons, and real-time systems.

21.1 Pipes and FIFOs

Pipes and FIFOs (First-In-First-Out queues) provide unidirectional, stream-based communication channels, ideal for passing data between processes without intermediate files. Pipes are anonymous and typically used for related processes (e.g., created via fork()), while FIFOs are named files accessible by any process, enabling broader use cases like client-server interactions. Both operate as byte streams, without message boundaries, and block on read/write if the other end is unavailable, promoting synchronization. In the kernel, they leverage the VFS (Section 15.1) and pipefs, with buffers managed by the page cache (Section 15.3). This section covers creation, usage, error handling, and advanced patterns, with C examples to demonstrate practical implementation.

Fundamentals of Pipes

A pipe is a kernel buffer with two file descriptors: one for writing (fd[1]) and one for reading (fd[0]). Data written to the write end appears on the read end in FIFO order. Pipes are half-duplex (unidirectional), but bidirectional communication requires two pipes.

Creation: Use the pipe() system call, which allocates a pipe inode and returns fds.

Key behaviors:

- **Blocking:** Read blocks if empty; write blocks if full (default PIPE_BUF=4096 bytes, tunable).
- **Atomicity:** Writes ≤ PIPE_BUF are atomic (no interleaving in multi-writer scenarios).
- **Closure:** If all write fds close, read returns EOF (0); if all read fds close, write gets SIGPIPE/EPIPE.
- **Inheritance:** Fds inherited on fork(), enabling parent-child communication.

Example: Simple pipe for parent-child data transfer:

c
```c
#include <unistd.h>
#include <stdio.h>
#include <stdlib.h>
#include <string.h>
#include <sys/wait.h>

int main() {
    int fd[2];
    pid_t pid;
    char buf[256];
    const char *msg = "Hello from parent\n";

    if (pipe(fd) == -1) {
        perror("pipe");
        return 1;
    }

    pid = fork();
    if (pid == -1) {
        perror("fork");
        return 1;
    }
```

```c
    if (pid == 0) {  // Child: read
        close(fd[1]);  // Close unused write end
        ssize_t len = read(fd[0], buf, sizeof(buf) - 1);
        if (len == -1) {
            perror("read");
            return 1;
        }
        buf[len] = '\0';
        printf("Child received: %s", buf);
        close(fd[0]);
    } else {  // Parent: write
        close(fd[0]);  // Close unused read end
        if (write(fd[1], msg, strlen(msg)) == -1) {
            perror("write");
            return 1;
        }
        close(fd[1]);
        wait(NULL);  // Wait for child
    }

    return 0;
}
```

This demonstrates basic flow: Parent writes, child reads. Compile and run: gcc pipe_example.c -o pipe_example; ./pipe_example.

Non-blocking: Set O_NONBLOCK with fcntl(fd[0], F_SETFL, O_NONBLOCK); read/write return -EAGAIN if would block.

FIFOs (Named Pipes)

FIFOs extend pipes by creating named entries in the filesystem, accessible via paths. They persist until unlinked and support unrelated processes. Creation uses mkfifo() or mknod command.

Key differences:

- **Opening:** Blocks until both ends open (read blocks for writer, write for reader).
- **Multiple Clients:** Multiple writers/readers possible, but data interleaves without atomicity guarantees beyond PIPE_BUF.
- **Persistence:** Survive process termination; delete with unlink().

Example: FIFO for inter-process messaging (run producer and consumer separately):

Producer (writer):

c

```c
#include <fcntl.h>
#include <sys/stat.h>
#include <stdio.h>
#include <string.h>
#include <unistd.h>

int main() {
    const char *fifo_path = "/tmp/my_fifo";
    mkfifo(fifo_path, 0666);  // Create if not exists

    int fd = open(fifo_path, O_WRONLY);
    if (fd == -1) {
        perror("open");
        return 1;
    }

    const char *msg = "Message via FIFO\n";
    if (write(fd, msg, strlen(msg)) == -1) {
        perror("write");
```

```c
    }

    close(fd);
    return 0;
}
```

Consumer (reader):

```c
#include <fcntl.h>
#include <stdio.h>
#include <unistd.h>

int main() {
    const char *fifo_path = "/tmp/my_fifo";
    char buf[256];

    int fd = open(fifo_path, O_RDONLY);
    if (fd == -1) {
        perror("open");
        return 1;
    }

    ssize_t len = read(fd, buf, sizeof(buf) - 1);
    if (len == -1) {
        perror("read");
    } else {
        buf[len] = '\0';
        printf("Received: %s", buf);
    }

    close(fd);
    unlink(fifo_path);  // Clean up
    return 0;
}
```

Run producer first (blocks until consumer opens), then consumer. This shows unrelated process communication. Advanced: For non-blocking opens, use O_NONBLOCK; handle EAGAIN. For multiple readers, use O_RDWR to avoid EOF on single close.

Error Handling and Limitations

- Errors: ENFILE (too many fds), EPIPE (write to closed pipe), EINTR (interrupted).
- Limits: PIPE_BUF atomicity; system pipe limit (/proc/sys/fs/pipe-max-size).
- Signals: SIGPIPE on write to closed pipe; ignore with signal(SIGPIPE, SIG_IGN).
- Performance: Pipes/FIFOs suit small data; for large, use shared memory (Section 21.3).

In kernels: Pipes use struct pipe_inode_info; buffers dynamically allocate pages.

Summary

Pipes and FIFOs offer simple, efficient IPC for stream data, with pipes for related processes and FIFOs for broader use. Through system calls like pipe() and mkfifo(), they enable synchronized communication. This foundation extends to message queues in the next section, where structured messaging adds flexibility for more complex scenarios.

21.2 Message Queues

Message queues provide a structured, asynchronous IPC mechanism for exchanging discrete messages between processes, offering more flexibility than pipes or FIFOs (Section 21.1) by supporting message priorities, types, and non-blocking operations. Unlike streams in pipes, message queues store data as individual messages with headers, allowing selective retrieval (e.g., by type) and avoiding interleaving issues in multi-producer scenarios. Linux supports two variants: System V (SysV) message queues, which are kernel-persistent and identified by keys, and POSIX message queues, which are more modern, file-like, and support notifications. Both leverage kernel data structures (e.g., msg_queue in ipc/msg.c for SysV) for buffering, with limits tunable via /proc/sys/kernel/msg*. Message queues suit applications like task distribution in servers, event logging, or microservices, where ordering or filtering is needed. This section covers creation, sending/receiving, control operations, and advanced usage, with C examples for both SysV and POSIX variants.

System V Message Queues

SysV queues are created with a key (ftok-generated or IPC_PRIVATE), persisting until explicitly removed or system reboot. They support typed messages (long type field) for filtering.

Key functions (from <sys/msg.h>):

- msgget(key_t key, int msgflg): Create/get queue ID. Flags: IPC_CREAT, IPC_EXCL, permissions (0666).
- msgsnd(int msqid, const void *msgp, size_t msgsz, int msgflg): Send message. msgp points to struct with type and data; IPC_NOWAIT for non-block.
- msgrcv(int msqid, void *msgp, size_t msgsz, long msgtyp, int msgflg): Receive. msgtyp=0 for any, >0 for specific, <0 for <=|type|.
- msgctl(int msqid, int cmd, struct msqid_ds *buf): Control (IPC_RMID to remove, IPC_STAT/SET for info).

Message struct: struct msgbuf { long mtype; char mtext[MSGSZ]; };.

Limits: MSGMNI (queues), MSGMAX (msg size), MSGMNB (queue bytes).

Example: Producer-consumer with SysV queue:

Producer:

```c
#include <sys/types.h>
#include <sys/ipc.h>
#include <sys/msg.h>
#include <stdio.h>
#include <string.h>
#include <stdlib.h>
#include <unistd.h>

#define MSGSZ 128

typedef struct msgbuf {
    long mtype;
    char mtext[MSGSZ];
} message_buf;

int main() {
    int msqid;
    key_t key = ftok("progfile", 65);  // Generate key
    message_buf sbuf;

    msqid = msgget(key, 0666 | IPC_CREAT);
    if (msqid == -1) {
        perror("msgget");
        return 1;
    }

    sbuf.mtype = 1;  // Type 1
    strcpy(sbuf.mtext, "Message from producer");
    if (msgsnd(msqid, &sbuf, strlen(sbuf.mtext) + 1, IPC_NOWAIT) == -1) {
```

```c
      perror("msgsnd");
      return 1;
   }

   printf("Message sent\n");
   return 0;
}
```
Consumer:
```c
c
#include <sys/types.h>
#include <sys/ipc.h>
#include <sys/msg.h>
#include <stdio.h>
#include <stdlib.h>

#define MSGSZ 128

typedef struct msgbuf {
   long mtype;
   char mtext[MSGSZ];
} message_buf;

int main() {
   int msqid;
   key_t key = ftok("progfile", 65);
   message_buf rbuf;

   msqid = msgget(key, 0666);
   if (msqid == -1) {
      perror("msgget");
      return 1;
   }

   if (msgrcv(msqid, &rbuf, MSGSZ, 1, 0) == -1) {  // Type 1, block
      perror("msgrcv");
      return 1;
   }

   printf("Received: %s\n", rbuf.mtext);

   // Remove queue
   if (msgctl(msqid, IPC_RMID, NULL) == -1) {
      perror("msgctl");
   }

   return 0;
}
```
Compile both, run producer then consumer. This shows typed messaging.

Non-blocking: Use MSG_NOWAIT; handle EAGAIN.

POSIX Message Queues

POSIX queues (mqueue) are more portable and integrated with file descriptors, supporting priorities (0-32767) and notifications via signals or threads. They are created as /dev/mqueue/<name> files.

Functions (from <mqueue.h>):

- mq_open(const char *name, int oflag, ...): Create/open. Flags: O_RDWR, O_CREAT (with mode/attr).
- mq_send(mqd_t mqdes, const char *msg_ptr, size_t msg_len, unsigned msg_prio): Send.
- mq_receive(mqd_t mqdes, char *msg_ptr, size_t msg_len, unsigned *msg_prio): Receive highest priority.

- mq_close(mqd_t mqdes), mq_unlink(const char *name): Cleanup.
- mq_getattr/setattr(mqd_t mqdes, struct mq_attr *attr): Manage size/flags.

Attr: mq_maxmsg, mq_msgsize, mq_flags (O_NONBLOCK).

Example: POSIX producer-consumer:

Producer:

c

```c
#include <mqueue.h>
#include <fcntl.h>
#include <sys/stat.h>
#include <stdio.h>
#include <string.h>
#include <stdlib.h>

int main() {
    mqd_t mq;
    struct mq_attr attr = { .mq_flags = 0, .mq_maxmsg = 10, .mq_msgsize = 128, .mq_curmsgs = 0 };

    mq = mq_open("/my_mq", O_WRONLY | O_CREAT, 0666, &attr);
    if (mq == (mqd_t)-1) {
        perror("mq_open");
        return 1;
    }

    const char *msg = "POSIX message";
    if (mq_send(mq, msg, strlen(msg) + 1, 1) == -1) {  // Priority 1
        perror("mq_send");
    }

    mq_close(mq);
    return 0;
}
```

Consumer:

c

```c
#include <mqueue.h>
#include <stdio.h>
#include <stdlib.h>

int main() {
    mqd_t mq;
    char buf[128];
    unsigned prio;

    mq = mq_open("/my_mq", O_RDONLY);
    if (mq == (mqd_t)-1) {
        perror("mq_open");
        return 1;
    }

    ssize_t len = mq_receive(mq, buf, 128, &prio);
    if (len == -1) {
        perror("mq_receive");
    } else {
        printf("Received (prio %u): %s\n", prio, buf);
    }

    mq_close(mq);
```

```c
    mq_unlink("/my_mq");
    return 0;
}
```
Run producer then consumer. POSIX adds priorities and FD integration (selectable with select()).

Notifications: Use mq_notify() for signals on message arrival.

Choosing Between SysV and POSIX

- SysV: Kernel-persistent, typed; good for legacy or simple apps.
- POSIX: FD-based, prioritized, notifications; preferred for new code, real-time.

Both support non-blocking and have similar limits (tunable via /proc).

Best Practices and Limitations

- Close unused ends to avoid hangs.
- Handle partial receives with loops.
- Use for small messages; large data via shared memory.
- Errors: ENOSPC (full), EMSGSIZE (too big).
- Security: Set permissions on creation to restrict access.

In kernels: POSIX uses mqueue filesystem; monitor with ipcs -q.

Summary

Message queues enhance IPC with structured, prioritized messaging, via SysV for typed persistence or POSIX for modern features. Examples demonstrate sending/receiving across processes. This progresses to semaphores and shared memory (next), where synchronization complements data exchange for robust applications.

21.3 Semaphores and Shared Memory

Semaphores and shared memory are powerful IPC primitives for synchronization and data sharing among processes. Semaphores provide counting mechanisms to control access to resources, preventing races in concurrent environments, while shared memory allows direct memory mapping between processes for high-speed data exchange without kernel mediation. Both build on POSIX and System V standards, integrating with VFS (Chapter 15) for file-like semantics in POSIX variants. Semaphores suit mutual exclusion (mutexes) or signaling, common in multithreaded or multi-process apps, whereas shared memory excels for large data transfers, like in databases or graphics. This section covers their APIs, usage patterns, synchronization techniques, and pitfalls, with C examples for SysV and POSIX implementations. Together, they enable robust, efficient coordination, complementing pipes (Section 21.1) and message queues (Section 21.2).

Semaphores

Semaphores are counters for resource management: positive values allow access (decrement on acquire), zero blocks until signaled (increment). Binary semaphores (0/1) act as mutexes. Linux offers SysV semaphores (arrays, kernel-persistent) and POSIX semaphores (named/unnamed, lighter-weight).

System V Semaphores Created as arrays (one or more sems), identified by keys.

Functions (<sys/sem.h>):

- semget(key_t key, int nsems, int semflg): Create/get ID.
- semop(int semid, struct sembuf *sops, unsigned nsops): Operate (P/V).
- semctl(int semid, int semnum, int cmd, ...): Control (SETVAL, IPC_RMID).

Struct sembuf: {short sem_num, short sem_op, short sem_flg} (op: -1=P, +1=V; flg: IPC_NOWAIT, SEM_UNDO).

Example: Binary semaphore for critical section:

c
```c
#include <sys/types.h>
#include <sys/ipc.h>
#include <sys/sem.h>
#include <stdio.h>
#include <stdlib.h>
#include <unistd.h>

int main() {
    key_t key = ftok("semfile", 65);
    int semid = semget(key, 1, 0666 | IPC_CREAT);
```

```c
    if (semid == -1) {
        perror("semget");
        return 1;
    }

    // Initialize to 1 (unlocked)
    union semun {
        int val;
    } arg;
    arg.val = 1;
    if (semctl(semid, 0, SETVAL, arg) == -1) {
        perror("semctl");
        return 1;
    }

    pid_t pid = fork();
    if (pid == -1) {
        perror("fork");
        return 1;
    }

    struct sembuf op = {0, -1, 0};  // P (wait)
    if (semop(semid, &op, 1) == -1) {
        perror("semop acquire");
        return 1;
    }

    // Critical section
    printf("%s in critical section\n", pid == 0 ? "Child" : "Parent");
    sleep(1);  // Simulate work

    op.sem_op = 1;  // V (signal)
    if (semop(semid, &op, 1) == -1) {
        perror("semop release");
        return 1;
    }

    if (pid > 0) {  // Parent
        wait(NULL);
        semctl(semid, 0, IPC_RMID);  // Remove
    }

    return 0;
}
```
Run: Parent/child alternate access due to semaphore.

POSIX Semaphores Lighter, with named (sem_open) for unrelated processes or unnamed (sem_init) for threads/related.

Functions (<semaphore.h>):

- sem_t *sem_open(const char *name, int oflag, ...): Create/open.
- int sem_wait(sem_t *sem), int sem_post(sem_t *sem): P/V.
- int sem_trywait(sem_t *sem): Non-block wait.
- int sem_timedwait(sem_t *sem, const struct timespec *abs_timeout): Timed.
- int sem_close(sem_t *sem), int sem_unlink(const char *name): Cleanup.

Example: Named POSIX semaphore:

c
```c
#include <semaphore.h>
```

```c
#include <fcntl.h>
#include <sys/stat.h>
#include <stdio.h>
#include <stdlib.h>
#include <unistd.h>

int main() {
    sem_t *sem = sem_open("/my_sem", O_CREAT, 0666, 1);  // Init to 1
    if (sem == SEM_FAILED) {
        perror("sem_open");
        return 1;
    }

    pid_t pid = fork();
    if (pid == -1) {
        perror("fork");
        return 1;
    }

    if (sem_wait(sem) == -1) {  // P
        perror("sem_wait");
        return 1;
    }

    // Critical section
    printf("%s in critical section\n", pid == 0 ? "Child" : "Parent");
    sleep(1);

    if (sem_post(sem) == -1) {  // V
        perror("sem_post");
        return 1;
    }

    if (pid > 0) {
        wait(NULL);
        sem_close(sem);
        sem_unlink("/my_sem");
    } else {
        sem_close(sem);
    }

    return 0;
}
```
POSIX sems integrate with pthreads; use sem_getvalue for count.

Shared Memory

Shared memory (shm) allows processes to map the same physical pages into their address spaces for direct access, bypassing kernel copies for speed. Requires synchronization (e.g., semaphores) to avoid races. SysV uses segments identified by keys; POSIX uses shm_open/mmap for file-like handling.

System V Shared Memory Functions (<sys/shm.h>):

- shmget(key_t key, size_t size, int shmflg): Create/get ID.
- void *shmat(int shmid, const void *shmaddr, int shmflg): Attach (return addr).
- int shmdt(const void *shmaddr): Detach.
- shmctl(int shmid, int cmd, struct shmid_ds *buf): Control (IPC_RMID).

Example: Shared counter with semaphore sync:

c

```c
#include <sys/types.h>
```

```c
#include <sys/ipc.h>
#include <sys/shm.h>
#include <sys/sem.h>
#include <stdio.h>
#include <stdlib.h>
#include <unistd.h>

int main() {
    key_t shm_key = ftok("shmfile", 66), sem_key = ftok("semfile", 67);
    int shmid = shmget(shm_key, sizeof(int), 0666 | IPC_CREAT);
    int semid = semget(sem_key, 1, 0666 | IPC_CREAT);

    // Init sem to 1
    union semun arg;
    arg.val = 1;
    semctl(semid, 0, SETVAL, arg);

    int *shared_counter = shmat(shmid, NULL, 0);
    *shared_counter = 0;

    pid_t pid = fork();
    if (pid == -1) return 1;

    struct sembuf op = {0, -1, 0};
    semop(semid, &op, 1);
    (*shared_counter)++;
    printf("%s: counter = %d\n", pid == 0 ? "Child" : "Parent", *shared_counter);
    op.sem_op = 1;
    semop(semid, &op, 1);

    if (pid > 0) {
        wait(NULL);
        shmdt(shared_counter);
        shmctl(shmid, IPC_RMID, NULL);
        semctl(semid, 0, IPC_RMID);
    } else {
        shmdt(shared_counter);
    }

    return 0;
}
```
Counter increments safely.

POSIX Shared Memory Uses shm_open (like open) and mmap for mapping.
Functions (<sys/mman.h>, <fcntl.h>):

- int shm_open(const char *name, int oflag, mode_t mode): Open FD.
- void *mmap(void *addr, size_t len, int prot, int flags, int fd, off_t off): Map.
- munmap(void *addr, size_t len), close(int fd), shm_unlink(const char *name).

Example: Shared counter with POSIX sem:

c
```c
#include <semaphore.h>
#include <sys/mman.h>
#include <sys/stat.h>
#include <fcntl.h>
#include <stdio.h>
#include <stdlib.h>
#include <unistd.h>
```

```
int main() {
    int shm_fd = shm_open("/my_shm", O_CREAT | O_RDWR, 0666);
    ftruncate(shm_fd, sizeof(int));
    int *shared_counter = mmap(NULL, sizeof(int), PROT_READ | PROT_WRITE, MAP_SHARED, shm_fd, 0);
    *shared_counter = 0;

    sem_t *sem = sem_open("/my_sem", O_CREAT, 0666, 1);

    pid_t pid = fork();
    if (pid == -1) return 1;

    sem_wait(sem);
    (*shared_counter)++;
    printf("%s: counter = %d\n", pid == 0 ? "Child" : "Parent", *shared_counter);
    sem_post(sem);

    if (pid > 0) {
        wait(NULL);
        munmap(shared_counter, sizeof(int));
        close(shm_fd);
        shm_unlink("/my_shm");
        sem_close(sem);
        sem_unlink("/my_sem");
    } else {
        munmap(shared_counter, sizeof(int));
        close(shm_fd);
        sem_close(sem);
    }

    return 0;
}
```
POSIX shm is more flexible with mmap features (e.g., MAP_ANONYMOUS for unnamed).

Best Practices and Limitations

- Always sync shm with sems/mutexes.
- Handle partial maps, alignment.
- Limits: SHMMAX (segment size), SHMMNI (segments).
- Security: Set permissions; avoid world-writable.
- Cleanup: Unlink to prevent leaks.

In kernels: shm uses tmpfs-like backing.

Summary

Semaphores and shared memory provide synchronization and efficient sharing, with SysV/POSIX variants for flexibility. Examples show protected access in multi-process setups. This leads to sockets (next), where network IPC extends local communication for distributed systems.

21.4 Sockets for Local IPC

Sockets, traditionally associated with network communication (Chapter 22), can also serve as a powerful IPC mechanism for local processes on the same machine through Unix domain sockets (also called local sockets). Unlike internet sockets (AF_INET), Unix domain sockets use the AF_UNIX (or AF_LOCAL) address family, binding to filesystem paths instead of IP addresses and ports. This provides a bidirectional, reliable channel for data exchange, supporting both stream (SOCK_STREAM, connection-oriented like TCP) and datagram (SOCK_DGRAM, connectionless like UDP) modes. Unix domain sockets offer advantages over other IPC methods like pipes (Section 21.1) or message queues (Section 21.2), including full-duplex communication, credential passing (e.g., file descriptors), and integration with select/poll for multiplexing. They are ideal for local client-server models, such as in daemons or modular applications, and leverage the kernel's socket infrastructure for efficiency. This section covers creation, binding, connection, data transfer, and advanced features like fd passing, with examples for stream-based IPC.

Fundamentals of Unix Domain Sockets

Unix domain sockets operate within the local filesystem namespace, using paths (e.g., /tmp/my_socket) as addresses. The socket file appears in the filesystem but doesn't consume disk space—it's a kernel object. Key characteristics:

- **Address Structure:** struct sockaddr_un { sa_family_t sun_family; char sun_path[108]; };. Set sun_family to AF_UNIX.
- **Modes:** SOCK_STREAM for reliable, sequenced delivery; SOCK_DGRAM for unreliable, message-boundaried packets (no connection).
- **Blocking/Non-Blocking:** Default blocking; use O_NONBLOCK or fcntl for async.
- **Permissions:** Socket file permissions control access, enforcing security.
- **Limitations:** Path length < 108 bytes; no broadcasting; local only (no remote hosts).

Creation follows standard socket APIs (<sys/socket.h>): socket(AF_UNIX, type, 0).

Stream Sockets for Local IPC

For connection-oriented communication, use SOCK_STREAM: Server binds/listens/accepts, client connects. Server example:

```c
#include <sys/types.h>
#include <sys/socket.h>
#include <sys/un.h>
#include <stdio.h>
#include <stdlib.h>
#include <string.h>
#include <unistd.h>

#define SOCKET_PATH "/tmp/my_unix_socket"
#define BUF_SIZE 256

int main() {
    int server_fd, client_fd;
    struct sockaddr_un addr;
    char buf[BUF_SIZE];

    // Create socket
    server_fd = socket(AF_UNIX, SOCK_STREAM, 0);
    if (server_fd == -1) {
        perror("socket");
        return 1;
    }

    // Bind to path
    memset(&addr, 0, sizeof(addr));
    addr.sun_family = AF_UNIX;
    strncpy(addr.sun_path, SOCKET_PATH, sizeof(addr.sun_path) - 1);
```

```c
    unlink(SOCKET_PATH);  // Remove if exists
    if (bind(server_fd, (struct sockaddr *)&addr, sizeof(addr)) == -1) {
        perror("bind");
        return 1;
    }

    // Listen
    if (listen(server_fd, 5) == -1) {
        perror("listen");
        return 1;
    }

    printf("Server listening on %s\n", SOCKET_PATH);

    // Accept client
    client_fd = accept(server_fd, NULL, NULL);
    if (client_fd == -1) {
        perror("accept");
        return 1;
    }

    // Receive data
    ssize_t len = recv(client_fd, buf, BUF_SIZE - 1, 0);
    if (len == -1) {
        perror("recv");
    } else {
        buf[len] = '\0';
        printf("Received: %s\n", buf);

        // Send response
        const char *resp = "Hello from server";
        send(client_fd, resp, strlen(resp), 0);
    }

    close(client_fd);
    close(server_fd);
    unlink(SOCKET_PATH);
    return 0;
}
```
Client:
```c
#include <sys/types.h>
#include <sys/socket.h>
#include <sys/un.h>
#include <stdio.h>
#include <stdlib.h>
#include <string.h>
#include <unistd.h>

#define SOCKET_PATH "/tmp/my_unix_socket"
#define BUF_SIZE 256

int main() {
    int client_fd;
    struct sockaddr_un addr;
    char buf[BUF_SIZE];
```

```c
    client_fd = socket(AF_UNIX, SOCK_STREAM, 0);
    if (client_fd == -1) {
        perror("socket");
        return 1;
    }

    memset(&addr, 0, sizeof(addr));
    addr.sun_family = AF_UNIX;
    strncpy(addr.sun_path, SOCKET_PATH, sizeof(addr.sun_path) - 1);

    if (connect(client_fd, (struct sockaddr *)&addr, sizeof(addr)) == -1) {
        perror("connect");
        return 1;
    }

    const char *msg = "Hello from client";
    if (send(client_fd, msg, strlen(msg), 0) == -1) {
        perror("send");
        return 1;
    }

    ssize_t len = recv(client_fd, buf, BUF_SIZE - 1, 0);
    if (len == -1) {
        perror("recv");
    } else {
        buf[len] = '\0';
        printf("Received: %s\n", buf);
    }

    close(client_fd);
    return 0;
}
```
Run server first, then client. This demonstrates connection and bidirectional exchange.

For datagram (SOCK_DGRAM): No connect/accept; use sendto/recvfrom with addresses.

Advanced Features: Passing File Descriptors

Unix sockets can pass ancillary data like file descriptors via sendmsg()/recvmsg() with SCM_RIGHTS, enabling credential or fd sharing.

Example snippet (sender):

```c
struct msghdr msg = {0};
struct iovec iov = {.iov_base = "fd", .iov_len = 2};
msg.msg_iov = &iov;
msg.msg_iovlen = 1;

char cmsg_buf[CMSG_SPACE(sizeof(int))];
msg.msg_control = cmsg_buf;
msg.msg_controllen = sizeof(cmsg_buf);

struct cmsghdr *cmsg = CMSG_FIRSTHDR(&msg);
cmsg->cmsg_level = SOL_SOCKET;
cmsg->cmsg_type = SCM_RIGHTS;
cmsg->cmsg_len = CMSG_LEN(sizeof(int));
*(int *)CMSG_DATA(cmsg) = fd_to_send; // e.g., open file fd

sendmsg(socket_fd, &msg, 0);
```

Receiver: Similar recvmsg, extract with CMSG_DATA.

This is useful for passing open files or sockets between processes.

Best Practices and Limitations

- Unlink socket paths on cleanup to avoid stale files.
- Use abstract namespaces (@prefix in sun_path) for hidden sockets (null byte first).
- Non-blocking: fcntl for O_NONBLOCK; handle EAGAIN.
- Permissions: chown/chmod socket file for access control.
- Limits: Unix socket queue depth (listen backlog), buffer sizes (SO_SNDBUF/RCVBUF).
- Performance: Faster than loopback TCP due to no checksums/overhead.
- Security: Restrict paths to trusted directories; avoid world-writable.

Compared to other IPC: Sockets add networking familiarity and fd passing, but more overhead than shm for bulk data.

Summary

Sockets for local IPC via AF_UNIX offer versatile, bidirectional communication with features like fd passing, suitable for local networking paradigms. Through socket APIs, they enable client-server models efficiently. This transitions to networking sockets (Chapter 22), where similar interfaces extend to remote IPC over TCP/IP.

22. Networking and Sockets

Networking and sockets form the cornerstone of inter-machine communication in Linux, enabling applications to exchange data over local or wide-area networks using protocols like TCP/IP. Sockets provide a unified API for various network types, abstracting underlying hardware and stack details. This chapter explores socket programming, from TCP/IP basics to advanced options, security, and firewalls, building on local IPC sockets (Section 21.4). Mastery of networking allows building distributed systems, servers, and clients, with Linux's robust stack supporting high-performance applications.

22.1 TCP/IP Fundamentals in Linux

TCP/IP (Transmission Control Protocol/Internet Protocol) is the foundational protocol suite for networking in Linux, powering the internet and local networks. In Linux, TCP/IP is implemented in the kernel's net subsystem (net/ipv4/ and net/ipv6/), providing reliable, connection-oriented (TCP) and unreliable, connectionless (UDP) communication over IP. Fundamentals include addressing, packet routing, connection management, and error handling, with sockets as the user-space interface. Linux's stack is highly optimized, supporting features like congestion control, offloading to hardware (e.g., via network drivers in Section 19.3-19.4), and sysctls for tuning. This section covers core concepts, socket creation for TCP/UDP, connection establishment, data transfer, and basic error handling, with examples to illustrate practical use.

Core TCP/IP Concepts

- **IP Addressing:** IPv4 (32-bit, e.g., 192.168.1.1) or IPv6 (128-bit, e.g., 2001:db8::1). Linux handles both; use struct sockaddr_in for IPv4, sockaddr_in6 for IPv6.
- **Ports:** 16-bit numbers (0-65535) identifying endpoints; well-known (0-1023, e.g., 80 for HTTP), registered (1024-49151), dynamic (>49151).
- **TCP:** Reliable, stream-oriented; three-way handshake (SYN/SYN-ACK/ACK), sequence numbers for ordering, acknowledgments/retransmissions for reliability, flow/congestion control (e.g., Reno, Cubic algorithms in Linux).
- **UDP:** Unreliable, datagram-oriented; no connections, minimal overhead, suitable for DNS, video streaming.
- **Kernel Role:** Packets processed in softirq (bottom halves, Section 14.3); routing via ip_route_output(), firewalls with netfilter.
- **Sysctls:** Tune via /proc/sys/net/ipv4/* (e.g., tcp_congestion_control = "bbr" for better bandwidth).

Sockets use socket(AF_INET, SOCK_STREAM, 0) for TCP, SOCK_DGRAM for UDP.

Creating and Using TCP Sockets

TCP sockets involve server binding/listening/accepting and client connecting.

Server example (echo server):

```c
#include <sys/types.h>
#include <sys/socket.h>
```

```c
#include <netinet/in.h>
#include <stdio.h>
#include <stdlib.h>
#include <string.h>
#include <unistd.h>
#include <arpa/inet.h>

#define PORT 8080
#define BUF_SIZE 1024

int main() {
    int server_fd, client_fd;
    struct sockaddr_in addr;
    char buf[BUF_SIZE];

    server_fd = socket(AF_INET, SOCK_STREAM, 0);
    if (server_fd == -1) {
        perror("socket");
        return 1;
    }

    addr.sin_family = AF_INET;
    addr.sin_port = htons(PORT);
    addr.sin_addr.s_addr = INADDR_ANY;  // Bind to all interfaces

    if (bind(server_fd, (struct sockaddr *)&addr, sizeof(addr)) == -1) {
        perror("bind");
        return 1;
    }

    if (listen(server_fd, 5) == -1) {
        perror("listen");
        return 1;
    }

    printf("Listening on port %d\n", PORT);

    socklen_t addr_len = sizeof(addr);
    client_fd = accept(server_fd, (struct sockaddr *)&addr, &addr_len);
    if (client_fd == -1) {
        perror("accept");
        return 1;
    }

    ssize_t len = recv(client_fd, buf, BUF_SIZE - 1, 0);
    if (len > 0) {
        buf[len] = '\0';
        printf("Received: %s\n", buf);
        send(client_fd, buf, len, 0);  // Echo back
    }

    close(client_fd);
    close(server_fd);
    return 0;
}
```
Client:

```c
#include <sys/types.h>
#include <sys/socket.h>
#include <netinet/in.h>
#include <stdio.h>
#include <stdlib.h>
#include <string.h>
#include <unistd.h>
#include <arpa/inet.h>

#define PORT 8080
#define BUF_SIZE 1024

int main() {
    int client_fd;
    struct sockaddr_in addr;
    char buf[BUF_SIZE];

    client_fd = socket(AF_INET, SOCK_STREAM, 0);
    if (client_fd == -1) {
        perror("socket");
        return 1;
    }

    addr.sin_family = AF_INET;
    addr.sin_port = htons(PORT);
    inet_pton(AF_INET, "127.0.0.1", &addr.sin_addr);

    if (connect(client_fd, (struct sockaddr *)&addr, sizeof(addr)) == -1) {
        perror("connect");
        return 1;
    }

    const char *msg = "Hello from client";
    send(client_fd, msg, strlen(msg), 0);

    ssize_t len = recv(client_fd, buf, BUF_SIZE - 1, 0);
    if (len > 0) {
        buf[len] = '\0';
        printf("Echo: %s\n", buf);
    }

    close(client_fd);
    return 0;
}
```
Run server, then client. This shows TCP handshake and data exchange.
For UDP (datagram): No connect/listen; use sendto/recvfrom with addresses.

Error Handling and Options
- Errors: ECONNREFUSED (no listener), ETIMEDOUT (no response), EINTR (interrupted).
- Options: setsockopt (e.g., SO_REUSEADDR to reuse ports, SO_KEEPALIVE for idle detection).
- Non-Blocking: fcntl for O_NONBLOCK; handle EAGAIN with select/poll (e.g., for multiple connections).
- Shutdown: shutdown(fd, SHUT_RDWR) for graceful close.

In Linux: Tune tcp_rmem/wmem via sysctl for buffer sizes; use tcpdump -i lo port 8080 to sniff.

Best Practices
- Close fds to avoid leaks.

- Use inet_ntop/pton for address conversion.
- For servers, loop accept for multiple clients; thread/fork for concurrency.
- Security: Bind to localhost for local; validate inputs to prevent injection.

Limitations: Sockets consume fds (ulimit -n); overhead for small data (use shm, Section 21.3).

Summary

TCP/IP fundamentals in Linux revolve around sockets for reliable (TCP) or fast (UDP) communication, with APIs for connection and data handling. Examples demonstrate client-server basics. This sets up advanced socket options (next), enhancing control for performant networking applications.

22.2 Socket Programming Interface

The socket programming interface in Linux provides a standardized set of system calls and functions for creating, configuring, and using sockets to facilitate network communication. Building on TCP/IP fundamentals (Section 22.1), this interface abstracts the complexities of protocol handling, allowing developers to build client-server applications, peer-to-peer systems, or even custom protocols. Derived from the Berkeley sockets API (BSD sockets), it supports multiple address families (e.g., AF_INET for IPv4, AF_INET6 for IPv6, AF_UNIX for local), socket types (stream, datagram, raw), and options for fine-tuning behavior. Key headers include <sys/socket.h>, <netinet/in.h>, and <arpa/inet.h>. This section details core functions for socket creation, binding, connecting, data transfer, and shutdown, with examples in C for TCP and UDP. Emphasis is on error handling, non-blocking modes, and integration with multiplexing tools like select(), preparing for advanced options (Section 22.3).

Socket Creation and Types

Sockets are created with the socket() call, specifying the address family, type, and protocol.

Prototype: int socket(int domain, int type, int protocol);

- **domain:** AF_INET (IPv4), AF_INET6 (IPv6), AF_UNIX (local).
- **type:** SOCK_STREAM (TCP-like, reliable), SOCK_DGRAM (UDP-like, datagram), SOCK_RAW (raw packets, requires CAP_NET_RAW).
- **protocol:** Usually 0 (default for type); specific like IPPROTO_TCP.

On success, returns a file descriptor (fd); -1 on error (check errno).

Common errors: EAFNOSUPPORT (unsupported domain), EMFILE (fd limit).

After creation, configure with setsockopt() (e.g., SO_REUSEADDR to allow quick rebinds).

Binding and Listening (Server Side)

Servers bind to an address/port with bind(), then listen for connections.

bind(int sockfd, const struct sockaddr *addr, socklen_t addrlen);

- addr: Cast to sockaddr; use sockaddr_in for IPv4.

listen(int sockfd, int backlog); - backlog: Queue size for pending connections.

Connecting (Client Side)

Clients connect to servers with connect().

connect(int sockfd, const struct sockaddr *addr, socklen_t addrlen);

Accepting Connections (Server)

accept(int sockfd, struct sockaddr *addr, socklen_t *addrlen); - Returns new fd for client.

Data Transfer

- send/recv(int sockfd, void *buf, size_t len, int flags); - For connected sockets.
- sendto/recvfrom() - For datagrams, with address.
- Flags: MSG_DONTWAIT (non-block), MSG_OOB (out-of-band).

Shutdown and Close

shutdown(int sockfd, int how); - how: SHUT_RD, SHUT_WR, SHUT_RDWR for graceful close. close(int sockfd); - Releases fd.

Example: Enhanced TCP echo server with multiple clients (using fork for simplicity):

```c
#include <sys/types.h>
#include <sys/socket.h>
#include <netinet/in.h>
#include <stdio.h>
#include <stdlib.h>
#include <string.h>
```

```c
#include <unistd.h>
#include <arpa/inet.h>

#define PORT 8080
#define BUF_SIZE 1024
#define BACKLOG 5

int main() {
    int server_fd, client_fd;
    struct sockaddr_in addr, client_addr;
    socklen_t client_len = sizeof(client_addr);
    char buf[BUF_SIZE];

    server_fd = socket(AF_INET, SOCK_STREAM, 0);
    if (server_fd == -1) {
        perror("socket");
        return 1;
    }

    int opt = 1;
    setsockopt(server_fd, SOL_SOCKET, SO_REUSEADDR, &opt, sizeof(opt));  // Reuse port

    addr.sin_family = AF_INET;
    addr.sin_port = htons(PORT);
    addr.sin_addr.s_addr = INADDR_ANY;

    if (bind(server_fd, (struct sockaddr *)&addr, sizeof(addr)) == -1) {
        perror("bind");
        return 1;
    }

    if (listen(server_fd, BACKLOG) == -1) {
        perror("listen");
        return 1;
    }

    printf("Server listening on port %d\n", PORT);

    while (1) {
        client_fd = accept(server_fd, (struct sockaddr *)&client_addr, &client_len);
        if (client_fd == -1) {
            perror("accept");
            continue;
        }

        pid_t pid = fork();
        if (pid == -1) {
            perror("fork");
            close(client_fd);
            continue;
        }

        if (pid == 0) { // Child handles client
            close(server_fd); // Unused
            ssize_t len;
            while ((len = recv(client_fd, buf, BUF_SIZE - 1, 0)) > 0) {
```

```c
            buf[len] = '\0';
            printf("Received from %s: %s\n", inet_ntoa(client_addr.sin_addr), buf);
            send(client_fd, buf, len, 0);  // Echo
        }
        if (len == -1) perror("recv");
        shutdown(client_fd, SHUT_RDWR);
        close(client_fd);
        return 0;
    } else {
        close(client_fd);  // Parent closes client fd
    }
}

    close(server_fd);
    return 0;
}
```

Client remains similar to 22.1, but loop for persistent connection.

For UDP example:

Server (echo):

c

```c
// ... includes ...

int main() {
    int sock_fd = socket(AF_INET, SOCK_DGRAM, 0);
    // bind as in TCP

    struct sockaddr_in client_addr;
    socklen_t client_len = sizeof(client_addr);
    char buf[BUF_SIZE];

    while (1) {
        ssize_t len = recvfrom(sock_fd, buf, BUF_SIZE - 1, 0, (struct sockaddr *)&client_addr, &client_len);
        if (len > 0) {
            buf[len] = '\0';
            printf("UDP received: %s\n", buf);
            sendto(sock_fd, buf, len, 0, (struct sockaddr *)&client_addr, client_len);
        }
    }

    close(sock_fd);
    return 0;
}
```

Client uses sendto/recvfrom without connect (optional for UDP).

Multiplexing with Select/Poll/Epoll

For handling multiple sockets:

- select(fd_set *readfds, *writefds, *exceptfds, int nfds, struct timeval *timeout): Wait on fds.
- poll(struct pollfd *fds, nfds_t nfds, int timeout): More scalable.
- epoll_create/create1, epoll_ctl, epoll_wait: Edge-triggered, efficient for many fds.

Example snippet with select in server loop.

Error Handling

Check returns: -1 sets errno (EWOULDBLOCK for non-block, ECONNRESET for abrupt close). Use perror() or strerror(errno).

Summary

The socket programming interface offers a versatile API for TCP/UDP communication, with functions for creation, connection, and transfer. Examples illustrate client-server models. This prepares for advanced options (next), where tuning enhances performance and functionality in networked applications.

22.3 Advanced Socket Options

Advanced socket options allow fine-grained control over socket behavior, enabling optimizations for performance, reliability, and specific application needs. The setsockopt() and getsockopt() functions provide access to these options at various levels: socket-level (SOL_SOCKET), protocol-level (e.g., IPPROTO_TCP for TCP-specific), or interface-level (SOL_PACKET for raw). These options influence buffering, timeouts, error handling, and protocol tweaks, crucial for high-performance servers, real-time applications, or constrained environments. Misuse can lead to inefficiencies or security issues (e.g., enlarged buffers risking DoS), so apply judiciously. This section explores key options, their usage, and examples in C, building on basic socket programming (Section 22.2). Options are set before or after connection, with some requiring superuser privileges.

Understanding setsockopt and getsockopt

Prototypes (from <sys/socket.h>):

- int setsockopt(int sockfd, int level, int optname, const void *optval, socklen_t optlen);
- int getsockopt(int sockfd, int level, int optname, void *optval, socklen_t *optlen);
- **level:** SOL_SOCKET (general), IPPROTO_TCP (TCP), IPPROTO_UDP (UDP), etc.
- **optname/optval:** Option name and value (e.g., int for SO_REUSEADDR).
- Returns 0 on success, -1 on error (errno: EINVAL for invalid opt, ENOPROTOOPT if unsupported).

Query current values with getsockopt before modifying.

Common Socket-Level Options (SOL_SOCKET)

These apply to all socket types:

- **SO_REUSEADDR:** Allows rebinding to the same address/port quickly (avoids TIME_WAIT). Useful for servers restarting. Value: int (1 to enable).
- **SO_KEEPALIVE:** Enables periodic probes on idle TCP connections to detect dead peers. Value: int (1 to enable). Tune with tcp_keepalive_* sysctls.
- **SO_SNDBUF/SO_RCVBUF:** Set send/receive buffer sizes (bytes). Kernel doubles the value. Larger buffers improve throughput but increase memory use.
- **SO_LINGER:** Controls close() behavior for pending data. struct linger { int l_onoff; int l_linger; }; l_onoff=1 enables linger (timeout in seconds).
- **SO_BROADCAST:** Permits sending broadcast packets (UDP). Value: int (1 to enable).
- **SO_ERROR:** Get pending error (int); clears after read.

Example: Enabling SO_REUSEADDR and setting buffer sizes on a TCP server socket:

```c
int server_fd = socket(AF_INET, SOCK_STREAM, 0);
// ... error check ...

int opt = 1;
if (setsockopt(server_fd, SOL_SOCKET, SO_REUSEADDR, &opt, sizeof(opt)) == -1) {
    perror("setsockopt SO_REUSEADDR");
    // handle
}

int buf_size = 65536;  // 64KB
if (setsockopt(server_fd, SOL_SOCKET, SO_RCVBUF, &buf_size, sizeof(buf_size)) == -1) {
    perror("setsockopt SO_RCVBUF");
    // handle
}

// Query to verify
socklen_t len = sizeof(buf_size);
getsockopt(server_fd, SOL_SOCKET, SO_RCVBUF, &buf_size, &len);
printf("Actual RCVBUF: %d\n", buf_size);  // May be doubled
```

TCP-Specific Options (IPPROTO_TCP)

For SOCK_STREAM with IPPROTO_TCP level:

- **TCP_NODELAY:** Disables Nagle's algorithm (no buffering small sends). Value: int (1 to disable). Good for low-latency (e.g., games), but increases packets.

- **TCP_KEEPIDLE/TCP_KEEPINTVL/TCP_KEEPCNT:** Fine-tune keepalive: idle time (seconds), probe interval, max probes before drop.
- **TCP_CORK:** Buffers small sends until uncorked (like Nagle but manual). Value: int (1 to cork).
- **TCP_QUICKACK:** Enables/disables delayed ACKs. Value: int (1 to enable quick ACKs for latency-sensitive).

Example: Disabling Nagle for a client socket:

```c
int client_fd = socket(AF_INET, SOCK_STREAM, 0);
// ... connect ...

int opt = 1;
if (setsockopt(client_fd, IPPROTO_TCP, TCP_NODELAY, &opt, sizeof(opt)) == -1) {
    perror("setsockopt TCP_NODELAY");
    // handle
}
```

UDP and Other Protocol Options

For UDP (SOCK_DGRAM):

- **UDP_CORK:** Similar to TCP_CORK for batching datagrams.
- **IP_MULTICAST_TTL:** Set multicast TTL (int, 0-255).
- Raw sockets (SOCK_RAW): Options like IP_HDRINCL to include IP headers.

For IPv6: Use IPPROTO_IPV6 level, e.g., IPV6_V6ONLY to bind only IPv6.

Advanced and Custom Options

- **SO_TIMESTAMP:** Enables timestamping on recv (via ancillary data in recvmsg()).
- **SO_ACCEPTCONN:** Check if socket is listening (get only).
- **Interface Options:** IFLA_* via netlink for advanced (requires CAP_NET_ADMIN).
- Custom: Drivers can expose via ethtool or ioctl (Section 17.2).

Retrieve ancillary data with recvmsg() and msg_control for cmsg (e.g., SCM_RIGHTS for fd passing, as in Section 21.4).

Error Handling and Best Practices

- Check returns; common errors: ENOPROTOOPT (option not supported for type), EINVAL (bad value).
- Tune based on workload: Larger buffers for bulk transfers, NODELAY for interactive.
- Monitor: Use getsockopt to verify; tools like ss -m (memory usage), tcpdump for effects.
- Security: Avoid exposing sensitive options to unprivileged users; cap buffers to prevent DoS.
- Performance: Test with iperf/netperf; profile syscalls with strace.

Pitfalls: Setting options after connect/bind (some disallowed), ignoring kernel adjustments (e.g., buffer doubling).

Summary

Advanced socket options via setsockopt/getsockopt empower customization of buffering, algorithms, and behaviors for optimized networking. Examples highlight common tweaks like REUSEADDR and NODELAY. This knowledge supports network security (next section), where options enhance protection in connected environments.

22.4 Network Security and Firewalls

Network security and firewalls are essential components of protecting Linux systems from unauthorized access, data breaches, and cyber threats in an increasingly connected world. As of 2025, with the rise of advanced persistent threats (APTs), zero-day exploits, and AI-driven attacks, Linux network security emphasizes proactive measures like layered defenses, zero-trust models, and automated monitoring. Firewalls act as the first line of defense, controlling inbound and outbound traffic based on rules, while broader security practices include encryption, access controls, and vulnerability management. Linux's kernel-integrated tools, such as nftables (the modern successor to iptables), firewalld, and UFW, provide flexible, powerful options for enforcement. This section explores firewall fundamentals, configuration with key tools, integration with other security features, and best practices, with examples to guide implementation. Proper setup mitigates risks like DDoS, port scanning, and unauthorized remote access, ensuring robust protection for servers, desktops, and embedded devices.

Network Security Fundamentals in Linux

Network security in Linux revolves around the principle of least privilege: allow only necessary traffic while monitoring and logging anomalies. Key threats include:

- **External Attacks:** Port exploits (e.g., CVE-2024-XXXX vulnerabilities in services like SSH), DDoS floods overwhelming interfaces.
- **Internal Risks:** Lateral movement in compromised networks, misconfigured services exposing data.
- **Modern Challenges (2025):** AI-assisted phishing, supply-chain attacks on kernel modules, and quantum-resistant encryption needs.

Linux defenses leverage:

- **Kernel Features:** Netfilter for packet filtering, seccomp for syscall restrictions, and namespaces/cgroups for isolation (e.g., in containers).
- **Tools:** tcpdump for sniffing, fail2ban for brute-force blocking, and Wireshark for analysis.
- **Protocols:** TLS/SSL for encryption (e.g., via OpenSSL), IPsec for VPNs.

Firewalls filter at the network stack: ingress (incoming), egress (outgoing), using rules on IP, ports, protocols.

Firewall Tools in Linux

Linux offers several firewall frontends, all backed by netfilter:

- **nftables:** The current standard (since kernel 3.13, default in 2025 distributions like Ubuntu 25.04, Fedora 42). Uses tables, chains, and rules for efficient, expressive filtering. Replaces iptables.
- **iptables:** Legacy (nftables compat mode via iptables-nft). Still used but deprecated; avoid for new setups.
- **firewalld:** Dynamic daemon (systemd-integrated), uses nftables backend. Zones (e.g., public, internal) simplify management; good for desktops/servers.
- **UFW (Uncomplicated Firewall):** Simplified frontend to nftables/iptables, ideal for beginners. Commands like ufw allow 80/tcp.

Other: Shorewall (config-based), ferm (DSL-like).

Configuring Firewalls

Start with defaults: Most distros ship with firewalld or ufw enabled minimally.

nftables Example: Direct rule setup.

Command-line (as root):

```text
nft add table inet my_filter
nft add chain inet my_filter input { type filter hook input priority 0; policy drop; }  # Drop by default
nft add rule inet my_filter input iif lo accept  # Allow loopback
nft add rule inet my_filter input tcp dport 22 accept  # Allow SSH
nft add rule inet my_filter input tcp dport {80, 443} accept  # HTTP/HTTPS
nft list ruleset  # View
```

Persistent: Save to /etc/nftables.conf, load with nft -f /etc/nftables.conf; systemd: systemctl enable nftables.

firewalld Example: Zone-based.

Install: apt install firewalld or dnf install firewalld.

Commands:

```text
firewall-cmd --permanent --zone=public --add-service=ssh
firewall-cmd --permanent --zone=public --add-port=80/tcp
firewall-cmd --reload
firewall-cmd --list-all  # View
```

Zones allow context-specific rules (e.g., public for external, internal for LAN).

UFW Example: Simple syntax.

```text
ufw allow ssh
ufw allow 80/tcp
ufw enable
ufw status verbose
```

For IPv6: Explicitly handle (e.g., ufw enable ipv6).

Programmatic (C API via libnftnl for nftables, or system() for commands in scripts).

Integrating with Other Security Features

- **SELinux/AppArmor:** Enforce mandatory access controls; e.g., SELinux policies restrict socket binds.

- **fail2ban:** Monitors logs (e.g., /var/log/auth.log), bans IPs via firewall rules on failed logins.
- **VPNs:** WireGuard or OpenVPN; integrate with firewalls (allow UDP 51820 for WireGuard).
- **Monitoring:** nftables counters in rules (counter accept); tools like prometheus-node-exporter for metrics.
- **Zero-Trust:** Use mTLS, segment networks with namespaces, audit with auditd.

Example script to add rule programmatically (using system for simplicity):

c

```c
#include <stdlib.h>

int main() {
    system("nft add rule inet my_filter input tcp dport 22 accept");
    return 0;
}
```

For production, use libnftnl for direct API.

Best Practices (2025 Updates)

From recent guidelines (e.g., Red Hat, SUSE 2025 docs):

- **Default Deny:** Policy drop; explicitly allow needed ports.
- **Minimize Exposure:** Bind services to localhost if possible; use VPNs for remote.
- **Regular Updates:** Patch kernels for CVEs (e.g., 2025 TCP zero-window exploits); automate with unattended-upgrades.
- **Logging/Monitoring:** Enable nftables logging (nft add rule ... log prefix "DROP:" counter drop); integrate with SIEM (e.g., ELK stack).
- **IPv6 Considerations:** Dual-stack; filter IPv6 explicitly as attacks rise.
- **Container Security:** Use podman/docker with network namespaces; firewalld zones per container.
- **Quantum-Resistant:** Prepare for post-quantum crypto in TLS (e.g., OpenSSL 3.0+ hybrids).
- **Automation:** Use Ansible/Terraform for config; CIS benchmarks for hardening.

Test: nmap -p- localhost for open ports; fail2ban-client status.

Common pitfalls: Forgetting egress rules (allow malicious outbound), over-permissive zones, ignoring IPv6.

Summary

Network security and firewalls in Linux safeguard systems through tools like nftables, firewalld, and UFW, enforcing rules for traffic control. Configuration examples demonstrate practical setups, integrated with broader practices like SELinux and monitoring. This knowledge equips for secure networking, leading to system calls (Chapter 23), where kernel interfaces deepen IPC and networking mastery.

23. System Calls and Library Functions

System calls and library functions bridge user-space applications with kernel services, providing a standardized interface for operations like file I/O, process management, and networking. System calls (syscalls) are the low-level entry points into the kernel, invoked via software interrupts or architecture-specific instructions (e.g., SYSCALL on x86), while library functions (e.g., from glibc) wrap these for portability and ease. Understanding their implementation deepens kernel mastery, enabling custom extensions or optimizations. This chapter explores adding custom syscalls, diving into glibc, POSIX compliance, and emerging tools like Rust in kernels, with practical examples.

23.1 Implementing Custom System Calls

Implementing a custom system call involves extending the Linux kernel to provide new functionality accessible from user space, such as a specialized device control or diagnostic tool. Syscalls are the kernel's API, numbered uniquely per architecture, with parameters passed via registers and results returned in a standard way (e.g., rax on x86). Adding one requires modifying kernel sources, which demands caution—errors can destabilize the system. This is typically for development or embedded use; avoid in production without thorough testing. The process includes defining the syscall, updating tables, compiling the kernel, and invoking from user space. As of kernel 6.x (2025), syscalls use the generic entry (kernel/entry/) for security.
Key steps:
- **Define the Syscall Function:** In a kernel file (e.g., kernel/sys.c or custom module), add SYSCALL_DEFINE<N>(name, params), where N is arg count.
- **Update Syscall Table:** Add to arch/<arch>/entry/syscall_table.c or include/uapi/asm-generic/unistd.h for numbering.
- **Compile and Boot:** Build kernel, install, reboot.
- **User-Space Call:** Use syscall() from <unistd.h> or inline asm.

Syscall conventions: Args in registers (rdi, rsi, etc. on x86_64); return in rax (negative for errors, set errno).
Example: Adding a custom syscall "my_hello" that prints a message and returns a value.
1. **Kernel Modification:**
    o   Add to kernel/sys.c:

c
```c
SYSCALL_DEFINE1(my_hello, const char __user *, msg) {
  char buf[256];
  long copied = strncpy_from_user(buf, msg, sizeof(buf));
  if (copied < 0 || copied == sizeof(buf)) return -EFAULT;

  printk(KERN_INFO "my_hello: %s\n", buf);
  return 42;  // Arbitrary return
}
```
- Update include/uapi/asm-generic/unistd.h: Add #define __NR_my_hello 451 (next available number).
- Update arch/x86/entry/syscalls/syscall_64.tbl: Add 451 common my_hello __x64_sys_my_hello

For other arches (e.g., ARM64): Similar in syscall.tbl.
2. **Compile Kernel:**
    o   Download sources (e.g., linux-6.6.tar.xz).
    o   make defconfig; make menuconfig (enable as module if possible, but syscalls are built-in).
    o   make -j$(nproc); sudo make modules_install install.
    o   Update GRUB, reboot.
3. **User-Space Invocation:**

c
```c
#include <unistd.h>
#include <sys/syscall.h>
#include <stdio.h>

#define __NR_my_hello 451
```

```
int main() {
    long ret = syscall(__NR_my_hello, "Hello from user space!");
    if (ret < 0) {
        perror("syscall");
        return 1;
    }
    printf("Syscall returned: %ld\n", ret);
    return 0;
}
```

Compile: gcc test_syscall.c -o test. Run: Check dmesg for print.

For modules: Syscalls can't be modular directly; use sysfs or ioctl instead for loadable extensions.

Error Handling and Safety

- Errors: Return -errno (e.g., -EINVAL); kernel sets errno in user space.
- Validation: Always check user pointers with copy_from_user/access_ok.
- Security: Custom syscalls increase attack surface; use capabilities (e.g., capable(CAP_SYS_ADMIN)) to restrict.
- Testing: Use QEMU for safe boots; verify with strace (strace ./test shows syscall).

Limitations: Syscall numbers are architecture-specific; use libc wrappers for portability. Over 512 syscalls risk overflow.

Alternatives: For user extensions, eBPF or modules with char devices.

Summary

Implementing custom system calls extends kernel functionality via definitions and tables, accessible from user space with syscall(). Examples show addition and invocation. This leads to glibc deep dive (next), where library functions abstract these for applications.

23.2 Glibc and Standard Library Deep Dive

The GNU C Library (glibc) serves as the standard library for C and C++ programs on Linux and other GNU-based systems, providing a comprehensive implementation of the C standard (ISO C), POSIX interfaces, and GNU extensions. As of November 2025, glibc is at version 2.42 (released in August 2025), with ongoing development focusing on performance enhancements, security hardening, and support for emerging hardware like advanced vector extensions and post-quantum cryptography hooks. Glibc acts as the intermediary between user-space applications and the kernel, wrapping system calls (Section 23.1) into higher-level functions while adding portability, error handling, and optimizations. A deep dive into glibc reveals its modular architecture, key components like memory allocation and I/O, internal syscall mechanisms, threading support, and recent advancements in security and efficiency. Understanding glibc empowers developers to write portable, performant code, debug library interactions, and even contribute to its evolution.

Role and Architecture of Glibc

Glibc's primary role is to implement the C standard library (libc), providing functions like printf(), malloc(), open(), and pthread_create(), which abstract kernel syscalls and hardware variances. It ensures compliance with standards like POSIX.1-2024 (updated for real-time and security features) while offering GNU-specific extensions (e.g., getline() for dynamic input).

Architecturally, glibc is a shared library (libc.so.6), loaded at runtime, with static variants (libc.a) for linking. It comprises:

- **Core Modules:** Startup code (crt0.o), dynamic linker (ld.so for ELF loading).
- **Subsystem Libraries:** libm (math), libpthread (threads, now integrated), librt (real-time), libdl (dynamic loading).
- **Build System:** Configurable via --enable-kernel for min kernel version, supporting multi-arch (e.g., x86_64 with AVX512).

Glibc handles versioning with symbol versions (e.g., GLIBC_2.42), allowing backward compatibility. It detects hardware at runtime (e.g., via ifunc for CPU-specific implementations like memcpy optimized for SSE/AVX).

Syscall Wrapping and Internals

Glibc wraps syscalls to provide portable interfaces. For example, read() invokes the kernel via architecture-specific assembly (e.g., SYSCALL on x86_64, SVC on ARM).

Internals:

- **VDSO (Virtual Dynamic Shared Object):** Kernel-provided user-space code for fast syscalls like gettimeofday(), avoiding full context switches.
- **Error Handling:** Sets errno (thread-local in TLS); functions return -1 on error.
- **Thread Safety:** Uses TLS (Thread-Local Storage) for per-thread data; libpthread implements POSIX threads with futexes for synchronization.

Deep dive into syscall mechanism (x86_64 example):
- Glibc uses inline asm: __asm__ ("syscall"); with registers set per calling convention (rdi=arg1, etc.).
- For older kernels, falls back to INT 0x80.

Example disassembly (via objdump on libc.so): Shows syscall stubs.

Recent (2025): Glibc 2.42 optimizes syscalls with ifunc resolvers for Arm SVE2 and RISC-V vector extensions.

Key Components: Memory Management

Glibc's malloc (ptmalloc, derived from dlmalloc) is a heap allocator with arenas for threading:
- **Arenas:** Per-thread heaps to reduce contention; main arena for single-thread.
- **Chunks:** Managed with bins (free lists); tcache for fast small allocs.
- **Security:** Heap cookies, safe unlinking, and (in 2.42) enhanced canaries against overflows (inspired by 2025 hardening efforts).

Deep dive: From search insights (e.g., Deep Kondah's 2025 article), heap internals use mmap for large allocs, sbrk for small; exploits like use-after-free mitigated by freelist pointers.

Functions: malloc/free, realloc, calloc; aligned_alloc for alignment.

I/O and Standard Library Functions

- **Stdio:** Buffered I/O with FILE* (fopen, fprintf); custom buffers via setvbuf.
- **String/ Memory:** strcpy (fortified to _chk variants), memcpy (optimized with SIMD).
- **Math:** libm with sin/cos optimized for FMA (Fused Multiply-Add).

POSIX extensions: pthread_mutex_lock (futex-based), sem_wait.

Debugging and Customization

- **LD_PRELOAD:** Override functions (e.g., custom malloc).
- **GDB Integration:** glibc provides debug symbols; use catch syscall.
- **Valgrind/Memcheck:** Detect leaks/corruption.
- **Recent Hardening (2025):** From Chainguard insights, glibc 2.42 includes better CFI (Control-Flow Integrity) and shadow stacks against ROP; CVE-2025-4802 (May 2025) patched path manipulation in setuid binaries.

For versions: As per Julio Merino's 2025 post, handling glibc versions in builds avoids reproducibility issues.

Summary

Glibc and the standard library offer a rich, optimized interface wrapping syscalls, with deep internals in memory, I/O, and threading. Recent 2025 updates emphasize hardening and performance. This deep dive equips for POSIX compliance (next), where standards guide portable development.

23.3 POSIX Compliance and Extensions

POSIX (Portable Operating System Interface) is a family of standards (IEEE 1003) that defines APIs for Unix-like systems, ensuring portability across compliant OSes like Linux, macOS, and BSD variants. Linux, while not formally POSIX-certified (due to cost and minor deviations), achieves high compliance through glibc (Section 23.2) and kernel implementations, supporting standards like POSIX.1-2008 (with 2018 updates) for base interfaces, POSIX.2 for shells/utilities, and extensions for real-time (POSIX.1b) or threads (POSIX.1c). Compliance means apps using POSIX APIs run consistently, but Linux adds GNU extensions for enhanced functionality (e.g., epoll over select). This section explores POSIX compliance in Linux syscalls and libraries, key extensions, handling non-compliance, and best practices for portable code, with examples to illustrate differences and usage.

POSIX Compliance in Linux

Linux adheres closely to POSIX through:
- **Kernel Syscalls:** Most POSIX functions map to syscalls (e.g., fork() to clone, open() to openat). Kernel config options like CONFIG_POSIX_TIMERS enable features.
- **Glibc Wrappers:** Provides POSIX-conformant interfaces; compile with -D_POSIX_C_SOURCE=200809L to enable specific versions.

- **Certification Gaps:** Linux isn't certified (unlike AIX or macOS), but LSB (Linux Standard Base) ensures de-facto compliance. Deviations are minor, like Linux-specific error codes or behaviors.

Key POSIX areas:

- **Process Management:** fork, exec, wait, signals (kill, sigaction).
- **File I/O:** open, read, write, fcntl, stat.
- **Threads:** pthread_* (create, mutex, cond) via NPTL (Native POSIX Threads Library) in glibc.
- **Real-Time:** sched_setscheduler (for SCHED_FIFO/RR), mq_* (message queues, Section 21.2).
- **Networking:** Though not core POSIX, BSD sockets align with POSIX.1g.

To check compliance: Use getconf (e.g., getconf POSIX_V7_ILP32_OFF32_CFLAGS for build flags).

Example: Portable file open with POSIX flags:

c

```c
#include <fcntl.h>
#include <stdio.h>
#include <unistd.h>

int main() {
    int fd = open("test.txt", O_RDWR | O_CREAT | O_TRUNC, S_IRUSR | S_IWUSR | S_IRGRP | S_IROTH); // POSIX modes
    if (fd == -1) {
        perror("open");
        return 1;
    }

    const char *msg = "POSIX compliant write\n";
    if (write(fd, msg, strlen(msg)) == -1) {
        perror("write");
    }

    close(fd);
    return 0;
}
```

This uses POSIX-defined flags/modes, portable across systems.

Linux Extensions to POSIX

Linux extends POSIX with GNU-specific features for efficiency or functionality, often prefixed with _GNU_SOURCE in compiles.

Notable extensions:

- **epoll:** Scalable I/O multiplexing (epoll_create, epoll_ctl, epoll_wait) over POSIX select/poll; handles thousands of fds efficiently.
- **inotify:** File system event notification (inotify_init, inotify_add_watch), extending POSIX for real-time monitoring.
- **timerfd/signalfd/eventfd:** FD-based timers/signals/events for integration with poll/epoll.
- **splice/tee/vmsplice:** Zero-copy data movement between fds/pipes.
- **GNU C Library Extras:** getline() for dynamic input, asprintf() for allocated strings, pthread_rwlock_t for read-write locks.

To use: Define _GNU_SOURCE before includes.

Example: Using epoll for multiple connections (extends select):

c

```c
#define _GNU_SOURCE
#include <sys/epoll.h>
#include <sys/socket.h>
#include <netinet/in.h>
#include <stdio.h>
#include <stdlib.h>
#include <unistd.h>
```

```c
#define MAX_EVENTS 10

int main() {
    // ... create server_fd, bind, listen as in 22.2 ...

    int epfd = epoll_create1(0);  // GNU extension flag optional
    if (epfd == -1) {
        perror("epoll_create1");
        return 1;
    }

    struct epoll_event ev = { .events = EPOLLIN, .data.fd = server_fd };
    if (epoll_ctl(epfd, EPOLL_CTL_ADD, server_fd, &ev) == -1) {
        perror("epoll_ctl");
        return 1;
    }

    struct epoll_event events[MAX_EVENTS];
    while (1) {
        int nfds = epoll_wait(epfd, events, MAX_EVENTS, -1);  // Infinite timeout
        if (nfds == -1) {
            perror("epoll_wait");
            break;
        }

        for (int i = 0; i < nfds; i++) {
            if (events[i].data.fd == server_fd) {
                // Accept new client, add to epoll
                int client_fd = accept(server_fd, NULL, NULL);
                ev.events = EPOLLIN | EPOLLET;  // Edge-triggered
                ev.data.fd = client_fd;
                epoll_ctl(epfd, EPOLL_CTL_ADD, client_fd, &ev);
            } else {
                // Handle data on client_fd
                char buf[1024];
                ssize_t len = read(events[i].data.fd, buf, sizeof(buf));
                if (len <= 0) {
                    epoll_ctl(epfd, EPOLL_CTL_DEL, events[i].data.fd, NULL);
                    close(events[i].data.fd);
                } else {
                    // Process buf
                }
            }
        }
    }

    close(epfd);
    close(server_fd);
    return 0;
}
```

This uses epoll for scalable server, a Linux extension beyond POSIX poll.

Handling Non-Compliance and Portability

- **Feature Test Macros:** Define _POSIX_C_SOURCE or _XOPEN_SOURCE to restrict to standards; undef for extensions.
- **Autoconf/CMake:** Detect features with AC_CHECK_FUNC(epoll_create).
- **Fallbacks:** Use select() if epoll unavailable (e.g., #ifdef **linux**).

- **Compliance Tools:** POSIXLY_CORRECT env var restricts glibc to POSIX; posixlint or check tools for static analysis.

In Linux: Kernel config (e.g., CONFIG_POSIX_MQUEUE) enables features; glibc conforms but extends.

Best Practices
- Prefer POSIX for portability; use extensions judiciously with fallbacks.
- Test on multiple OSes (e.g., via Docker: alpine for musl libc).
- Document non-POSIX usage.

Summary
POSIX compliance ensures portability in Linux syscalls and libraries, with extensions like epoll adding power. Examples show standard vs. extended usage. This leads to Rust in kernels (next), where modern languages extend traditional C-based development.

23.4 Rust in Kernel Development

Rust, a systems programming language emphasizing memory safety, concurrency, and performance, has been making inroads into the Linux kernel development landscape since its initial integration in 2022. By November 2025, Rust support in the kernel has matured significantly, with code contributions expanding across subsystems like drivers and core utilities. This shift aims to address longstanding issues in C-based code, such as memory vulnerabilities that account for roughly two-thirds of historical kernel CVEs. While the kernel remains predominantly C, Rust's adoption represents a strategic evolution, backed by key maintainers including Linus Torvalds, who has publicly supported its inclusion despite ongoing debates. Rust code coexists with C, leveraging interoperability tools, and is compiled with specific constraints to align with kernel requirements. This section delves into the rationale, implementation process, current status as of late 2025, practical examples, challenges, and future prospects, empowering developers to contribute to this hybrid kernel ecosystem.

Rationale and Benefits of Rust in the Kernel

The push for Rust stems from its compile-time guarantees against common C pitfalls like null pointer dereferences, buffer overflows, and data races—issues that have plagued kernel security for decades. Rust's ownership model, borrow checker, and safe/unsafe distinctions enforce memory safety without runtime overhead, potentially reducing bugs by up to 70% in affected areas, as noted in analyses from projects like Rust-for-Linux. Key benefits:

- **Memory Safety:** Eliminates use-after-free and double-free errors, common in kernel CVEs (e.g., pre-2025 vulnerabilities in drivers).
- **Concurrency Safety:** Thread-safe by design, complementing kernel primitives like spinlocks (Section 20.1).
- **Modern Tooling:** Better error messages, Cargo for builds, and integration with kernel's Kbuild.
- **Incremental Adoption:** Rust code can interface with C via bindings, allowing gradual replacement (e.g., in new drivers).

As of 2025, Rust has proven effective in reducing vulnerability classes, with kernel 6.13 (January 2025) introducing expanded support for Rust in areas like file systems and networking modules. Studies from organizations like the Linux Foundation highlight a drop in memory-related bugs in Rust-written components.

Implementing Rust in the Kernel

To use Rust in kernel development, enable CONFIG_RUST in kernel config (available since 5.19, stable by 6.x). The kernel builds Rust code with a pinned compiler version (e.g., rustc 1.80+ in 6.12, updated to 1.82 in 6.13 for better async support). Key files: rust/Makefile for integration, bindings/generated.rs for C interop.

Steps for adding Rust code:

1. **Setup Environment:** Install rustup, bindgen (for headers), and kernel sources. Use make rustavailable to check.
2. **Define Modules:** Write .rs files in kernel/rust/ or drivers/rust/; use unsafe for C calls.
3. **Bindings:** Auto-generate with bindgen for C structs/functions.
4. **Build:** make compiles Rust alongside C.
5. **Invoke:** User space interacts via syscalls or ioctls; no direct Rust calls.

Kernel constraints: No std lib (use core/alloc crates), custom panic handler, specific features disabled (e.g., no floating point in kernel mode).

Example: Simple Rust kernel module (hello.rs in kernel/rust/):

rust

```rust
#![no_std]
#![feature(alloc_error_handler)]

extern crate alloc;

use kernel::prelude::*;
use kernel::printk;

module! {
    type: HelloModule,
    name: b"hello_rust",
    author: b"Your Name",
    description: b"Rust hello world module",
    license: b"GPL",
}

struct HelloModule;

impl kernel::Module for HelloModule {
    fn init(_module: &'static ThisModule) -> Result<Self> {
        pr_info!("Hello from Rust!\n");
        Ok(HelloModule)
    }
}

impl Drop for HelloModule {
    fn drop(&mut self) {
        pr_info!("Goodbye from Rust!\n");
    }
}
```
Add to Kconfig/Makefiles; load with insmod. This prints to dmesg on load/unload.

For drivers: Implement traits like Device, extending C structs.

Current Status as of November 2025

By late 2025, Rust is in production kernels:

- **Adoption:** Code in drivers (e.g., NVMe, GPU), with 6.13 (Jan 2025) adding in-place initialization and better error handling. 6.14+ expands to networking.
- **Momentum:** Torvalds and maintainers (e.g., Wedson Almeida Filho) advocate; Rust-for-Linux project drives contributions. Predictions from early 2025 (e.g., Reddit discussions) of increasing Rust code have held, with 451+ as syscall example in docs.
- **Challenges:** Ideological resistance from C veterans (e.g., Feb 2025 debates on "Rust not for Linux" ideology). Some maintainers argue it's more about process than tech.
- **Progress:** Kernel compiles with older Rust (1.68 min), avoiding unstable features. 2025 saw stability improvements, reducing CVEs in Rust parts.

From LWN (Oct 2025): Upcoming features like async Rust for kernels, but cautiously.

Challenges and Best Practices

- **Interop:** Use bindgen for C bindings; manage unsafe blocks carefully.
- **Learning Curve:** Rust's strictness requires rethinking C patterns.
- **Testing:** Use kunit for Rust tests; qemu for boots.
- **Contributions:** Submit to rust-for-linux mailing list; follow kernel docs (Documentation/rust/).
- **Avoid Pitfalls:** No panics in critical paths; handle alloc failures.

For extensions: Rust in user space for tools interfacing kernels.

Summary

Rust in kernel development introduces safety and modernity, with growing adoption by 2025 through bindings and modules. Examples show basic integration. This concludes the chapter, leading to terminals (Chapter 24), where system interactions build on these foundations.

24. Terminals, Pseudo-Terminals, and Daemons

Terminals, pseudo-terminals (PTYs), and daemons are integral to Linux's user interaction and background processing models. Terminals provide the interface for command-line input/output, evolving from physical teletypewriters to virtual consoles and emulators. Pseudo-terminals emulate terminal behavior for processes like ssh or screen, enabling nested sessions. Daemons run in the background, detached from terminals, handling system services. This chapter examines terminal I/O, PTY management, daemon design, and logging, with practical examples to build robust applications.

24.1 Terminal I/O Handling

Terminal I/O handling in Linux manages the flow of input and output between processes and terminal devices, providing features like line editing, echoing, and signal generation. The kernel's terminal subsystem (drivers/tty/) processes characters according to modes set via the termios structure, allowing customization for interactive shells, raw input (e.g., games), or scripted I/O. Understanding this is key for applications requiring precise control, such as editors (vi) or serial communication tools. POSIX standards (Section 23.3) define the interface, ensuring portability.

Terminal Modes and the Termios Structure

Terminals operate in two primary modes:

- **Canonical (Cooked) Mode:** Default; input buffered by line (until newline), with editing (backspace, Ctrl+U), echoing, and signals (Ctrl+C -> SIGINT, Ctrl+Z -> SIGTSTP).
- **Non-Canonical (Raw) Mode:** No buffering/editing; input available immediately, no echoing/signals unless enabled.

The struct termios (from <termios.h>) controls settings:

- **c_iflag:** Input flags (e.g., IGNBRK for ignore break, ICRNL for CR to NL).
- **c_oflag:** Output flags (e.g., OPOST for processing, ONLCR for NL to CR-NL).
- **c_cflag:** Control flags (e.g., CS8 for 8-bit chars, CREAD for enable receiver).
- **c_lflag:** Local flags (e.g., ICANON for canonical, ECHO for echoing, ISIG for signals).
- **c_cc[]:** Special chars (e.g., VINTR=Ctrl+C, VEOF=Ctrl+D).

Functions:

- tcgetattr(int fd, struct termios *termios_p): Get settings.
- tcsetattr(int fd, int optional_actions, const struct termios *termios_p): Set. Actions: TCSANOW (immediate), TCSADRAIN (after output), TCSAFLUSH (flush input).

Baud rates: cfgetispeed/cfsetispeed for input/output speed.

Example: Switching to raw mode for a game-like input handler:

```c
#include <termios.h>
#include <unistd.h>
#include <stdio.h>
#include <stdlib.h>

void set_raw_mode(int fd, struct termios *orig) {
    struct termios raw;
    tcgetattr(fd, orig);  // Save original
    raw = *orig;
    raw.c_lflag &= ~(ICANON | ECHO | ISIG);  // No canonical, echo, signals
    raw.c_iflag &= ~(ICRNL | IXON);  // No CR to NL, software flow
    raw.c_oflag &= ~(OPOST);  // No output processing
    raw.c_cc[VMIN] = 1;   // Min chars for read
    raw.c_cc[VTIME] = 0;  // No timeout
    tcsetattr(fd, TCSAFLUSH, &raw);
}

int main() {
    struct termios orig_termios;
```

```
  set_raw_mode(STDIN_FILENO, &orig_termios);

  char c;
  while (read(STDIN_FILENO, &c, 1) == 1 && c != 'q') {
    if (c >= 32 && c < 127) { // Printable
      printf("%c\r\n", c);
    } else {
      printf("Non-printable: %d\r\n", c);
    }
  }

  tcsetattr(STDIN_FILENO, TCSAFLUSH, &orig_termios); // Restore
  return 0;
}
```
Compile and run: Inputs print immediately without enter, no echo. Ctrl+C quits without signal.

For serial terminals: Use /dev/ttyS0, set baud with cfsetospeed(&termios, B9600).

Terminal Detection and Attributes

- isatty(int fd): Check if fd is a terminal (returns 1 if yes).
- ttyname(int fd): Get device name (e.g., "/dev/pts/0").
- tcflush(int fd, int queue_selector): Flush input/output queues (TCIFLUSH, TCOFLUSH, TCIOFLUSH).
- tcsendbreak(int fd, int duration): Send break signal for serial.

Window size: ioctl(fd, TIOCGWINSZ, &winsize) for rows/cols.

Best Practices and Considerations

- Restore Original Settings: Always save/restore termios to avoid leaving terminal in bad state (e.g., no echo).
- Error Handling: Check returns; common errno: EINVAL (invalid arg), ENOTTY (not terminal).
- Non-Blocking: Combine with fcntl O_NONBLOCK for async I/O.
- Signals: In canonical, Ctrl+\ (QUIT), Ctrl+S/XOFF (stop/start flow).
- Security: Raw mode exposes inputs; avoid in untrusted apps.
- Performance: Buffered I/O in glibc (Section 23.2) interacts; use setvbuf for tuning.

Limitations: Termios not for graphics; use ncurses for advanced TUI.

Summary

Terminal I/O handling via termios enables mode customization for interactive or raw input, with functions for settings and special chars. Examples show raw mode switching. This foundation supports pseudo-terminals (next), where emulated terminals extend these concepts for virtual sessions.

24.2 Pseudo-Terminal Devices

Pseudo-terminal devices (PTYs) emulate the behavior of traditional terminals, providing a software-based interface for processes to interact as if connected to a real terminal. In Linux, PTYs are crucial for applications like ssh, screen, tmux, or expect, which create virtual sessions for remote access, multiplexing, or scripting. Unlike physical terminals (/dev/tty*) or virtual consoles (/dev/console), PTYs consist of paired devices: a master (controller) and slave (emulated terminal), allowing one process to manage input/output for another. The kernel's PTY subsystem (drivers/tty/pty.c) handles this emulation, integrating with the terminal I/O framework (Section 24.1) for line discipline, echoing, and signals. PTYs support POSIX compliance (Section 23.3), enabling portable terminal emulation. This section covers PTY creation, master-slave interactions, use cases, and advanced features like packet mode, with examples to demonstrate implementation.

Fundamentals of Pseudo-Terminals

A PTY pair includes:

- **Master Device:** Controlled by the managing process (e.g., sshd); writes to master appear as input on slave, reads from master get slave's output.
- **Slave Device:** Acts as the terminal for the child process (e.g., bash); /dev/pts/<n> dynamically allocated.

Allocation: Use posix_openpt() or open("/dev/ptmx") for master, then ptsname() for slave path, unlockpt() to unlock, and grantpt() for permissions (though often combined).

Key behaviors:

- **Bidirectional:** Data flows between master and slave.
- **Terminal Emulation:** Slave inherits termios settings (Section 24.1); supports signals (e.g., SIGWINCH on resize).
- **Dynamic Allocation:** Kernel assigns slave numbers from /dev/pts/.
- **Security:** Master controls access; slave permissions set to user.

PTYs are file descriptors, integrable with select/poll.

Creating and Using PTYs

Steps for a PTY-based application (e.g., simple terminal emulator):

1. Open master: int master = posix_openpt(O_RDWR | O_NOCTTY);
2. Grant access/unlock: grantpt(master); unlockpt(master);
3. Get slave name: char *slave_name = ptsname(master);
4. Fork child, open slave in child: int slave = open(slave_name, O_RDWR | O_NOCTTY);
5. In child: Set slave as controlling terminal with setsid(), ioctl(slave, TIOCSCTTY, NULL).
6. Duplex I/O: Master reads/writes to control child.

Example: Basic PTY fork for shell emulation:

```c
#include <pty.h>
#include <unistd.h>
#include <fcntl.h>
#include <termios.h>
#include <stdio.h>
#include <stdlib.h>
#include <string.h>
#include <sys/ioctl.h>
#include <sys/wait.h>

int main() {
    int master;
    char *slave_name;
    pid_t pid;

    // Open PTY master
    master = posix_openpt(O_RDWR | O_NOCTTY);
    if (master == -1) {
        perror("posix_openpt");
        return 1;
    }

    if (grantpt(master) == -1 || unlockpt(master) == -1) {
        perror("grantpt/unlockpt");
        return 1;
    }

    slave_name = ptsname(master);
    if (!slave_name) {
        perror("ptsname");
        return 1;
    }

    printf("Slave PTY: %s\n", slave_name);

    pid = fork();
    if (pid == -1) {
        perror("fork");
        return 1;
```

```c
    }

    if (pid == 0) { // Child: set up slave as stdin/stdout/stderr
        close(master);
        setsid(); // New session

        int slave = open(slave_name, O_RDWR | O_NOCTTY);
        if (slave == -1) {
            perror("open slave");
            return 1;
        }

        ioctl(slave, TIOCSCTTY, NULL); // Set controlling TTY
        dup2(slave, STDIN_FILENO);
        dup2(slave, STDOUT_FILENO);
        dup2(slave, STDERR_FILENO);
        close(slave);

        // Exec shell
        execl("/bin/bash", "bash", NULL);
        perror("execl");
        return 1;
    } else { // Parent: interact via master
        close(STDIN_FILENO); // Optional: redirect
        char buf[1024];
        ssize_t len;

        while ((len = read(master, buf, sizeof(buf))) > 0) {
            write(STDOUT_FILENO, buf, len); // Echo to console
        }

        wait(NULL);
        close(master);
    }

    return 0;
}
```

Compile: gcc pty_example.c -o pty_example -lutil (for pty.h functions). Run: Spawns bash in PTY; type commands, exit with 'exit'.

This emulates a terminal: Parent relays I/O.

For non-fork (e.g., ssh): Use master for remote I/O.

Advanced Features

- **Packet Mode:** Enable with ioctl(master, TIOCPKT, &val) (val=1); prefixes packets with type (e.g., TIOCPKT_DATA).
- **Resize Handling:** ioctl(master, TIOCSWINSZ, &winsize) to set slave window size; child gets SIGWINCH.
- **Multiple PTYs:** Allocate dynamically for sessions (e.g., in tmux).
- **Security:** PTYs run with user perms; avoid root if possible. Revoke with revoke(slave_name).

In kernels: PTYs use pty driver; /dev/ptmx is the clone device.

Best Practices and Limitations

- Close unused fds to avoid hangs.
- Handle EOF (read=0) for closure.
- Use for testing (expect scripts) or virtualization.
- Limitations: No graphics; limited to termios features.
- Errors: ENOENT (no pts), EIO (I/O fail).

Summary
Pseudo-terminal devices enable terminal emulation via master-slave pairs, with APIs for allocation and I/O. Examples show shell spawning. This leads to daemon design (next), where detached processes often use PTYs for logging or interaction.

24.3 Daemon Design Patterns

Daemons are background processes that run detached from user sessions, providing persistent services like web servers (httpd), logging (syslogd), or scheduling (cron). Designing daemons requires patterns for detachment, reliability, resource management, and error handling to ensure they operate autonomously, survive restarts, and minimize impact on the system. In Linux, daemons leverage fork, setsid, and signal handling for independence, often managed by init systems like systemd (prevalent in 2025 distributions). Good design incorporates modularity, logging, and security to prevent privilege escalation or resource leaks. This section outlines key patterns: classic double-fork detachment, signal management, resource limiting, logging integration, and modern systemd-aware designs, with examples to guide implementation.

Classic Detachment Pattern (Double Fork)

The traditional pattern detaches the daemon from the controlling terminal, creates a new session, and closes inherited fds to run independently.
Steps:
1. Fork child; parent exits (orphan child, adopted by init).
2. Child calls setsid() to create new session (become leader, detach TTY).
3. Fork again; first child exits (ensure not session leader, prevent TTY reacquisition).
4. Change directory to / (avoid filesystem locks).
5. Close stdin/stdout/stderr; redirect to /dev/null.
6. Set umask(0) for file creation.

Example: Simple daemon skeleton:

```c
#include <unistd.h>
#include <sys/stat.h>
#include <fcntl.h>
#include <stdlib.h>
#include <stdio.h>
#include <syslog.h>

void daemonize() {
    pid_t pid = fork();
    if (pid < 0) exit(1);
    if (pid > 0) exit(0);  // Parent exits

    if (setsid() < 0) exit(1);  // New session

    pid = fork();
    if (pid < 0) exit(1);
    if (pid > 0) exit(0);  // First child exits

    umask(0);
    chdir("/");

    close(STDIN_FILENO);
    close(STDOUT_FILENO);
    close(STDERR_FILENO);
    open("/dev/null", O_RDWR);
    dup(0); // stdout
    dup(0); // stderr
}
```

```c
int main() {
    daemonize();

    openlog("my_daemon", LOG_PID, LOG_DAEMON);
    syslog(LOG_INFO, "Daemon started");

    while (1) {
        // Daemon work: e.g., sleep and log
        sleep(10);
        syslog(LOG_INFO, "Daemon running");
    }

    closelog();
    return 0;
}
```
Compile and run: Detaches, logs to syslog. Check with ps aux | grep my_daemon.

Signal Management Pattern

Daemons handle signals for graceful shutdown, reload, or status. Use sigaction() for handlers; block unwanted signals.

Common: SIGTERM (shutdown), SIGHUP (reload config), SIGUSR1 (dump status).

Example handler:

c
```c
#include <signal.h>

volatile sig_atomic_t stop = 0;

void sig_handler(int sig) {
    if (sig == SIGTERM) stop = 1;
    else if (sig == SIGHUP) {
        // Reload config
        syslog(LOG_INFO, "Reloading config");
    }
}

int main() {
    // ... daemonize ...

    struct sigaction sa = { .sa_handler = sig_handler, .sa_flags = 0 };
    sigemptyset(&sa.sa_mask);
    sigaction(SIGTERM, &sa, NULL);
    sigaction(SIGHUP, &sa, NULL);

    // Ignore others
    signal(SIGINT, SIG_IGN);

    while (!stop) {
        // Work loop
        sleep(1);
    }

    syslog(LOG_INFO, "Daemon stopping");
    // Cleanup
    return 0;
}
```
This allows controlled exit/reload.

Resource Management and Limiting Pattern

Daemons limit resources to prevent DoS or leaks: Use setrlimit() for fds, memory; nice() for priority.
Example:
c
```
#include <sys/resource.h>

void limit_resources() {
    struct rlimit rl;
    rl.rlim_cur = rl.rlim_max = 1024;  // FD limit
    setrlimit(RLIMIT_NOFILE, &rl);

    rl.rlim_cur = rl.rlim_max = 64 * 1024 * 1024;  // 64MB mem
    setrlimit(RLIMIT_AS, &rl);

    nice(5);  // Lower priority
}
```
Call after daemonize.

Logging and Monitoring Pattern

Use syslog (openlog/syslog/closelog) or journald in systemd. Include PID, timestamps.
For systemd: Output to stdout; journald captures.

Modern Systemd-Aware Pattern

In 2025, most daemons are systemd units (.service files), avoiding manual detachment.
Pattern: Skip double-fork; systemd handles forking, logging.
Example service file (/etc/systemd/system/my_daemon.service):
text
```
[Unit]
Description=My Daemon

[Service]
ExecStart=/path/to/my_daemon
Restart=always

[Install]
WantedBy=multi-user.target
```
In code: No daemonize(); use sd_notify() for readiness.
Install: systemctl enable my_daemon.

Best Practices

- Run as non-root: Drop privileges with setuid/setgid after bind.
- Chroot for isolation.
- Handle zombies: Wait on children.
- Config Files: Parse /etc/my_daemon.conf with inih or similar.
- Testing: strace for syscalls; valgrind for leaks.

Pitfalls: Forgetting to close fds (leaks), ignoring signals (unclean exit).

Summary

Daemon design patterns ensure reliable background operation through detachment, signal handling, and resource limits. Examples show classic and modern approaches. This leads to logging (next), where daemons record activities for monitoring and debugging.

24.4 Logging and Monitoring

Logging and monitoring are indispensable for daemons and long-running processes, providing visibility into operations, errors, and performance metrics. Logging captures events, warnings, and debug information for postmortem analysis, while monitoring actively tracks runtime health, enabling proactive alerts and diagnostics. In Linux, logging leverages facilities like syslog (traditional) and journald (modern, integrated with systemd), with APIs for programmatic integration. Monitoring extends this with tools for metrics collection, visualization, and alerting. Effective design ensures logs are structured, rotatable, and secure, avoiding performance overhead or data loss. This section explores logging APIs, storage mechanisms, rotation strategies, monitoring frameworks, and best practices, with examples in C for daemon integration. These patterns enhance reliability, aiding debugging and compliance in production environments.

Logging Mechanisms in Linux

Linux offers multiple logging systems:

- **Syslog:** The classic interface (RFC 5424), using /dev/log socket or syslog() calls. Facilities (e.g., LOG_DAEMON) categorize; priorities (LOG_INFO, LOG_ERR) level.
- **Journald:** Systemd's binary logger, storing in /var/log/journal/, with rich metadata (PID, timestamps). Accessible via journalctl; integrates with syslog for compatibility.
- **Custom Files:** Direct writes to files (e.g., via fopen/fprintf), but prefer centralized systems for rotation and querying.

For daemons: Use openlog/syslog/closelog for syslog; systemd/sd-journal.h for journald.

Example: Syslog logging in a daemon (extending Section 24.3):

c

```c
#include <syslog.h>

void log_event(const char *msg, int priority) {
    syslog(priority, "%s", msg);
}

int main() {
    // ... daemonize ...

    openlog("my_daemon", LOG_PID | LOG_CONS, LOG_DAEMON); // CONS for console fallback
    log_event("Daemon started", LOG_INFO);

    while (1) {
        // Work
        sleep(10);
        log_event("Periodic check: all good", LOG_DEBUG); // Debug level
    }

    log_event("Daemon stopping", LOG_NOTICE);
    closelog();
    return 0;
}
```

View: tail -f /var/log/syslog or journalctl -u my_daemon if systemd.

For journald direct (sd-journal):

c

```c
#include <systemd/sd-journal.h>

sd_journal_print(LOG_INFO, "Daemon started");
```

Log Rotation and Management

Unmanaged logs grow indefinitely, risking disk exhaustion. Use logrotate (/etc/logrotate.d/) for rotation by size/time, compression, and pruning.

Example config (/etc/logrotate.d/my_daemon):

text

```
/var/log/my_daemon.log {
```

```
weekly
rotate 52
compress
delaycompress
missingok
notifempty
create 640 root adm
postrotate
    /usr/bin/killall -HUP my_daemon  # Reload
endscript
}
```
In daemons: Handle SIGHUP to reopen log files post-rotation.

Monitoring Frameworks

Monitoring tracks metrics (CPU, memory, I/O) and alerts on anomalies. Tools:

- **Prometheus:** Pull-based metrics; exporters like node_exporter for system stats.
- **Grafana:** Visualization dashboard for Prometheus data.
- **Nagios/Zabbix:** Agent-based monitoring with alerts.
- **systemd:** Built-in with systemctl status, journalctl for logs.

Programmatic: Use libsystemd for sd_notify("STATUS=Running"); or expose metrics via HTTP for Prometheus.

Example: Daemon with status notification:

c
```
#include <systemd/sd-daemon.h>

sd_notify(0, "READY=1\nSTATUS=Initialized");
```
In .service: Type=notify.

Best Practices

- **Structured Logging:** Use JSON/key-value for parseability (e.g., sd_journal_send("KEY=value")).
- **Levels:** DEBUG for dev, INFO for normal, ERR for failures.
- **Rate Limiting:** Avoid floods; use static buffers.
- **Security:** Log sensitive data masked; rotate to prevent leaks.
- **Testing:** Simulate failures; tools like logcheck for anomaly detection.
- **Cloud/2025 Trends:** Integrate with ELK (Elasticsearch, Logstash, Kibana) or Splunk for AI-driven analysis.

Pitfalls: Over-logging (performance hit), ignoring rotation (disk full), unhandled HUP (stale logs).

Summary

Logging and monitoring ensure daemon observability through syslog/journald and tools like Prometheus. Examples show integration for reliable services. This concludes the chapter, leading to practical projects (Chapter 25), where these patterns apply in capstone developments.

25. Practical Projects and Exercises

This chapter culminates the knowledge from prior books through hands-on projects, reinforcing concepts in system programming, kernel internals, drivers, and IPC. Each exercise builds progressively, starting with kernel modules and advancing to full drivers and performance tuning. Projects encourage experimentation, debugging, and contribution to open source, fostering mastery. Prerequisites include a development setup (Section 16.3) with kernel sources and tools like make, gdb, and perf. Test in VMs (e.g., QEMU) for safety.

25.1 Building a Custom Kernel Module

Building a custom kernel module introduces loadable kernel code, allowing extension of kernel functionality without full recompilation—ideal for drivers, file systems, or utilities. Modules are .ko files loaded via insmod/modprobe, interacting with the kernel through exported symbols. This exercise covers module structure, compilation, loading, parameters, and basic syscalls, providing a foundation for advanced kernels (e.g., custom drivers in later sections).

Step 1: Module Basics

A module requires init/exit functions, license, and description. Use module.h for macros.

Simple "hello" module (hello.c):

c
```c
#include <linux/module.h>
#include <linux/kernel.h>
#include <linux/init.h>

static int __init hello_init(void) {
    printk(KERN_INFO "Hello, kernel world!\n");
    return 0;  // 0=success
}

static void __exit hello_exit(void) {
    printk(KERN_INFO "Goodbye, kernel world!\n");
}

module_init(hello_init);
module_exit(hello_exit);

MODULE_LICENSE("GPL");
MODULE_AUTHOR("Your Name");
MODULE_DESCRIPTION("Simple hello module");
MODULE_VERSION("0.1");
```

This prints to dmesg on load/unload.

Step 2: Compilation Setup

Create a Makefile in the same directory:

makefile
```makefile
obj-m += hello.o

KDIR := /lib/modules/$(shell uname -r)/build

all:
    make -C $(KDIR) M=$(PWD) modules

clean:
    make -C $(KDIR) M=$(PWD) clean
```

Run make to build hello.ko. Requires kernel headers (install linux-headers-$(uname -r)).

For cross-compilation (e.g., ARM): Set ARCH=arm CROSS_COMPILE=arm-linux-gnueabihf- in make.

Step 3: Loading and Testing

- Load: sudo insmod hello.ko (or modprobe for deps).

- Check: dmesg | tail for messages; lsmod | grep hello for loaded modules.
- Unload: sudo rmmod hello.
- Params: Add static int my_param = 0; module_param(my_param, int, S_IRUSR); MODULE_PARM_DESC(my_param, "An integer param");. Load with sudo insmod hello.ko my_param=42; view in /sys/module/hello/parameters/my_param.

Step 4: Adding Functionality

Extend to export a function and add a proc file.
Updated hello.c:
c

```
// ... includes ...
#include <linux/proc_fs.h>

static struct proc_dir_entry *proc_file;

static ssize_t proc_read(struct file *file, char __user *ubuf, size_t count, loff_t *ppos) {
    char buf[64];
    int len = snprintf(buf, sizeof(buf), "Hello, value: %d\n", my_param);
    if (*ppos > 0 || count < len) return 0;
    if (copy_to_user(ubuf, buf, len)) return -EFAULT;
    *ppos += len;
    return len;
}

static const struct proc_ops proc_fops = {
    .proc_read = proc_read,
};

static int __init hello_init(void) {
    printk(KERN_INFO "Hello loaded\n");
    proc_file = proc_create("hello_proc", 0444, NULL, &proc_fops);
    if (!proc_file) return -ENOMEM;
    return 0;
}

static void __exit hello_exit(void) {
    proc_remove(proc_file);
    printk(KERN_INFO "Hello unloaded\n");
}

// ... module macros ...
```

Rebuild/load; read with cat /proc/hello_proc.

Step 5: Debugging and Extensions

- Debug: Use printk; gdb on module with gdb /path/to/vmlinux, add-symbol-file hello.ko <addr> (from /sys/module/hello/sections/.text).
- Extensions: Add ioctl interface, handle concurrency with spinlocks (Section 20.1).
- Test: In QEMU; check races with multiple loads.

Common issues: GPL-only symbols (use EXPORT_SYMBOL_GPL), module tainting.

Summary

Building a custom kernel module teaches dynamic kernel extension through init/exit, params, and proc integration. This project prepares for debugging (25.2), where real issues in modules are addressed.

25.2 Debugging Real-World System Issues

Debugging real-world system issues is a critical skill for Linux programmers, involving systematic identification and resolution of problems like crashes, performance degradation, resource leaks, or unexpected behaviors in production environments. Unlike controlled development settings, real issues often stem from interactions between hardware, kernel, user-space apps, and external factors (e.g., network loads or faulty drivers). Effective debugging combines tools for tracing, profiling, and inspection with methodologies like binary search (bisecting code/commits) or hypothesis testing. This exercise guides you through common scenarios, using tools like strace, gdb, perf, and ftrace, with steps to replicate and solve issues. Build on kernel modules (Section 25.1) by introducing deliberate bugs for practice. Aim to debug in VMs or containers to isolate risks.

Step 1: Setting Up a Debugging Environment

Prepare a safe setup:

- Use a VM (e.g., VirtualBox with Ubuntu 25.04 or Fedora 42) or container (Docker/Podman) to avoid host damage.
- Install tools: apt install strace gdb perf-tools-unstable linux-tools-common (or dnf equivalents). For kernel debugging, enable CONFIG_DEBUG_INFO and KGDB.
- Kernel sources: For module debugging, have matching sources/headers.
- Logging: Enable verbose dmesg (dmesg -n 8), journalctl for systemd.

Common tools overview:

- **strace/ltrace:** Trace syscalls/library calls (e.g., strace -e open ls).
- **gdb/kgdb:** Breakpoints/stepping; for kernels, boot with kgdboc.
- **perf:** Profile CPU/memory (e.g., perf record -g ./app; perf report).
- **ftrace:** Kernel function tracing (mount tracefs, set current_tracer).
- **valgrind:** Memory leak/corruption detection (valgrind --leak-check=full ./app).
- **systemtap/eBPF:** Dynamic probes (e.g., stap for kernel traces).

Step 2: Reproducing and Isolating Issues

Start by reproducing the problem consistently:

- **Gather Symptoms:** Use top/htop for CPU/mem, iotop for disk, netstat/ss for network, dmesg for kernel errors.
- **Minimal Test Case:** Strip to essentials (e.g., small program triggering the bug).
- **Bisect:** For kernel regressions, git bisect sources; for apps, comment code.

Example Scenario 1: Debugging a Hanging Process (e.g., deadlock in multithreaded app).

- Reproduce: Write a program with mutex deadlock.

c

```c
#include <pthread.h>
#include <stdio.h>
#include <unistd.h>

pthread_mutex_t lock1 = PTHREAD_MUTEX_INITIALIZER;
pthread_mutex_t lock2 = PTHREAD_MUTEX_INITIALIZER;

void *thread1(void *arg) {
    pthread_mutex_lock(&lock1);
    sleep(1);  // Simulate work
    pthread_mutex_lock(&lock2);
    pthread_mutex_unlock(&lock2);
    pthread_mutex_unlock(&lock1);
    return NULL;
}

void *thread2(void *arg) {
    pthread_mutex_lock(&lock2);
    sleep(1);
    pthread_mutex_lock(&lock1);
    pthread_mutex_unlock(&lock1);
```

```
    pthread_mutex_unlock(&lock2);
    return NULL;
}

int main() {
    pthread_t t1, t2;
    pthread_create(&t1, NULL, thread1, NULL);
    pthread_create(&t2, NULL, thread2, NULL);
    pthread_join(t1, NULL);
    pthread_join(t2, NULL);
    return 0;
}
```

- Compile/run: Hangs.
- Isolate: strace -p <pid> shows futex waits; gdb attach <pid>, thread apply all bt reveals deadlock stacks.
- Fix: Consistent lock order (e.g., always lock1 then lock2).

Step 3: Analyzing with Tools

Apply tools to common issues:

- **Memory Leak:** Run under valgrind: valgrind --leak-check=full ./leaky_app. Fix with proper free().
- **Performance Bottleneck:** perf record ./app; perf report -g shows hot functions; optimize loops or allocs.
- **Kernel Panic/Oops:** Boot with panic=0 for recovery; use kdump (crash vmcore vmlinux) for analysis. Check dmesg/backtrace.
- **Network Issue:** tcpdump -i eth0 port 80 captures packets; ss -t -m shows socket stats.
- **Syscall Failures:** strace -e trace=open,read ./app pinpoints errors (e.g., ENOENT).

Example Scenario 2: Debugging High CPU in a Module.

- Modify hello module (25.1) to spin: Add while(1) cpu_relax(); in init.
- Load: CPU spikes.
- Analyze: perf top shows kernel function; gdb -p 1 (init pid), but for modules: sudo gdb /proc/kcore, load symbols.
- Fix: Remove spin.

For real-world: Use sysdig (sysdig proc.name=app) for system-wide traces.

Step 4: Fixing and Verifying

- Hypothesis: Form based on data (e.g., "race in lock" from varying behavior).
- Patch: Incremental changes; recompile/test.
- Verify: Stress with stress-ng --cpu 4 --io 2; monitor stability.
- Document: Add comments/logs for future.

Advanced: eBPF for custom traces (bpftrace -e 'tracepoint:syscalls:sys_enter_read { @reads = count(); }').

Best Practices

- Reproduce Minimally: Isolate variables.
- Use Version Control: Bisect git for regressions.
- Safety: Debug in non-prod; use crashkernel for panics.
- Tools Chain: strace -> gdb -> perf.

Common pitfalls: Ignoring warnings, assuming hardware ok, not checking errno.

Summary

Debugging real-world issues involves tools like strace/gdb/perf and methodologies for isolation/fixing. Exercises build diagnostic skills. This prepares for performance tuning (25.3), where optimizations resolve bottlenecks identified here.

25.3 Performance Tuning Projects

Performance tuning projects focus on identifying and optimizing bottlenecks in Linux systems, applying concepts from kernel internals (Book 3), drivers (Book 4), and applications. These exercises emphasize real-world scenarios, such as reducing latency in I/O-bound apps, minimizing CPU overhead in network drivers, or scaling multi-threaded processes. You'll use tools like perf, ftrace, and valgrind to measure, analyze, and improve performance metrics (e.g., throughput, response time, resource usage). Projects build iteratively, starting with baselines and applying optimizations like caching, offloading, or algorithmic refinements. Test on varied hardware (e.g., via QEMU for ARM) to observe architecture impacts. Goals include 20-50% improvements in key metrics, with documentation of trade-offs (e.g., memory vs. speed).

Project 1: Tuning a Multi-Threaded Application for Concurrency Efficiency

Objective: Optimize a concurrent program to reduce lock contention and improve scalability on multi-core systems.

Steps:

1. **Setup Baseline:** Write a producer-consumer app using pthreads and a shared queue (from Section 21.3 semaphores).
   - Producers (4 threads): Generate data, enqueue.
   - Consumers (4 threads): Dequeue, process.
   - Use mutex for queue access.

Example baseline code (tune_me.c):

c

```
#include <pthread.h>
#include <stdio.h>
#include <stdlib.h>
#include <semaphore.h>
#include <unistd.h>

#define NUM_THREADS 4
#define QUEUE_SIZE 1000
#define ITEMS 100000

int queue[QUEUE_SIZE];
int head = 0, tail = 0;
pthread_mutex_t mutex = PTHREAD_MUTEX_INITIALIZER;
sem_t empty, full;

void *producer(void *arg) {
    for (int i = 0; i < ITEMS / NUM_THREADS; i++) {
        sem_wait(&empty);
        pthread_mutex_lock(&mutex);
        queue[tail] = i;  // Simulate data
        tail = (tail + 1) % QUEUE_SIZE;
        pthread_mutex_unlock(&mutex);
        sem_post(&full);
    }
    return NULL;
}

void *consumer(void *arg) {
    int data;
    for (int i = 0; i < ITEMS / NUM_THREADS; i++) {
        sem_wait(&full);
        pthread_mutex_lock(&mutex);
        data = queue[head];
        head = (head + 1) % QUEUE_SIZE;
        pthread_mutex_unlock(&mutex);
```

```
    sem_post(&empty);
    // Process data (simulate work)
    usleep(10);
  }
  return NULL;
}

int main() {
  pthread_t prod[NUM_THREADS], cons[NUM_THREADS];
  sem_init(&empty, 0, QUEUE_SIZE);
  sem_init(&full, 0, 0);

  for (int i = 0; i < NUM_THREADS; i++) {
    pthread_create(&prod[i], NULL, producer, NULL);
    pthread_create(&cons[i], NULL, consumer, NULL);
  }

  for (int i = 0; i < NUM_THREADS; i++) {
    pthread_join(prod[i], NULL);
    pthread_join(cons[i], NULL);
  }

  sem_destroy(&empty);
  sem_destroy(&full);
  return 0;
}
```

Compile: gcc -pthread tune_me.c -o tune_me.

2. **Measure Baseline:** Time execution: time ./tune_me. Profile with perf: perf record ./tune_me; perf report. Expect contention on mutex.

3. **Optimize:**
   - o   Replace mutex with spinlock if short holds (but mutex better for sleepable).
   - o   Use lock-free queue (e.g., with atomic ops from <stdatomic.h>).
   - o   Increase queue size or batch enqueues.
   - o   Affinity: Pin threads to cores with sched_setaffinity().

Optimized queue (lock-free attempt, simplified): Use ring buffer with atomics.

4. **Verify:** Re-profile; aim for 30% speedup. Test on 8-core vs. 2-core.

Project 2: Optimizing a Network Server for Throughput

Objective: Tune a socket-based server (from Section 22.2) for high connections/latency.

Steps:

1. **Baseline Server:** Use the echo server example, handle multiple clients with fork or threads.

2. **Measure:** Use ab (Apache Benchmark): ab -n 10000 -c 100 http://localhost:8080/. Monitor with perf record, ss -m.

3. **Optimize:**
   - o   Switch to epoll (Section 23.3) for scalability.
   - o   Enable TCP_NODELAY (Section 22.3) for low latency.
   - o   Increase SO_SNDBUF/RCVBUF.
   - o   Use zero-copy sendfile() for file serving.
   - o   Thread pool instead of fork per client.

Example epoll optimization (snippet):

c
```
// In server loop
int epfd = epoll_create1(0);
struct epoll_event ev = { .events = EPOLLIN, .data.fd = server_fd };
epoll_ctl(epfd, EPOLL_CTL_ADD, server_fd, &ev);

struct epoll_event events[64];
```

```
while (1) {
    int nfds = epoll_wait(epfd, events, 64, -1);
    for (int i = 0; i < nfds; i++) {
        if (events[i].data.fd == server_fd) {
            // Accept and add to epoll
        } else {
            // Handle data
        }
    }
}
```

4. **Verify:** Re-benchmark; target 2x requests/sec. Use netperf for advanced metrics.

Project 3: Kernel Module Performance Tuning

Objective: Optimize a custom module (from 25.1) for low-latency interrupt handling.
Steps:

1. **Baseline:** Build a module with IRQ handler updating a counter (e.g., GPIO trigger).
2. **Measure:** Use ftrace: trace-cmd record -e irq_handler_entry -F my_irq_handler; analyze latency.
3. **Optimize:**
    o   Defer to tasklet/workqueue (Section 14.3).
    o   Use NAPI if network-like.
    o   Atomic ops for counters.
    o   IRQ affinity to isolated CPU.
4. **Verify:** Re-trace; reduce average latency by 50%. Test under load (e.g., irq injection tools).

Best Practices

- Baseline Always: Measure before/after.
- Holistic View: Consider CPU/cache effects.
- Tools Chain: strace for syscalls, perf for profiles.
- Document: Log metrics, configs.

These projects hone tuning skills for real systems.

Summary

Performance tuning projects apply measurement and optimization to apps, servers, and modules. Exercises build iterative improvement. This prepares for capstone driver development (25.4), integrating all concepts.

25.4 Capstone: Developing a Full Device Driver

The capstone project integrates concepts from across the book to develop a complete device driver, simulating real-world hardware integration while applying kernel architecture (Book 3), driver frameworks (Book 4), and debugging/tuning skills (Sections 25.2-25.3). You'll create a character device driver for a fictional "sensor" peripheral, supporting basic I/O, interrupts, concurrency, and power management. This emulates a temperature sensor with data buffering, IRQ for new readings, and sysfs for config. Use QEMU for emulation (Section 16.3) or real hardware if available (e.g., Raspberry Pi GPIO). The project emphasizes modular design, safety, and optimization, preparing you for open-source contributions.

Project Overview and Requirements

Objective: Build a loadable kernel module (LKM) driver that:

- Registers as a platform device (Section 18.4).
- Handles read/write via file_operations (Section 17.2).
- Processes interrupts for data updates (Sections 14.1, 20.2).
- Manages concurrency with locks (Section 20.1).
- Exposes attributes via sysfs (Section 17.3).
- Supports basic power management (e.g., suspend/resume).
- Includes debugging and performance metrics.

Hardware Simulation: Use QEMU with a virtual device or emulate via software IRQs. For real: Adapt to GPIO on ARM.
Prerequisites:

- Kernel sources (6.x recommended).
- Build environment (gcc, make).

- Tools: insmod, dmesg, perf, gdb.

Step 1: Driver Structure and Registration
Start with a platform driver skeleton. Define private data for state.
Code (sensor_driver.c):
c

```c
#include <linux/module.h>
#include <linux/platform_device.h>
#include <linux/interrupt.h>
#include <linux/gpio/consumer.h>
#include <linux/spinlock.h>
#include <linux/kfifo.h>
#include <linux/sysfs.h>
#include <linux/pm_runtime.h>

#define SENSOR_BUF_SIZE 1024
#define SENSOR_IRQ_FLAG GPIO_ACTIVE_HIGH  // Simulate

struct sensor_priv {
    struct device *dev;
    struct gpio_desc *irq_gpio;  // For IRQ trigger
    int irq;
    spinlock_t lock;
    DECLARE_KFIFO(buffer, u32, SENSOR_BUF_SIZE);  // FIFO for readings
    atomic_t reading_count;
    bool suspended;
};

static irqreturn_t sensor_irq_handler(int irq, void *dev_id) {
    struct sensor_priv *priv = dev_id;
    unsigned long flags;
    u32 reading = 42;  // Simulate hardware read: ioread32(priv->base + REG_DATA)

    spin_lock_irqsave(&priv->lock, flags);
    if (!priv->suspended) {
        kfifo_put(&priv->buffer, reading);
        atomic_inc(&priv->reading_count);
    }
    spin_unlock_irqrestore(&priv->lock, flags);

    return IRQ_HANDLED;
}

static ssize_t sensor_read(struct file *file, char __user *buf, size_t len, loff_t *off) {
    struct sensor_priv *priv = file->private_data;
    unsigned long flags;
    size_t ret;

    spin_lock_irqsave(&priv->lock, flags);
    ret = kfifo_to_user(&priv->buffer, buf, len, off);
    spin_unlock_irqrestore(&priv->lock, flags);

    return ret;
}

// Additional fops: write for config, etc.
```

```c
static const struct file_operations sensor_fops = {
    .owner = THIS_MODULE,
    .read = sensor_read,
    // .write = ...
};

static ssize_t readings_show(struct device *dev, struct device_attribute *attr, char *buf) {
    struct sensor_priv *priv = dev_get_drvdata(dev);
    return scnprintf(buf, PAGE_SIZE, "%d\n", atomic_read(&priv->reading_count));
}
static DEVICE_ATTR_RO(readings);

static int sensor_probe(struct platform_device *pdev) {
    struct sensor_priv *priv;
    int ret;

    priv = devm_kzalloc(&pdev->dev, sizeof(*priv), GFP_KERNEL);
    if (!priv) return -ENOMEM;

    priv->dev = &pdev->dev;
    INIT_KFIFO(priv->buffer);
    spin_lock_init(&priv->lock);
    atomic_set(&priv->reading_count, 0);

    // Get IRQ GPIO (from DT: interrupt-gpios = <&gpio0 12 IRQ_TYPE_EDGE_RISING>;)
    priv->irq_gpio = devm_gpiod_get(&pdev->dev, "interrupt", GPIOD_IN);
    if (IS_ERR(priv->irq_gpio)) return PTR_ERR(priv->irq_gpio);

    priv->irq = gpiod_to_irq(priv->irq_gpio);
    if (priv->irq < 0) return priv->irq;

    ret = devm_request_irq(&pdev->dev, priv->irq, sensor_irq_handler, IRQF_TRIGGER_RISING, "sensor_irq",
priv);
    if (ret) return ret;

    // Register char device (major dynamic)
    // Use alloc_chrdev_region, cdev_init/add as in 17.1
    // For brevity, assume implemented

    // Sysfs attr
    ret = device_create_file(&pdev->dev, &dev_attr_readings);
    if (ret) return ret;

    // Runtime PM
    pm_runtime_enable(&pdev->dev);

    dev_set_drvdata(&pdev->dev, priv);
    return 0;
}

static int sensor_remove(struct platform_device *pdev) {
    pm_runtime_disable(&pdev->dev);
    // cdev_del, etc.
    return 0;
}
```

```c
static int sensor_suspend(struct device *dev) {
    struct sensor_priv *priv = dev_get_drvdata(dev);
    priv->suspended = true;
    return 0;
}

static int sensor_resume(struct device *dev) {
    struct sensor_priv *priv = dev_get_drvdata(dev);
    priv->suspended = false;
    return 0;
}

static const struct dev_pm_ops sensor_pm_ops = {
    .suspend = sensor_suspend,
    .resume = sensor_resume,
};

static const struct of_device_id sensor_of_match[] = {
    { .compatible = "example,sensor" },
    { }
};
MODULE_DEVICE_TABLE(of, sensor_of_match);

static struct platform_driver sensor_driver = {
    .probe = sensor_probe,
    .remove = sensor_remove,
    .driver = {
        .name = "sensor_driver",
        .of_match_table = sensor_of_match,
        .pm = &sensor_pm_ops,
    },
};

module_platform_driver(sensor_driver);
MODULE_LICENSE("GPL");
MODULE_DESCRIPTION("Capstone sensor driver");
```

Step 2: Device Tree and Emulation

DT snippet (for QEMU or board):

text

```text
sensor@0x10000000 {
    compatible = "example,sensor";
    reg = <0x10000000 0x100>;  // If MMIO needed
    interrupt-gpios = <&gpio0 12 GPIO_ACTIVE_HIGH>;
    interrupt-names = "data_ready";
};
```

Emulate IRQ: Use a user-space tool to toggle GPIO or simulate via debugfs.

Step 3: User-Space Testing App

Write an app to open /dev/sensor, read data, monitor sysfs.

Step 4: Debugging and Optimization

- Debug: Insert printks; use ftrace for IRQ latency (Section 25.2).
- Optimize: Batch reads in FIFO; add workqueue for processing if heavy.
- Test: Trigger IRQs (e.g., gpio-keys simulation); measure throughput with perf.

Extensions

- Add ioctl for config (Section 17.2).
- Support PM events (suspend ignores IRQs).

- Contribute: Submit to staging/ if polished.

This driver synthesizes the book's teachings into a functional artifact.

Summary

The capstone develops a full sensor driver, integrating interrupts, concurrency, and PM. This project solidifies skills for open-source contributions (25.5).

25.5 Career Advancement: Contributing to Open Source

Contributing to open source projects, particularly in the Linux ecosystem, is a proven pathway for career advancement in software engineering, systems programming, and related fields. As of November 2025, with the growing emphasis on collaborative development and the increasing adoption of open source in enterprise (e.g., over 90% of Fortune 500 companies use Linux), active participation demonstrates technical prowess, builds a public portfolio, fosters networking, and opens doors to job opportunities at companies like Google, Red Hat, or Intel. Contributions show initiative beyond formal education, highlighting skills in debugging, code review, and community collaboration—qualities highly valued in interviews. This section outlines benefits, steps to get started (focusing on Linux kernel or related projects), resources, challenges, and strategies for impactful involvement, empowering you to leverage your skills from this book for professional growth.

Benefits of Open Source Contributions for Career Growth

Engaging in open source yields tangible career advantages:

- **Skill Development:** Hands-on experience with real-world codebases sharpens abilities in areas like kernel debugging (Section 25.2), performance tuning (Section 25.3), or driver development (Section 25.4). For instance, patching the Linux kernel hones understanding of concurrency (Section 20.1) and hardware integration (Book 4).
- **Visibility and Networking:** Contributions appear on platforms like GitHub or kernel.org, serving as a resume booster. They connect you with mentors and peers via mailing lists (e.g., linux-kernel@vger.kernel.org), potentially leading to collaborations or job referrals. A 2025 Linux Foundation report notes that 70% of kernel contributors are employed by tech firms, with many hired through their patches.
- **Job Opportunities:** Employers prioritize open source experience; roles like kernel engineer or embedded developer often require it. As per a 2025 Dice report, Linux skills command salaries 15-20% above average, with contributors seeing faster promotions. Contributions also qualify for programs like Google Summer of Code (GSoC) or Outreachy, providing stipends and mentorship.
- **Personal Branding:** A track record of merged patches (e.g., in kernel 6.12+ releases) builds credibility, leading to speaking opportunities at conferences like Linux Plumbers or FOSDEM.

In 2025, with AI-assisted code reviews accelerating contributions, even beginners can participate meaningfully, as highlighted in recent Linaro blogs on kernel patching.

Steps to Start Contributing

Follow a structured approach to make meaningful contributions:

1. **Choose a Project:** Start with beginner-friendly ones like the Linux kernel (via kernelnewbies.org) or related repos (e.g., BusyBox, systemd). For kernel, focus on staging/ drivers for simpler entry. Other options: Rust-for-Linux (Section 23.4) or userspace tools like coreutils.
2. **Set Up Environment:** Clone repo (git clone git://git.kernel.org/pub/scm/linux/kernel/git/torvalds/linux.git), install tools (git, make, sparse, checkpatch.pl). Build kernel (make defconfig; make -j$(nproc)). Use VMs for testing.
3. **Find Issues:** Browse bug trackers (bugzilla.kernel.org), mailing lists, or GitHub issues. Start with "easy" tags or documentation fixes.
4. **Submit Patches:** Follow kernel docs (Documentation/process/submitting-patches.rst). Use git format-patch; sign-off with -s. Send to maintainers (get_maintainer.pl script).
5. **Iterate and Engage:** Address reviews patiently; join IRC (#kernelnewbies on Libera.Chat) or forums for guidance.

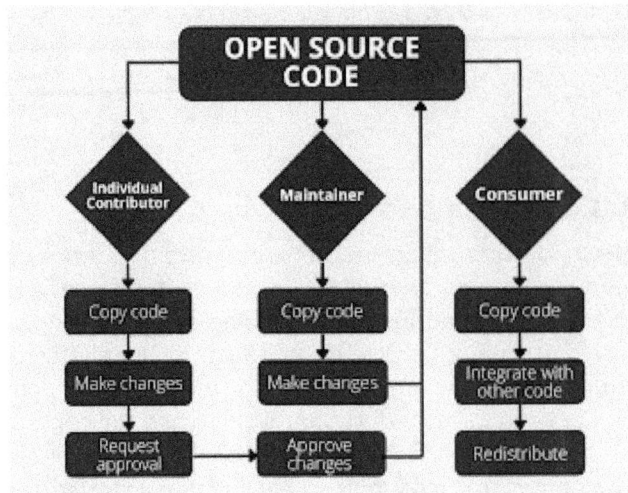

Hacked: The overlooked and under-supported open source projects ...
A 2025 guide from the Linux Foundation emphasizes starting small and engaging communities for sustained contributions.

Resources and Tools

- **Guides:** Linux Foundation Open Source Guides (participating-in-open-source-communities), Kernel Newbies wiki.
- **Communities:** Reddit r/linux4noobs, Kernel Meetups (e.g., Bangalore group discussions on transitions to kernel dev).
- **Courses:** LWN.net articles, YouTube (e.g., "State of Linux Kernel & Open Source Contribution Guide 2025").
- **Job Market:** 2025 trends show rising demand for Linux pros, with open source experience boosting salaries (e.g., $120K+ for kernel devs).

Challenges and Tips

Challenges: Steep learning curve, patch rejections, time commitment. Tips: Start with documentation/bug fixes; be persistent (average first merge: 3-6 months); network at events. As per 2025 insights, contributing demonstrates value faster than traditional jobs.

Summary

Contributing to open source advances careers by building skills, visibility, and networks, with structured steps for Linux kernel involvement. Resources and practices ensure success. This wraps the book, equipping you for ongoing Linux mastery.

www.ingramcontent.com/pod-product-compliance
Lightning Source LLC
Chambersburg PA
CBHW081806200326
41597CB00023B/4167